Use these handy Zagat bookmarks to mark your favorites and the places you'd like to try. Plus, we've included re-useable blank bookmarks for you to write on (and wipe off). Browsing through your Zagat guide has never been easier!

Must Try
Must Try
Love it!
Love it!
Like it!
Top Pick

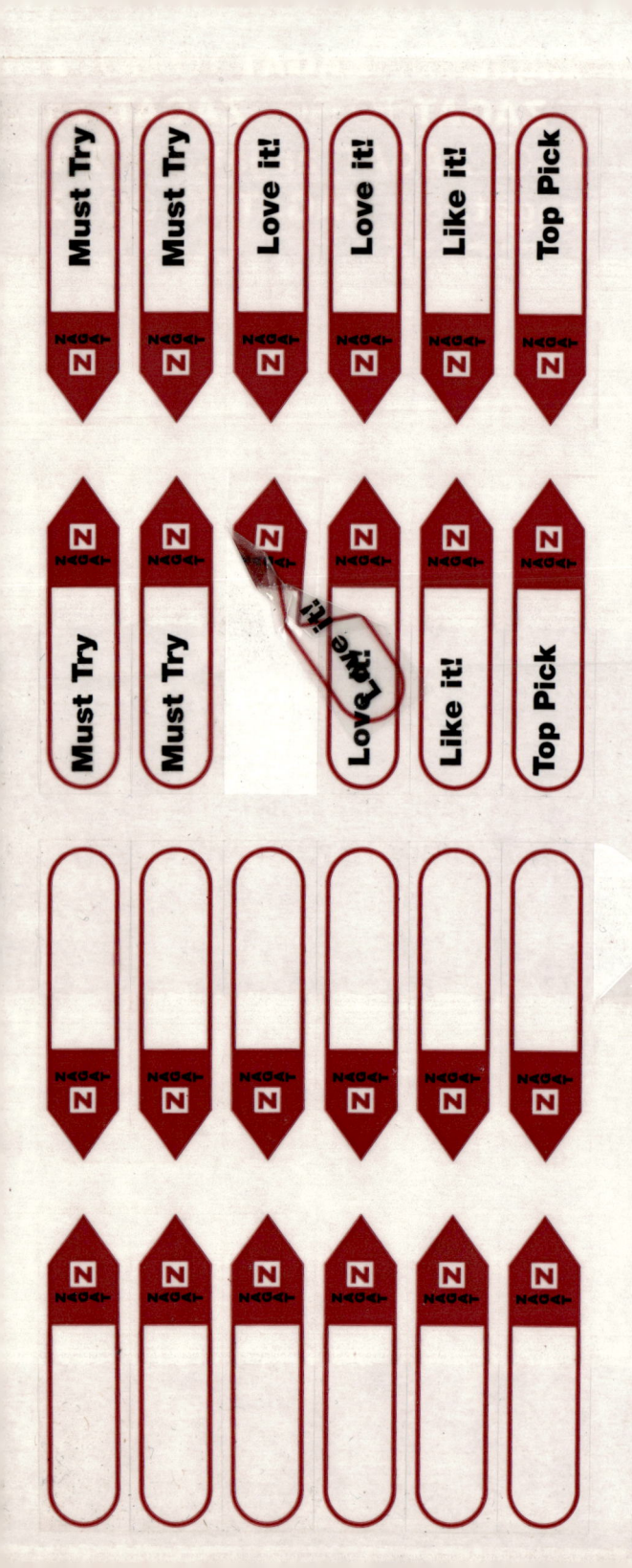

Must Try
Must Try
Love it!
Love it!
Like it!
Top Pick

ZAGAT SURVEY

Celebrating 30 Years

Back in 1979, we never imagined that an idea born during a wine-fueled dinner with friends would take us on an adventure that's lasted three decades – and counting.

The idea – that the collective opinions of avid consumers can be more accurate than the judgments of an individual critic – led to a hobby involving friends rating NYC restaurants. And that hobby grew into Zagat Survey, which today has over 350,000 participants worldwide weighing in on everything from airlines, bars, dining and golf to hotels, movies, shopping, tourist attractions and more.

By giving consumers a voice, we – and our surveyors – had unwittingly joined a revolution whose concepts (user-generated content, social networking) were largely unknown 30 years ago. However, those concepts caught fire with the rise of the Internet and have since transformed not only restaurant criticism but also virtually every aspect of the media, and we feel lucky to have been at the start of it all.

As we celebrate Zagat's 30th year, we'd like to thank everyone who has participated in our surveys. We've enjoyed hearing and sharing your frank opinions and look forward to doing so for many years to come. As we always say, our guides and online content are really "yours."

We'd also like to express our gratitude by supporting **Action Against Hunger,** an organization that works to meet the needs of the hungry in over 40 countries. To find out more, visit www.zagat.com/action.

Nina and Tim Zagat

ZAGAT®
CELEBRATING 30 YEARS

Las Vegas
2009

LOCAL EDITORS
Heidi Knapp Rinella and Jason Bracelin

STAFF EDITOR
Michelle Golden

Published and distributed by
Zagat Survey, LLC
4 Columbus Circle
New York, NY 10019
T: 212.977.6000
E: lasvegas@zagat.com
www.zagat.com

ACKNOWLEDGMENTS

We thank Bernard Onken and Steven Shukow, as well as the following members of our staff: Caitlin Eichelberger (assistant editor), Brian Albert, Sean Beachell, Maryanne Bertollo, Jane Chang, Sandy Cheng, Reni Chin, Larry Cohn, Bill Corsello, Alison Flick, Jeff Freier, Andrew Gelardi, Justin Hartung, Karen Hudes, Roy Jacob, Garth Johnston, Ashunta Joseph, Cynthia Kilian, Natalie Lebert, Mike Liao, Dave Makulec, Andre Pilette, Kimberly Rosado, Becky Ruthenburg, Aleksandra Shander, Jacqueline Wasilczyk, Liz Borod Wright, Sharon Yates, Anna Zappia and Kyle Zolner.

The reviews published in this guide are based on public opinion surveys. The numerical ratings reflect the average scores given by all survey participants who voted on each establishment. The text is based on direct quotes from, or fair paraphrasings of, participants' comments. Phone numbers, addresses and other factual information were correct to the best of our knowledge when published in this guide.

© 2008 Zagat Survey, LLC
ISBN-13: 978-1-60478-018-5
ISBN-10: 1-60478-018-5
Printed in the
United States of America

Contents

Ratings & Symbols	4
About This Survey	5
What's New	6
A Las Vegas Primer	7

MAPS

The Strip	8
Greater Las Vegas	10

DINING

Top Lists:

Most Popular	12
Key Newcomers	12
Food	13
Decor	16
Service	17
Best Buys	18

Names, Locations, Contact Info, Ratings & Reviews — 19

NIGHTLIFE

Top Lists:

Most Popular	88
Key Newcomers	88
Appeal	89
Decor	89
Service	89

Names, Locations, Contact Info, Ratings & Reviews — 90

SHOPPING

Top Lists:

Most Popular	112
Key Newcomers	112
Quality	113
Display	113
Service	113

Names, Locations, Contact Info, Ratings & Reviews — 114

SITES & ATTRACTIONS

Top Lists — 132

Names, Locations, Contact Info, Ratings & Reviews — 132

GOLF

Top Lists — 140

Names, Locations, Contact Info, Ratings & Reviews — 140

HOTELS

Top Lists — 146

Names, Locations, Contact Info, Ratings & Reviews — 146

INDEXES

Dining:

Cuisines	156
Locations	162
Special Features	168

Nightlife:

Locations	187
Special Appeals	189

Shopping:

Merchandise	198
Locations	200
Special Features	202

Sites & Attractions:

Types	205
Locations	206

Golf:

Features	207

Hotels:

Locations	209
Special Features	210

Alphabetical Page Index — 213

Ratings & Symbols

	Zagat Top Spot	Name	Symbols	Cuisine	Zagat Ratings			
					FOOD	DECOR	SERVICE	COST

Area, Address & Contact	ⓩ **Tim & Nina's** ◐ *Steak* ▽ 23 | 9 | 13 | $15 **Strip** | 88 Gambling Way (Blackjack Rd.) | 702-555-1212 | www.zagat.com
Review, surveyor comments in quotes	"You're more likely to see Tim and Nina at the slots" than run into them at their Asian-, Armenian-, Aleutian-accented steakhouse off the Strip, where the "ambitions are as frighteningly elevated as the prices"; maybe the staff got "waylayed by baccarat" during the "long, forced march through the casino" to get to this "chintz-infested tomb" where "a table by the peephole" offers a "glimpse of the construction site" next door.

Ratings	Ratings are on the following 0 to 30 scale:
	0 – 9 poor to fair
	10 – 15 fair to good
	16 – 19 good to very good
	20 – 25 very good to excellent
	26 – 30 extraordinary to perfection
	▽ low response | less reliable

Cost	Cost is covered differently, as noted in the Ratings & Symbols keys at the beginning of each section.

Symbols	ⓩ highest ratings, popularity and importance
	◐ open late (hours vary by section)
	Ⓢ closed on Sunday
	Ⓜ closed on Monday
	⌀ no credit cards accepted
	See also the Ratings & Symbols key in each section.

Index	All establishments are listed in the Alphabetical Index at the back of the book.

About This Survey

This **2009 Las Vegas Survey** is an update reflecting significant developments since our last Survey was published. It covers 796 of the city's finest restaurants, nightspots, shops, attractions, golf courses and hotels. We've also indicated new addresses, phone numbers, chef changes and other major alterations to bring this guide up to the minute.

WHO PARTICIPATED: Input from 5,279 enthusiasts forms the basis for the ratings and reviews in this guide (their comments are shown in quotation marks within the reviews). Collectively they bring vast experience and knowledge to this Survey. We sincerely thank each of these participants – this book is really "theirs."

HELPFUL LISTS: Our top lists and indexes can help you find exactly the right place for any occasion. See the lists that begin each section: Dining (pages 12–18); Nightlife (pages 88–89); Shopping (pages 112–113); Sites & Attractions (page 132); Golf (page 140) and Hotels (page 146). We've also provided 107 handy indexes.

OUR EDITORS: Special thanks go to our local editors for this update, Heidi Knapp Rinella, the restaurant critic and a features writer for the *Las Vegas Review-Journal*, and Jason Bracelin, the entertainment writer at the newspaper.

ABOUT ZAGAT: This marks our 30th year reporting on the shared experiences of consumers like you. What started in 1979 as a hobby has come a long way. Today we have over 350,000 surveyors and now cover airlines, bars, dining, entertaining, fast food, golf, hotels, movies, music, resorts, shopping, spas, theater and tourist attractions in over 100 countries.

INTERACTIVE: Up-to-the-minute news about restaurant openings plus menus, photos and more are free on **ZAGAT.com** and the award-winning **ZAGAT.mobi** (for web-enabled mobile devices). They also enable reserving at thousands of places with just one click.

VOTE AND COMMENT: We invite you to join any of our surveys at **ZAGAT.com**. There you can rate and review establishments year-round. In exchange for doing so, you'll receive a free copy of the resulting guide when published.

AVAILABILITY: Zagat guides are available in all major bookstores as well as on **ZAGAT.com**. You can also access our content when on the go via **ZAGAT.mobi** and **ZAGAT TO GO** (for smartphones).

FEEDBACK: There is always room for improvement, thus we invite your comments about any aspect of our performance. Did we miss anything? Just contact us at **lasvegas@zagat.com**.

New York, NY
December 10, 2008

Nina and Tim Zagat

Let your voice be heard - visit ZAGAT.com/vote

What's New

The chips may be down, but you wouldn't know it from a glance at the Strip. With two flashy new megaresorts and dozens of restaurants opening their doors this year, Las Vegas defiantly continues to grow, in spite of the current economic slump.

FEELING THE SQUEEZE: Though Las Vegas is famously resilient, it's not entirely immune to the rest of the country's fiscal woes. Notable closings since the downturn include Louis Osteen's Louis's Fish Camp – a casual annex to **Louis's Las Vegas** in Town Square – and off-Strip mom-and-pop shops like Anna Bella and Becker's Steakhouse. Donald Trump's **DJT,** the fine-dining venue in his new hotel/condo tower, was reinventing itself at press time with a lower-priced menu. Meanwhile, construction on Echelon Place – bringing lodging, gaming and 30 bars and restaurants to the old Stardust site – has been delayed because of financing issues.

YET STILL GOING STRONG: New resorts – all of which were planned before the market slowdown – continue to recruit celeb chefs in droves, invigorating the city's restaurant scene. At the Palazzo on the Strip, Charlie Trotter returned with the seafooder **Restaurant Charlie,** Wolfgang Puck cloned his LA steakhouse **CUT** and Emeril Lagasse and Mario Batali unveiled **Table 10** and **Carnevino,** serving their signature New Orleans–inflected cooking and meaty Italian cuisine, respectively. Encore, the sister resort to the Wynn, is slated to keep the boldface-names coming when it opens at the end of this year with high-profile eateries from Mark LoRusso (ex **Tableau**) who will headline the hotel's steakhouse, and Theo Schoenegger (ex Patina in Los Angeles), whose **Theo's** will showcase Cal-Italian fare. Looking ahead, Aria, the forthcoming casino at City Center on the Strip, has announced their dining lineup, which includes entries from MGM-Mirage vets Sirio Maccioni, Michael Mina and Jean-Georges Vongerichten, plus Vegas neophytes Masayoshi Takayama of Masa in New York and Shawn McClain of Spring in Chicago.

AFTER HOURS: Though 2008 ushered in a slew of posh nightclubs like **The Bank, CatHouse** and **Privé,** midlevel venues are working to keep their capacity numbers up in the wake of the flagging economy. As a result, some, like the new **Rok** at New York-New York, are offering half-bottle service, while others are drastically reducing what they pay for celebrity appearances. Meanwhile, the more affordable Downtown district continues to thrive with entries like **Gold Diggers** at the Golden Nugget and the **Canyon Club** at the Four Queens. Even so, with the luxurious City Center still moving forward along with Encore's aptly named new club, **XS,** don't expect Sin City to repent for its lavishness any time soon.

MONEY MATTERS: With an average meal cost of $44.44, Las Vegas ranks as the most expensive dining city in the country with New York City ($40.78) and Miami ($38.86) trailing behind. But Vegas still has plenty of bargains – from noodle shops to nouveau burger joints.

Las Vegas, NV	Heidi Knapp Rinella
December 10, 2008	Jason Bracelin

A Las Vegas Primer

ARRIVING: Most visitors to Las Vegas will pass through McCarran International Airport – one of the nation's busiest, and equipped with its own slot machines – located off the south end of the Strip. Shuttles, rental cars and taxis are readily available, with cab fares running from around $12–$15 to the Strip and $40 to Downtown hotels.

GETTING ORIENTED: [see map, page 8] Navigating Las Vegas' tourism corridor is a cinch. Most major resorts are situated on the famed, four-mile-long Strip (aka Las Vegas Boulevard South), which runs north to south. The convention center as well as many restaurants and non-gaming hotels lie on Paradise Road, just east of the Strip. Lost? Get reoriented easily by looking for the Stratosphere Hotel, the city's tallest building, which anchors the Strip's north end.

GETTING AROUND: You may not want to walk long distances in Las Vegas (especially when it's 112 degrees outside), but there's plenty of public transportation, so a car isn't essential. Taxis, trolleys and buses service most areas, and a monorail runs from the MGM Grand to the Convention Center, with many stops in between. Visit www.lvmonorail.com or www.rtcsouthernnevada.com for monorail or bus information. Also, many off-Strip hotels run their own shuttles – just ask your concierge.

SIGHTSEEING: [see map, page 10] Many visitors to Las Vegas aren't aware of the spectacular sights just beyond its borders. Companies offering tours include Gray Line (www.graylinelasvegas.com) and Pink Jeep (www.pinkjeep.com), which go to the Grand Canyon and Hoover Dam, and Las Vegas Grand Canyon Tours (www.lasvegasgrandcanyontour.com), which provides bus and air tours of those destinations as well as Death Valley, plus river rafting and horseback riding. And don't overlook historic Downtown – it may not be as glossy as the Strip, but it's full of old-time charm.

GAMBLING: Part of the fun of Vegas is hitting the tables. If you're new to gambling, you might want to start off on some cheaper games – minimums are often lower in mornings and afternoons or in Downtown casinos. And while dealers can seem intimidating, their job is to explain how the game works, and they're often happy to do so, if it's not busy. Generally, if you're winning or have spent a lot of time at a table, it's customary to leave a gratuity (in the form of a few chips) for the dealer. Finally, don't forget to inquire about Players Club cards, available at most casinos, which allow you to accrue credit toward meals, room expenses or entertainment.

WHEN TO VISIT: Las Vegas' desert climate is most pleasant during the spring and fall. Winters tend to be chilly (though snow is very rare), but that doesn't stop revelers who pour into the Strip on New Year's Eve, one of the biggest nights of the year. Prices are generally lower during the week and in January. For a list of annual events, go to the Las Vegas Convention and Visitors Authority website, www.visitlasvegas.com.

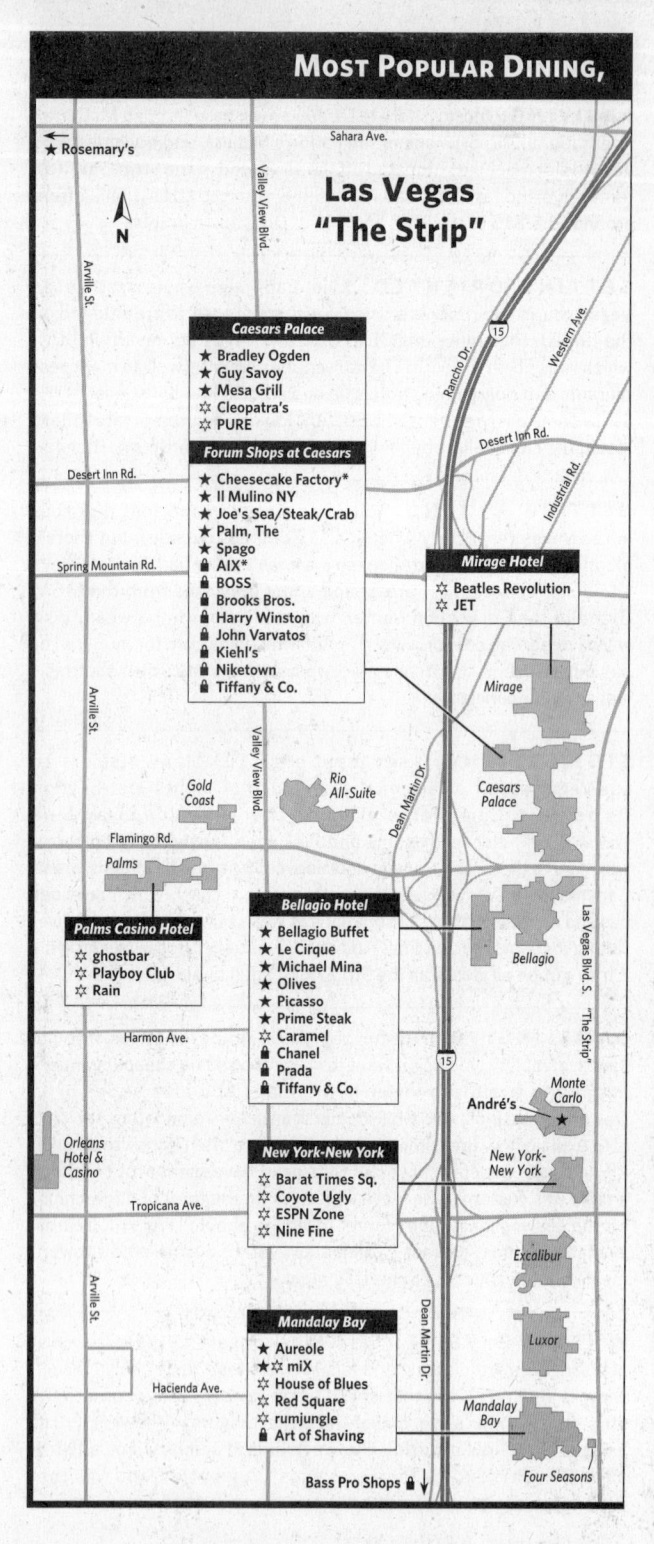

MOST POPULAR DINING,

Las Vegas "The Strip"

← ★ Rosemary's

Caesars Palace
- ★ Bradley Ogden
- ★ Guy Savoy
- ★ Mesa Grill
- ☆ Cleopatra's
- ☆ PURE

Forum Shops at Caesars
- ★ Cheesecake Factory*
- ★ Il Mulino NY
- ★ Joe's Sea/Steak/Crab
- ★ Palm, The
- ★ Spago
- 🔒 AIX*
- 🔒 BOSS
- 🔒 Brooks Bros.
- 🔒 Harry Winston
- 🔒 John Varvatos
- 🔒 Kiehl's
- 🔒 Niketown
- 🔒 Tiffany & Co.

Mirage Hotel
- ☆ Beatles Revolution
- ☆ JET

Palms Casino Hotel
- ☆ ghostbar
- ☆ Playboy Club
- ☆ Rain

Bellagio Hotel
- ★ Bellagio Buffet
- ★ Le Cirque
- ★ Michael Mina
- ★ Olives
- ★ Picasso
- ★ Prime Steak
- ☆ Caramel
- 🔒 Chanel
- 🔒 Prada
- 🔒 Tiffany & Co.

★ André's

New York-New York
- ☆ Bar at Times Sq.
- ☆ Coyote Ugly
- ☆ ESPN Zone
- ☆ Nine Fine

Mandalay Bay
- ★ Aureole
- ★☆ miX
- ☆ House of Blues
- ☆ Red Square
- ☆ rumjungle
- 🔒 Art of Shaving

Bass Pro Shops 🔒

8   40,000 places to eat, drink, stay & play – free at ZAGAT.com

NIGHTLIFE, SHOPPING

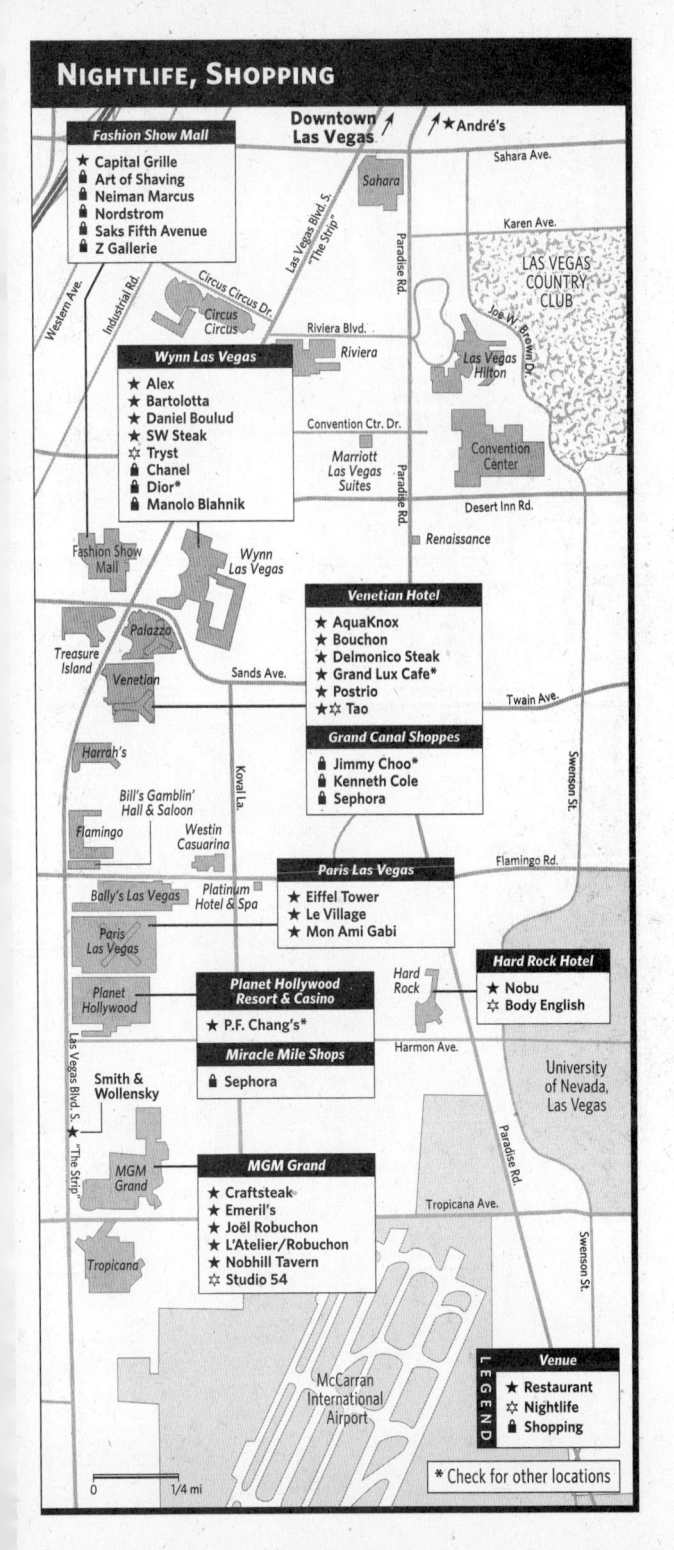

Downtown Las Vegas ↗ ↗ ★ André's

Fashion Show Mall
- ★ Capital Grille
- 🛍 Art of Shaving
- 🛍 Neiman Marcus
- 🛍 Nordstrom
- 🛍 Saks Fifth Avenue
- 🛍 Z Gallerie

Wynn Las Vegas
- ★ Alex
- ★ Bartolotta
- ★ Daniel Boulud
- ★ SW Steak
- ☆ Tryst
- 🛍 Chanel
- 🛍 Dior*
- 🛍 Manolo Blahnik

Venetian Hotel
- ★ AquaKnox
- ★ Bouchon
- ★ Delmonico Steak
- ★ Grand Lux Cafe*
- ★ Postrio
- ★☆ Tao

Grand Canal Shoppes
- 🛍 Jimmy Choo*
- 🛍 Kenneth Cole
- 🛍 Sephora

Paris Las Vegas
- ★ Eiffel Tower
- ★ Le Village
- ★ Mon Ami Gabi

Hard Rock Hotel
- ★ Nobu
- ☆ Body English

Planet Hollywood Resort & Casino
- ★ P.F. Chang's*

Miracle Mile Shops
- 🛍 Sephora

MGM Grand
- ★ Craftsteak
- ★ Emeril's
- ★ Joël Robuchon
- ★ L'Atelier/Robuchon
- ★ Nobhill Tavern
- ☆ Studio 54

LEGEND

Venue	
★	Restaurant
☆	Nightlife
🛍	Shopping

* Check for other locations

Let your voice be heard – visit ZAGAT.com/vote

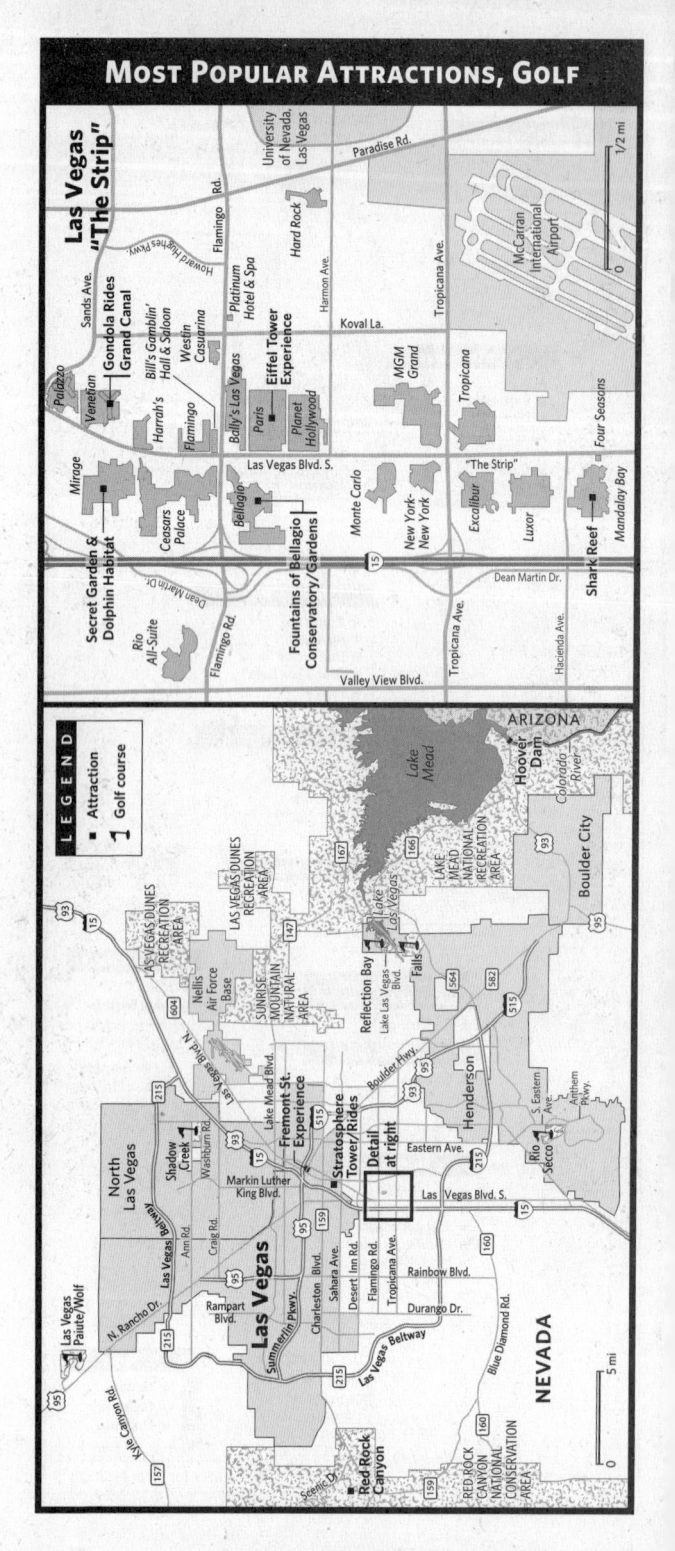

MOST POPULAR ATTRACTIONS, GOLF

DINING

Most Popular

1. Picasso | *French*
2. Bouchon | *French*
3. Delmonico Steak | *Steak*
4. Bellagio Buffet | *Eclectic*
5. Aureole | *American*
6. Mon Ami Gabi | *French*
7. Mesa Grill | *Southwestern*
8. Prime Steak | *Steak*
9. Olives | *Mediterranean*
10. Rosemary's | *American*
11. Emeril's | *Seafood*
12. Michael Mina* | *Seafood*
13. Daniel Boulud | *French*
14. Le Cirque | *French*
15. Bradley Ogden | *American*
16. Spago | *American*
17. Nobu | *Japanese*
18. Joe's | *Seafood/Steak*
19. Joël Robuchon | *French*
20. Palm, The* | *Seafood/Steak*
21. Craftsteak | *Seafood/Steak*
22. Alex | *French*
23. Il Mulino NY | *Italian*
24. Eiffel Tower | *French*
25. Cheesecake Factory | *American*
26. miX | *American/French*
27. André's | *French*
28. Bartolotta* | *Italian/Seafood*
29. Tao | *Pan-Asian*
30. Le Village | *French*
31. P.F. Chang's | *Chinese*
32. L'Atelier/Robuchon | *French*
33. SW Steak | *Steak*
34. Smith & Wollensky | *Steak*
35. Postrio | *American/Med.*
36. Guy Savoy | *French*
37. AquaKnox | *Seafood*
38. Capital Grille | *Steak*
39. Grand Lux Cafe | *Eclectic*
40. Nobhill Tavern | *Californian*

It's obvious that many of the above restaurants are among the Las Vegas area's most expensive, but if popularity were calibrated to price, we suspect that a number of others would join their ranks. Thus, we have added two lists comprising 80 Best Buys on page 18.

KEY NEWCOMERS

Our editors' take on the year's top arrivals. See page 168 for a full list.

Ago | *Italian*
BLT Burger | *Burgers*
Brand Steak | *Steak*
Brio | *Italian*
Carnevino | *Italian/Steak*
CatHouse | *American*
Company | *American*
CUT | *Steak*
Dos Caminos | *Mexican*
Galerias Gourmet | *Mexican*
Lavo | *Mediterranean*

Morels | *French/Steak*
Payard | *French*
Rest. Charlie | *Seafood*
RUB | *BBQ*
Simon | *American*
Stratta | *Italian*
SushiSamba | *Eclectic*
Table 10 | *American*
V Thai | *Thai*
Woo | *Pan-Asian*
Yellowtail | *Japanese*

* Indicates a tie with restaurant above

Top Food Ratings

Excludes places with low votes.

28 L'Atelier/Robuchon | *French*
Joël Robuchon | *French*
Rosemary's | *American*
Nobu | *Japanese*
Todd's Unique Dining | *Eclectic*
Guy Savoy | *French*

27 Picasso | *French*
Lotus of Siam | *Thai*
Alex | *French*
Tableau | *American*
Michael Mina | *Seafood*

26 Del Frisco's Steak | *Steak*
André's | *French*
B&B Ristorante | *Italian*
Prime Steak | *Steak*
Alizé | *French*
Le Cirque | *French*
Jean Philippe | *Dessert*
Sterling Brunch | *Eclectic*
SW Steak | *Steak*

Ferraro's | *Italian*
Nobhill Tavern | *Californian*
Delmonico Steak | *Steak*
Michael's | *Continental*
Bradley Ogden | *American*
Hugo's Cellar | *Continental*
Capital Grille | *Steak*
Daniel Boulud | *French*
Il Mulino NY | *Italian*

25 N9ne Steak | *Steak*
Fleur de Lys | *French*
Wing Lei | *Chinese*
Joe's | *Seafood/Steak*
Okada | *Japanese*
Charlie Palmer | *Steak*
Craftsteak | *Seafood/Steak*
Social House | *Pan-Asian*
StripSteak | *Steak*
Bouchon | *French*
T-Bones | *Steak*

BY CUISINE

AMERICAN (NEW)
28 Rosemary's
27 Tableau
26 Bradley Ogden
25 Aureole
24 David Burke

AMERICAN (TRAD.)
23 Fix
21 Egg & I
Triple 7
20 Cheesecake Factory
Hash House A Go Go

BURGERS
24 In-N-Out
23 Burger Bar
21 Fatburger
20 All-American B&G
17 Big Dog's

CHINESE
25 Wing Lei
Fin
23 Jasmine
Pearl
22 Shanghai Lilly

ECLECTIC
28 Todd's Unique Dining
26 Sterling Brunch
24 Bellagio Buffet
22 Cravings
Spice Market

FRENCH
26 André's
25 Pamplemousse
24 Marché Bacchus
23 Le Village
22 Eiffel Tower

FRENCH (NEW)
28 L'Atelier/Robuchon
Joël Robuchon
Guy Savoy
27 Picasso
Alex

ITALIAN
26 B&B Ristorante
Ferraro's
Il Mulino NY
25 Antonio's
Circo

Let your voice be heard – visit ZAGAT.com/vote

JAPANESE

- [28] Nobu
- [25] Okada
- Shibuya
- [24] I Love Sushi
- Sushi Roku

MEXICAN

- [23] Isla
- [22] Border Grill
- [21] Diego
- [20] Chipotle
- Taqueria Cañonita

PAN-ASIAN

- [25] Social House
- [23] Tao
- Red 8
- [22] Noodles
- [20] Ah Sin

PIZZA

- [24] Metro Pizza
- [23] Spago
- [22] Le Provençal
- [21] Canaletto
- Trattoria del Lupo

SEAFOOD

- [27] Michael Mina
- [25] Joe's
- Craftsteak
- Sensi
- Palm, The

STEAKHOUSES

- [26] Del Frisco's
- Prime Steak
- SW Steak
- Delmonico Steak
- Capital Grille

BY SPECIAL FEATURE

BREAKFAST

- [27] Tableau
- [26] Jean Philippe
- [25] Bouchon
- [24] Bellagio Buffet
- [23] Verandah, The

BRUNCH

- [27] Tableau
- [26] Sterling Brunch
- [25] Bouchon
- Mesa Grill
- Steak House

BUFFET

- [26] Sterling Brunch
- [24] Bellagio Buffet
- [23] Le Village
- [22] Cravings
- Spice Market

BUSINESS DINING

- [28] Rosemary's
- Todd's Unique Dining
- [26] B&B Ristorante
- Prime Steak
- SW Steak

CHILD-FRIENDLY

- [28] Rosemary's
- [27] Lotus of Siam
- [24] Metro Pizza
- [21] Sammy's
- [15] Salt Lick BBQ

DINING ALONE

- [28] Rosemary's
- [27] Lotus of Siam
- [26] Jean Philippe
- Daniel Boulud
- [25] Fleming's Prime

OFFBEAT

- [24] Firefly
- [22] Cafe Ba Ba Reeba!
- [21] Yolie's
- Melting Pot
- [19] Benihana

OPEN 24 HOURS

- [20] Grand Lux Cafe (Venetian)
- Café Bellagio
- [19] Bootlegger Bistro
- Mr. Lucky's
- [17] Black Mountain

OUTDOOR DINING

- [28] Joël Robuchon
- [27] Picasso
- Alex
- Tableau
- [26] André's

PEOPLE-WATCHING

- [28] Nobu
- [27] Picasso
- Alex
- Michael Mina
- [26] B&B Ristorante

QUIET CONVERSATION

- 28 Todd's Unique Dining
- Guy Savoy
- 26 Alizé
- Le Cirque
- SW Steak

SINGLES SCENES

- 28 Nobu
- 25 N9ne Steak
- Sensi
- Fleming's Prime
- 24 Little Buddha

TRENDY

- 28 Nobu
- 26 B&B Ristorante
- Bradley Ogden
- 25 Craftsteak
- 23 Tao

WINNING WINE LISTS

- 28 Guy Savoy
- 27 Picasso
- Alex
- Tableau
- Michael Mina

BY LOCATION

DOWNTOWN

- 26 André's
- Hugo's Cellar
- 25 Vic & Anthony's
- 24 Redwood B&G
- Binion's Ranch

EAST OF STRIP

- 28 Nobu
- 26 Del Frisco's
- 25 Lawry's
- Morton's Steak
- 24 Ruth's Chris

EAST SIDE

- 27 Lotus of Siam
- 25 Pamplemousse
- 24 Billy Bob's
- In-N-Out
- Metro Pizza

HENDERSON

- 28 Todd's Unique Dining
- 24 I Love Sushi
- In-N-Out
- Metro Pizza
- 23 Hank's

NORTHWEST

- 25 T-Bones
- 24 Nora's

- In-N-Out
- Roy's
- Marché Bacchus

SOUTH OF STRIP

- 26 Michael's
- 24 In-N-Out
- 23 Capriotti's
- 21 Panevino
- 20 Famous Dave's

STRIP

- 28 L'Atelier/Robuchon
- Joël Robuchon
- Guy Savoy
- 27 Picasso
- Alex

WEST OF STRIP

- 26 Alizé
- 25 N9ne Steak
- Antonio's
- 24 Buzio's
- In-N-Out

WEST SIDE

- 28 Rosemary's
- 26 Ferraro's
- 25 Fleming's Prime
- 24 Nora's
- Ruth's Chris

Let your voice be heard – visit ZAGAT.com/vote

Top Decor Ratings

29 Picasso	25 Tableau
28 Alex	Daniel Boulud
27 Joël Robuchon	Jasmine
Alizé	Wing Lei
miX	Fin
Le Cirque	Sensi*
Tao	Circo
Okada	Agave
Prime Steak	Shibuya
T-Bones	AquaKnox
Aureole	Shanghai Lilly
26 Eiffel Tower	24 L'Atelier/Robuchon
Hank's	Medici Café
SW Steak	André's
Fleur de Lys	Japonais
Guy Savoy	Michael Mina
Social House	Nobhill Tavern
Bartolotta	Sapporo
Top of the World	Capital Grille
Little Buddha	Bouchon

OUTDOORS

Agave	Okada
Border Grill	Olives
Firefly	T-Bones
Luna Rossa	Trader Vic's
Mon Ami Gabi	Verandah, The

ROMANCE

André's	Le Cirque
Eiffel Tower	Melting Pot
Fleur de Lys	Pamplemousse
Hugo's Cellar	Panevino
Joël Robuchon	Top of the World

ROOMS

Alex	L'Atelier/Robuchon
Aureole	Little Buddha
B&B Ristorante	Origin India
Bouchon	Pullman Grille
Guy Savoy	Tao

VIEWS

Alizé	Eiffel Tower
Binion's Ranch	Medici Café
Capital Grille	miX
Circo	Taqueria Cañonita
Daniel Boulud	Top of the World

Top Service Ratings

28 Joël Robuchon

27 Picasso
Hugo's Cellar
Guy Savoy
Tableau
Michael's
Alex

26 Rosemary's
André's
Le Cirque
L'Atelier/Robuchon
Ferraro's
Alizé
Michael Mina
Prime Steak
Medici Café

25 Todd's Unique Dining
Delmonico Steak
Pamplemousse
Fleur de Lys
Capital Grille
Sterling Brunch
Del Frisco's
Charlie Palmer
Nobhill Tavern
SW Steak
Bradley Ogden
Fin
Verandah, The
Antonio's
Lawry's

24 Daniel Boulud
Morton's Steak
Okada
Redwood B&G
B&B Ristorante
Il Mulino NY
Marché Bacchus
Fellini's
Bartolotta

Best Buys

In order of Bang for the Buck rating.

1. In-N-Out
2. Capriotti's
3. Fatburger
4. Chipotle
5. Baja Fresh
6. Rubio's
7. Ethel's Chocolate
8. Garden Court
9. Chocolate Swan
10. Jean Philippe
11. Egg & I
12. Metro Pizza
13. Triple 7
14. Feast, The
15. Roxy's
16. 'wichcraft
17. Big Dog's
18. Doña Maria
19. Mr. Lucky's
20. Feast Around World
21. Paymon's
22. Sammy's
23. Crown & Anchor
24. Chicago Brewing Co.
25. Carson St.
26. Hash House A Go Go
27. French Market
28. Tintoretto
29. El Jefe's
30. Famous Dave's
31. Memphis BBQ
32. Chili's
33. La Salsa
34. Roadrunner
35. Buffet, The (Hilton)
36. Flavors
37. Elephant Bar
38. Gandhi
39. Agave
40. Cravings

OTHER GOOD VALUES

Archi's Thai Kitchen
Auld Dubliner
Binion's Ranch
BLT Burger
Bootlegger Bistro
Border Grill
Burger Bar
Café Bellagio
California Pizza
Dick's Last Resort
El Sombrero
Firefly
Fix
Florida Café
Grand Lux Cafe
Grape St.
I Love Sushi
Joyful House
Kathy's
Le Provençal
Little Buddha
Lotus of Siam
Makino
Noodles
Nora's
Pasta Shop
Ping Pang Pong
Potato Valley
Pullman Grille
Redwood B&G
RUB BBQ
Salt Lick BBQ
Sam Woo BBQ
Stage Deli
Terra Verde
Thai Spice
Tinoco's
Todd's Unique Dining
Viva Mercado's
Wolfgang Puck B&G

FOOD DECOR SERVICE COST

Dining

Ratings & Symbols

Food, **Decor** and **Service** are rated on the Zagat 0 to 30 scale.

Cost reflects our surveyors' estimate of the price of dinner with one drink and tip and is a benchmark only. Lunch is usually 25 to 30% less. For places without ratings, cost is shown as follows:

| ⌐ $25 and below | E $41 to $65 |
| M $26 to $40 | VE $66 or more |

● serves after 11 PM M closed on Monday
Ø closed on Sunday

Agave ● *Mexican* 18 | 25 | 18 | $27

NW | Pavilion Ctr. | 10820 W. Charleston Blvd. (Hwy. 215) | 702-214-3500 | www.agavelasvegas.com

"A visual treat" thanks to its "colorful", "artistic" decor with soaring ceilings, wrought-iron details and an "amazing" patio, this "happening" Northwest Mexican lures "after-work" crowds with its "festive" atmosphere and "impressive tequila selection"; a few find the "creative" cuisine, while often "tasty", "doesn't match the promise of the decor" (or the moderately "pricey" tabs) while critics say sometimes "lackluster" service "could be improved upon" as well; N.B. the bar now closes at 2 AM.

NEW Ago *Italian* - | - | - | E

E of Strip | Hard Rock Hotel | 4455 Paradise Rd. (bet. Flamingo Rd. & Harmon Ave.) | 702-693-4440 | www.hardrockhotel.com

The buff-and-brown color scheme is about the only thing that's neutral in this hopping enclave in the Hard Rock Hotel east of the Strip, a clone of the LA original that's been a longtime celeb magnet (maybe because Robert De Niro is a partner); expect updated versions of classic Italian fare ranging from *zuppe* to *noci*.

Ah Sin M *Pan-Asian* 20 | 20 | 20 | $44

Strip | Paris Las Vegas | 3655 Las Vegas Blvd. S. (bet. Flamingo Rd. & Harmon Ave.) | 702-946-7000 | www.parislasvegas.com

"Ah, full!" is what you'll be after grazing on "everything from dim sum to chow mein to fancy whole fish" to "fresh, abundant sushi" at the Paris' "total Asian experience"; still, critics say the kitchen could "try a bit" harder to turn out "more creative" plates for the "quick" waiters to ferry; the "patio seating is barely one step up from picnic tables" in comparison to the "beautifully decorated" room, but dine alfresco anyway for "great views of the Bellagio fountains."

AJ's Steakhouse Ø M *Steak* 23 | 22 | 24 | $60

E of Strip | Hard Rock Hotel | 4455 Paradise Rd. (bet. Flamingo Rd. & Harmon Ave.) | 702-693-5500 | www.hardrockhotel.com

"Dean Martin's kind of restaurant" in a Van Halen kind of hotel, the Hard Rock's "retro" chophouse serves up "the swankiest, sexiest nods to Rat Pack culture"; in the "cozy, cool" classic-style room, "gorgeous"

Let your voice be heard – visit ZAGAT.com/vote

DINING

| | FOOD | DECOR | SERVICE | COST |

"eye candy" caddies "incredible martinis" and "rocking steaks" for a dining experience that's "truly hip in its own quiet way."

Alan Albert's *Steak* | 22 | 19 | 22 | $67 |
Strip | 3763 Las Vegas Blvd. S. (bet. Harmon & Tropicana Aves.) | 702-795-4006

"You feel like you've been transported back in time" at this "pricey", "old-fashioned" steakhouse on the Strip that "holds its own" with "huge" and "dependable" steaks, crab legs and sides; service is "top of the line", but some surveyors suggest they "spend a little" on the "boring" teak wood decor and move out of "1978."

al Dente ⓜ *Italian* | 19 | 18 | 20 | $47 |
Strip | Bally's Las Vegas | 3645 Las Vegas Blvd. S. (Flamingo Rd.) | 702-967-7999 | www.ballyslasvegas.com

"As is indicated by the name, pasta is the specialty" of this traditional Italian in Bally's where the only complaint about the "very good" linguine with baby clams is that there isn't enough of it; "small portions" aside, the "routine" plates are "ok for a fast meal", and the "courteous staff" obliges you in your rush, while the "blah" decor has some yearning to leave quickly.

🆉 Alex *French* | 27 | 28 | 27 | $200 |
Strip | Wynn Las Vegas | 3131 Las Vegas Blvd. S. (bet. Desert Inn & Spring Mountain Rds.) | 888-352-3463 | www.wynnlasvegas.com

"No detail is left undone" at "genius" chef Alex Stratta's "foodie fantasy come true" in the Wynn, where "achingly delicious" prix fixe meals of New French cuisine "hit their mark perfectly", "exceptional" servers "treat everyone like a high roller" and "even your purse gets a fancy chair"; from the first step "down the grand staircase" into the "opulent" room to the last "sublime" bite of dessert, it's a "luxurious" "over-the-top experience" that has some "big spenders" swearing it's "worth repeating"; next time "skip the gambling and invest your money here."

Alizé *French* | 26 | 27 | 26 | $86 |
W of Strip | Palms Casino Hotel | 4321 W. Flamingo Rd. (Arville St.) | 702-951-7000 | www.alizelv.com

"Oh-la-la – fine dining with magnificent views to boot" enthuse fans of this "sophisticated" André Rochat–owned French perched atop the Palms Hotel west of the Strip where the "phenomenal" dishes are best enjoyed when "day turns into night" and you can "watch the city come alive"; "impeccable" service from the "surprisingly unpretentious" staff and an "elegant" room that oozes with "romance" mean that most have no regrets about "offloading some winnings" here; N.B. jacket and tie suggested, and no children under 12 please.

All-American Bar & Grille ⓢ *American* | 20 | 16 | 19 | $36 |
W of Strip | Rio All-Suite Hotel | 3700 W. Flamingo Rd. (bet. I-15 & Valley View Blvd.) | 702-777-7767 | www.playrio.com

"We're talkin' half-pounder cooked to order, juicy, with a great bun" at this "easy" "all-American spot" at the Rio for "big" burgers or "solid steak", "chops and chix" that make "decent late-night meaty snacks"; the vibe is "laid-back", the "cost isn't bad" and the "friendly" crowd is mostly focused around the "sports plasma screens."

DINING

| | FOOD | DECOR | SERVICE | COST |

America ◐ *American* — 15 | 17 | 15 | $21

Strip | New York-New York Hotel | 3790 Las Vegas Blvd. S. (Tropicana Ave.) | 702-740-6451 | www.arkvegas.com

The eponymous "land of abundance" is represented by the "plethora of choices" "from each state in the country" at this 24/7 New York-New York theme eatery; though "slow service leaves time to view" the "gigantic U.S. map" dominating the "red, white and blue" room, it can seem that the "waiters are actually going to some of those far-reaching places to get the food" – and, if they are, some feel it's "not worth the trip" for what amounts to rather "pedestrian" "coffee-shop fare."

Z André's *French* — 26 | 24 | 26 | $80

Downtown | 401 S. Sixth St. (bet. Bonneville St. & Bridger Ave.) | 702-385-5016 ⓢ
Strip | Monte Carlo Resort | 3770 Las Vegas Blvd. S. (bet. Harmon & Tropicana Aves.) | 702-798-7151
www.andrelv.com

"Old Las Vegas" comes alive at this Downtown "classic" from André Rochat that's "been here for decades" serving "rich" French fare ("even the butter is sautéed in butter") in a venerable converted house with plenty of "charm"; the newer Strip outpost offers the same "excellent" food but in more "elegant", "Louis XIV–style" quarters, while both pamper patrons with "impeccably polite service" that makes it all "worth the splurge"; N.B. the Decor score does not reflect a recent spruce-up at the Monte Carlo locale.

Antonio's Ⓜ *Italian* — 25 | 23 | 25 | $56

W of Strip | Rio All-Suite Hotel | 3700 W. Flamingo Rd. (bet. I-15 & Valley View Blvd.) | 702-777-7777 | www.playrio.com

"Classic old-school Italian" cuisine is the draw at this "upscale" "New York"–style spot in the Rio just west of the Strip turning out "huge portions" of "innovatively prepared standards" (like osso buco) brought by waiters who treat you "just right"; if a few are "put off by the location" steps away from "the casino floor", others insist it's not only "quiet", but "comfortable" and "elegant" with a dining area decorated in muted tones that faces onto an open kitchen.

Applebee's *American* — 13 | 13 | 15 | $19

E Side | Boulevard Mall | 3340 S. Maryland Pkwy. (Desert Inn Rd.) | 702-737-4990
E Side | Smith's Shopping Ctr. | 500 N. Nellis Blvd. (Stewart Ave.) | 702-452-7155
Henderson | 699 N. Stephanie St. (Sunset Rd.) | 702-433-6339
NW | Best of the West | 2070 N. Rainbow Blvd. (Lake Mead Blvd.) | 702-648-1065
S of Strip | 820 E. Warm Springs Rd. (Hwy. 215) | 702-837-8733
SW | 5010 S. Fort Apache Rd. (Tropicana Ave.) | 702-221-1061
W Side | 3501 S. Rainbow Blvd. (Spring Mountain Rd.) | 702-220-3070
W Side | Westland Fair | 4605 W. Charleston Blvd. (Decatur Blvd.) | 702-870-5973
W Side | 8730 W. Charleston Blvd. (Durango Dr.) | 702-946-6104
www.applebees.com

"If you're looking for a quick lunch" after days of haute fressing, "you could do worse than a salad" from the "great Weight Watchers menu" at this "low-end" Traditional American chain that's "thriving" in

DINING

                                        FOOD | DECOR | SERVICE | COST

Vegas; critics say "if the service were any worse, it would be a buffet", but at least it "beats standing in line at a hotel coffee shop."

AquaKnox *Seafood*   23 | 25 | 22 | $68

Strip | Venetian Hotel | 3355 Las Vegas Blvd. S. (bet. Flamingo & Spring Mountain Rds.) | 702-414-3772 | www.aquaknox.net

"A cool blue" "aquarium"-like room with a water-encased wine cellar provides the perfect setting to indulge in "sumptuous" seafood dishes (like "heaping" platters of oysters) and "fabulous" vintages at this "outstanding" "gem" set inside the Venetian on the Strip; though service is "attentive and professional", a few find it "pricey for what it is" and add that the "noisy" environs and "slick", "clublike setting" seem like they're better suited to "a bar [than] a restaurant."

Archi's Thai Kitchen ⓂThai   ▽ 24 | 11 | 20 | $20

W Side | 6360 W. Flamingo Rd. (bet. Jones Blvd. & Torrey Pines) | 702-880-5550

It's "not fancy", but what this "quaint" West Side Thai "lacks in decor, it makes up for in flavor and spice" say surveyors citing "top-tier" dishes like "excellent" curries that are "cheap" too (the $5.95 "lunchtime special" "can't be beat"); regulars note that its "small" size and "popular" status mean that "wait times can be long depending on the time of day."

Artem ●Ⓜ *Russian*   ▽ 21 | 16 | 19 | $28
(aka Eliseevsky)

W Side | 4825 W. Flamingo Rd. (Decatur Blvd.) | 702-247-8766 | www.russianrest.russianvegas.com

Every place in Vegas has a shtick, but this one's bona fide: expats (including off-hours Cirque du Soleil performers) will tell you this West Side spot is "almost like stepping into a little eatery in the Ukraine" where the "good, basic Russian food" pairs with "icy vodka shots" brought by "surly" old-country waiters; it's so "authentic", "they should give women babushkas when entering."

Auld Dubliner Irish Pub *Irish*   ▽ 20 | 19 | 19 | $21

Lake LV | MonteLago Vill. | 40 Via Bel Canto (Via Brianza) | Henderson | 702-567-8002 | www.aulddubliner.com

Those "in search of the perfect pint" seek out this "solid-all-around" Lake Las Vegas pub where they "pour a good Guinness" and the "traditional" Irish "grub", while "nothing unique", is "well done"; patio seating and a view of the water add to the "nice atmosphere", as do live "fiddlers" (Thursdays–Saturdays) who inspire many a customer to dance a "jig."

ⓩ Aureole *American*   25 | 27 | 24 | $101

Strip | Mandalay Bay Resort | 3950 Las Vegas Blvd. S. (Mandalay Bay Rd.) | 702-632-7401 | www.charliepalmer.com

"It feels like walking into a dream" swoon surveyors "wowed" by chef Charlie Palmer's "NYC transplant" in Mandalay Bay where a "dramatic entranceway" opens into a "beautiful" room with a multistory wine tower famously attended to by "harnessed" "angels" who "elegantly ascend" to retrieve vintages from a "tremendous" collection; "first-class" New American cuisine "rises to new heights" as well in a "superb" prix fixe menu while near "flawless" service "makes you feel like a million bucks"; in all it's an experience of "sensory overload" that

DINING

| | FOOD | DECOR | SERVICE | COST |

"more than satisfies", especially if "someone else is paying" the "insanely expensive" bill.

Austins Steakhouse Steak   ▽ 24 | 20 | 24 | $52

N Las Vegas | Texas Station Hotel | 2101 Texas Star Ln. (bet. Lake Mead Blvd. & Rancho Dr.) | North Las Vegas | 702-631-1033 | www.stationcasinos.com

If "you're tired of buffets and food courts" – heck, if you need "a break from the Strip" altogether – high-tail it to North Vegas where "wonderful steaks", a "nice atmosphere" and "outstanding service" await at this Texas Station chophouse; when you're done with your meal, "you can hit the $5 craps tables" in the hotel's "locals' casino."

Baja Fresh Mexican Grill Mexican   19 | 11 | 14 | $11

E Side | Target Shopping Ctr. | 1292 S. Nellis Blvd. (Charleston Blvd.) | 702-641-6770
E Side | Mission Ctr. | 1380 E. Flamingo Rd. (Maryland Pkwy.) | 702-699-8920
E Side | 3347 E. Russell Rd. (Pecos Rd.) | 702-212-6800
NW | 4343 N. Rancho Dr. (Craig Rd.) | 702-396-2553
NW | Summerhill Plaza | 7501 W. Lake Mead Blvd. (Buffalo Dr.) | 702-838-4100
NW | 7930 W. Tropical Pkwy. (Centennial Center Blvd.) | 702-307-2345
SW | Tropicana Beltway | 4916 S. Fort Apache Rd. (Tropicana Ave.) | 702-871-4260
W Side | 4190 S. Rainbow Blvd. (Flamingo Rd.) | 702-876-4193
W Side | Sahara Pavillion Shopping Ctr. | 4760 W. Sahara Ave. (Decatur Blvd.) | 702-878-7772
W Side | The Lakes | 8780 W. Charleston Blvd. (bet. Durango Dr. & Rampart Blvd.) | 702-948-4043
www.bajafresh.com
Additional locations throughout the Las Vegas area

"Fresh fast food" might sound like an "oxymoron", but given the "healthy" staples "made right in front of you" and a "rapidly replenished fixings bar", the cuisine at this Mexican chain fits the description; ok, it's "not a place for a romantic dinner", but it's "simple", "inexpensive" and turns out your "delicious, filling" order quicker than you can throw "two thumbs up" for its burritos.

Bally's Steakhouse Steak   22 | 19 | 22 | $60

Strip | Bally's Las Vegas | 3645 Las Vegas Blvd. S. (Flamingo Rd.) | 702-967-7999 | www.ballyslasvegas.com

"When it's raining and you don't want to leave the premises", you're in luck at Bally's where "solid" beef and lobster come "with all the comforts you would expect" from "a man's steakhouse out of the '60s" (1973, to be exact), including "old-world service" and a "clubby" ambiance; perhaps the "decor and menu are dated, but the food is good", not only for dinner but on Sundays when it transforms into the "quintessentially old-school" Sterling Brunch with champagne and caviar aplenty.

☒ B&B Ristorante Italian   26 | 24 | 24 | $75

Strip | Venetian Hotel | 3355 Las Vegas Blvd. S. (bet. Flamingo & Spring Mountain Rds.) | 702-266-9977 | www.bandbristorante.com

"Finally", "just what Vegas was missing" declare "foodies" "delighted" with Mario Batali's pricey Venetian venture that mirrors the experience of NYC's Babbo with "phenomenal wines" and "ingenious" "twists on classic Italian dishes" like the "amazing" signature beef

DINING

| | FOOD | DECOR | SERVICE | COST |

cheek ravioli; a "knowledgeable" staff and "intimate" digs decked out in dark woods also win raves, and if a few find "they still have a few kinks to work out", the majority is convinced this "exciting" arrival "will only get better."

Bartolotta Ristorante di Mare *Italian/Seafood*   24 | 26 | 24 | $91

Strip | Wynn Las Vegas | 3131 Las Vegas Blvd. S. (bet. Desert Inn & Spring Mountain Rds.) | 888-352-3463 | www.wynnlasvegas.com

Connoisseurs claim they're "transported to a seaside village" thanks to a "unique assortment" of "fantastically fresh fish" from the Mediterranean at chef Paul Bartolotta's "simply outstanding" Italian seafooder at the Wynn with "romantic" lakefront seating available in one of the private cabanas; "top-notch" staffers "aim to please" with "superb" service (including "tableside presentations"), making this local "treasure" a "memorable" experience, and one that's "way worth" the "truly outrageous" final bill.

Battista's Hole in the Wall *Italian*   17 | 17 | 19 | $31

E of Strip | 4041 Audrie St. (Las Vegas Blvd.) | 702-732-1424 | www.battistaslasvegas.com

"Something with soul" in Sin City say surveyors stuffing themselves on "red-sauce" "package deals", "great garlic bread and as much wine as you can drink" at this "old Vegas" "dive" east of the Strip that offers "passable" Italian with faux "Queens ambiance" on the side; sure, some say it's "tacky" and "out of date", but everyone "treats you like a human", including the "campy" "accordion guy" who "has a song and something to say about each state" in the nation.

Bay Side Buffet *Eclectic*   19 | 19 | 19 | $28

Strip | Mandalay Bay Resort | 3950 Las Vegas Blvd. S. (Mandalay Bay Rd.) | 702-632-7402 | www.mandalaybay.com

"Lots of choices" – including "roasted meats", a "good pasta station" and a "nice selection of desserts" – might sound heavy, but it's balanced by the "light and airy" view of the "amazing" Mandalay Bay pools and gardens at this Eclectic buffet that's "above and beyond" the pack of wolf-downs on the Strip; still, even fans admit "it is what it is": "just another cafeteria" in which to "use your comps to get a free meal."

☒ Bellagio Buffet *Eclectic*   24 | 19 | 19 | $34

Strip | Bellagio Hotel | 3600 Las Vegas Blvd. S. (Flamingo Rd.) | 702-693-8255 | www.bellagio.com

"A certain diet destroyer" say the legions of surveyors who endure almost "constant lines" for what they call the "mac daddy" of all buffets, with a "vast" spread of Eclectic dishes from "Buffalo wings to wild boar", "bountiful quantities" of seafood, plus a "fantastic" brunch on Saturdays and Sundays where the champagne "flows like the Bellagio fountains themselves"; some contend it's more "expensive" than competitors, though defenders justify the "high" prices declaring "it's the only meal you need for the day."

Benihana ● *Japanese*   19 | 18 | 19 | $44

E of Strip | Las Vegas Hilton | 3000 Paradise Rd. (bet. Desert Inn Rd. & Karen Ave.) | 702-732-5334 | www.benihana.com

Amid an east-of-the-Strip landscape "replete with koi ponds, waterfalls and replica huts" lies the "most lavish" link in this "standard-model chop

DINING

| | FOOD | DECOR | SERVICE | COST |

'n' dice" Japanese chain; the "chefs put on quite a show" for "conventioneers" slurping "umbrella drinks", but the fare is "trite" to some, so the "shrimp-and-knives juggling" act quickly becomes "old-hat."

Big Al's Oyster Bar *Seafood* 19 | 12 | 17 | $26
W of Strip | Orleans Hotel | 4500 W. Tropicana Ave. (Arville St.) | 702-365-7111 | www.orleanscasino.com

"Sit at the counter and watch 'em make your meal" in the open kitchen at this raw bar/casual seafooder in a "heavily trafficked area of the Orleans" west of the Strip where fans claim the "affordable" eats are "not damn bad at all"; critics, however, aren't nearly as "friendly" toward the place as the staff is toward them: asked "how can you mess up an oyster?", they suggest visiting this "perfect combination" of "disappointing" fare and "unending racket" to find out.

Big Dog's ☻ *American* 17 | 14 | 19 | $18
E Side | 1511 N. Nellis Blvd. (bet. Owens & Washington Aves.) | 702-459-1099
W Side | 4543 N. Rancho Dr. (Craig Rd.) | 702-645-1404
W Side | 6390 W. Sahara Ave. (Torrey Pines Dr.) | 702-876-3647
www.bigdogsbrews.com

"Great for Green Bay Packer cheeseheads", this "pub-grub" trio wags the tail with "Wisconsin specialties", including brats and steaks; the "cute roadhouses" serve "nothing fancy", just "tasty", "modestly priced" comfort food (plus "their own beer brewed on-site" at Rancho Drive) dished out in a four-legged-friend-themed "sports-bar" atmosphere – bring "earplugs" lest the howling "during playoffs" nips at your nerves.

Big Kitchen Buffet *Eclectic* 16 | 12 | 16 | $23
Strip | Bally's Las Vegas | 3645 Las Vegas Blvd. S. (Flamingo Rd.) | 702-967-4930 | www.ballyslasvegas.com

It's "not the newest kid on the block", but "if you want a hearty meal (and who doesn't when they're losing money?)", this matron of "midlevel buffets" in Bally's churns out the "usual" belt-buster suspects, from "regular American" to Italian and Chinese; the "sterile room" feels like a "cafeteria", and "nothing will knock your socks off", but it might make you pop your pants – eat enough of the "hometown potluck" cuisine, and you'll "have to buy a sweat suit to be comfortable for the rest of the day."

Billy Bob's *Seafood/Steak* 24 | 19 | 21 | $40
E Side | Sam's Town Hotel | 5111 Boulder Hwy. (Nellis Blvd.) | 702-454-8031 | www.samstownlv.com

"Ah, be still my clogged arteries" sigh carnivores tucking into "juicy" "perfectly cooked steaks" served in "great, big portions" at this rustic, Old West–themed surf 'n' turfer with "real character" on the East Side; "casual, comfortable" quarters and "good value" make it a "favorite" for locals and visitors alike.

Binion's Ranch Steakhouse *Steak* 24 | 19 | 22 | $47
Downtown | Binion's Hotel | 128 E. Fremont St., 24th fl. (bet. Casino Center Blvd. & 1st St.) | 702-382-1600 | www.binions.com

"The view alone is worth the trip" to this Downtown chophouse on the 24th floor of the "historic" Binion's Hotel offering "superior" sights of

DINING

the city below, "plenty of beef" and an "outstanding" "price/value" ratio; a few find the "decor needs a little refreshing", but that's no matter to insiders who'd rather "let the tourists hit the big Strip chains" and keep this "local" "favorite" to themselves.

Black Mountain Grill ● *Eclectic*   17 | 17 | 17 | $26

Henderson | 11021 S. Eastern Ave. (Sunridge Hts. Pkwy.) | 702-990-0990

"For a solid meal without the tourists", hang out with Henderson "locals" at this "lodge-style" Eclectic covering everything from steakhouse specialties to wood-fired pizzas to Pacific Rim flavors; "the fireplace is a nice touch", but while "the food is good", some say "it takes forever for it to come out of the kitchen" – lucky that the place is open 24 hours a day.

NEW BLT Burger ● *Burgers*   - | - | - | M

Strip | Mirage Hotel | 3400 Las Vegas Blvd. S. (Spring Mountain Rd.) | 702-792-7888 | www.bltrestaurants.com

Celeb chef Laurent Tourondel joins the boutique burger fray with this moderately priced entry at the Mirage on the Strip where prime beef, lamb and turkey patties are joined up with unusual draft beers, house cocktails and more than 10 varieties of milkshakes (including alcohol-spiked versions); its casually trendy setup includes a curvy open kitchen, flat-screen video wall and rock 'n' roll soundtrack.

Boa Steakhouse *Steak*   24 | 23 | 22 | $67

Strip | Forum Shops at Caesars Palace | 3500 Las Vegas Blvd. S. (Flamingo Rd.) | 702-733-7373 | www.innovativedining.com

"Mind-blowing cocktails" fuel the "sexy" scene at this "way too hip" LA chophouse import in the Forum Shops at Caesars Palace featuring "excellent" dry-aged steaks paired with "superb sauces" and served in "sleek", "modern" quarters; "plenty of hustle and bustle" accounts for some "incredible people-watching" (especially if you snag a seat in the patio section), and if a few deem service "uneven" and say the "loud" environs are strictly "for the young", most consider it the epitome of "chic" and well worth the "pricey" tabs, in spite of its "mall location."

Bob Taylor's Ranch House *Steak*   20 | 17 | 18 | $34

NW | 6250 Rio Vista St. (Ann Rd.) | 702-645-1399 | www.bobtaylorsranchhouse.com

This "vintage" (circa 1955) midpriced steakhouse in the Northwest part of the valley draws local supporters who suggest the appeal here is quite simple: "just good steaks" "grilled over an open flame"; the converted ranch house setting and its working fireplace lend it "rustic charm", so even if some find the food simply "average", it's still "worth the trip" for something a little "different" from the chains proliferating on the Strip.

Bonefish Grill *Seafood*   21 | 21 | 20 | $34

Henderson | 10839 S. Eastern Ave. (Horizon Ridge Pkwy.) | 702-228-3474 | www.bonefishgrill.com

"Fresh fresh fish" at "reasonable prices" reel 'em in to this Henderson chain seafooder where "competently prepared" finned favorites from a "rotating" menu are delivered by an "attentive", "well-trained" staff; "attractive", "yuppieish" decor makes it "more of a grown-up place", even if detractors declare digs a bit on the "noisy" side.

DINING

| | FOOD | DECOR | SERVICE | COST |

Bootlegger Bistro ◐ *Italian* — 19 | 19 | 21 | $32
S of Strip | 7700 Las Vegas Blvd. S. (Robindale Rd.) | 702-736-4939 | www.bootleggerlasvegas.com
"It's easy to imagine mob guys hanging out" at this "kitschy", "old-fashioned" south-of-the-Strip Italian where "family recipes" served up 24/7 are the draw for assorted "locals", "old-timers" and a handful of "celebrities"; "noisy" and "crowded" conditions add to the "charm", though some skip the cuisine entirely and focus on the festive "atmosphere" and entertainment like "excellent jazz bands."

Border Grill *Mexican* — 22 | 18 | 19 | $34
Strip | Mandalay Bay Resort | 3950 Las Vegas Blvd. S. (Mandalay Bay Rd.) | 702-632-7403 | www.bordergrill.com
"Don't look for the Taco Bell dog" at this "elevated Mexican" by TV's *Two Hot Tamales* where "reasonably priced", "creative" *comidas* are created with "plenty of spice" and "a dash of tradition"; the "margaritas could knock you on your ass" – if you weren't already sitting down in the colorful, bi-level interior or outside "overlooking the Mandalay Bay pool gardens" slur "crowds" who cause such a ruckus that "a bullfight ring is more subdued"; N.B. the Decor score does not reflect a 2008 spruce-up.

Z Bouchon *French* — 25 | 24 | 24 | $60
Strip | Venetian Hotel | 3355 Las Vegas Blvd. S. (bet. Flamingo & Spring Mountain Rds.) | 702-414-6200 | www.bouchonbistro.com
Thomas Keller's "relatively affordable" "outpost of gastronomy" in the Venetian is "absolutely true to his Yountville original" with "perfectly executed French bistro fare", from "heavenly breakfasts" ("light-as-a-feather waffles", a cheese Danish "to dream about") to "indescribably delicious" dinners; the "beautiful" Adam Tihany-designed dining area includes "relaxing" patio seating "overlooking a quiet, well-shaded pool" that "makes you forget where you are", so even if service is sometimes "a little lacking", patrons proclaim it all "thoroughly enjoyable" nonetheless.

Z Bradley Ogden *American* — 26 | 24 | 25 | $85
Strip | Caesars Palace | 3570 Las Vegas Blvd. S. (Flamingo Rd.) | 702-731-7731 | www.caesarspalace.com
A "serene", "elegant" "oasis" amid the "clanging bells" of Caesars Palace, this upscale New American from "Bay Area wonder chef" Bradley Ogden "charms" with "inspired" dishes so full of "fresh", "wonderful flavors" that "you forget how much you lost at the craps table"; the staff is "experienced" and "well-informed", though regulars note that "what really makes it best" is that the owner himself is often "on-site" (his "tours of the kitchen" are another "nice touch"); N.B. wallet-watchers say the bar menu is a less-expensive dining option.

NEW Brand Steakhouse *Steak* — - | - | - | E
Strip | Monte Carlo Resort | 3770 Las Vegas Blvd. S. (bet. Harmon & Tropicana Aves.) | 702-730-6705 | www.montecarlo.com
A far cry from your father's steakhouse, this stylish new entry at the Monte Carlo on the Strip is a restaurant/club hybrid with an open, loungelike layout and live DJs every weekend; although the pricey menu features updated surf 'n' turf classics like king-crab scampi,

DINING

make no mistake that cattle is king here with a 120-oz. porterhouse on offer in case you and five of your friends are unusually hungry.

NEW Brio Tuscan Grille Italian | - | - | - | M |

S of Strip | Town Square | 6605 Las Vegas Blvd. S. (bet. I-215 & Sunset Rd.) | 702-914-9145 | www.brioitalian.com

Soaring ceilings and Venetian plaster accents give a villalike feel to this Italian chain link housed south of the Strip in Town Square; its moderately priced dishes include lobster risotto, bistecca alla fiorentina and a signature sampling of bruschettas.

Broiler Seafood/Steak | ▽ 21 | 15 | 19 | $37 |

E Side | Boulder Station Hotel | 4111 Boulder Hwy. (Lamb Blvd.) | 702-432-7777 | www.boulderstation.com

W of Strip | Palace Station Hotel | 2411 W. Sahara Ave. (Rancho Dr.) | 702-367-2408 | www.stationcasinos.com

"Adding an entree can be gilding the lily" when the "excellent soup-and-salad bar" is this "extensive", but make room anyway for the "good" meat and "great" seafood at this "casual" surf 'n' turf duo in the Station casinos on the East Side and west of the Strip; they're "fantastic" for a "reliable" meal, with plenty left over to "wrap up and take away."

Buffet, The Eclectic | - | - | - | E |

Strip | Wynn Las Vegas | 3131 Las Vegas Blvd. S. (bet. Desert Inn & Spring Mountain Rds.) | 702-770-7000 | www.wynnlasvegas.com

Serving items like jerk chicken, wood-fired pizza and several types of ceviche, this Eclectic buffet at the Wynn goes a step further than some of its many competitors; highlights include an attractive dining space with – surprise – natural light, plus an impressive lineup of desserts.

Buffet, The American | 17 | 15 | 16 | $22 |

Downtown | Golden Nugget Hotel | 129 E. Fremont St. (Main St.) | 702-385-7111 | www.goldennugget.com

The "very good combination" of "casual" environs and "fulfilling" fare awaits at this Golden Nugget buffet; the "traditional Downtown setting" and "safe-for-American-tastes" cuisine might be "nothing special", but Friday's seafood is "plentiful", Sunday brunch's "champagne flows freely" and, as opposed to other "cheap" spreads, "some of the food here even has flavor" – particularly the "to-die-for bread pudding."

Buffet, The Eclectic | 17 | 13 | 16 | $19 |

E of Strip | Las Vegas Hilton | 3000 Paradise Rd. (bet. Desert Inn Rd. & Karen Ave.) | 702-732-5111 | www.lvhilton.com

Even if "cabbies and locals" recommend this all-you-can-eat chowdown amid the "flashing lights and singing slots" of the Las Vegas Hilton's sportsbook east of the Strip, tourists find it "nothing to write home about"; there's "lots of variety" to the "decent" Eclectic offerings, but like others of its ilk, it's "known for speed, not quality dining."

Burger Bar Burgers | 23 | 17 | 18 | $26 |

Strip | Mandalay Place | 3930 Las Vegas Blvd. S. (Mandalay Bay Rd.) | 702-632-9364 | www.burgerbarlv.com

From the "Zen-like simplicity" of a plain patty to the "baroque opulence" of "Kobe beef with foie gras and black truffles", the "possibili-

DINING

| | FOOD | DECOR | SERVICE | COST |

ties are unlimited" for "building your own" version of that "old American favorite" at this "great concept" in Mandalay Place from chef-owner Hubert Keller (Fleur de Lys); not only can you choose from "an array of tasty toppings", but the burgers themselves come in a "huge variety" – at a "wide range of prices"; beyond monitors broadcasting sports events, the "casual" place isn't nearly as well dressed as the namesakes.

Buzio's *Seafood* 24 | 19 | 22 | $48

W of Strip | Rio All-Suite Hotel | 3700 W. Flamingo Rd. (bet. I-15 & Valley View Blvd.) | 702-252-7697 | www.playrio.com

The "cioppino is wonderful" and a "bargain, for all you get" at this "terrific" fish house in the Rio that also offers "oversized cocktails" and the "biggest lobster ever"; still, those who knew it when feel it's "getting a bit dated", citing the kitchen's "lack of imagination", not to mention "slow service" and a "so-so setting."

Cafe, The *American* 19 | 19 | 17 | $30

Strip | Mandalay Bay Resort | 3950 Las Vegas Blvd. S. (Mandalay Bay Rd.) | 702-632-9250 | www.mandalaybay.com

This "cut-above" cafe in THEhotel at Mandalay Bay is a "stylish" setting for "casual" but "relaxing" dining; though the menu choices are "standard" for this type of Traditional American, they're "well prepared" and it's a "hoot" watching the "parade of interesting people going to miX" while remaining at a safe distance from the "hustle and bustle."

Cafe Ba Ba Reeba! *Spanish* 22 | 20 | 20 | $34

Strip | Fashion Show Mall | 3200 Las Vegas Blvd. S. (Spring Mountain Rd.) | 702-258-1211 | www.cafebabareeba.com

They "should open in Madrid and teach Spaniards how good their food can be" argue admirers of this Fashion Show Mall outpost of a Chicago institution serving "little morsels of heaven"; there are "no bad picks" among their "amazing" paellas and "huge variety" of "excellent tapas", while the festive "indoor/outdoor" seating helps make it the "place for celebrating", "sampling" and "sipping sangria."

Café Bellagio ● *American* 20 | 20 | 20 | $31

Strip | Bellagio Hotel | 3600 Las Vegas Blvd. S. (Flamingo Rd.) | 702-693-8255 | www.bellagio.com

"Even at 3 AM" when "you want to get back to the tables quickly", the casual New American food is "fresh and plentiful" and the staff "accommodating" at this around-the-clock, "upscale coffee shop" that's the "most reasonable place to eat" in the namesake hotel; a "lovely view" of the conservatory's "ever-fabulous", ever-changing floral garden makes this "quiet oasis" all the more "pleasant."

Cafe Heidelberg *German* 22 | 17 | 20 | $27

E of Strip | 610 E. Sahara Ave. (bet. Maryland Pkwy. & Paradise Rd.) | 702-731-5310

"Not for the faint of appetite", this "fast, fun German" east of the Strip rolls out "huge portions" of "excellent" wurst, schnitzel and sauerbraten and frosty pints of beer; a weekend band playing oompahs and "cheery maidens" who seem "fresh out of their show-girl costumes" bring on "Oktober" where "far too much of a good thing" includes takeaway tastes from the "nice" deli/grocery.

DINING

	FOOD	DECOR	SERVICE	COST

Cafe Lago *Eclectic* — 17 | 18 | 18 | $29
Strip | Caesars Palace | 3570 Las Vegas Blvd. S. (Flamingo Rd.) | 702-731-7110 | www.caesarspalace.com
"Slightly more sophisticated" than most "typical hotel cafes", this "mellow" spot in Caesars with "short waits" is a "good choice" for Eclectic selections served in a buffet format; sit outside on the patio or inside by the "big windows" for a view of the "hot bodies surrounding the huge pool."

Cafe Martorano ☻ *Italian* — ▽ 25 | 21 | 23 | $72
W of Strip | Rio All-Suite Hotel | 3700 W. Flamingo Rd. (bet. I-15 & Valley View Blvd.) | 702-221-8279 | www.harrahs.com
Italian cuisine with "Philly flair" awaits at this "upscale" yearling in the Rio where chef-owner Steve Martorano "follows up" his Ft. Lauderdale original with this Vegas version offering the same "top-notch", "family-style" fare that's both "edgy and traditional at the same time"; a "lively" setting with DJs spinning nightly have critics complaining that "too loud" environs mean you "can't count on having a conversation here."

Café Wasabi ⓈPacific Rim — ▽ 21 | 16 | 19 | $33
W Side | 7365 W. Sahara Ave. (Tenaya Way) | 702-804-9652
"Tasty", "innovative" Pacific Rim dishes like chicken lettuce wraps and wasabi cheesecake are the draw at this "funky" West Sider set in a "nondescript strip mall"; in spite of complaints of "inconsistent" food, "friendly service" and gentle prices mean that locals still recommend it "if you're craving something a little different."

California Pizza Kitchen *Pizza* — 18 | 14 | 17 | $23
NEW **S of Strip** | Town Square | 6659 Las Vegas Blvd. S. (bet. I-215 & Sunset Rd.) | 702-896-5154
Strip | Fashion Show Mall | 3200 Las Vegas Blvd. S. (Spring Mountain Rd.) | 702-893-1370
Strip | Mirage Hotel | 3400 Las Vegas Blvd. S. (Spring Mountain Rd.) | 702-791-7357 ☻
www.cpk.com
"Same ol', same ol'", but it's all "decent" at this "reliable chain" for "twists" on pizza, pasta and salad near the Strip or in the Fashion Show Mall; the "reasonably priced", "kid-friendly" menu offers "enough options to please any crew", so "bring the gang", "especially to the Mirage location" where a "great view of the sportsbook" and "good people-watching" keep the urchins occupied during the "long wait" for a table.

NEW **Caminos de Morelia** *Mexican* — - | - | - | I
W Side | 3713 W. Sahara Ave. (Valley View Blvd.) | 702-364-9657
This West Side newcomer showcases inexpensive renditions of classic Mexican specialties from chef Miguel Magana (ex The Tillerman); the decor has a sports-bar feel with multiple TVs and gaming machines, but service is warm and the food's the real deal.

Canaletto *Italian* — 21 | 22 | 20 | $46
Strip | Venetian Hotel | 3355 Las Vegas Blvd. S. (bet. Flamingo & Spring Mountain Rds.) | 702-733-0070 | www.venetian.com
The "delicious" Northern Italian dishes "almost make the canal seem real" on the terrace of this "charming" trattoria in the Venetian's

DINING

                          FOOD DECOR SERVICE COST

"'open-air' replica of St. Mark's Square"; delight your date with "a late lunch and a good bottle of wine" – accompanied by "faux sunsets", "singing gondoliers and lapping water", it's "as romantic as outdoors created indoors can get."

Canal Street *Seafood/Steak* ▽ 22 | 20 | 20 | $41
W of Strip | Orleans Hotel | 4500 W. Tropicana Ave. (Arville St.) | 702-365-7111 | www.orleanscasino.com
This Big Easy-styled surf 'n' turfer in the Orleans Hotel west of the Strip augments its meat-heavy menu with classic NOLA dishes like oysters Rockefeller while salads get tableside presentations; the upscale atmosphere with a mural of a Louisiana bayou belies the "moderate" tabs – in ever-escalating Las Vegas, this steakhouse is "popular for a reason – fair prices."

Canter's Deli ● *Deli* 18 | 11 | 12 | $19
Strip | Treasure Island Hotel | 3300 Las Vegas Blvd. S. (Spring Mountain Rd.) | 702-894-7111 | www.cantersdeli.com
"Skinny girls beware": though it's the "sister" of a Los Angeles institution, this "casual" joint doesn't peddle celebrity-diet fare; instead, "if you need a pastrami fix or a bowl of matzo-ball soup", its deli dishes "meet expectations" for a "huge", "quick bite"; TI's take is "almost authentic", though fans feel it's "missing the attitude" and "gritty charm" of the SoCal original.

Canyon Ranch Café *American/Health Food* 21 | 16 | 20 | $29
Strip | Venetian Hotel | 3355 Las Vegas Blvd. S., 4th fl. (bet. Flamingo & Spring Mountain Rds.) | 702-414-3633 | www.venetian.com
NEW Canyon Ranch Grill *American/Health Food*
Strip | Palazzo Hotel | 3325 Las Vegas Blvd. S. (Sands Ave.) | 702-414-3600 | www.palazzolasvegas.com
"Detox" from "gluttony" with a "light, delicious" daytime meal at this "healthy" New American near the Venetian's namesake spa; it may seem "weird sitting next to bathrobed clients", but an egg-white omelet in a "cool, chic" setting "without the slot-machine noise" is a "nice way to start a day", even if foes grumble "I had to go get some breakfast after breakfast" here; N.B. the newer Palazzo outpost also offers dinner and a full bar.

Capital Grille, The *Steak* 26 | 24 | 25 | $66
Strip | Fashion Show Mall | 3200 Las Vegas Blvd. S. (Spring Mountain Rd.) | 702-932-6631 | www.thecapitalgrille.com
"Damn good" steaks "without a lot of showy frills" are the main attraction at this chain chophouse in the Fashion Show Mall that's also "worthy of praise" for its "solid" sides, "divine wines" and "personable" servers; the decor has a "swanky" "boys' club feel" with dark wood and brass detailing, and if a few quibble it's "pricey" and "a bit generic", hey – at least it's "never a gamble"; P.S. "if you want the best view, ask for a corner table overlooking the Strip."

Capriotti's Sandwich Shop *Sandwiches* 23 | 7 | 18 | $10
E Side | Paradise Mktpl. | 3830 E. Flamingo Rd. (Sandhill Rd.) | 702-454-2430
E Side | 3981 E. Sunset Rd. (Annie Oakley Dr.) | 702-898-4904

(continued)

Let your voice be heard – visit ZAGAT.com/vote   31

DINING

FOOD | DECOR | SERVICE | COST

(continued)

Capriotti's Sandwich Shop
E Side | 4747 S. Maryland Pkwy. (bet. Tropicana & University Sts.) | 702-736-6166
E Side | Warm Springs Mktpl. | 7291 S. Eastern Ave. (Warm Springs Rd.) | 702-260-4334
NW | 7440 Cheyenne Ave. (Buffalo Dr.) | 702-656-7779
S of Strip | Silverado | 9620 Las Vegas Blvd. S. (Silverado Ranch Blvd.) | 702-407-5602
SW | 4825 S. Fort Apache Rd. (Tropicana Ave.) | 702-873-4682
W of Strip | 322 W. Sahara Ave. (bet. Industrial Rd. & Las Vegas Blvd.) | 702-474-0229
W Side | 4983 W. Flamingo Rd. (bet. Decatur Blvd. & Edmond St.) | 702-222-3331
W Side | 8450 W. Sahara Ave. (Durango Dr.) | 702-562-0440
www.capriottis.com
Additional locations throughout the Las Vegas area

The "Capastrami is awesome", the "cheese steaks are heavenly" and the "famous Bobbie" (a turkey-and-trimmings sub that's "like Thanksgiving without the work") is "sooo delicious" at these "excellent sandwich shops" dotting the desert; "what they lack in decor, they make up for in the quality", so get yours to go before you leave Vegas – then unwrap an "enormous" feast on your flight and "receive a lot of envious stares."

Caribe Café ● *American*   17 | 15 | 17 | $25
Strip | Mirage Hotel | 3400 Las Vegas Blvd. S. (Spring Mountain Rd.) | 702-791-7356 | www.mirage.com

When you come down with gambling fever, try the "great chicken noodle soup" for comfort at this "solid" late-nighter in the Mirage; "more than a glorified hotel coffee shop" but less than "special", it efficiently serves "reliable" Traditional American eats that belie its name – in other words, "there's nothing Caribe about it."

Carluccio's Tivoli Gardens Ⓜ *Italian*   ▽ 21 | 15 | 18 | $25
E Side | Liberace Plaza | 1775 E. Tropicana Ave. (Spencer St.) | 702-795-3236

If you "love a cheesy night out", you can get your "Liberace" on at this "glitzy", "old-school Vegas" East Side "holdover" once owned and said to be "haunted" by the besequined one himself; the "'70s-style" setting and pricing are "so retro", you get a "good value" on a "kitschy", "hearty" Italian meal; N.B. Mr. Showmanship's museum is right next door.

Carnegie Deli ● *Deli*   21 | 13 | 15 | $24
Strip | Mirage Hotel | 3400 Las Vegas Blvd. S. (Spring Mountain Rd.) | 702-791-7371 | www.mirage.com

As "obscenely large" as its "towering" Gotham prototype, a skyscraping sandwich from the Mirage's deli offshoot "could literally feed three", if they had a "forklift" to handle it; the corned beef and pastrami are "musts", but the soup is also "rich and steaming" and the half-sours are "tart and plentiful"; even New Yorkers who say "the original, it ain't" concede that "it does the trick."

NEW Carnevino *Italian/Steak*   - | - | - | VE
Strip | Palazzo Hotel | 3325 Las Vegas Blvd. S. (Sands Ave.) | 702-789-4141 | www.carnevino.com

From NY superstars Mario Batali and Joe Bastianich comes this new Italian steakhouse in the Palazzo that's a fine companion piece

DINING

| | FOOD | DECOR | SERVICE | COST |

to their Enoteca San Marco and B&B Ristorante next door at the Venetian; fashioned like a Mediterranean villa with a liberal use of marble, crystal and wood, it serves pricey vittles that go beyond beef to include seafood, pasta and antipasti, all washed down with an impressive wine list.

Carnival World Buffet *Eclectic*   20 | 16 | 16 | $26

W of Strip | Rio All-Suite Hotel | 3700 W. Flamingo Rd. (bet. I-15 & Valley View Blvd.) | 702-252-7757 | www.playrio.com

One G-rated reason to "undo your pants" in Vegas is this "massive" International buffet west of the Strip where a trip around the room takes you "around the world" cuisinewise; be careful of the ballast you load at each of the "ethnically grouped" ports of call, as the space can be "too difficult to navigate to get back to your table" with all that "quantity that supercedes quality."

Carson Street Cafe ● *Eclectic*   17 | 15 | 18 | $20

Downtown | Golden Nugget Hotel | 129 E. Fremont St. (Main St.) | 702-385-7111 | www.goldennugget.com

"As pleasant a coffee shop as you can find" "when nothing else is open" Downtown is this 24-hour Eclectic in the Golden Nugget where the "amazing variety" of eats suits the "wide range of visitors and locals"; "if you don't like buffets", or you're too "hungover" to stomach the lines at the feeding troughs, this sit-down restaurant is "good in a pinch" for breakfast or lunch, despite sometimes "slow" service.

Casa Nicola *Italian/Mediterranean*   ▽ 20 | 19 | 20 | $46

E of Strip | Las Vegas Hilton | 3000 Paradise Rd. (bet. Desert Inn Rd. & Karen Ave.) | 702-732-5664 | www.lvhilton.com

If you're "going to the Manilow show", a "great find" for a pre-'Mandy' meal is this "hidden gem in the maze of the Las Vegas Hilton" with a "wonderful, open-kitchen ambiance" and "roomy seating" ripe for ripping through "reliably good" pasta and other Northern Italian–Med specialties; the "attentive, assertive staff" will get you out in time for Barry, but barring the chance to hear 'Copacabana' one more time, critics "wouldn't go out of their way" for the "uninspired" eats.

Cathay House *Chinese*   21 | 13 | 17 | $23

W Side | 5300 Spring Mountain Rd. (bet. Decatur & Jones Blvds.) | 702-876-3838 | www.cathayhouse.com

"Excellent" dim sum is served every day till 10 PM at this little bit of "Hong Kong" on the city's West Side, where the "terrific" Chinese dishes earn points, as does the "nice view of the Strip" from the "great, big picture windows"; tabs are inexpensive, so the biggest downside is the "language barrier" with the staff, but that's ok – "it's really just point and eat."

NEW CatHouse *American*   - | - | - | E

Strip | Luxor Hotel | 3900 Las Vegas Blvd. S. (Reno Ave.) | 702-262-4228 | www.cathouselv.com

Nineteenth-century bordello is the theme of this new eatery in the Strip's Luxor Hotel where chef Kerry Simon offers a New American small-plates menu with Asian-European accents and cutesy names (pigs in a duvet, anyone?); after the dinner hour, the place morphs into an ultralounge complete with dancers provocatively clad in lingerie.

DINING

| | FOOD | DECOR | SERVICE | COST |

Chang's *Chinese* — 21 | 16 | 17 | $35

W of Strip | Palace Station Hotel | 2411 W. Sahara Ave. (Rancho Dr.) | 702-367-2411 | www.palacestation.com ◐
W Side | 4670 S. Decatur Blvd. (Tropicana Ave.) | 702-362-3663

For the "real deal in Hong Kong–style" dining, "plenty of Asians" will direct you toward these "classy" west of the Strip Chinese spots where shark-fin soup, dim sum and other "neat stuff" "only slightly modified for the Anglo palate" coexist with more "Americanized" dishes; the decor may be "no-frills", but regulars assure you'll be "treated like family."

Charlie Palmer Steak *Steak* — 25 | 24 | 25 | $82

Strip | Four Seasons Hotel | 3960 Las Vegas Blvd. S. (Four Seasons Dr.) | 702-632-5120 | www.charliepalmer.com

An "oasis" of "civility" "hidden away" in the Four Seasons Hotel, this "understated" steakhouse represents "dining at its finest" with "polished service", "sumptuous" cuisine and "a wine list that is sure to please"; the "elegant" Spanish-styled room with "room between the tables" means "you can actually hear the person sitting across from you", so while a few find it "overpriced", even those who agree attest they'll be "returning" nonetheless.

Cheesecake Factory *American* — 20 | 19 | 19 | $28

Henderson | The District at Green Valley Ranch | 160 S. Green Valley Pkwy. (Paseo Verde Pkwy.) | 702-207-6372
NW | 750 S. Rampart Blvd. (Alta Dr.) | 702-951-3800
Strip | Forum Shops at Caesars Palace | 3500 Las Vegas Blvd. S. (Flamingo Rd.) | 702-792-6888 ◐
www.thecheesecakefactory.com

Boosters boast they're "never disappointed" at the Henderson, Northwest and Strip links of this "reliable" chain proffering "tasty" but "formulaic" American eats in "out-of-control" portions; "noisy", "family-friendly" environs often include "long lines" that are "a bit of a hassle", but the biggest drawback is that "there's never room" for their "heavenly" signature desserts ("if you really want one, have it first").

Chevys Fresh Mex *Mexican* — 14 | 14 | 14 | $20

Henderson | Galleria Mall | 1300 W. Sunset Rd. (Stephanie St.) | 702-434-8323 | www.chevys.com

A "cheap" pit stop for shoppers cruising Henderson's Galleria, this California Mexican chainster rolls out a "filling" meal made of "fresh ingredients and tortillas" and sided by "light, crispy chips"; if critics claim the "cookie-cutter" comidas "lack in creativity", the fruity margaritas are "really good" for a Vegas-style refueling.

Chicago Brewing Company ◐ *American* — 17 | 17 | 20 | $21

Downtown | Four Queens Hotel | 202 Fremont St. (Casino Center Blvd.) | 702-385-4011
W Side | 2201 S. Fort Apache Rd. (bet. Charleston & Sahara Aves.) | 702-254-3333
www.chicagobrewingcolv.com

The "garlic cheese knots rule" and the ales are "even better" at these "solid" Downtown and West Side American microbreweries where the "pub grub" is a "great" accompaniment when "watching sports events", followed by a stogie in the cigar lounge; not all of those "giant vats" are filled with hops, though – they also make their own root beer.

DINING

| | FOOD | DECOR | SERVICE | COST |

Chicago Joe's 🚫 M *Italian* — ▽ 21 | 14 | 18 | $23
Downtown | 820 S. Fourth St. (bet. Gass & Hoover Aves.) | 702-382-5637 | www.chicagojoesrestaurant.com

Chicago Joes and Janes jump for the "real" Windy City chow at this "longtime locals' favorite" in a "tiny cottage nestled among the legal offices" Downtown; it might be a "hole-in-the-wall", but its "consistently good red-sauce Italian food" will "make your mouth happy", and the "genial *Goodfellas* vibe" clinches it as a "choice for a lawyers' power lunch" in the "old-fashioned" tradition.

Chili's Grill & Bar *American/Tex-Mex* — 16 | 14 | 16 | $19
E Side | 10080 S. Eastern Ave. (St. Rose Pkwy.) | 702-407-6924
Henderson | 2751 N. Green Valley Pkwy. (Sunset Rd.) | 702-433-3333
NW | 2011 N. Rainbow Blvd. (Lake Mead Blvd.) | 702-638-1482
NW | 9051 W. Charleston Blvd. (Rampart Blvd.) | 702-228-0479
S of Strip | 7530 Las Vegas Blvd. S. (Warm Springs Rd.) | 702-270-2818
W Side | 2520 S. Decatur Blvd. (Sahara Ave.) | 702-871-0500
www.chilis.com

"When you're too tired to cook or live it up" or even go for something that's not "predictable", this "good family chain" may be "nothing special", but it "does just what it says it will": serve "a decent fajita, a medium-rare burger" or some other Traditional American or Tex-Mex "standard" along with "great chips", salsa and margaritas at "moderate prices"; sometimes it's soothing to "know what you'll get."

China Grill *Asian* — 23 | 23 | 21 | $55
Strip | Mandalay Bay Resort | 3950 Las Vegas Blvd. S. (Mandalay Bay Rd.) | 702-632-7404 | www.chinagrillmgt.com

"A lot of imagination" was sunk into the menu and decor at this "funky, loud" Asian fusion "madhouse" that "fits the bill" for fans of "hip places"; the Mandalay Bay outpost of the NYC original "beautifully presents" "family-style" "creativity" in entrees like signature Shanghai lobster followed by "Disney-esque desserts"; after a few "delicious" concoctions poured by the "talent" that stirs up the "outstanding bar scene", you'll want to stop into "the coolest bathrooms in town."

Chin Chin *Chinese* — 20 | 16 | 17 | $30
Strip | New York-New York Hotel | 3790 Las Vegas Blvd. S. (Tropicana Ave.) | 702-740-6300 | www.chinchin.com

A "Chinese breakfast is a good choice after all-night partying" at New York-New York, so stop into this Sino to soothe yourself with 7:30 AM dim sum; "bargain" pricing for "huge portions" is also a relief "after a long day of gambling" all your money away, but as for the flavor, critics aren't rushing to cash in their chips for "ersatz Asian-themed food."

Chinois *Asian* — 22 | 19 | 20 | $45
Strip | Forum Shops at Caesars Palace | 3500 Las Vegas Blvd. S. (Flamingo Rd.) | 702-737-9700 | www.wolfgangpuck.com

"Life isn't complete unless you've had the Chinois chicken salad" at the Forum Shops' "roomier" sibling to LA's original Peking Puck palace; though this branch "doesn't have Wolfgang's touch, some of the magic can be sensed" in the Asian fare's "impressive flavor combinations"; the "casual" vibe is just the thing for "unwinding after shopping" with a "mai tai" along with "family-style" plates and "excellent sushi."

Let your voice be heard – visit ZAGAT.com/vote

DINING

	FOOD	DECOR	SERVICE	COST

Chipotle *Mexican*   20 | 12 | 15 | $11
E Side | 4530 S. Maryland Pkwy. (Harmon Ave.) | 702-436-9177
Henderson | 10251 S. Eastern Ave. (Sahara Ave.) | 702-361-6438
Henderson | 1311 W. Sunset Rd. (Stephanie St.) | 702-436-7740
NW | 7150 N. Durango Dr. (Elkhorn Rd.) | 702-656-9885
NW | Rock Springs Shopping Ctr. | 7175 W. Lake Mead Blvd. (Rock Springs Dr.) | 702-233-3199
Strip | 3475 Las Vegas Blvd. S. (Flamingo Rd.) | 702-836-0804 ●
Strip | 7370 Las Vegas Blvd. S. (Warm Springs Rd.) | 702-270-1973
www.chipotle.com

"Whether you're a high roller or just lost your shirt", you get the same "cheap", "quick bites between bets" at this Mexican chain where "high-quality ingredients" are rolled into "spaceship-size burritos" right before your eyes; it's "not exceptional", but if you're "drunk and hungry", it "seems much more natural than McDonald's fare, even though it's owned by them."

Chocolate Swan *Dessert*   23 | 17 | 18 | $17
Strip | Mandalay Place | 3930 Las Vegas Blvd. S. (Mandalay Bay Rd.) | 702-632-9366 | www.chocolateswan.com

One of the "hardest working kitchens" in a town of hard-working kitchens just might lie in this "decadent" cafe at Mandalay Bay, a "pricey" but "great place to satisfy your sweet tooth" on "delicious frozen custard", "heavenly" pies and "kick-ass" cocoa-based creations; it's an opportunity to "chocolate out", "sip coffee" or wine and "watch the world go by."

Circo *Italian*   25 | 25 | 23 | $70
(aka Osteria del Circo)
Strip | Bellagio Hotel | 3600 Las Vegas Blvd. S. (Flamingo Rd.) | 702-693-8150 | www.bellagio.com

The name has been tweaked but the rest of this "solid performer" from the Maccioni family remains the same with "wonderfully prepared" Tuscan cuisine and "fantastic Italian wines" served up in a "playful", "harlequin"-inspired dining room with an "amazing view of the Bellagio fountains"; service is "efficient", if sometimes "a little snooty", and even though "it's not cheap", most take comfort that it "offers better value than big sister Le Cirque."

Claim Jumper *American*   - | - | - | M
NEW Henderson | 601 N. Green Valley Pkwy. (Corporate Circle) | 702-933-0880
NEW S of Strip | Town Square | 6629 Las Vegas Blvd. S. (bet. I-215 & Sunset Rd.) | 702-270-2509
Summerlin | 1100 S. Ft. Apache Rd. (Charleston Blvd.) | 702-243-8751
www.claimjumper.com

These family-friendly chain links in Henderson, Summerlin and at Town Square pay homage to the Old West with a rustic, woodsy design incorporating real Douglas Fir logs; the Traditional American menu mixes comfort fare with international crowd-pleasers, all served in mammoth portions by cheerful staffers.

Coffee Pub *Diner*   ▽ 19 | 12 | 14 | $17
W of Strip | 2800 W. Sahara Ave. (Paseo Del Prado) | 702-367-1913

This coffee shop west of the Strip is hailed for "basic" breakfasts and wallet-friendly lunches, pleasing "business" types and tourists alike;

DINING

| | FOOD | DECOR | SERVICE | COST |

service "needs improvement", but the country-kitsch decor and "outdoor seating" with "big umbrellas" "make you feel like you're in a small town – a nice thing when you're visiting Vegas."

NEW Company American Bistro ⓈⓂ *American* | - | - | - | E |

Strip | Luxor Hotel | 3900 Las Vegas Blvd. S. (bet. Mandalay Bay Rd. & Reno Ave.) | 702-262-4702 | www.luxor.com

Nicky Hilton and Wilmer Valderrama are among the celebs behind this high-end New American at the Luxor on the Strip specializing in a small- and large-plates menu of Asian-inflected classics like duck confit potstickers and yuzu chili chicken wings; while service may be chilly, at least the cozy, chalet-inspired decor provides a touch of warmth.

Craftsteak *Seafood/Steak* | 25 | 23 | 24 | $79 |

Strip | MGM Grand Hotel | 3799 Las Vegas Blvd. S. (Tropicana Ave.) | 702-891-7318 | www.mgmgrand.com

"Truly exceptional" steaks and "marvelously simple" sides showcasing "artisanal" ingredients are the hallmarks of chef Tom Colicchio's "exorbitantly priced" surf 'n' turfer in the MGM Grand where the "fantastic food" is supported by an "unbelievable wine list" and a selection of 140 single-malt scotches; surroundings are "sleek" and "nontraditional" while "ever-so-attentive" servers ensure an experience so "outstanding" it makes any night "feel like an occasion."

Cravings *Eclectic* | 22 | 18 | 18 | $26 |
(aka The Ultimate Buffet)

Strip | Mirage Hotel | 3400 Las Vegas Blvd. S. (Spring Mountain Rd.) | 702-791-7111 | www.mirage.com

On the heels of Adam Tihany's "hip" "makeover", the "Mirage buffet has left the 20th century and entered the 21st"; when you browse the dozen or so "separate stations" manned by chefs offering "personalized" dishes "from every corner of the world", "if you can't find something" to satisfy the "craving to fill your empty stomach without making a hole in your wallet", you're "food-phobic" say fans; those who find it "sterile" say the über-designer may have "taken the Zen, clean-lines thing a little too far."

Crown & Anchor British Pub ● *British* | 16 | 19 | 14 | $19 |

E Side | 1350 E. Tropicana Ave. (bet. Eastern Ave. & Maryland Pkwy.) | 702-739-8676 | www.crownandanchorlv.com

"A friendly locals' hangout", this "authentic" 24/7 British pub on the East Side draws "blokes straight off the boat from England" and "college students" who "crowd" in for football matches on the telly and a "huge selection" of brews on tap; the food is "decent" enough, though the real appeal are the "cute waitresses" and "noisy" scene that grows more "bacchanalian" as the night wears on.

NEW CUT *Steak* | - | - | - | VE |

Strip | Palazzo Hotel | 3325 Las Vegas Blvd. S. (Sands Ave.) | 702-607-6300 | www.palazzolasvegas.com

Wolfgang Puck puts a contemporary spin on the traditional steakhouse at this sleek addition to the Palazzo on the Strip; mirrored surfaces and modern art and furnishings in neutral hues set the scene for dramatic (and dramatically priced) cuts of beef, from rib-eye to

Let your voice be heard - visit ZAGAT.com/vote

DINING

| | FOOD | DECOR | SERVICE | COST |

Wagyu, plus an edited selection of imaginatively prepared pork, lamb and fish; lesser appetites can hit the bar where the Rough Cuts nibbles menu features Kobe sliders, tuna tartare and the like.

NEW Dal Toro ● *Italian* — | — | — | M

Strip | Palazzo Hotel | 3327 Las Vegas Blvd. S. (Sands Ave.) | 702-437-9800 | www.palazzolasvegas.com

There's no fast food in sight but there's plenty of speed at this casual Italian at the Palazzo whose contemporary marble-clad dining area is squeezed in next to a Lamborghini showroom; if the cars are too rich for your blood, take solace in the moderately priced menu of substantial from-The-Boot standards like pizzas and pastas, plus meat and seafood entrees.

Z Daniel Boulud Brasserie *French* 26 | 25 | 24 | $78

Strip | Wynn Las Vegas | 3131 Las Vegas Blvd. S. (bet. Desert Inn & Spring Mountain Rds.) | 702-770-3463 | www.wynnlasvegas.com

"Master" chef Daniel Boulud's "showstopping" brasserie in the Wynn "does nothing less than impress" say those savoring the "brilliantly conceived and executed" New French cuisine (the DB burger stuffed with short ribs and foie gras is "a must"), "superb" wines and "exceptional" service; the "beautiful lakeside location" encourages many a diner to "snag a seat outside" and take in the "glitzy" light and fountain show – think of it as "dinner theater" and the meal will feel like a relative "bargain", especially if you opt for the $48 prix fixe early-bird special.

David Burke 24 | 24 | 23 | $76
Modern American Cuisine *American*

Strip | Venetian Hotel | 3355 Las Vegas Blvd. S. (bet. Flamingo & Spring Mountain Rds.) | 702-414-7111 | www.venetian.com

"Culinary rock 'n' roll" is how fans of chef David Burke describe his "extremely inventive" and "appealingly presented" New American dishes like pretzel-crusted crab cakes and cheesecake lollipops at this "fabulous" entry in the Venetian; yet in spite of a "whimsical" menu, skeptics "can't help but feeling it's more about image than substance", citing the "loud", "high-energy" digs that are "very much a scene" – either way, prepare for some major "sticker shock."

Z Del Frisco's 26 | 23 | 25 | $67
Double Eagle Steak House *Steak*

E of Strip | 3925 Paradise Rd. (Corporate Dr.) | 702-796-0063 | www.delfriscos.com

"A mix of locals and tourists" puts this east of the Strip chain beef bonanza "at the top of the list" saying "you can't go wrong" with its "divine" steaks, "extraordinary wines" and "remarkable" service even if prices nearly "break the bank"; diners, however, take opposing sides on the mahogany wood and white-tablecloth decor, with some deeming it "classy" and others insisting it's "bland" and in need of an "update."

Z Delmonico Steakhouse *Steak* 26 | 23 | 25 | $76

Strip | Venetian Hotel | 3355 Las Vegas Blvd. S. (bet. Flamingo & Spring Mountain Rds.) | 702-414-3737 | www.emerils.com

"Emeril has it all together here" gush groupies of celebrity chef Lagasse, whose "absolute hunk-o-meat perfection" in the Venetian

DINING

pleases with "fabulous cuts" of beef (including a "primo" bone-in ribeye), "wonderful Caesar salad" prepared tableside and an "amazing", "unending" wine list; in spite of a few "lapses", servers "take care of your every need" so the only complaint is the "monasterylike" atmosphere, which some say needs to be "kicked up a notch" – most would "prefer a little more grandeur" given the "high prices."

Diablo's Cantina ● *Mexican* — | — | — | M

Strip | Monte Carlo Resort | 3770 Las Vegas Blvd. S. (bet. Harmon & Tropicana Aves.) | 702-693-8300 | www.lightgroup.com

Spring break comes to Vegas at this open-air cantina at the Monte Carlo, where cross-the-border Mexican, Southwestern and American fare is served in a multilevel space adorned with hand-painted murals, rustic tiles and vibrant colors; with 75 types of tequila, 10 large-screen plasma TVs and live music, expect a nonstop fiesta.

Dick's Last Resort ● *American* — | — | — | I

Strip | Excalibur Hotel | 3850 Las Vegas Blvd. S. (Tropicana Ave.) | 702-597-7991 | www.excalibur.com

"Shame o' the Strip" is a label that would make most places cringe, but it's self-proclaimed and worn proudly at this raucous, beach-styled spot in the Excalibur where almost anything goes; the inexpensive American menu includes hamburgers and finger foods, but the biggest draws are frozen, fruity cocktails and an impressive assortment of beers.

Diego *Mexican* — 21 | 22 | 19 | $42

Strip | MGM Grand Hotel | 3799 Las Vegas Blvd. S. (Tropicana Ave.) | 702-891-3200 | www.mgmgrand.com

What's the specialty of this "snazzy" cantina in the MGM Grand?; "authentic Mexican with a flair" and even more so, to quote The Champs' 1958 classic, "tequila!" – 100-plus varieties, poured plain or stirred into the slurringly "bestest mahhhgaaahritas"; the "wonderful" fare is "more than tacos", so "look for the goat on the menu."

NEW DJT *American* — | — | — | E

Strip | Trump International Hotel & Tower | 2000 Fashion Show Dr. (Las Vegas Blvd.) | 702-982-0000 | www.trumplasvegashotel.com

The signature restaurant at Trump International Hotel & Tower on the Strip seems to reflect the sartorial tastes of the man himself with a dining room done up in all shades of dignified neutrals; the straightforward American menu offers flashy flourishes and is backed by a selection of signature cocktails.

Doña Maria *Mexican* — 19 | 13 | 17 | $18

Central | 910 Las Vegas Blvd. S. (Charleston Blvd.) | 702-382-6538
NW | 3205 N. Tenaya Way (Cheyenne Ave.) | 702-656-1600
www.donamariatamales.com

Amigos who eschew "Anglicized" Mexican head to these Central and Northwest "institutions" for "authentic", inexpensive south-of-the-border fare including "fantastic" tamales that are a house "specialty"; "service is quick", especially at lunch, and colorful murals and shiny saltillo tiles create a "homey" respite that's generally "quiet" except when soccer games are beamed in on big-screen TVs.

Let your voice be heard – visit ZAGAT.com/vote

DINING

| | FOOD | DECOR | SERVICE | COST |

Don Miguel's Mexican   ▽ 19 | 15 | 19 | $21

W of Strip | Orleans Hotel | 4500 W. Tropicana Ave. (Arville St.) | 702-365-7111 | www.orleanscasino.com

"At the end of a long day" of craps and slots when you thirst for an "exceptional margarita", this dinner-only casita in the Orleans west of the Strip has 'em with "good, warm chips served with nice salsa, guacamole and refried beans"; the entrees are "ample" and "inexpensive", though "spotty service" and "little innovation" in the kitchen lead south-of-the-border intelligentsia to label it "mindless Mexican."

NEW Dos Caminos Mexican   - | - | - | M

Strip | Palazzo Hotel | 3325 Las Vegas Blvd. S. (Sands Ave.) | 702-577-9600 | www.brguestrestaurants.com

A dramatic David Rockwell–designed space is the backdrop for this Mexican arrival at the Palazzo on the Strip, a New York import proffering fancied up plates of chipotle BBQ ribs, chicken tinga tacos and made-to-order guacamole; a lounge area features DJs nightly with VIP service and a late-night bar menu, not to mention over 100 tequilas.

Dragon Noodle Co. Chinese   18 | 16 | 17 | $30

Strip | Monte Carlo Resort | 3770 Las Vegas Blvd. S. (bet. Harmon & Tropicana Aves.) | 702-730-7965 | www.dragonnoodleco.com

Noodles and other Cantonese dishes are "nicely prepped and served" at this "casual" Asian in the Monte Carlo with "quite good sushi" as well (at dinner only); it might be "a little pricey for what you get", but if you don't want to "make the drive to Chinatown", the lengthy tea list and fully feng-shui'd space make this convenient option all the more "pleasant."

Egg & I American   21 | 12 | 20 | $16

W Side | West Lake Plaza | 4533 W. Sahara Ave. (bet. Arville St. & Decatur Blvd.) | 702-364-9686 | www.eggandi.com

Yes, it's "in a strip mall", but "cast all fears aside" assure "local celebrities" and plebeians, because "breakfast in Las Vegas doesn't get any better" than "perfect" "eggs any way you like 'em" (including in "unusual" omelets, frittatas and scrambles) at this Traditional American "family place"; look for "interesting sandwich combinations" during lunch and clues during Wednesday–Saturday "murder-mystery dinner theater."

Eiffel Tower French   22 | 26 | 22 | $76

Strip | Paris Las Vegas | 3655 Las Vegas Blvd. S. (bet. Flamingo Rd. & Harmon Ave.) | 702-948-6937 | www.eiffeltowerrestaurant.com

Those expecting "a gimmick" may be "surprised" by the "fine" French fare (including "perfectly executed soufflés") served in a "spectacular" "romantic" setting with vistas of the city and the Bellagio fountains at this Paris Las Vegas destination; the staff is "knowledgeable" if a bit "stiff", and though the whole experience strikes most as "*magnifique*", a minority claims it wasn't "blown away", citing "pedestrian" eats and "hefty price tags" as cause for complaint.

Elephant Bar Eclectic   17 | 19 | 17 | $24

Henderson | The District | 2270 Village Walk Dr. (Green Valley Pkwy.) | 702-361-7468 | www.elephantbar.com

"Your loud friends" in Henderson might trumpet this "popular" Eclectic chain in a "nice location" in The District mall; it's "big, noisy and crowded", but it's a "great place to meet at the bar" for a "quick

DINING

| | FOOD | DECOR | SERVICE | COST |

bite" and a cocktail in a "friendly atmosphere"; don't expect more than a "just-average" meal, though: the "service is high-school level", and as for the "inconsistent kitchen", "it's a jungle in there."

El Jefe's Mexican Restaurant & Cantina *Mexican* | 17 | 18 | 18 | $22 |

Henderson | 9925 S. Eastern Ave. (St. Rose Pkwy.) | 702-453-5333 | www.eljefesrestaurant.com

"Decent, but not outstanding" sums up this Henderson Mexican where the "tasty margaritas" and free-flowing sangria outshine the "contemporary" dishes; still, a "varied menu" plus patio seating and "friendly and attentive" servers mean it "satisfies" for "lunch" or happy hour when the drinks are "cheap" (3-6 PM every day).

El Sombrero Café ⊠ *Mexican* | - | - | - | I |

Downtown | 807 S. Main St. (Gass Ave.) | 702-382-9234

"A Vegas institution", this family-run Downtown "gem" lures "locals" and tourists in-the-know for "very cheap" Sonoran-style Mexican fare like primo posole and green-chile pork; in spite of hole-in-the-wall decor, insiders insist "you won't find a friendlier place"; N.B. closed Sundays.

☑ Emeril's New Orleans Fish House *Seafood* | 23 | 21 | 22 | $57 |

Strip | MGM Grand Hotel | 3799 Las Vegas Blvd. S. (Tropicana Ave.) | 702-891-7374 | www.emerils.com

"Awfully good for this far west of the bayou", Emeril's Cajun-Creole seafooder in the MGM Grand is a "solid introduction to the Lagasse style" with "huge portions" of "terrific", "spicy" eats and a "don't-miss" banana cream pie served in a "nicely redone" interior; yet in spite of a staff that "will bend over backward for you", some are left "disappointed" by food and service they say "doesn't live up to the hype" or the "high prices."

Empress Court Ⓜ *Chinese* | 22 | 23 | 23 | $57 |

Strip | Caesars Palace | 3570 Las Vegas Blvd. S. (Flamingo Rd.) | 702-731-7731 | www.caesarspalace.com

This "Hong Kong regional" restaurant in Caesars offers "beautifully served" Cantonese and "great dim sum" amid "nice comfort" graced with "a touch of elegance"; still, "kung pao with no pow", "impassive waiters" and an "old-style" vibe have modernists urging "get with it!"

Enoteca San Marco *Italian* | 21 | 20 | 18 | $46 |

Strip | Venetian Hotel | 3355 Las Vegas Blvd. S. (bet. Flamingo & Spring Mountain Rds.) | 702-677-3390 | www.enotecasanmarco.com

"All of Mario's touches" are to be found in Batali and Joe Bastianich's "casual" yearling in the Venetian where a "wide array" of "wonderful" "snackable" Italian bites like "excellent salumi", "unbelievable pizzas" and "homemade gelati" get a boost from a "fantastic wine list" available by the bottle or quartino; "spotty" service hits a snag, but the St. Mark's Square setting redeems with patio seating providing perfect "people-watching" as well as soothing canal views.

Envy Steakhouse *Steak* | 21 | 23 | 22 | $57 |

E of Strip | Renaissance Las Vegas Hotel | 3400 Paradise Rd. (Desert Inn Rd.) | 702-733-6533 | www.envysteakhouse.com

"Chic" quarters marry with "convention-center convenience" at this "under-the-radar" east-of-the-Strip spot in the Renaissance Las Vegas

DINING

FOOD | DECOR | SERVICE | COST

that owes its "loungey" feel to cushy leather booths and a "dressed-to-kill" crimson room; "excellent" (if "overpriced") steaks are elevated by "delicious sides", and while "service can be a bit spotty", at least "getting a table isn't too difficult."

Ethel's Chocolate Lounge *Dessert* 21 | 19 | 20 | $16

Henderson | Sunset Mountain Vista Plaza | 2 Cactus Garden Dr. (Sunset Way) | 702-435-2655
Henderson | The District | 2235 Village Walk Dr. (Green Valley Pkwy.) | 702-492-1130
Strip | Fashion Show Mall | 3200 Las Vegas Blvd. S. (Spring Mountain Rd.) | 702-796-6662
www.ethelschocolate.com

"A chocoholic must", these "cute" pink-and-brown chain outposts allow "tired shoppers" the chance to "sip a mocha" or indulge in "sinful" desserts like fondue for two, "awesome" hot cocoa and "beautiful and innovative" candies; the staff is "friendly" too, leaving some visiting patrons to pine "please, Ethel, open a branch in NYC"; P.S. "if you have time and a car, take a drive out to their factory in Henderson."

Famous Dave's *BBQ* 20 | 15 | 19 | $22

NW | 1951 N. Rainbow Blvd. (Lake Mead Blvd.) | 702-646-5631
S of Strip | 4390 Blue Diamond Rd. (Arville St.) | 702-633-7427
W Side | 9695 W. Flamingo Rd. (off Rte. 215) | 702-871-5631
www.famousdaves.com

"Come early or expect a wait" at these off-Strip outposts of the Minnesota-based 'cue chain, where "smiling" servers deliver "filling" plates of "melt-in-your-mouth" smoked goods in a backwoods lodge setup; a choice of six different sauces and "a lot of food for the buck" clinch their claim to fame, causing "long lines on weekends."

Fatburger ● *Burgers* 21 | 9 | 14 | $10

E Side | Albertson's Shopping Ctr. | 2845 S. Nellis Blvd. (Vegas Valley Dr.) | 702-457-1727
Henderson | Sunset Station Hotel | 1301 W. Sunset Rd. (Stephanie St.) | 702-450-7820
Henderson | Green Valley Ranch | 2300 Paseo Verde Pkwy. (Green Valley Pkwy.) | 702-617-2209
Henderson | 4663 E. Sunset Rd. (bet. Green Valley Pkwy. & Mountain Vista Rd.) | 702-898-7200
NW | 4199 S. Fort Apache (Nevso Dr.) | 702-368-1244
NW | 4525 N. Rancho Dr. (Craig Rd.) | 702-658-4604
NW | Santa Fe Station Hotel | 4949 N. Rancho Dr. (bet. Lone Mountain Rd. & Rainbow Blvd.) | 702-839-9610
Strip | 3763 Las Vegas Blvd. S. (bet. Harmon & Tropicana Aves.) | 702-736-4733
W Side | 4851 W. Charleston Blvd. (Decatur Blvd.) | 702-870-4933
W Side | 6775 W. Flamingo Rd. (Rainbow Blvd.) | 702-889-9009
www.fatburger.net
Additional locations throughout the Las Vegas area

"Best burger west of the Mississippi" sigh devotees of this "classic" fast-food chain, where "phat" patties, "perfectly greasy" onion rings and "amazing" shakes are "hangover cure" and "cardiac nightmare" all rolled into one; ok, "service can be slow" (the grub's "cooked to order", after all), so "bring your quarters" to play the "great jukebox" while you wait.

DINING

	FOOD	DECOR	SERVICE	COST

Feast, The *Eclectic* — 18 | 17 | 17 | $17

E Side | Boulder Station Hotel | 4111 Boulder Hwy. (Lamb Blvd.) | 702-432-7777
Henderson | Sunset Station Hotel | 1301 W. Sunset Rd. (Stephanie St.) | 702-547-7777
NW | Red Rock Casino | 11011 W. Charleston Blvd. (Hwy. 215) | 702-797-7777
W of Strip | Palace Station Hotel | 2411 W. Sahara Ave. (Rancho Dr.) | 702-367-2411
www.stationcasinos.com

They're "nothing fancy", but "locals" find these "affordable" buffets off the Strip are "a good place to fill up" on a "huge selection" of Eclectic dishes; the Red Rock Casino outpost is deemed the most "impressive" of the bunch, although skeptics say that all locations suffer from "long lines" and "service that could be better."

Feast Around The World Buffet *Eclectic* — 18 | 15 | 16 | $18

Henderson | Green Valley Ranch | 2300 Paseo Verde Pkwy. (Green Valley Pkwy.) | 702-617-7777 | www.greenvalleyranchresort.com
N Las Vegas | Texas Station Hotel | 2101 Texas Star Ln. (bet. Lake Mead Blvd. & Rancho Dr.) | North Las Vegas | 702-631-1000 | www.stationcasinos.com

"There is a lot of variety at these budget-friendly buffets" with live-action cooking areas in Henderson's Green Valley Ranch and North Vegas' Texas Station, but there's also plenty of interest among "locals", so "go at off-times, as it gets busy", and "the wait" for the "constantly rotated" items "can make you even hungrier than you already are."

Fellini's *Italian* — 24 | 21 | 24 | $42

Strip | Stratosphere Hotel | 2000 Las Vegas Blvd. S. (north of Sahara Ave.) | 702-380-7777 | www.fellinislv.com

"Hearty" pastas served in "elegant, but unpretentious" surroundings draw "Las Vegas bigwigs" and "the occasional out-of-towner" to this "old-time" Italian offering "good value" plus plenty of "charm"; service is "pleasant", while occasional live music adds to the "nostalgic" feel.

Ferraro's *Italian* — 26 | 19 | 26 | $52

W Side | 5900 W. Flamingo Rd. (bet. Decatur & Jones Blvds.) | 702-364-5300 | www.ferraroslasvegas.com

This "joint always jumps" say those who know it's "worth the trip" to this West Side stalwart where "live piano" on most nights sets the scene for "fabulous" meals of "old-world" Italian cuisine; despite a few grumbles about "high prices", most find it a "delightful" experience enhanced by a "friendly" chef and "superb" service.

Festival Buffet *Eclectic* — ▽ 14 | 11 | 14 | $12

Henderson | Fiesta Henderson Hotel | 777 W. Lake Mead Pkwy. (S. 4th St.) | 702-558-7000
NW | Fiesta Rancho Hotel | 2400 N. Rancho Dr. (Lake Mead Blvd.) | 702-631-7000
www.fiestacasino.com

"Saturday brunch is the buy of the century" rave hyperbolic types clamoring for the "cheap" eats at these Eclectic gorgefests in the Northwest and Henderson; if you happen to be at either of the Fiestas, they'll do just "fine", particularly given "some excellent baked goods

DINING

| | FOOD | DECOR | SERVICE | COST |

that lend them something to stand above the crowd" of joints at the "low end."

Fiamma Trattoria *Italian*   22 | 22 | 21 | $58
Strip | MGM Grand Hotel | 3799 Las Vegas Blvd. S. (Tropicana Ave.) | 702-891-7600 | www.brguestrestaurants.com

"Another good example of the food renaissance at the MGM Grand", Steve Hanson's "sexy" SoHo import features "upscale" Italian dishes like "short rib ravioli" and "lobster gnocchi to dream about"; the "dark, ultramodern decor is perfect for a first date", whom you could even meet amid "an awesome bar scene filled with hip people" sipping "to-die-for specialty cocktails"; unfortunately, you might "part with more money than you should" for "small portions."

Fin *Chinese*   25 | 25 | 25 | $58
Strip | Mirage Hotel | 3400 Las Vegas Blvd. S. (Spring Mountain Rd.) | 702-791-7353 | www.mirage.com

Forget about "your father's takeout", this "first-class" Cantonese seafooder in the Mirage delivers "divine" "upscale" dishes like Santa Barbara prawns and wok-fried sea bass in a "sleek, chic" setting decked out in rich woods and fine fabrics; though a few find it "fussy", most say the "attention to detail" – including "wonderful service" – makes this "authentic dining experience" "pricey, but worth it"; N.B. no children under five allowed.

Firefly ● *Spanish*   24 | 18 | 21 | $28
E of Strip | 3900 Paradise Rd. (bet. Flamingo Rd. & Twain Ave.) | 702-369-3971 | www.fireflylv.com

"Tasty little plates" of "easy-to-share" tapas "keep on comin'" to your table thanks to "helpful" servers at this East Side Spaniard that's "nowhere near as stuffy or expensive" as its Strip counterparts, and does without those "ringing slot machines" too; decorwise it may be a bit "blasé" inside, so "sit on the patio" instead, where pitchers of "dangerous" sangria go down easier.

Firelight Buffet *Eclectic*   ▽ 15 | 15 | 16 | $15
E Side | Sam's Town Hotel | 5111 Boulder Hwy. (Nellis Blvd.) | 702-454-8044 | www.samstownlv.com

Like moths to the light, "locals throng" to this "typical", "cheap buffet" in Sam's Town on the East Side; luckily, "the serving area has a good flow and doesn't bunch people up" on Wednesday's "don't-miss steak night" and other special evenings; still, "you pay for what you get", so if you're seeking something "outstanding", "don't make a special trip here."

Fix ● *American*   23 | 23 | 22 | $57
Strip | Bellagio Hotel | 3600 Las Vegas Blvd. S. (Flamingo Rd.) | 702-693-8844 | www.fixlasvegas.com

"Could the crowd or decor be any groovier" at this "eye-catching", dinner-only American "hot spot" that opens onto the Bellagio casino?; "sink into a deep booth" beneath an "artistic, wooden" ceiling that's "as curvy as the hostess" and order up a fix of "brilliant" "gourmet" comfort grub to "see and be seen" with – though the "flash" of the "loud" "bar scene blurs the palate", a "damn-hot staff serving great-looking", "young" "bachelorette partyers" makes the "people-watching" a "total experience."

DINING

	FOOD	DECOR	SERVICE	COST

Flavors Buffet *Eclectic* — 18 | 16 | 18 | $22

Strip | Harrah's Las Vegas | 3475 Las Vegas Blvd. S. (Flamingo Rd.) | 702-369-5000 | www.harrahs.com

"Surprisingly good" sum up supporters of this "middle-range" Eclectic smorgasbord in Harrah's where folks line up for "basic" breakfasts and "solid", if "unoriginal" dinners that are a "good value" (and "even better if you can snag a coupon"); servers rate "compliments", so even if some say it's "below other buffets on the Strip", it works for a "basic" meal.

Fleming's Prime Steakhouse & Wine Bar *Steak* — 25 | 23 | 22 | $54

W Side | 8721 W. Charleston Blvd. (bet. Durango Dr. & Rampart Blvd.) | 702-838-4774 | www.flemingssteakhouse.com

"Huge", "shockingly delicious" filets paired with "giant" sides ("it was practically a head of broccoli") and an "excellent" selection of wines by the glass help make this "clubby" satellite of the "high-end" national beef chain "the social hub of the West Side" (read: it's "very loud"); there may be "better ones on the Strip", but if you're caught further out, this one will make the cut.

Fleur de Lys *French* — 25 | 26 | 25 | $93

Strip | Mandalay Bay Resort | 3950 Las Vegas Blvd. S. (Mandalay Bay Rd.) | 702-632-9400 | www.fleurdelyssf.com

The "pinnacle" of Vegas dining declare those dazzled by Hubert Keller's "jewel" in the Mandalay Bay Resort that "honors his San Francisco flagship" with "outrageously good" New French dishes presented in such "exquisite arrangements" they "look too good to eat"; servers "go out of their way to please you" in the "gorgeous" flower-filled dining room with "romantic" "private booths"; it's a "special place" to either "spend your winnings" or "console your losses"; P.S. "if you don't want to commit to dinner, sample small plates in the lounge."

Florida Café *Cuban* — ∇ 19 | 13 | 15 | $19

Central | Howard Johnson Hotel | 1401 Las Vegas Blvd. S. (bet. Charleston & Oakey Blvds.) | 702-385-3013 | www.floridacafecuban.com

Despite residency in a Howard Johnson's on a "seedy" stretch of Las Vegas Boulevard, this "Cuban oasis" manages to be "*the* place for ex-Miamians" to feast on "exemplary *croquetas*" and satisfy "café con leche cravings"; drivers take note: parking can be "hard to find."

French Market Buffet *Eclectic* — 19 | 17 | 18 | $22

W of Strip | Orleans Hotel | 4500 W. Tropicana Ave. (Arville St.) | 702-365-7111 | www.orleanscasino.com

You can score "really tasty" "treats" at this Eclectic extravaganza situated west of the Strip where "insiders" praise the "wide selection of international food" and steak and seafood nights (Wednesdays and Fridays); add in "solid" service and "for the price it can't be beat."

Fusia *Asian* — ∇ 21 | 21 | 22 | $48

Strip | Luxor Hotel | 3900 Las Vegas Blvd. S. (bet. Mandalay Bay Rd. & Reno Ave.) | 702-262-4774 | www.luxor.com

Surveyors split on whether the "food as art" concept works at this mid-priced Luxor Asian; fans swear the fare "can't be beat" while detractors dis a "mind-numbing blend of East, West and everything in between" and add that "slow" service and an "uninspired" setting also disappoint.

DINING

| | FOOD | DECOR | SERVICE | COST |

Gaetano's *Italian* | 23 | 22 | 23 | $42 |
Henderson | Siena Promenade | 10271 S. Eastern Ave. (Siena Heights Dr.) | 702-361-1661 | www.gaetanoslasvegas.com

"Real class act" Gaetano Palmeri "makes you feel at home" in his "wonderfully friendly" yet "elegant", "family-operated" namesake in Henderson where "the customer is first" on the list for "personal care"; "it's not the cheapest Italian in town", but it's "worth the price" for "excellent", "authentic Northern" standards and "innovative specials" – even snobs call it "not bad for a neighborhood place."

NEW Galerias Gourmet *Mexican* | – | – | – | I |
NW | 1780 N. Buffalo Dr. (bet. Vegas Dr. & Lake Mead Blvd.) | 702-243-3003 | www.galeriasgourmet.net

Going beyond the usual Mexican clichés, this new Northwesterner serves innovative dishes (like the Salvador Dali – pork with guava, rose petals and herbs) in a handsome, low-key space done in natural woods; service is casual but sincere, while modest prices feel right on the money.

Gallagher's Steakhouse *Steak* | 24 | 19 | 21 | $65 |
Strip | New York-New York Hotel | 3790 Las Vegas Blvd. S. (Tropicana Ave.) | 702-740-6450 | www.nynyhotelcasino.com

On your way into this "dark" New York-New York chophouse (a takeoff on the Gotham "original"), "you can see" the "incredible" cuts "hanging in the windows" "in giant coolers", and they're "exactly what you would hope for", i.e. "mouthwateringly aged" and "big" say supporters who "can't believe they ate the whole thing"; "disappointed" carnivores counter that "there are better options at Vegas' top-tier steak level" than the "tough" chews in this "noisy" "blah environment."

Gandhi India's Cuisine *Indian* | 21 | 15 | 16 | $23 |
E of Strip | 4080 Paradise Rd. (Flamingo Rd.) | 702-734-0094 | www.gandhicuisine.com

The "great lunch buffet" is the standout (and a "deal" as well) at this east of the Strip Indian that's "popular with the local community" for its "spicy" "quality" cuisine; service is usually "prompt", though style mavens say that the traditional decor "could use a little updating."

Garden Court Buffet *Eclectic* | 19 | 19 | 19 | $16 |
Downtown | Main Street Station Hotel | 200 N. Main St. (Ogden Ave.) | 702-387-1896 | www.mainstreetcasino.com

"There are so many tasting stations that you can't sample all the varieties of foods in just one day" at this "shockingly good" Downtown multi-disher's depot say repeat eaters who pop in on "specialty nights" like seafood Friday and Saturday or "go early to avoid the big crowds" "in line for the good stuff at the grill"; "one of the most pleasant buffet dining environments" in town also includes a gardenlike setting.

Garduño's *Mexican/Southwestern* | 20 | 18 | 16 | $25 |
NW | Fiesta Rancho Hotel | 2400 N. Rancho Dr. (Lake Mead Blvd.) | 702-631-7000
W of Strip | Palms Casino Hotel | 4321 W. Flamingo Rd. (Arville St.) | 702-942-7777
www.gardunosrestaurants.com

West of the Strip and in the Northwest, these Mexican-Southwestern cantinas originally out of Albuquerque are "great for drinks and gabbing"

DINING

| | FOOD | DECOR | SERVICE | COST |

with gringos while gobbling "spicy", traditional grub; "sopaipillas plus a salsa bar" "with some kickin' margaritas to boot" "equals a very happy tummy" tout amigos who "like it *mucho*" for a "reasonably priced" dinner, while the word on the "great Sunday buffet" is "*que bueno!*"

Gaylord's *Indian* ▽ 20 | 21 | 19 | $42

W of Strip | Rio All-Suite Hotel | 3700 W. Flamingo Rd. (bet. I-15 & Valley View Blvd.) | 702-777-2277 | www.playrio.com

"A world away from the noisy casino", this "small" "hideaway" tucked into the Rio west of the Strip offers "rightly spiced" Indian dishes (including "great vegetarian options") ferried by an "attentive" staff in a low-lit setting draped with colorful fabrics; detractors deem it "plain-Jane", and slipping Food scores indicate the experience "may not be worth" the somewhat "outrageous prices."

Giorgio Ristorante & Caffè *Italian* 20 | 16 | 18 | $45

Strip | Mandalay Place | 3930 Las Vegas Blvd. S. (Mandalay Bay Rd.) | 702-920-2700 | www.caffegiorgio.com

"It's nice to watch the shoppers go by" Piero Selvaggio's "cute place for lunch" in Mandalay Place where a "reasonably priced" Italian meal might include antipasto, "well-prepared" pasta and wine from the 20-strong by-the-glass list; it's a "winner", if you don't mind that it's "a serious step below" Valentino, the restaurateur's upscale spot.

Golden Steer Steak House *Steak* 22 | 18 | 22 | $55

W of Strip | 308 W. Sahara Ave. (bet. Fairfield Ave. & Tam Dr.) | 702-384-4470 | www.goldensteerlv.com

This former "Rat Pack hangout" is "as close to an eternal institution" as this town has, so "check your gun at the door" (proverbially speaking), "cozy up in a booth and enjoy a good piece of meat" and a healthy dose of "Old West-bordello" "kitsch" west of the Strip; it's "great for bachelor parties", but some former regulars "no longer shine the banquettes with their bottoms" because the "service is marginal" compared to the "dozens of great steakhouses" competing with it now.

Grand Lux Cafe ● *Eclectic* 20 | 18 | 19 | $29

NEW **Strip** | Palazzo Hotel | 3327 Las Vegas Blvd. S. (Sands Ave.) | 702-733-7411

Strip | Venetian Hotel | 3355 Las Vegas Blvd. S. (bet. Flamingo & Spring Mountain Rds.) | 702-414-3888
www.grandluxcafe.com

The folks behind the Cheesecake Factory "take the coffee shop concept to the next level" with this "cavernous" 24/7 chain outpost in the Venetian that "satisfies any craving" with "gigantic portions" of Eclectic fare including "carb-loaded breakfasts that hit the hangover spot", "tasty appetizers" and a "staggering" array of desserts; "prices are decent for Vegas", and though "long waits" are par for the course, guests are grateful that "it takes longer to make up your mind than it does to get your order"; N.B. the Palazzo branch opened post-Survey, and serves till 3 AM.

Grape Street Café *Mediterranean* 23 | 20 | 21 | $31

NW | Summerhill Plaza | 7501 W. Lake Mead Blvd. (Buffalo Dr.) | 702-228-9463 | www.grapestreetcafe.com

Oenophiles opine the "fantabulous flights" are "made in heaven" at this "local" wine lover's "paradise" in Northwest's Summerhill Plaza;

Let your voice be heard – visit ZAGAT.com/vote

DINING

| | FOOD | DECOR | SERVICE | COST |

the "super" Eclectic-Mediterranean entrees, "fun-to-share"-and-"rave-about" chocolate fondue and 75 "interesting" grapes by the glass are "good for a yuppie dinner out", particularly if you avoid the "crowded" inside (where "they play the music too loud at dinner") and take a table on the "adorable" patio.

Guadalajara Bar & Grille *Mexican* ▽ 19 | 15 | 16 | $20

E Side | Boulder Station Hotel | 4111 Boulder Hwy. (Lamb Blvd.) | 702-432-7777
Henderson | Sunset Station Hotel | 1301 W. Sunset Rd. (Stephanie St.) | 702-547-7777
www.stationcasinos.com

A "great family dining spot" for clans composed of "people of differing heat tolerances" is this "inexpensive" Mexican with locations in the "noisy" Station casinos where "the top-notch salsa bar" runs the gamut from blistering to mellow; "if you don't want authentic", the "Americanized" menu is "not bad", and the "big" margaritas suffice for a buzz, if you can get served – the staff seems to "make a point of looking the other way all night."

Z Guy Savoy Ⓜ *French* 28 | 26 | 27 | $195

Strip | Caesars Palace | 3570 Las Vegas Blvd. S. (Flamingo Rd.) | 877-346-4642 | www.caesarspalace.com

"How do you say 'beyond perfect' *en français*?" ask acolytes of "genius" chef Guy Savoy, who has "outdone himself" with this "gastronomic adventure" in Caesars Palace, which some say is "better than the three-star Paris original" with "brilliantly presented" New French cuisine served à la carte or in an "exquisite" tasting menu plus a "terrific" wine list with 1,500 labels; also "memorable" is "impeccable", "unpretentious" service (ladies like the "purse perches") and a "stylish" setting done up in dark, rich woods, while "breathtaking prices" are commensurate with the "once-in-a-lifetime" experience; N.B. the Bubbles Bar inside the restaurant offers a small-bites menu.

Hamada *Japanese* 19 | 17 | 19 | $44

E of Strip | 365 E. Flamingo Rd. (Paradise Rd.) | 702-733-3005 ◑
Strip | Flamingo Las Vegas | 3555 Las Vegas Blvd. S. (Flamingo Rd.) | 702-733-3455
W of Strip | Rio All-Suite Hotel | 3700 W. Flamingo Rd. (bet. I-15 & Valley View Blvd.) | 702-777-2770
www.hamadaofjapan.com

"Three restaurants in one", the branches of this Vegas "classic" offer "good" "Benihana-style, sushi-bar and sit-down-Japanese" dining, all at "affordable prices"; no, there's "no karaoke", but the east-of-the-Strip original entertains with "fantastic people-watching after 10 PM"; since many say it's "nothing special" with "decor in need of upkeep", those who knew it when say "expansion has not helped" it.

Hank's *Steak* 23 | 26 | 22 | $70

Henderson | Green Valley Ranch | 2300 Paseo Verde Pkwy. (Green Valley Pkwy.) | 702-617-7515 | www.greenvalleyranchresort.com

"Top-notch steaks" and seafood are supported by "strong martinis" and a stable of "highly addictive" sides (like truffle tater tots and creamed corn) at this "special-occasion" chophouse in Henderson's Green Valley Ranch; the "lovely atmosphere" comes courtesy of "pro-

DINING

| | FOOD | DECOR | SERVICE | COST |

fessional" service and a "luxurious" dining room with "plush" powder-blue velvet booths and chocolate-brown walls illuminated by "crystal chandeliers", while live piano music adds the final "swanky" touch.

Hard Rock Cafe ◐ *American* | 15 | 21 | 15 | $26 |
E of Strip | 4475 Paradise Rd. (Harmon Ave.) | 702-733-7625 | www.hardrock.com

For diners who love rock 'n' roll, this "typical" East Side branch of the music-themed chain is still singin' that same old song, with "lots of memorabilia", "loud" tunes, "overpriced T-shirts" and "juicy burgers"; the rest of the American menu is "hackneyed" and the service "indifferent", but when you're itching to mix with "hungover twentysomethings", "older biker types" and "festive tourists", "ya just gotta go there."

Harley-Davidson Cafe *American* | 15 | 20 | 17 | $26 |
Strip | 3725 Las Vegas Blvd. S. (Harmon Ave.) | 702-740-4555

Don't dare tell the hog riders here that they're drinking out of "adult sippy cups"; not only are the mugs unusual, but with "a U.S. flag made of chain taking up an entire wall", motorcycles "whirling overhead" and the chance to snap "your very own pic as a Harley babe", the entire vibe at this easy-ridin' American "gimmick" is "interesting"; "get out your temporary tatoos and leather" for "cheap", "heaping burgers, a mishmash of bar food" and "lots of 'tude on the Strip."

Hash House A Go Go *American* | 20 | 18 | 20 | $24 |
W Side | 6800 W. Sahara Ave. (Rainbow Blvd.) | 702-804-4646 | www.hashhouseagogo.com

Like "a Denny's on steroids", this urban farmhouse-styled West Sider lures "hungry" hopefuls with "freshly prepared" American fare – like especially "tasty" breakfasts – served in portions that are beyond "bountiful", moving into "mutated science experiment" territory with "skillet-sized" flapjacks and entrees "big enough to feed three teenage boys"; skeptics say it's "overkill", with "quantity" emphasized "over quality", but in excess-heavy Vegas, it suits most as a "great value" that's "worth a try", "even if they have to roll you out of there."

NEW Hawaiian Tropic Zone ◐ *American* | - | - | - | M |
Strip | Miracle Mile Shops | 3663 Las Vegas Blvd. S. (Harmon Ave.) | 702-731-4858 | www.hawaiiantropiczone.com

Fuchsia bikinis and floral sarongs (those would be on the 'table concierges', aka servers) set the tone at this tropical-themed New American at the Miracle Mile Shops at Planet Hollywood on the Strip; an outpost of the New York original, it serves pricey fare by David Burke, including his iconic cheesecake lollipops; N.B. it's open for lunch, but go for dinner to catch the servers' nightly beauty pageant.

Z Hugo's Cellar *Continental* | 26 | 22 | 27 | $56 |
Downtown | Four Queens Hotel | 202 Fremont St. (Casino Center Blvd.) | 702-385-4011 | www.fourqueens.com

"If you're looking for bright, new and open, this is not for you", but if you like it "dank and delicious", this "amazing '70s throwback" Downtown is a "gem", even if it's set in the basement of a "grungy casino"; expect "expertly prepared" Continental dining presided over by an "unsurpassed" staff that sees to "all the extras", including a "roving

DINING

salad cart", "old-fashioned flaming desserts" and a "long-stemmed rose for every lady."

Hush Puppy Seafood/Southern   ▽ 22 | 12 | 18 | $22

E Side | 1820 N. Nellis Blvd. (Lake Mead Blvd.) | 702-438-0005
W Side | 7185 W. Charleston Blvd. (bet. Buffalo Dr. & Rainbow Blvd.) | 702-363-5988

"The all-you-can-eat catfish will cure your Southern nostalgia" at this down-home duo on the East and West Sides where diners in a hurry make "repeat visits" to the drive-up window; sure, they're "dumps", but the "coleslaw is great" and you can score "outta-sight" deals on shrimp, frogs' legs and snow crab, all of which are "not bad."

Hyakumi Japanese   24 | 18 | 20 | $57

Strip | Caesars Palace | 3570 Las Vegas Blvd. S. (Flamingo Rd.) | 702-731-7110 | www.caesarspalace.com

Get a "quick unagi power boost" before muscling into the madness of Cleopatra's Barge, which rocks beneath this "happening" Japanese where the sushi is "fresh, sweet" and "generous" and the tempura and teppanaki are "excellent"; the "seasoned chefs" "dazzle and delight" with their slice it-and-dice it show, and the rest of the staff is "marvelously attentive", though the "noisy" location above the hydraulized party scene can be a "turnoff."

Il Fornaio ● Italian   20 | 19 | 20 | $37

Strip | New York-New York Hotel | 3790 Las Vegas Blvd. S. (Tropicana Ave.) | 702-650-6500 | www.ilfornaio.com

Carb-loving clans clamor for the "delicious pasta", claiming your "grandfather would love this" "affordable" chain link at NY-NY on the Strip, "and grandma would finally get to enjoy dinner with *la famiglia*" if they had a "classic Italian" meal here; insiders advise you "sit on the patio and feel like you're in Central Park – well, Central Park with slot machines and fake foliage."

Il Mulino New York Italian   26 | 23 | 24 | $79

Strip | Forum Shops at Caesars Palace | 3500 Las Vegas Blvd. S. (Flamingo Rd.) | 702-492-6000 | www.ilmulinonewyork.com

"Be very hungry" because "from the moment you walk in" you'll be "bombarded with goodies" at this "New York-style" Italian in the Forum Shops, where "high rollers on a winning streak" indulge in "huge portions" of "fabulous" "garlicky" fare and finish with a complimentary taste of grappa all served by "hardworking waiters" who "don't rush you"; "spacious" chandeliered digs may "lack some of the ambiance" of the Greenwich Village original, but it's "close enough" say East Coast expats who attest that "expense-account" pricing reigns at both locations.

I Love Sushi Japanese   24 | 14 | 20 | $30

Henderson | 11041 S. Eastern Ave. (Sunridge Heights Pkwy.) | 702-990-4055

Locals craving "unbelievably fresh" sushi hit this "always packed" Henderson Japanese for creatively named maki (sex on the beach rolls anyone?) that are considered some of the "best in town"; "on the ball" waitresses provide "fast service" and prices are a "real bargain" too, so insiders insist you overlook the strip-mall setting and "hole-in-the-wall" decor.

DINING

	FOOD	DECOR	SERVICE	COST

India Palace *Indian* ▽ 24 | 12 | 19 | $26
E of Strip | 505 E. Twain Ave. (bet. Paradise Rd. & Swenson St.) | 702-796-4177

"All the food is nice", but the "lunch buffet" is the best "deal" at this "favorite Indian restaurant" of "lucky" in-the-know locals; though regulars report its east-of-the-Strip location is "sketchy" and the interior may be "getting long in the tooth", the "inexpensive" eats are still "worth the visit."

In-N-Out Burger ● *Burgers* 24 | 11 | 19 | $8
E Side | 4705 S. Maryland Pkwy. (bet. Harmon & Tropicana Aves.)
E Side | 51 N. Nellis Blvd. (Charleston Blvd.)
Henderson | 1051 W. Sunset Rd. (Marks St.)
NW | 1960 Rock Springs Dr. (Lake Mead Blvd.)
NW | 5690 Centennial Center Blvd. (Ann Rd.)
S of Strip | 9240 S. Eastern Ave. (Serene Ave.)
W of Strip | 2900 W. Sahara Ave. (bet. Richfield Blvd. & Teddy Dr.)
W of Strip | 4888 Dean Martin Dr. (Tropicana Ave.)
800-786-1000 | www.in-n-out.com

Even "if you lose your shirt, save enough for" the "best hamburger in the whole dang world" scored from these Southern Californian "legends" where "nothing is frozen" and everything is "fast, cheap" and "outstanding", including the "crisp" hand-cut fries and "awesome shakes", eaten in or taken out via the drive-thru; the only problem with Vegas' "finest hangover fare" and biggest Bang for the Buck is that it "goes down too fast"; in other words, "burp!"

Isla ● *Mexican* 23 | 20 | 20 | $41
Strip | Treasure Island Hotel | 3300 Las Vegas Blvd. S. (Spring Mountain Rd.) | 702-894-7349 | www.treasureisland.com

"It's nice to see TI update their food" say fans of this "innovative" Mexican by NY chef Richard Sandoval; the "creative" fare pairs well with the "lively" room's "bold colors", not to mention "hundreds of different" pours from the resident Tequila Goddess; the "delightful staff" takes good care of you, and the "relaxed" room is more than "comfy."

NEW Jade Dim Sum Noodles ● *Pan-Asian* - | - | - | M
Strip | Palazzo Hotel | 3325 Las Vegas Blvd. S. (Sands Ave.) | 702-414-1000 | www.palazzolasvegas.com

Contemporary Pan-Asian dishes comprise the menu at this new arrival on the casino level of the Palazzo Hotel, where the specialty noodles and dim sum are borrowed from the traditions of Taiwan and Vietnam, as well as the Canton and Sichuan provinces of China; service is quick and capable, while prices feel reasonable given its prime Strip location.

Japonais *Japanese* 23 | 24 | 20 | $64
Strip | Mirage Hotel | 3400 Las Vegas Blvd. S. (Spring Mountain Rd.) | 702-792-7800 | www.mirage.com

"Breathtaking decor" with cascading palm trees and a waterfall "takes you far from the madness of the casino floor" at this Mirage outpost of a Chicago original that's "fast becoming a favorite" for its "imaginative" Japanese dishes, many of which are designed for sharing; on the downside, service is a little "rough around the edges" and prices require you to "dig really deep"; N.B. they now serve lunch.

Let your voice be heard - visit ZAGAT.com/vote

DINING

| | FOOD | DECOR | SERVICE | COST |

Jasmine Chinese 　　　　　　　　23 | 25 | 23 | $69

Strip | Bellagio Hotel | 3600 Las Vegas Blvd. S. (Flamingo Rd.) | 702-693-8166 | www.bellagio.com

"Outstanding views of the fountains" and "exquisite" Asian cuisine come together in this "elegant" chintz-filled "oasis" in the Bellagio where "unusual" Hong Kong–style dishes round out a menu of Cantonese, Sichuan and Hunan classics; service strikes most as "impeccable", but a few find fault with the "hefty" prices, especially given portions that sometimes require a "magnifying glass."

Jean Philippe Patisserie Dessert 　　　26 | 22 | 18 | $19

Strip | Bellagio Hotel | 3600 Las Vegas Blvd. S. (Flamingo Rd.) | 702-693-7111 | www.bellagio.com

"Delectable desserts" as "sinful" as Vegas itself inspire some to "order too many" at this Bellagio patisserie also offering "fabulous croissants", "tasty sandwiches" and "excellent" crêpes; since seating is scarce and decor minimal beyond the "hypnotizing" multistory chocolate fountain, most order at the counter and then opt to "carry out."

Jimmy Buffett's Margaritaville ● American 17 | 21 | 18 | $27

Strip | Flamingo Las Vegas | 3555 Las Vegas Blvd. S. (Flamingo Rd.) | 702-733-3302 | www.margaritavillelasvegas.com

"Nothing says 'restaurant entertainment' like a server who is 'sacrificed' to an indoor volcano, only to emerge in a bikini and slide into an oversized margarita blender" at this perennial Parrot Head "party", a Flamingo-based themester that's "all about life with one simple song"; "sit in fishing boats", soak up the "continuous Buffett music", live acts and "Hawaiian-shirt" shtick and reel in an "average" cheeseburger among other American eats or, for "originality", the conch fritters.

ⓩ Joël Robuchon French 　　　　　　28 | 27 | 28 | $251

Strip | MGM Grand Hotel | 3799 Las Vegas Blvd. S. (Tropicana Ave.) | 702-891-7925 | www.mgmgrand.com

"Truly an experience for the ages" swoon surveyors "savoring each moment" of chef Joël Robuchon's "life-altering" New French in the MGM Grand, where the "exquisite" tasting menus "build to a crescendo of amazing intensity", rendering "all other [meals] a mere blur"; so don a jacket, "buckle in" and revel in the "elegant lavender and cream interior" and "pampering" treatment (earning it Las Vegas' No. 1 score for Service) – and if you're daunted by the "three-hour-plus" meal (not to mention the "stratospheric prices"), gastronomes advise "pace yourself, breathe deeply and keep looking at the dessert cart for motivation."

Joe's Seafood, Prime Steak & 　　　　25 | 21 | 24 | $66
Stone Crab Seafood/Steak

Strip | Forum Shops at Caesars Palace | 3500 Las Vegas Blvd. S. (Flamingo Rd.) | 702-792-9222 | www.leye.com

"The stone crab is king" at this "wildly popular" steak-and-seafood import from Miami and Chicago that brings a "welcome breath of fresh salt air" to the Forum Shops with their "phenomenal" namesake crustaceans (available both in- and off-season), "fab steaks cooked to perfection" and an especially noteworthy bread basket; sure, the "mall location" may be a far cry from South Beach, but "polished service"

DINING

| | FOOD | DECOR | SERVICE | COST |

and a reservations policy (unlike the original) convince more than a few customers that it's "worth the splurge", even without the waves.

Joyful House Chinese Cuisine ● *Chinese* ▽ 21 | 12 | 15 | $29
W Side | 4601 Spring Mountain Rd. (Stober Blvd.) | 702-889-8881
"Try ordering from the Chinese specialty list" at this West Side "anti-P.F. Chang's" – it's even "more authentic than the regular menu", which itself features "a number of unique dishes", including "very fresh seafood"; the "hurried" but efficient staff is "reminiscent of New York's" frenetic Chinatown, but "who cares with food this good?"; N.B. cook your own after 9 PM, courtesy of the late-night shabu-shabu buffet.

NEW Kabuki *Japanese* — | — | — | M
S of Strip | Town Square | 6605 Las Vegas Blvd. S. (bet. I-215 & Sunset Rd.) | 702-896-7440 | www.kabukirestaurants.com
This new link in a California-based Japanese chain brings midpriced sushi, teriyaki and over 200 beers to Town Square south of the Strip; the spacious black-and-red interior includes a lively bar area whose happy-hour specials (Mondays–Fridays, 3-6 PM) feature deals on drinks and apps.

Kathy's Southern Cooking ⓂӨ *Southern* ▽ 24 | 6 | 14 | $19
Henderson | Sunset Mountain Vista Plaza | 6407 Mountain Vista St. (Sunset Rd.) | 702-433-1005
"Honest soul food" including homemade sweet potato pie and some of "the best fried chicken in Vegas" make this "spartan" strip-mall joint a Henderson "neighborhood favorite"; though some find fault with "painfully slow" service, allies insist that those who are "patient" will be "well-rewarded"; N.B. cash and debit cards only.

King's Fish House *Seafood* 23 | 19 | 21 | $33
Henderson | The District | 2255 Village Walk Dr. (Green Valley Pkwy.) | 702-835-8900 | www.kingsseafood.com
You "can almost smell the Atlantic" at the Henderson branch of this seafood chain where you "can't beat the freshness" of the dozen different types of fish on offer daily; since this "family place" serves "seasonal items, the menu changes constantly" and keeps the "noisy" crowds coming back; for a quieter time, escape to the "wonderful" patio and enjoy "a nice selection of oysters" while "watching people go by."

NEW Koi *Japanese* — | — | — | E
Strip | Planet Hollywood Resort | 3667 Las Vegas Blvd. S (Harmon Ave.) | 702-454-4555 | www.koirestaurant.com
LA comes to Vegas in this new Planet Hollywood clone of the infamous celeb hangout where pretty people nibble on sushi rolls and signature Japanese dishes like spicy tuna on crispy rice; the earth-toned Zen-chic decor features low-slung tables with stellar sight lines and a lounge area with floor-to-ceiling windows affording spectacular views of the Strip.

Kona Grill *American* 18 | 18 | 18 | $31
NW | Boca Park | 750 S. Rampart Blvd. (Charleston Blvd.) | 702-547-5552 | www.konagrill.com
"Hang out with the hip crowd" while sipping and nibbling "happy-hour specials that can't be beat" at the "inside/outside bar" at this Pacific

Let your voice be heard – visit ZAGAT.com/vote 53

DINING

| | FOOD | DECOR | SERVICE | COST |

Rim-inspired New American in the Northwest's Boca Park; plenty of partyers dig the "trendy atmosphere" and "great sushi", even if critics crab "it's not worth going out of the way for" "hit-or-miss" fare at just "another 'in' spot that ought to be 'out.'"

Lake Mead Cruises American — | — | — | E
Boulder City | Lake Mead Nat'l Recreation Area | 490B Horsepower Cove (I-93) | 702-293-6180 | www.lakemeadcruises.com

The dinner cruises on these paddlewheelers offer "a great view" of "magnificent Hoover Dam" and "beautiful Lake Mead" while passengers sample simple American fare like prime rib and baked chicken; the April–October Sunday brunch tour is "fun and filling" and makes for a "nice day away from Sin City."

NEW La Madonna ☒ Mexican — | — | — | M
SW | 6115 S. Fort Apache Rd. (Patrick Ln.) | 702-586-0925 | www.lamadonnarestaurant.com

This self-proclaimed 'avant-garde' Southwest Mexican features border-bending interpretations of authentic dishes like crab cakes with chipotle aïoli and filet mignon with charred peppers; the decor offers a similar edgy take on the traditional with punched-tin stars, lots of candles and dark-wood tables lending a modern, romantic feel.

La Salsa Mexican 15 | 11 | 13 | $17
E Side | Boulevard Mall | 3480 S. Maryland Pkwy. (Desert Inn Rd.) | 702-369-1234
E Side | Riviera Hotel | 9000 Las Vegas Blvd. S. (Pebble Rd.) | 702-697-4401 ◑
Henderson | The District | 2265 Village Walk Dr. (Green Valley Pkwy.) | 702-263-8233
Strip | Forum Shops at Caesars Palace | 3500 Las Vegas Blvd. S. (Flamingo Rd.) | 702-735-8226 ◑
Strip | Miracle Mile Shops | 3663 Las Vegas Blvd. S. (Harmon Ave.) | 702-892-0645 ◑
Strip | Showcase Mall | 3785 Las Vegas Blvd. S. (Tropicana Ave.) | 702-240-6944 ◑
www.lasalsa.com

"Terrific" salsas made from "very fresh ingredients" are the trademark of this Mexican chain that's also famed for "fabulous [yard-long] margaritas" that "come in a variety of flavors" and are great for washing down "cheap", "monstrous burritos"; those who bemoan the "drunk, rowdy crowd" should head for Boulevard Mall (the only location that doesn't serve booze).

☒ L'Atelier de Joël Robuchon French 28 | 24 | 26 | $118
Strip | MGM Grand Hotel | 3799 Las Vegas Blvd. S. (Tropicana Ave.) | 702-891-7358 | www.mgmgrand.com

This downscaled (but still "staggeringly" expensive) sister to Joël Robuchon in the MGM Grand is "a less stuffy way" for "hard-core foodies" to experience "the master's" "stunning" New French cuisine, which earns it the No. 1 Food score in Las Vegas thanks to "memorable" small plates best appreciated from the U-shaped bar where "you can marvel at the action" in the open kitchen; refreshingly "unpretentious" service makes the black-and-red interior feel both "sleek" and "casual" at the same time, setting the scene for "one of the single best dining experiences in Vegas" – just bring your "sense of adventure."

DINING

| | FOOD | DECOR | SERVICE | COST |

🆕 Lavo ● *Mediterranean* — | — | — | E

Strip | Palazzo Hotel | 3327 Las Vegas Blvd. S. (Sands Ave.) | 702-791-1800 | www.lavolv.com

The owners of Tao are behind this new entry in the Palazzo that takes its inspiration from the bathhouses of ancient Rome, with an AvroKO-designed space done up in tile and stone and illuminated by lots of candles; chef Ludo Lefebvre (recently of LA's Bastide) presents a broad menu of pricey Med small plates that includes prosciutto fig panini and sardines à la plancha as well as upmarket pizzas and sliders; N.B. also on-site is a nightclub with DJs and bottle service.

Lawry's The Prime Rib *Steak* — 25 | 21 | 25 | $53

E of Strip | Hughes Ctr. | 4043 Howard Hughes Pkwy. (Flamingo Rd.) | 702-893-2223 | www.lawrysonline.com

"If you don't love steak, stay away" from this slice of "prime-rib heaven" east of the Strip; otherwise, "unleash the carnivore within" and "gorge yourself" on "outstanding" beef carved tableside by the "old-school staff" in a "dignified", "art deco" space that's "always crowded" "but worth the wait", even if a handful feels this ritual is "tired"; N.B. they now serve lunch on weekdays at their Ale & Sandwich Bar.

🅩 Le Cirque *French* — 26 | 27 | 26 | $96

Strip | Bellagio Hotel | 3600 Las Vegas Blvd. S. (Flamingo Rd.) | 702-693-8100 | www.bellagio.com

"A class act", this "extravagant" New York offshoot in the Bellagio is "delightful in every way" say those savoring "exceptional" repasts of New French cuisine, "smooth service" from waiters who "anticipate your every desire" and "spectacular views of the fountains" from the "playful" silk-tented dining room; in short, "it's simply one of the best" – so "bring a jacket" and a fat wallet; N.B. no children under 12 allowed.

🆕 Le Golosita *Italian* — — | — | — | M

Henderson | Sansone Park Place Ctr. | 9500 S. Eastern Ave. (bet. Serene Ave. & Silverado Ranch Blvd.) | 702-216-4080 | www.legolositarestaurant.com

A laid-back and more modestly priced sibling of Zeffirino in the Venetian, this new Henderson trattoria serves up familiar Italian favorites like pastas and veal scaloppini in a sepia-toned space with marble floors; with a gelateria, pizzeria and bakery also on the premises, it's already become a popular one-stop shop for families seeking takeout.

Le Provençal *French/Italian* — 22 | 21 | 21 | $40

Strip | Paris Las Vegas | 3655 Las Vegas Blvd. S. (bet. Flamingo Rd. & Harmon Ave.) | 702-946-4656 | www.parislasvegas.com

At this "well-kept secret" in the Paris, "singing servers" deliver Italian-French bistro fare like "sublime crêpes" and bouillabaisse as well as "some of the best pizza in Vegas"; some feel the "food is good enough without the show", and others find the songs "fun" and "entertaining", but all agree the "charming farmhouse" setting is "excellent for lunch."

Les Artistes Steakhouse *French/Steak* — 22 | 23 | 21 | $63

Strip | Paris Las Vegas | 3655 Las Vegas Blvd. S. (bet. Flamingo Rd. & Harmon Ave.) | 702-946-4663 | www.parislasvegas.com

The "two-level dining room" of this New French beefery in the Paris is "classy and beautiful" with high ceilings and Impressionist artwork that create a "romantic" atmosphere in which to enjoy "fantastic

DINING

| | FOOD | DECOR | SERVICE | COST |

bone-in filet" and "splendid lobster tails"; though a few find it "pricey, pretentious" and "not particularly exceptional", most agree "it's a safe bet" for "delicious" if "basic steakhouse fare."

Le Village Buffet French   23 | 21 | 18 | $29
Strip | Paris Las Vegas | 3655 Las Vegas Blvd. S. (bet. Flamingo Rd. & Harmon Ave.) | 702-946-4966 | www.parislasvegas.com

This "top-tier" buffet at Paris Las Vegas "works the French angle" with an "eye-popping spread" of "well-executed" Gallic dishes including "regional" specialties, "freshly made crêpes" and "scrumptious" breakfasts and desserts served in a "picturesque" setting; it's all so "charming" that it conjures up a "country village", so long as you can avert your eyes from the "long lines."

Lindo Michoacan Mexican   - | - | - | M
E Side | 2655 E. Desert Inn Rd. (bet. Eastern Ave & McLeod Dr.) | 702-735-6828 | www.usmenuguide.com/lindomichoacan.html
NEW **W Side** | 10082 W. Flamingo Rd. (Hualapai Way) | 702-838-9990

South-of-the-border posters and artifacts from the Michoacan region adorn the walls of this popular, family-owned Mexican on the East Side, where handmade tortillas, bean and salsa dips and hearty dishes such as goat with dried chiles and beer are brought to table by a friendly staff; expect a casual atmosphere and live music each evening; N.B. the West Side branch is new.

Little Buddha Asian   24 | 26 | 22 | $47
W of Strip | Palms Casino Hotel | 4321 W. Flamingo Rd. (Arville St.) | 702-942-7778 | www.littlebuddhalasvegas.com

"Excellent" French-inspired Asian fare varied enough "to please everyone" and some "mind-blowing" sushi are served up in a "cool", "round" room at this moderately priced sis to France's Buddha Bar situated in the Palms west of the Strip; "fun drinks" plus an "inviting staff" make it an appealing stop "before going out on the town", although given the "trendy" atmosphere and the DJ who "spins a great mix", some prefer to hunker down and stay the night.

Lombardi's Italian   ▽ 20 | 17 | 21 | $37
Strip | Miracle Mile Shops | 3663 Las Vegas Blvd. S. (Harmon Ave.) | 702-731-1755 | www.lombardisrestaurants.com

Those who've stumbled upon this "tried-and-true" Northern Italian in the Miracle Mile Shops in Planet Hollywood praise the "ideal location" and "relaxing environment"; savor the "consistently good", "reasonable priced" fare while sitting "on the patio that provides a view" of the musicians, magicians and tourists that frequent this section of the mall.

ⓩ Lotus of Siam Thai   27 | 10 | 20 | $28
E Side | Commercial Ctr. | 953 E. Sahara Ave. (bet. Maryland Pkwy. & Paradise Rd.) | 702-735-3033 | www.lotusofsiamlv.com

"Hitchhike if you have to" but "don't leave town" without a stop at this "local treasure" east of the Strip that intrepid eaters rank as the "best Thai restaurant in the country" with a "dazzling" "affordable" array of "complex" dishes including "exquisite" Northern-style "gems" like jackfruit curry that pair well with sips from an "excellent list of German Rieslings"; "friendly service" helps you forget all about the "strip-mall" setting and "nondescript" decor; N.B. no lunch on Saturday or Sunday.

DINING

| | FOOD | DECOR | SERVICE | COST |

NEW Louis's Las Vegas *Southern* — | — | — | E
S of Strip | Town Square | 6605 Las Vegas Blvd. S. (bet. I-215 & Sunset Rd.) | 702-202-2400 | www.louislasvegas.com

James Beard Award–winner Louis Osteen gambled his name and reputation when he opened this sibling to the Pawleys Island, S.C., original at the Town Square center south of the Strip; Low Country cuisine classics such as she-crab soup and updated items like country-ham prosciutto are showcased in a gentrified interior designed to reflect the best of Southern hospitality.

Lucille's Smokehouse Bar-B-Que *BBQ* 22 | 19 | 18 | $28
Henderson | The District | 2245 Village Walk Dr. (Green Valley Pkwy.) | 702-257-7427 | www.lucillesbbq.com

"Bring your appetite" to The District branch of this barbecue chain: though the "portions are large" you'll still want a "second helping" of goodies like "lip-smacking babyback ribs", "tender brisket" and "irresistible" biscuits – if you can get the "really slow" staff to hustle it for you; N.B. dine on Saturdays and listen to live blues while sipping a mint julep.

NEW Lucio Ristorante *Italian* — | — | — | M
W Side | 8615 W. Sahara Ave. (Durango Dr.) | 702-233-2859 | www.lucioristorante.com

This Italian newcomer is somewhat hidden in its West Side strip-center home, but a committed cadre of fans seek it out for its modern takes on risottos, pastas and primo *primi* (and *secondi*) *piatti*; the airy layout boasts flowing drapes, textured walls and patio seating for balmy eves.

Luna Rossa *Italian* ▽ 20 | 19 | 18 | $36
Lake LV | MonteLago Vill. | 10 Via Bel Canto (Lake Las Vegas Pkwy.) | Henderson | 702-568-9921

"Lovely" patio seating affords "beautiful views" of Lake Las Vegas at this "cozy" white-tablecloth Italian restaurant in the cobblestoned MonteLago Village where the setting is so "quaint", it "makes you forget how close you are to the Strip"; "superb" homemade pastas stand out on the menu of Southern specialties, while "average" prices and solid (if sometimes "slow") service makes for an "enjoyable" evening.

Maggiano's Little Italy *Italian* 20 | 19 | 19 | $34
Strip | Fashion Show Mall | 3200 Las Vegas Blvd. S. (Spring Mountain Rd.) | 702-732-2550 | www.maggianos.com

Even for "the city of excess", this Italian chain's "heaping" servings are "mind-boggling"; "family-style is a great way to taste everything" on an "excellent-bargain" menu featuring "rich, flavorful sauces over a plethora of pastas and meats"; there are "no surprises", just lots of "*delizioso*" dishes delivered in a "finely lit", "dark-wood" space that's "as huge as its portions" – "with a great view of the Wynn" on the Strip to boot.

Makino *Japanese* 21 | 12 | 17 | $26
Downtown | Las Vegas Premium Outlets | 775 S. Grand Central Pkwy. (Bonneville Ave.) | 702-382-8848
Henderson | 9570 S. Eastern Ave. (Hardin Dr.) | 702-263-7837
W Side | 3965 S. Decatur Blvd. (Flamingo Rd.) | 702-889-4477
www.makinolasvegas.com

"If you're hungry, and you love sushi, this buffet is the deal!" rave fans fishing for all-you-can-eat bargains at this local chain; when "loading

DINING

up on the freshest, tastiest" raw ocean offerings "for the price" (plus "a crab feast at night" and "many hot items"), you'll "be in heaven" – just be warned that it "can get very crowded"; N.B. the Henderson branch opened post-Survey.

Marché Bacchus *French* — 24 | 21 | 24 | $40

NW | 2620 Regatta Dr. (Breakwater Dr.) | 702-804-8008 | www.marchebacchus.com

"Shhh... don't tell anyone about this hidden little gem" in the Northwest where "a little bit of France" can be had in the "romantic" interior or "delightfully alfresco" by the lake; "a knowledgeable staff" attends to the "eclectic" crowd munching on "basic" but "excellent" fare, but most "memorable" is the "full-on wine store" from which retail bottles can be purchased "off the shelf" and poured for an extra $10; N.B. the Food score does not reflect the departure of chef Jean-David Groff-Daudet.

Market City Caffe *Italian* — 18 | 16 | 19 | $24

Strip | Monte Carlo Resort | 3770 Las Vegas Blvd. S. (bet. Harmon & Tropicana Aves.) | 702-730-7777 | www.dragonnoodleco.com

For "some of the best Italian fare for the price", try this Strip trattoria featuring an all-you-can-eat antipasto bar and "good single-serving pizza"; sure, "service could be better", and the "small-ish", "quiet setting" is a far cry from glitz and glamour, but it's "reliable" when you're looking for a "quick break" from the "wallet crushing."

Marrakech *Moroccan* — ∇ 20 | 24 | 21 | $47

E of Strip | 3900 Paradise Rd. (bet. Flamingo Rd. & Twain Ave.) | 702-737-5611

"Watching the belly dancers helps with digestion", but "don't let the bare, undulating torsos distract you from the fabulous parade" of "tasty" Moroccan dishes brought by "friendly" servers at this "Marrakech-goes-Marra-kitsch" den east of the Strip; do let yourself slide into "another world" where diners "lay on a couch" under the "fabric-draped tent ceiling" in a "picturesque room with beautiful carpets" and "feast" their eyes, ears and stomachs.

Martinis ● *American* — - | - | - | M

NW | 1205 S. Fort Apache Rd. (Charleston Blvd.) | 702-242-8464

Specialty cocktails crafted from over 300 premium spirits pair with Traditional American dishes like bacon-wrapped prawns and savory crab dip at this sophisticated Northwesterner whose cherrywood walls are adorned with martini-themed *New Yorker* cartoon prints; it's open 24/7, though live music on Saturdays adds a swank touch to the weekend.

McCormick & Schmick's *Seafood* — 21 | 19 | 21 | $43

E of Strip | 335 Hughes Center Dr. (Paradise Rd.) | 702-836-9000 | www.mccormickandschmicks.com

"It's hard to believe you're in the middle of the desert with all the fresh fish on the menu" at this "dependably consistent" franchise for seafood east of the Strip; "far more upscale" than most chains and "definitely superior", it's a "nice place" to "see and be seen" on "a business lunch", but it can be "crowded" and "loud", especially "during happy hour" when "the killer $1.95 bar menu" reels 'em in.

DINING

| | FOOD | DECOR | SERVICE | COST |

Medici Café *American*   22 | 24 | 26 | $57
Lake LV | Ritz-Carlton, Lake Las Vegas | 1610 Lake Las Vegas Pkwy. (Grand Mediterra Blvd.) | Henderson | 702-567-4700 | www.ritz-carlton.com

So "relaxing" sigh supporters of this "lovely" New American set in the casino-free Ritz-Carlton on Lake Las Vegas where the "refined" cuisine is enjoyed in "romantic dinners" and "outstanding" lunches and brunches and prices are "more reasonable than the Strip"; insiders insist you "start with cocktails on the balcony overlooking the beach" then move to the "beautiful" dining room and "let the professional staff pamper you."

Melting Pot *Fondue*   21 | 19 | 21 | $49
Henderson | 8955 S. Eastern Ave. (Pebble Rd.) | 702-944-6358
NW | 8704 W. Charleston Blvd. (Merialdo Ln.) | 702-384-6358
www.meltingpot.com

A "cute idea for your teenager's birthday party", a "girls' night out" or a "first date", these Henderson and Northwest outposts of the nationwide chain are a "one-trick pony" for folks who are fond of fondue; all that melted "cholesterol" can be "great fun", but "expensive", leaving some dunksters wishing "they didn't have a monopoly" on the "novelty."

Memphis Championship Barbecue *BBQ*   21 | 17 | 20 | $24
E Side | 2250 E. Warm Springs Rd. (Eastern Ave.) | 702-260-6909
N Las Vegas | 4379 Las Vegas Blvd. N. (bet. Craig Rd. & Nellis Blvd.) | North Las Vegas | 702-644-0000
W Side | 1401 S. Rainbow Blvd. (Charleston Blvd.) | 702-254-0520
www.memphis-bbq.com

"Bring it on!" say surveyors salivating over "melt-in-your-mouth ribs, hot links, pulled pork and brisket" accompanied by two "to-die-for sides", "homemade iced tea in a Mason jar" and "service with a smile" at this "real-deal" 'cue trio; "portion control is not on the menu" but "jam-packed" lunchtimes are, so "stay away if you're on a diet" or craving quiet – otherwise, "there's only one word to describe it: mmmmmm!"

☒ Mesa Grill *Southwestern*   25 | 23 | 23 | $58
Strip | Caesars Palace | 3570 Las Vegas Blvd. S. (Flamingo Rd.) | 702-731-7731 | www.caesarspalace.com

Bobby Flay "delivers the goods" at this Caesars Palace "culinary oasis" whose "bold" Southwestern dishes – such as "awesome" chiles rellenos, "memorable" pork tenderloin and "extraordinary chipotle-glazed rib-eye" – offer a "distinctive" "change-up" from the rest of the Strip; with its "nice, open layout" and "standout" service, most agree it's a "near-perfect re-creation" of the NYC original.

Metro Pizza *Pizza*   24 | 13 | 17 | $17
E of Strip | Ellis Island Casino & Brewery | 4178 Koval Ln. (Flamingo Rd.) | 702-312-5888 ☾
E Side | 1395 E. Tropicana Ave. (Maryland Pkwy.) | 702-736-1955
E Side | Boulder Station Hotel | 4111 Boulder Hwy. (Lamb Blvd.) | 702-247-1980
Henderson | 1420 W. Horizon Ridge Pkwy. (Stephanie St.) | 702-458-4769
W Side | Renaissance Center W. | 4001 S. Decatur Blvd. (Flamingo Rd.) | 702-362-7896
www.metropizza.com

"Now we don't need to move back East" raves a "lively crowd" of pie-heads relieved to find these "locally owned" "joints" that put out "the

DINING

FOOD | DECOR | SERVICE | COST

best NY-style pizza in town"; "great crusts" topped with "tons" of "strong flavors" in "excellent combinations" make for "some serious 'za", washed down with "very cold beer"; "after a few nights of Strip extravagance, it's so comforting", "Brooklynites" sigh, to eat at a place that "makes me think of home."

MGM Grand Buffet *American* 17 | 13 | 15 | $26
Strip | MGM Grand Hotel | 3799 Las Vegas Blvd. S. (Tropicana Ave.) | 702-891-7314 | www.mgmgrand.com
For a chow break "when gambling", this "standard buffet" on the Strip is "convenient" for "piles" of "very decent, ordinary American food cooked well", but it really "has nothing to make it special"; given decor that "needs to be updated" and a staff that "ignores patrons", "underwhelmed" overeaters grumble that, despite its name, it's "not as grand as it could be."

Z Michael Mina *Seafood* 27 | 24 | 26 | $93
Strip | Bellagio Hotel | 3600 Las Vegas Blvd. S. (Flamingo Rd.) | 702-693-8255 | www.michaelmina.net
"Easily the best seafood on the Strip" rave regulars who savor the "divine scallops three ways", a lobster pot pie that's either "to die for" or "a reason to live", and other tastings that "tickle the senses" at chef/co-owner Michael Mina's "romantic", "beautiful and relaxing" Bellagio destination; a "superb" wine list and "marvelous" service help justify the "third mortgage required to fund the extravagance."

Z Michael's *Continental* 26 | 23 | 27 | $104
S of Strip | South Point Hotel | 9777 Las Vegas Blvd. S. (Flamingo Rd.) | 702-796-7111 | www.southpointcasino.com
"Its new locale at the South Point does its reputation justice" according to admirers of this "Vegas landmark" (relocated from the Barbary Coast to south of the Strip) serving such classic Continental dishes as "incomparable Dover sole", Châteaubriand and cherries jubilee; fittingly, its "bordello" decor is so "old-school" "you feel like the ghost of Baby Face is going to walk through the door", but even with "impeccable" service from the "same staff for years", critics contend "at these prices they should shine your shoes to boot."

MiraLago *Mediterranean* ▽ 21 | 20 | 19 | $45
Lake LV | Reflection Bay Golf Club | 75 Montelago Blvd. (Lake Las Vegas Pkwy.) | Henderson | 702-568-7383 | www.lakelasvegas.com
"Go while the sun is going down" to take in the view of Lake Las Vegas from this Mediterranean at Reflection Bay Golf Club, whose "outstanding" setting also makes it a "pleasant place for lunch" and Sunday brunch (even if the decor itself "could use a little refreshing"); the service is largely on par with the cuisine, which "almost measures up to the locale."

Z miX *American/French* 23 | 27 | 22 | $89
Strip | Mandalay Bay Resort | 3950 Las Vegas Blvd. S., 64th fl. (Mandalay Bay Rd.) | 702-632-9500 | www.chinagrillmgt.com
"Killer views" from "64 floors up" are "hard to beat" at Alain Ducasse's "gem" in THEhotel at Mandalay Bay, where the "gorgeous" *Austin Powers* interior with a chandelier of 15,000 blown-glass bubbles suggests "sitting in a glass of champagne"; fortunately its New American-

DINING

| | FOOD | DECOR | SERVICE | COST |

New French menu, running the gamut from "spectacular" bison to Gruyère mac 'n' cheese, is "memorable" too, and while the "amiable" staff is sometimes "spotty", fans call it "one of the few places that can almost justify the price"; P.S. "reserve an outside table and watch the sun set over the Strip."

Z Mon Ami Gabi *French* — 23 | 23 | 21 | $46

Strip | Paris Las Vegas | 3655 Las Vegas Blvd. S. (bet. Flamingo Rd. & Harmon Ave.) | 702-944-4224 | www.monamigabi.com

"The desserts will make you melt", and so will "the fountain show" visible from this "charming bistro" with sidewalk seating "spilling out toward the Bellagio lake"; featuring "authentic" French items such as "amazing pommes frites", "great hanger steak" and "a very good selection of wines and champagnes", it's a "lively", "packed" place and "possibly the only part of the Paris that actually feels like" the namesake city – yet with "better" service.

Montesano's ⓈItalian — ▽ 20 | 11 | 18 | $21

Henderson | 9905 S. Eastern Ave. (St. Rose Pkwy.) | 702-870-3287

"Everything is made from scratch, simply and lovingly" at this "real family-run Italian" in Henderson where the "pastas are all good" with "interesting combinations of ingredients" and it also boasts a take-out shop for homemade baked goods; yet just because the "owners are from Arthur Avenue in the Bronx" doesn't mean the eats are all that – some of the "sauces are way too sweet" say connoisseurs; N.B. the West Side locations have closed.

NEW Morels French Steakhouse *French/Steak* — - | - | - | E

Strip | Palazzo Hotel | 3325 Las Vegas Blvd. S. (Sands Ave.) | 702-607-6333 | www.palazzolasvegas.com

Attention to detail is held in high regard at this LA chophouse import in the Palazzo where some of the thoughtful touches include black napkins for dark-clad patrons and two types of salt (pink and fleur de sel) proffered by exacting servers; the understated gray-blue interior puts the focus on the food – prime steaks and French bistro standards – which get a boost from a deep wine list and a stellar cheese assortment; N.B. the patio affords one of the best views on the Strip.

Morton's The Steakhouse *Steak* — 25 | 22 | 24 | $67

E of Strip | 400 E. Flamingo Rd. (Paradise Rd.) | 702-893-0703 | www.mortons.com

"Morton's lives up to their reputation" at this east-of-the-Strip branch of the "top-notch" beef chain where the "old-style" dinner features "wonderful, aged" cuts, "huge sides" and "desserts to die for", all brought by "efficient servers"; those looking for a "hipper" vibe find the "classy" decor too "sober", and unless you "drink heavily", the "look-at-this-plate-of-raw-meat" "menu on wheels" is "not that exciting" either.

Mr. Lucky's 24/7 ☾ *Diner* — 19 | 17 | 17 | $19

E of Strip | Hard Rock Hotel | 4455 Paradise Rd. (bet. Flamingo Rd. & Harmon Ave.) | 702-693-5592 | www.hardrockhotel.com

"It's 3 AM, you've had a lot to drink, you need eggs and a burger", and you want them served by a "hot pants-clad, young staff" at "bargain" prices – where do you "drag your tired butt" but the Hard Rock's "trendy"

DINING

"all-nighter"?; given a "high-energy" vibe, "celebrity sightings" and "great" "all-around American junk food", this "always-happening" coffee shop is the place to "show off your new tatt" "any time of day."

Neros *Steak*   24 | 21 | 22 | $69
Strip | Caesars Palace | 3570 Las Vegas Blvd. S. (Flamingo Rd.) | 702-731-7110 | www.caesarspalace.com

Meat mavens say this "seriously underrated" "hidden jewel" in Caesars Palace "holds its own" against the onslaught of celebrity chefs with "exceptional" steaks and "gracious" service amid a recently renovated "modern and sleek" interior; it's "still a favorite" that's "well worth" the high prices.

NEW New Orleans Connection *Cajun/Creole*   - | - | - | I
E Side | 9711 S. Eastern Ave. (Silverado Ranch Blvd.) | 702-492-1650

The Katrina diaspora brought New Orleans refugees – and their food – to Las Vegas, hence this inexpensive Cajun-Creole BYO near Henderson; the digs are strictly no-frills and service is counter-style, but the hearty Louisiana-style dishes like étouffée, jambalaya and even alligator are already drawing a loyal following.

Nine Fine Irishmen *Irish*   17 | 22 | 18 | $30
Strip | New York-New York Hotel | 3790 Las Vegas Blvd. S. (Tropicana Ave.) | 702-740-6969 | www.ninefineirishmen.com

"Every kind of Irish drink you've ever heard of" can be downed at this pub in New York-New York where the "authentic" atmosphere features "the finest woods, cubbyholes for seating, just-right lighting and a noise level that's defeaning"; it's an "affordable" spot for an affable quaff amid a "high number of expats", who'll tell you that the "food is bland, just like in Ireland", but it "goes down well" with "group singing and lots of beer."

N9ne Steakhouse *Steak*   25 | 23 | 23 | $74
W of Strip | Palms Casino Hotel | 4321 W. Flamingo Rd. (Arville St.) | 702-933-9900 | www.n9negroup.com

"Those under 30 with money to burn" head to this "too cool for school" – and "too loud for conversation" – chophouse in the Palms Casino where "celebrity-spotting" is highly probable ("hello Miss Hilton") and "flirty waitresses" and "chic" decor replace the "tuxedoed waiters and red leather" of steakhouses of yore; it's a "total scene", but patrons are pleased to report that it "exceeds expectations" with "terrific" food – just watch they don't "rush you out to make room for someone prettier."

Nobhill Tavern *Californian*   26 | 24 | 25 | $88
Strip | MGM Grand Hotel | 3799 Las Vegas Blvd. S. (Tropicana Ave.) | 702-891-7337 | www.michaelmina.net

One of the "culinary treasures" of MGM Grand on the Strip, this "exquisite" Californian by chef/co-owner Michael Mina features "innovative cuisine of the high-calorie kind", complemented by "freshly baked" breads; an "exceptional" staff works the dining room whose savviest guests "book early to reserve one of the private booths", but also warn that dining here can "drain your wallet faster than the high-roller tables"; N.B. the above scores do not reflect a fall 2008 revamp, which introduced tavern-style menu items and more casual furnishings.

DINING

	FOOD	DECOR	SERVICE	COST

🏆 Nobu *Japanese* — 28 | 23 | 24 | $80

E of Strip | Hard Rock Hotel | 4455 Paradise Rd. (bet. Flamingo Rd. & Harmon Ave.) | 702-693-5090 | www.noburestaurants.com

"Exceptional raw fish in the desert" attracts seekers of the "absolute freshest" "sushi and sashimi creations" as well as "amazing cooked dishes" ("love the miso cod"), all served by a "superb" staff at Nobu Matsuhisa's outpost in the Hard Rock Hotel east of the Strip; sure, "they blast music like eardrums are going out of style" and you can expect a "flabbergasting bill", but many advise "just say omakase", "watch the masters at work at the bar" and "enjoy the ride."

Noodles ☻ *Pan-Asian* — 22 | 17 | 19 | $35

Strip | Bellagio Hotel | 3600 Las Vegas Blvd. S. (Flamingo Rd.) | 702-693-7111 | www.bellagio.com

"Bringing welcome variety to the Strip dining scene", this Bellagio eatery offers "every Asian noodle dish you can think of" and "solid weekend dim sum" on a Marco Polo-esque menu that roves the Far East; "simple" and "satisfying", it makes for a "nice little midnight snack", and you can feast your eyes on "numerous different types" of the "addictive" namesake that make up the "peculiar decor."

Noodle Shop *Chinese* — 19 | 15 | 17 | $27

Strip | Mandalay Bay Resort | 3950 Las Vegas Blvd. S. (Mandalay Bay Rd.) | 702-632-7777 | www.mandalaybay.com

"Waits" can be "interminable during busy hours" and the service can be "brusque" at what amounts to "basically your typical noodle joint from any Chinatown in America", transported to the casino in Mandalay Bay; nonetheless, you can score a "delicious won ton soup" "fix" on weekends till the wee hours, and "after a long night of losing, nothing tastes better."

Nora's Cuisine 🅩 *Italian* — 24 | 18 | 21 | $32

W Side | 6020 W. Flamingo Rd. (Jones Blvd.) | 702-873-8990 | www.norascuisine.com

Nora's Wine Bar & Osteria *Italian*

NW | 1031 S. Rampart Blvd. (W. Charleston Blvd.) | 702-940-6672 | www.noraswinebar.com

You'll find "families, older couples and young people having a good time" at this "creative" West Side Italian serving "down-home" "traditional" food, while its sleeker Northwest sister ("more of a hangout place") offers "top-notch" small plates, "delicious cheeses" and a "cool" Enomatic dispenser system that "lets you taste a variety of wines"; both provide "personal" service, a "neighborhood feel" and "reasonable prices" (a bit "higher" for vino), keeping them "mobbed with those in-the-know."

Nove Italiano *Italian* — ▽ 27 | 26 | 26 | $68

W of Strip | Palms Casino Hotel | 4321 W. Flamingo Rd., 51st fl. (Arville St.) | 702-942-6800 | www.n9negroup.com

The "food is as sumptuous as the view is magical" at this Italian offshoot of N9ne Steakhouse, both at the Palms just west of the Strip, which fans call "phenomenal from every perspective"; "beautiful" dishes such as osso buco, seafood crudo and savory cannoli are illuminated by crystal chandeliers and gilt-framed plasma screens display-

DINING

| | FOOD | DECOR | SERVICE | COST |

ing electronic art, while both the selection of super-Tuscans and often "flawless" service enhance the "exceptional" meal.

Z Okada *Japanese* | 25 | 27 | 24 | $78 |

Strip | Wynn Las Vegas | 3131 Las Vegas Blvd. S. (bet. Desert Inn & Spring Mountain Rds.) | 702-770-3320 | www.wynnlasvegas.com

"Delighted" diners say "Wynn Las Vegas offers another gem" gleaming with a "spectacular ambiance" – "especially if you have a table with a view of the waterfall" or one of the few in the "beautiful garden" – at this Japanese "oasis within an oasis"; boasting "fabulous" robata, teppanyaki and sushi, a "terrific" sake selection and "thoughtful" service, it's "expensive" but "not outrageously priced" for the Strip.

Z Olives *Mediterranean* | 23 | 23 | 22 | $57 |

Strip | Bellagio Hotel | 3600 Las Vegas Blvd. S. (Flamingo Rd.) | 702-693-8255 | www.toddenglish.com

"Another winner" by Todd English, this "little bit of heaven floating above the Bellagio lake" cooks up a "fairly priced" Medierreanean menu of "frolicky food", such as "amazing" flatbread pizzas and "fantastic" beef carpaccio served by a "solid" staff; while critics complain about "crowded" seating, those who nab an outdoor table "get an awesome view of the fountain show", leading fans to conclude it's the "best location on the Strip"; P.S. the "lively bar" is popular for "exotic cocktails" too.

Onda *Italian* | 22 | 22 | 23 | $58 |

Strip | Mirage Hotel | 3400 Las Vegas Blvd. S. (Spring Mountain Rd.) | 702-791-7223 | www.mirage.com

"The cha-chings of the slots start to disappear" as the bar area's music draws you into this "gentle respite" inside the Mirage; "if nothing really jumps out at you" on the "thin" Italian menu, at least everything is "solid", the staff "attentive" and it's "so quiet" in the dining room that you'll "think you're in another world."

Origin India ◐ *Indian* | ▽ 26 | 21 | 21 | $31 |

E of Strip | 4480 Paradise Rd. (Harmon Ave.) | 702-734-6342 | www.originindiarestaurant.com

"Creative twists on traditional dishes" lead those who've discovered this "authentic" east-of-the-Strip newcomer to dub it "one of the best Indian restaurants in town" and a boon for vegetarians; despite its "bland" strip-mall exterior, the dining room is "peaceful" with graceful arches and rows of candles suspended from the ceiling, and the "friendly" service makes it a "favorite."

Osaka Japanese Bistro ◐ *Japanese* | 22 | 15 | 20 | $37 |

Henderson | 10920 S. Eastern Ave. (Sunridge Heights Pkwy.) | 702-616-3788
W Side | 4205 W. Sahara Ave. (Valley View Blvd.) | 702-876-4988
www.lasvegas-sushi.com

"Like Benihana, only better" if simply because it's a Vegas "original", this West Side/Henderson duo boasts "fluffy, cloudlike tempura", "fresh, fresh, fresh sushi" and other "excellent" Japanese specialties; for a "great time", try the "lively" teppanyaki rooms where the "entertaining chefs" are "very good at throwing food in the air"; N.B. it's unaffiliated with Osaka Japanese Cuisine.

DINING

| | FOOD | DECOR | SERVICE | COST |

Osaka Japanese Cuisine *Japanese* ▽ 20 | 19 | 17 | $34

NW | 7511 W. Lake Mead Blvd. (Buffalo Dr.) | 702-869-9494

"One of the best sushi bars in town" enthuse those who also praise the potstickers and Pan-Asian fare at this Japanese in the Northwest, adding that the best deals on raw fish are during the "wonderful" happy hour when rolls are half-price; a cozy, understated Asian interior and prompt, efficient servers all add up to a "nice switch."

Outback Steakhouse *Steak* 18 | 15 | 18 | $30

E Side | 4141 S. Pecos Rd. (Flamingo Rd.) | 702-898-3801
Henderson | 4423 E. Sunset Rd. (Mountain Vista St.) | 702-451-7808
N Las Vegas | 2625 W. Craig Rd. (Fuselier Dr.) | North Las Vegas | 702-647-4152
NW | 1950 N. Rainbow Blvd. (Lake Mead Blvd.) | 702-647-1035
S of Strip | 7380 Las Vegas Blvd. S. (Warm Springs Rd.) | 702-643-3148
Strip | Casino Royale Hotel | 3411 Las Vegas Blvd. S. (Flamingo Rd.) | 702-251-7770 ◐
Strip | 3785 Las Vegas Blvd. (Tropicana Ave.) | 702-220-4185 ◐
W Side | 8671 W. Sahara Ave. (Durango Dr.) | 702-228-1088
www.outback.com

A "fair dinkum" "Aussie contribution to the USA", this "reliable steakhouse" chain serves meals that don't cost "an arm and a leg"; it's "not for business", it's "not for romance", but is "good for families" who "want to eat something familiar and save money for the casinos."

Pahrump Valley Winery *Continental* ▽ 21 | 20 | 24 | $35

Pahrump | 3810 Winery Rd. (east of Hwy. 160) | 775-727-6900 | www.pahrumpwinery.com

"Are we in wine country?" ask oenophiles visiting this "quaint" Pahrump destination that's "worth checking out" for a "fun side trip" (it's about an hour from Las Vegas); vino tastings and vineyard tours whet one's appetite for "wonderful" lunches and dinners of Continental cuisine taken in the French country–style dining room or out on the patio making for a "special experience" abetted by "attentive" servers.

Palm, The *Seafood/Steak* 25 | 19 | 23 | $65

Strip | Forum Shops at Caesars Palace | 3500 Las Vegas Blvd. S. (Flamingo Rd.) | 702-732-7256 | www.thepalm.com

"Testosterone-addled" "Palmophiles" patronize this surf 'n' turfer in the Forum Shops "ready to get stuffed" on steaks "the size of a roast" and lobsters so "big", "no one in their right mind or stomach would try and finish" one; the atmosphere is all "oak and alcohol and NYC-style loudness" (some of the latter in the form of the waiters' "sarcastic banter"), but the "food still rocks" and is a relative "bargain" during lunch.

Pampas Churrascaria *Brazilian/Steak* ▽ 22 | 17 | 20 | $38

Strip | Miracle Mile Shops | 3663 Las Vegas Blvd. S. (Harmon Ave.) | 702-737-4748 | www.pampasusa.com

"Meat is the main attraction" at this cavernous churrascaria in the Miracle Mile Shops at Planet Hollywood where those who "come hungry" are rewarded with "plentiful" quantities of Brazilian rotisserie (skewered sirloin, ribs, pork loin and sausages) that just "keep coming" until you cry uncle; price tags for the all-you-can-eat feasts are "reasonable", with deals for kids and lower tabs at lunch.

Let your voice be heard – visit ZAGAT.com/vote

DINING

| | FOOD | DECOR | SERVICE | COST |

Pamplemousse French | 25 | 21 | 25 | $56

E Side | 400 E. Sahara Ave. (bet. Joe W. Brown Dr. & Paradise Rd.) | 702-733-2066 | www.pamplemousserestaurant.com

This "lovely", "little" midpriced French east of the Strip "hasn't changed one iota" since it opened in 1976 and "thank God for that" proclaim patrons who cherish the "quirky" feel with a "recited menu" presented by "brilliant" waiters who guide you through "fabulous" traditional meals that begin with a basket of crudités; the "cozy converted home" setting may be "showing its age" (some say it resembles "a house of ill repute" from the outside), but it's "quite romantic", especially by the fireplace.

Panevino Ristorante & Gourmet Deli Italian | 21 | 24 | 21 | $47

S of Strip | 246 Via Antonio Ave. (Sunset Rd.) | 702-222-2400 | www.panevinolasvegas.com

Natives pop by this south-of-the-Strip Italian's "wonderful deli" for lunch and return in the evening to the "stunning" environs of the "terrific retro-populuxe" dining room to "have dinner and watch the planes take off at the airport"; "a nice place to go in an area that needs restaurants", it serves "rustic" cuisine, including pizza from a wood-burning oven and salads so "fresh", they "taste like they went out back and picked them."

Pasta Mia West Italian | ∇ 23 | 12 | 21 | $29

W Side | Flamingo & Arville Plaza | 4455 W. Flamingo Rd. (Arville St.) | 702-251-8871 | www.pastamiaw.com

The "aroma of garlic" wafts through this "Vegas favorite" for "huge" portions of "authentic Italian" entrees that "come with salad", a side of "superb pasta" and "terrific, homemade" bread; the West Side space is "comfortable" and filled with "locals" hip to its "reasonable prices."

Pasta Shop & Ristorante Italian | ∇ 24 | 14 | 23 | $30

E Side | Ocotilla Plaza | 2495 E. Tropicana Ave. (Eastern Ave.) | 702-451-1893 | www.pastashop.com

"Wonderful homemade pastas" head up the menu at this East Side Italian helmed by two brothers from New York where "warm" service "makes you feel at home"; some say the "not-so-attractive" strip-mall locale "keeps crowds away", but regulars insist that's a good thing since with fair prices and "only a few tables", the "only drawback is getting in."

NEW Payard Pâtisserie & Bistro French | - | - | - | E

Strip | Caesars Palace | 3570 Las Vegas Blvd. S. (Flamingo Rd.) | 702-731-7110 | www.harrahs.com

Chef François Payard duplicates his NYC namesake with this breakfast- and lunch-only French at Caesars Palace on the Strip turning out delectable pastries and bistro classics; customers can opt for full service in the elegant dining room or take out confections, coffee and sandwiches from a retail counter up front open till 11 PM.

Paymon's
Mediterranean Café ☻ Mediterranean/Mideastern | 23 | 16 | 20 | $22

E Side | Tiffany Square Shopping Plaza | 4147 S. Maryland Pkwy. (Flamingo Rd.) | 702-731-6030
W Side | 8380 W. Sahara Ave. (Durango Dr.) | 702-731-6030
www.paymons.com

"Grown more popular" and expanded to two locations "without sacrificing quality", this Med-Mideast pair in the East Side University

DINING

| | FOOD | DECOR | SERVICE | COST |

District and on the West Side proves itself to "authentic foodies" with a "wide variety" of "well-made, unusual flavors", taken in the cafe or the "adjoining hookah lounge"; though some complain about too "close" tables, at least the "low prices please the family scrooges."

Pearl *Chinese* | 23 | 24 | 22 | $64 |

Strip | MGM Grand Hotel | 3799 Las Vegas Blvd. S. (Tropicana Ave.) | 702-891-7380 | www.mgmgrand.com

"Each dish is a work of art", and the "hip" ambiance "fits the cuisine" at this French-influenced Chinese in the MGM Grand; the "inventive", "gourmet" offerings include a "fantastic tasting menu" and some of the "freshest seafood in LV", proferred by "expert" servers amid "contemporary" decor that manages to be both "trendy" and "relaxing."

Penazzi Ⓜ *Italian* | ▽ 22 | 21 | 26 | $55 |

Strip | Harrah's Las Vegas | 3475 Las Vegas Blvd. S. (Flamingo Rd.) | 702-369-5084 | www.harrahs.com

An "upscale" surprise in "middle-of-the-road" Harrah's, this Italian woos Strip-goers with "personable" service, "classic" dishes and an "extensive" selection of from-The-Boot vintages; the airy bi-level space includes an open kitchen plus a strolling guitarist crooning tunes, which adds up to a "very nice atmosphere", even though it's "right off the casino floor"; P.S. they have a "great raw bar" next door.

P.F. Chang's China Bistro *Chinese* | 21 | 19 | 19 | $31 |

E of Strip | 4165 Paradise Rd. (Flamingo Rd.) | 702-792-2207
Henderson | 101 S. Green Valley Pkwy. (Paseo Verde Pkwy.) | 702-361-3065
NW | 1095 S. Rampart Blvd. (Charleston Blvd.) | 702-968-8885
Strip | Planet Hollywood Resort | 3667 Las Vegas Blvd. S. (Harmon Ave.) | 702-836-0955 ☽
www.pfchangs.com

"In the middle of gambling, shopping and carousing", "you can't go wrong" at one of the town's four Chinese brothers from this extended family of "perennial favorites" where "reasonable prices", an "energetic staff" and "lots of action" at the "well-stocked bars" make them "fun places to meet and eat"; the "big portioned, bold flavored" fare is hardly "authentic", but the "crowds" don't seem to care.

🆉 Picasso *French* | 27 | 29 | 27 | $149 |

Strip | Bellagio Hotel | 3600 Las Vegas Blvd. S. (Flamingo Rd.) | 866-259-7111 | www.bellagio.com

"Perfection on a grand scale" comes via chef Julian Serrano's "lavish" New French palace in the Bellagio (voted tops for Decor as well as Most Popular in Las Vegas) where "high rollers" "live the luxe life" "surrounded by original Picassos" and an "abundance of fresh flowers" while tasting "transcendent" prix fixe meals paired with "fantastic" wines from an "extensive" European list; "polished" servers exhibit "pure finesse", making for a "sublime" experience that's sure to "break you out of your blue period" – at least until you get the check.

Piero's Italian Cuisine *Italian/Seafood* | 24 | 19 | 22 | $62 |

E of Strip | 355 Convention Center Dr. (Paradise Rd.) | 702-369-2305 | www.pieroscuisine.com

A "great old-time Vegas restaurant" where "ya would think Frank was there with his Pack", this east-of-the-Strip Italian "mainstay" serves

DINING

the "best osso buco" in town, "oh-so-tender and succulent", and "crab legs to die for"; service is "consistent" and reliable", although some complain that the "tired interior needs updating."

NEW Pie Town Pizza Pizza | - | - | - | I |
Henderson | 2833 N. Green Valley Pkwy. (Sunset Rd.) | 702-244-2246 | www.pietownpizza.com

This Chicago-centric Italian in a Henderson strip mall delivers authentic deep-dish pizza, beef sandwiches, hot dogs doused with sport peppers and other regional delights in a tiny brick-walled space with photographic murals of Windy City celebrities; counter service is fast and friendly, and though the eight-table setting is modest, so are the tabs.

Ping Pang Pong ● Chinese ▽ 21 | 11 | 14 | $25
W Side | Gold Coast Hotel | 4000 W. Flamingo Rd. (bet. Valley View Blvd. & Wynn Rd.) | 702-367-7111 | www.goldcoastcasino.com

"The won ton soup is won-derful" and all of the "creative Chinese" dishes are "not to be expected in such simple" "cafeteria decor", but here they are, at this "real surprise" on the West Side; open till 2:45 AM, it's "good for a late-night snack", if you can deal with the staff: "either the waiters won't leave you alone, or they won't come back."

Pink Taco Mexican 19 | 18 | 17 | $26
E of Strip | Hard Rock Hotel | 4455 Paradise Rd. (bet. Flamingo Rd. & Harmon Ave.) | 702-693-5525 | www.hardrockhotel.com

Your "perfect hangover cure"?: "tequila and tacos" "served alongside [and by] hard, beautiful bodies" at this "kick-ass Mexican" in the Hard Rock where the "intriguing decor" includes a "nice view of the pool" "if you sit outside"; they might be "more interested in selling alcohol than in culinary efforts" at this "meat market", but the "solid" fare is still "better than the locker room-inspired name."

Pinot Brasserie French 22 | 21 | 21 | $56
Strip | Venetian Hotel | 3355 Las Vegas Blvd. S. (bet. Flamingo & Spring Mountain Rds.) | 702-414-8888 | www.patinagroup.com

"Escape from the ringing slots" to "the Champs-Elysées" inside Joachim Splichal's French bistro at the Venetian where "authenticity" abounds in the "well-executed" fare, the "romantic" room and the staff's "snobby attitude"; still, though this spot is "cute" for a "moderately priced" "afternoon snack", fans find "the California outposts" in the "celeb chef's" Patina group "are decidedly better."

Planet Hollywood American 13 | 20 | 14 | $27
Strip | Forum Shops at Caesars Palace | 3500 Las Vegas Blvd. S. (Flamingo Rd.) | 702-791-7827 | www.planethollywood.com

"The family was shopping, the kids got hungry" and you needed "entertainment for young ones" - all reason enough to stop for American "pub grub" at this "movie memorabilia"-mobbed theme restaurant in the Forum Shops; foes fret about fare "lacking flavor" and "too commercial" decor, marveling "people still inhabit this Planet?"

Postrio American/Mediterranean 24 | 22 | 23 | $57
Strip | Venetian Hotel | 3355 Las Vegas Blvd. S. (bet. Flamingo & Spring Mountain Rds.) | 702-796-1110 | www.wolfgangpuck.com

Spinning off the "top of the Puck line", über-chef Wolfgang goes for a "serious contender" at this New American-Mediterranean in the

DINING

                             FOOD DECOR SERVICE COST

Venetian serving "fabulous" fare ferried by an "excellent" staff; some diners are "disappointed" in dishes that "don't always live up to their ambitions", but even they revel in the 'outside' seating for "serenading gondoliers" and "people-watching in Venice", "authentic-fabricated Vegas"-style; N.B. the Decor score does not reflect a fall 2008 redo.

Potato Valley Café ⓈAmerican   - | - | - | I

Downtown | 801 Las Vegas Blvd. S. (Charleston) | 702-363-7821 | www.potatovalley.net

The plain-old baked potato gets gussied up at this Downtown American where a myriad of versions like Broccoli Blue Cheese and Cuban Chicken elevate the spud to high art; counter service lends a casual vibe, suiting business types and tourists who file in for a quick, inexpensive lunch.

🄿 Prime Steakhouse Steak   26 | 27 | 26 | $92

Strip | Bellagio Hotel | 3600 Las Vegas Blvd. S. (Flamingo Rd.) | 866-259-7111 | www.bellagio.com

"Now *this* is what it's like in the lap of luxury" purr proponents of Jean-Georges Vongerichten's "posh" 1930s-style chophouse in the Bellagio that's "straight out of a movie set" with velvet drapes and Baccarat chandeliers setting the scene for a "high-rolling" "celebrity crowd" sipping "well-poured drinks" and nibbling "perfectly cooked" steaks; from the "superb" service to the "hard-to-beat" views of the fountains outside, it's a "prime" contender for "one of the most elegant dining experiences" in town.

Pullman Grille Ⓜ Steak   ▽ 24 | 24 | 22 | $40

Downtown | Main Street Station Hotel | 200 N. Main St. (Ogden Ave.) | 702-387-1896 | www.mainstreetcasino.com

This "true find" Downtown in the Main Street Station is a "bit out of the way" but "worth getting on board" to enjoy "excellent" steakhouse fare while "soaking up the atmosphere" of a "romantic Victorian" room that's "big on wood" and "antique furnishings"; polish off the evening with "after-dinner drinks" in the "actual rail car that belonged to Louisa May Alcott"; N.B. open Fridays–Sundays only.

Raffles Café ● Diner   16 | 16 | 14 | $27

Strip | Mandalay Bay Resort | 3950 Las Vegas Blvd. S. (Mandalay Bay Rd.) | 702-632-7406 | www.mandalaybay.com

"Far above the jingle" of the Mandalay Bay casino is this "solid" 24/7 coffee shop, a "benchmark" for "better-than-you'd-expect" Traditional American fare fit for "late-night cravings and hangover breakfasts"; "good-sized portions" make it a "terrific spot anytime", unless you stop by when "service is painfully slow."

Range Steakhouse Seafood/Steak   23 | 24 | 23 | $63

Strip | Harrah's Las Vegas | 3475 Las Vegas Blvd. S. (Flamingo Rd.) | 702-369-5000 | www.harrahs.com

With "floor-to-ceiling windows" offering a "commanding view of the Strip", this Harrah's surf 'n' turf is a "quiet place" to watch "the bustle" while attended to by a "super" staff; although some say the "standard steakhouse fare" "seems as dated" as the decor, it remains a "nice" choice "for before or after a show."

Let your voice be heard – visit ZAGAT.com/vote

DINING

| | FOOD | DECOR | SERVICE | COST |

Rao's *Italian* — 23 | 22 | 22 | $64
Strip | Caesars Palace | 3570 Las Vegas Blvd. S. (Flamingo Rd.) | 877-346-4642 | www.caesarspalace.com
"Finally" mere mortals can experience the "legendary" NYC eatery (that's usually "VIP" only) thanks to this Caesars Palace outpost offering similarly "bountiful feasts" of "rustic", "well-prepared" red-sauce fare – and a lemon chicken dish that's justifiably "famous" – in a "wonderful old-time atmosphere"; still, a befuddled few call it "nothing fancy" considering the "steep" prices, and don't get "what all the fuss is about."

Red 8 Asian Bistro *Pan-Asian* — 23 | 22 | 21 | $45
Strip | Wynn Las Vegas | 3131 Las Vegas Blvd. S. (bet. Desert Inn & Spring Mountain Rds.) | 702-770-9966 | www.wynnlasvegas.com
This "authentic" Pan-Asian noodle kitchen in the Wynn is "worth seeking out" for "excellent" dim sum and a "wide selection" of dishes that fuse flavors from the chef's native Malaysia with those of Thailand, Singapore and Canton; a "stylish, modern" setting "lush" with color distracts diners from sometimes "unavailable" service and "pricey" tabs.

Red, White and Blue *American* — 15 | 12 | 16 | $30
Strip | Mandalay Bay Resort | 3950 Las Vegas Blvd. S. (Mandalay Bay Rd.) | 702-632-7405 | www.chinagrillmgt.com
For a "reasonably priced" "change from buffet food", head to Mandalay Bay's "casual" "three-in-one" Traditional American, where the space and menu are sorted by the colors on Old Glory: 'red' for regional cuisine in the bistro, 'white' for desserts from the bakery and 'blue' for burgers and sandwiches in the deli; though the food's "nothing to wave a flag about", a "broad" selection and "friendly service" make it "good for a quick bite."

Redwood Bar & Grill *Seafood/Steak* — 24 | 21 | 24 | $36
Downtown | California Hotel | 12 E. Ogden Ave. (Main St.) | 702-385-1222 | www.thecal.com
A "hidden treasure" Downtown, this surf 'n' turfer parked in an "old-time casino" will "take you back" to Vegas' heyday with "professional service" and a "warm, relaxing" setting that's a "change from the hectic pace" of the Strip; nightly live piano music is a "nice touch" as are "value-for-the-dollar" entrees, including a porterhouse special that's "not on the menu."

NEW Restaurant Charlie *Seafood* — - | - | - | E
Strip | Palazzo Hotel | 3325 Las Vegas Blvd. S. (Sands Ave.) | 702-607-6336 | www.palazzolasvegas.com
Guests enter through a facade of etched-glass panels into a forest of lacewood piers before coming upon the centerpiece, a walk-through wine cellar, at famed Chicago chef Charlie Trotter's new seafood entry at the Palazzo on the Strip; the main dining area offers innovative fish preparations, while the adjacent 'restaurant-within-a-restaurant', Bar Charlie, offers supremely expensive eight- or 14-course kaiseki-style tasting menus; N.B. there's also a chef's table in a glass-and-steel loft suspended above the kitchen.

DINING

	FOOD	DECOR	SERVICE	COST

Rick Moonen's RM Seafood *Seafood* 24 | 21 | 22 | $70

Strip | Mandalay Place | 3930 Las Vegas Blvd. S. (Mandalay Bay Rd.) | 702-632-9300 | www.mandalaybay.com

Tucked away in Mandalay Bay, NYC chef Rick Moonen's "underrated gem" promises "nothing pretentious", just "straightforward", "terrific" dishes made from seafood so fresh, it's "better than if you caught it yourself"; the seafaring theme carries over into decor with a dining room decked out like a luxury yacht and "polite" staffers offering "high-level" service at appropriately lavish prices; N.B. downstairs is more casual and offers a less-expensive menu.

Rincon Criollo Ⓜ *Cuban* – | – | – | I

Downtown | 1145 Las Vegas Blvd. S. (Charleston Blvd.) | 702-388-1906

The "next best thing" to Miami's Calle Ocho, this intimate space Downtown near the Stratosphere is "the best of the local Cubans", serving such country-style fare as *Pierna de Puerco Asada* and *Bistec Criollo*; service is quick and efficient, and while the decor may be purely no-frills, it adds to the simple, country atmosphere.

Roadrunner ● *Southwestern* 16 | 18 | 17 | $22

E Side | 6910 E. Lake Mead Blvd. (Radwick Dr.) | 702-459-1889
NW | 5990 Centennial Center Blvd. (Azure Rd.) | 702-309-6015
NW | 921 N. Buffalo Dr. (Washington Ave.) | 702-242-2822
S of Strip | 2430 E. Pebble Rd. (Myrtle Beach Dr.) | 702-948-8282
SW | 9820 W. Flamingo Rd. (Grand Canyon Dr.) | 702-243-5329
www.roadrunnerlasvegas.com

There's "something for everyone" at these "Western-style" roadhouses serving "standard pub stuff", from "great cornbread" to "nachos large enough to feed a Mexican army"; "great drinking hangouts" for "boys watching sports", these joints remain "busy" with dudes huddling around the patio fire pits at the Flamingo and Pebble Road offshoots.

Romano's Macaroni Grill *Italian* 17 | 16 | 18 | $25

Henderson | 573 N. Stephanie St. (Sunset Rd.) | 702-433-2788
NW | 2001 N. Rainbow Blvd. (Lake Mead Blvd.) | 702-648-6688
W of Strip | 2400 W. Sahara Ave. (Rancho Dr.) | 702-248-9500
www.macaronigrill.com

At these "consistent" links in a national chain, "you know what you're getting": "basic Italian" in a "noisy", "step-above-standard" setting; sure, they're "nothing fancy", but "good-size portions", "reasonable prices" and free crayons for the kids make them "great family places."

🏆 Rosemary's *American* 28 | 20 | 26 | $58

W Side | West Sahara Promenade | 8125 W. Sahara Ave. (bet. Buffalo Dr. & Cimarron Rd.) | 702-869-2251 | www.rosemarysrestaurant.com

"A winner" that "hasn't lost its special touch", this West Sider proves "a tough act to follow" with chef-owners Michael and Wendy Jordan's "simply outstanding" New American cuisine showcasing "delicate flavors" and served à la carte or in an "excellent" $55 prix fixe meal available with "inspired" beer and wine pairings; "stellar" service makes the "pretty" (some say "dowdy") decor all the more "inviting", and though it's "quite a trip" from the Strip, most maintain they'd "go back in a heartbeat"; P.S. the "$28 three-course lunch may be the best deal in town."

Let your voice be heard – visit ZAGAT.com/vote

DINING

| | FOOD | DECOR | SERVICE | COST |

Rosewood Grille &   23 | 19 | 22 | $75
Lobster House ● *Seafood/Steak*
Strip | 3763 Las Vegas Blvd. S. (bet. Harmon & Tropicana Aves.) | 702-792-6719

"Size counts" at this "surf 'n' turf paradise" on the Strip where "monster steaks" and "giant lobsters" (not to mention "insane prices") are part of the shtick, as are "amusing", "pushy" waiters; the "clubby" low-lit interior is "loaded with pictures of the Rat Pack" exuding an "old Vegas charm" for some, while others suggest this stalwart is "past its prime" and in dire need of an "update."

Roxy's Diner *Diner*   16 | 19 | 18 | $18
Strip | Stratosphere Hotel | 2000 Las Vegas Blvd. S. (north of Sahara Ave.) | 702-383-4834 | www.stratospherehotel.com

"Just like the '50s diner it wants to be", this cafe at the Stratosphere on the Strip is a "trip down memory lane" where "the real draw is the entertainment" with singing waiters and waitresses who help make it "a great family place for a special trip"; the food is "just ok" – burgers, shakes, blue-plate specials and sandwiches – and though service may slow down when everyone's performing, "you have to enjoy" it nonetheless.

Roy's *Hawaiian*   24 | 21 | 22 | $54
E of Strip | 620 E. Flamingo Rd. (Swenson St.) | 702-691-2053
NW | 8701 W. Charleston Blvd. (Merialdo Ln.) | 702-838-3620
www.roysrestaurant.com

"Roy Yamaguchi groupies" say "*mahalo* for bringing the islands to the desert" at these east-of-the-Strip and Northwest "tropical delights" where "fresh", "creative combinations" make for "out-of-this-world" Hawaiian dishes (think "*misoyaki* butterfish that's the stuff of food dreams"); "camera-worthy" presentations, "attentive service" and an "aloha" ambiance mean this is "not your normal chain."

NEW RUB BBQ *BBQ*   - | - | - | M
W of Strip | Rio All-Suite Hotel | 3700 W. Flamingo Rd. (bet. I-15 & Valley View Blvd.) | 702-227-0779 | www.rubbbq.net

Rustled up from New York City, this new meat mecca west of the Strip in the Rio specializes in Righteous Urban Barbecue that's pit-smoked Kansas City–style; ok, the decor ain't fancy, but the price is right and fans are too busy licking their fingers to care.

Rubio's Fresh Mexican Grill *Mexican*   18 | 11 | 14 | $11
Henderson | Pebble Mkt. | 1500 N. Green Valley Pkwy. (Pebble Rd.) | 702-270-6097
NW | Red Rock Casino | 11011 W. Charleston Blvd. (Hwy. 215) | 702-254-7470
NW | 7290 W. Lake Mead Blvd. (Tenaya Way) | 702-233-0050
Strip | 3770 Las Vegas Blvd. S. (bet. Harmon & Tropicana Aves.) | 702-262-1988 ●
W Side | 9310 W. Sahara Ave. (Fort Apache Rd.) | 702-804-5860
www.rubios.com

A trip to one of these "semi-fast-food" chain Mexicans is "worth the drive" for "fresh", "filling" fare including what some amigos swear are the "best fish tacos north of Baja"; they're "good for a quick meal", but some say "you get what you pay for": "ok, but not great" dining.

DINING

| | FOOD | DECOR | SERVICE | COST |

Ruth's Chris Steak House *Steak* 24 | 19 | 22 | $67

E of Strip | Citibank Park Plaza | 3900 Paradise Rd. (bet. Flamingo Rd. & Twain Ave.) | 702-791-7011
W Side | Cameron Corner Shopping Ctr. | 4561 W. Flamingo Rd. (bet. Arville St. & Decatur Blvd.) | 702-248-7011 ☽
www.ruthschris.com

"Always winners" for "top-notch, sizzling steaks" broiled in butter, along with "huge portions" of "extra-tasty sides" and "very good seafood", these chophouse links east of the Strip and on the West Side "will make you forgive yourself for eating at a chain"; even so, the skeptical suggest that "service needs to improve" to match the "ouch"-inducing prices; P.S. the Flamingo Road outpost stays open till 3 AM.

Salt Lick Bar-BQ *BBQ* 15 | 15 | 16 | $26

NW | Red Rock Casino | 11011 W. Charleston Blvd. (Hwy. 215) | 702-797-7576 | www.redrocklasvegas.com

"Down-home" Texas BBQ comes to the Northwest via this easy-on-the-wallet Austin-area import at Red Rock Casino where slow-smoked brisket and ribs are washed down with microbrews and bourbons in "noisy", "barnlike" quarters; opinions are split on the food with a smattering of surveyors giving it a "sticky thumbs-up" and cons contending they're left "sorely disappointed" by "lackluster" 'cue that "falls short" of the "hype"; N.B. the Santa Fe Station branch has closed.

Samba Brazilian Steakhouse *Brazilian/Steak* 20 | 17 | 20 | $50

Strip | Mirage Hotel | 3400 Las Vegas Blvd. S. (Spring Mountain Rd.) | 702-791-7337 | www.mirage.com

"It's key to understand that the red side of the button means 'stop!'" at this Brazilian flesh "fiesta" in the Mirage where the waiters "keep coming" with "tasty all-you-can-eat" carnivorous cuts on "big swords"; the rodizio's "meaty menu pairs well with the sweet, strong drinks", "plentiful" sides and an "endless salad bowl", all of which "guarantee you get your money's worth"; though some find it a "disappointment", beef "gluttons" find themselves "too stuffed to move."

Sammy's Woodfired Pizza *Pizza* 21 | 15 | 17 | $20

Henderson | Town Center Shopping Plaza | 4300 E. Sunset Rd. (Green Valley Pkwy.) | 702-450-6664
NW | Montecito Mktpl. | 7160 N. Durango Dr. (Elkhorn Rd.) | 702-365-7777
W Side | 6500 W. Sahara Ave. (Torrey Pines Dr.) | 702-227-6000
www.sammyspizza.com

"Not a rip-off of California Pizza Kitchen but an homage", the Vegas-area branches of the La Jolla original turn out "decent" thin crusts with "traditional toppings as well as innovative ones", plus "can't-be-beat salads" and such; the "huge portions" are an "excellent value", and when you're urged to "leave room for the aptly named Messy Sundae", you can bet that "kids are welcome."

Sam Woo BBQ ⊉ *Chinese* 20 | 8 | 11 | $21

W Side | Chinatown Plaza | 4215 Spring Mountain Rd. (bet. Arville St. & Wynn Rd.) | 702-368-7628

"It isn't fusion, it isn't New Age, it isn't Americanized" – "in case you couldn't tell by the 95% Asian clientele, it is where you go for real

DINING

| | FOOD | DECOR | SERVICE | COST |

Chinese" dished up "fast", "cheap" and "family-style"; its West Side setting is "nothing fancy", and you might want to "BYOT (bring your own translator)" to get service from the "inattentive staff", but if you can deal with the fact that "the ducks still have heads and the chicken still have feet", it's an "adventure."

Sapporo *Japanese/Pacific Rim* 21 | 24 | 20 | $38

W Side | 9719 W. Flamingo Rd. (Grand Canyon Dr.) | 702-216-3080 | www.sappororestaurantgroup.com

It's "quite the scene" at this "cool" West Sider with a sleek, spacious setting that draws trendy tipplers for two happy hours daily (4–7 PM and 10 PM–1 AM) in the "loud" lounge area or on the roomy patio; the "many options for eating" run the gamut from "extremely fresh sushi" to "unique" Pacific Rim dishes and meats and veggies cooked up on teppanyaki tables by a rather "entertaining" staff.

Seablue *Seafood* 24 | 22 | 23 | $67

Strip | MGM Grand Hotel | 3799 Las Vegas Blvd. S. (Tropicana Ave.) | 702-891-3486 | www.michaelmina.net

The "knowledgeable servers are eager to describe the ultrafresh seafood preparations" on Michael Mina's "innovative" (but "not overly elaborate") menu at this "global" oceanic "experience" in the MGM Grand where other list "twists" include a "great build-your-own salad" and "melt-in-your-mouth Kobe rib-eye"; given prices that are "high but not off the charts" and "hip" decor including a "cool fish tank", "you won't feel blue" here.

Second Street Grill *Pacific Rim* ▽ 24 | 18 | 24 | $40

Downtown | Fremont Hotel | 200 E. Fremont St. (Casino Center Blvd.) | 702-385-6277 | www.fremontcasino.com

"Creative cuisine shines" at this "bargain" for "high-end dining in a surprising location" "in the middle of the Fremont casino floor" Downtown; a "best-kept secret" of those in-the-know, it's a "real treat" for "outstanding" Pacific Rim plates proffered in "intimate" digs with "art deco flair"; N.B. closed Tuesdays and Wednesdays.

Sen of Japan *Japanese* ▽ 27 | 21 | 26 | $44

W Side | 8480 W. Desert Inn Rd. (Durango Dr.) | 702-871-7781 | www.senofjapan.com

"Omakase is the way to go" at this "*sen*sational" West Side Japanese restaurant helmed by former Nobu chef Hiro Nakano who "keeps it new" every time with "excellent" "imaginative" sushi selections that "cost half of what you'd pay" on the Strip; a "soothing" atmosphere and "gracious service" appeal to all, though locals especially laud its "convenience."

Sensi *Asian/Italian* 25 | 25 | 24 | $62

Strip | Bellagio Hotel | 3600 Las Vegas Blvd. S. (Flamingo Rd.) | 702-693-8800 | www.bellagio.com

Forget gambling, "*this* is a reason to return to Las Vegas" swear surveyors smitten with this Bellagio boîte where the "stunning" setting with waterfalls and an "amazing" glass-enclosed kitchen is bested only by the "brilliant" Asian-Italian menu that includes "nice twists" on seafood dishes; yes, it's "expensive", but rest assured that "gracious" servers and a "buzzing" scene make it all "worthwhile."

DINING

| | FOOD | DECOR | SERVICE | COST |

Settebello *Pizza*   - | - | - | I
Henderson | The District at Green Valley Ranch | 140 S. Green Valley Pkwy. (Paseo Verde Pkwy.) | 702-222-3556 | www.settebello.net

Boasting the Italian government's official seal of approval for authentically prepared Neapolitan pie, this minimalist pizzeria in southern Henderson uses traditional brick, wood-fired ovens to turn out its specialty; fennel sausage, toasted pine nuts and peppered salami are among the toppings, all served aboard crusts made from imported flour; N.B. they relocated to The District in October 2008.

Shanghai Lilly *Chinese*   22 | 25 | 23 | $52
Strip | Mandalay Bay Resort | 3950 Las Vegas Blvd. S. (Mandalay Bay Rd.) | 702-632-7409 | www.mandalaybay.com

An "absolutely beautiful" room with "flowing draperies" and private booths conjures up a "magical" ambiance at this "elegant" eatery in Mandalay Bay where "sweet waitresses" shuttle "artistic" Cantonese and Sichuan dishes that showcase "first-rate ingredients" and "wonderful spices"; a few "can't wrap [their] head around paying top-dollar for Chinese food", but those who can assure it's "worth it."

Shibuya *Japanese*   25 | 25 | 23 | $78
Strip | MGM Grand Hotel | 3799 Las Vegas Blvd. S. (Tropicana Ave.) | 702-891-3001 | www.mgmgrand.com

"Astonishingly fresh fish" makes for an "outstanding" sushi experience at this "Rolls-Royce" of Japanese restaurants in the MGM Grand set in "dramatic" "techno-industrial" digs boasting an "amazing" 100-label sake cellar; pros proclaim it "perfection", though the less-starry-eyed say it "doesn't live up to the atmosphere" and are content to "leave it to the beautiful people with money to burn."

NEW Simon Restaurant & Lounge *American*   - | - | - | M
W of Strip | Palms Place | 4381 W. Flamingo Rd. (Arville St.) | 702-944-3292 | www.palmsplace.com

Lots of wood, glass and vaguely '70s decor accents characterize this hip, happening American overlooking the pool at Palms Place west of the Strip; the servers are as sexy as the view, and the coolness factor extends to Kerry Simon's midpriced menu of updated comfort classics like pizza, meatloaf and short ribs; N.B. breakfast, lunch and sushi are also offered.

Smith & Wollensky ● *Steak*   23 | 19 | 22 | $69
Strip | 3767 Las Vegas Blvd. S. (Tropicana Ave.) | 702-862-4100 | www.smithandwollensky.com

"*Flintstones*-sized cuts of meat" are served with a side of "NY attitude" from "tough-guy" servers at this beef behemoth on the Strip whose "pub-style dining room" adds to the "old-fashioned chophouse" feel; judging from the "hootin' and hollerin'" from "multiple bachelor parties" it's especially popular for a "boys' night out" in spite of "steep prices" that may "clean you out."

Social House ● *Pan-Asian*   25 | 26 | 23 | $63
Strip | Treasure Island Hotel | 3300 Las Vegas Blvd. S. (Spring Mountain Rd.) | 702-894-7223 | www.socialhouselv.com

"Celebs" and other assorted "under-25" revelers flock to this "loungey" venue that "spices up" Treasure Island with "creative"

Let your voice be heard – visit ZAGAT.com/vote

DINING

Pan-Asian plates perfect for "mixing-and-matching", "tasty" sushi and "incredible drinks" all enjoyed in "breathtaking" environs with a palm-shaded terrace overlooking the Strip; of course "being cool doesn't come cheap", so some suggest you keep an eye on tabs that can add up while others take issue with a staff that's sometimes "less than sociable"; still, it's a "no-brainer" for "late-night" (they serve a bar menu till 2 AM on weekends).

Spago *American*   23 | 19 | 21 | $54

Strip | Forum Shops at Caesars Palace | 3500 Las Vegas Blvd. S. (Flamingo Rd.) | 702-369-0360 | www.wolfgangpuck.com

"After all these years" Wolfgang Puck's venerable "classic" in the Forum Shops "still shines brightly" with its "fabulous", "trendy" pizzas and "creative" New American dishes that appease both "celebs and mere mortals" alike; but while it continues to be a "scene", cynics can't help feeling it's "living off its reputation" with "overrated" fare, "overcrowded" conditions and "mobs of shoppers" "detracting from the experience."

Spice Market Buffet *Eclectic*   22 | 15 | 17 | $28

Strip | Planet Hollywood Resort | 3667 Las Vegas Blvd. S. (Harmon Ave.) | 702-785-5555 | www.planethollywoodresort.com

There's "more variety than a Vegas talent show" at this "feast" in Planet Hollywood, where global dishes include a "wonderful Middle Eastern selection", all for a price so "reasonable" that "you'll be refilling until you explode"; N.B. the Decor score may not reflect a recent redo.

Spiedini *Italian*   21 | 22 | 21 | $39

NW | JW Marriott | 221 N. Rampart Blvd. (Summerlin Pkwy.) | 702-869-8500 | www.spiedini.com

"Well-known local chef" Gustav Mauler does a "nice job" at this Northwest "treat" where the "excellent Italian" fare includes "great spit-roasted dishes" "served quickly" at "non-Strip prices"; "ask to sit on the patio" and enjoy a bottle from the "impressive" wine list.

Stack *Steak*   24 | 23 | 22 | $56

Strip | Mirage Hotel | 3400 Las Vegas Blvd. S. (Spring Mountain Rd.) | 702-792-7800 | www.stacklasvegas.com

The classic steakhouse gets an "extremely stylish" makeover at this Mirage "hangout" catering to the "club crowd" with "loud music" ("my banquette was vibrating"), creative cocktails, "awesome" beef and "whimsical" small plates like "tater tots and jelly doughnuts worth the carb coma"; service is mostly "helpful", though some wonder if "stacked refers to the hostesses" and not the layered mahogany decor.

Stage Deli ● *Deli*   20 | 11 | 15 | $22

Strip | MGM Grand Hotel | 3799 Las Vegas Blvd. S. (Tropicana Ave.) | 702-891-3373 | www.mgmgrand.com

For "corned beef and pastrami heaped to the sky" (and "fabulous pickles") "without having to hail a cab to New York", go for a "gut-busting good" sandwich at this "true" deli in a "cafeterialike" setting in the MGM Grand; the "quick, casual meals" come with an authentically "saucy" "attitude", yet some Gothamites still grumble "there's nothing like the real thing, baby"; N.B. the Forum Shops outpost has closed.

DINING

| | FOOD | DECOR | SERVICE | COST |

Steak House *Steak* — 25 | 19 | 22 | $55

Strip | Circus Circus | 2880 Las Vegas Blvd. S. (bet. Desert Inn Rd. & Sahara Ave.) | 702-794-3767 | www.circuscircus.com

"Beef hanging in the cooler as you walk in sets the tone" at this "underappreciated" steakhouse at Circus Circus on the Strip, a "very surprising throwback to the old days of Vegas" where dry-aged cuts of cow are the draw; "great service" and "dark, elegant, upmarket" decor combine to make it "one of the best-kept secrets" in town.

Steak House, The *Steak* — 23 | 18 | 23 | $62

Strip | Treasure Island Hotel | 3300 Las Vegas Blvd. S. (Spring Mountain Rd.) | 702-894-7351 | www.treasureisland.com

"Better than you'd expect" "without all the hoopla of the brand-name-chef steakeries elsewhere on the Strip", this Treasure Islander serves up "fantastic" filets and other "traditional" fare in "understated" yet "inviting" digs; it's "not necessarily intimate", and it can be "a bit noisy", but the "excellent service" helps make it "worth every penny."

Steakhouse46 ⑤Ⓜ *Steak* — ▽ 26 | 22 | 27 | $77

Strip | Flamingo Las Vegas | 3555 Las Vegas Blvd. S. (Flamingo Rd.) | 702-733-3502 | www.flamingolasvegas.com

Though not exactly a "place to see and be seen", this "traditional" Flamingo chophouse comes through with "great steaks", including a "fantastic" rib-eye delivered in "classic" "supper-club" quarters; service is efficient, though some take issue with prices they find "expensive."

Sterling Brunch Ⓜ *Eclectic* — 26 | 22 | 25 | $71

Strip | Bally's Las Vegas | 3645 Las Vegas Blvd. S. (Flamingo Rd.) | 702-967-7999 | www.ballyslasvegas.com

"Decadence" is the theme of Bally's "ritzy" Sunday brunch (9:30 AM–2:30 PM) featuring an "over-the-top" Eclectic spread with "abundant lobsters" and "caviar aplenty" and where you'll "never lack for champagne", thanks to waiters in "tuxes and white gloves" who keep the Perrier Jouët "flowing"; "reservations" are a must, and while it may be "expensive" ($85 for adults), some wallet-watchers insist it's a relative deal - at least "you won't need dinner"; N.B. reservations recommended.

NEW Stratta *Italian* — - | - | - | E

Strip | Wynn Las Vegas | 3131 Las Vegas Blvd. S. (bet. Desert Inn & Spring Mountain Rds.) | 702-770-3463 | www.wynnlasvegas.com

Alex Stratta already has an eponymous restaurant at the Wynn Las Vegas on the Strip - that would be Alex - but he's added another with this more casual Italian with an open hearth; its less expensive (though still pricey) menu offers pizzas and pastas plus dishes more characteristic of the chef, such as tenderloin of beef with eggplant rollatini.

Strip House *Steak* — - | - | - | E

Strip | Planet Hollywood Resort | 3667 Las Vegas Blvd. S. (Harmon Ave.) | 702-737-5200 | www.planethollywood.com

Crimson decor and prints of Victorian-era hussies set a tone of delicious decadence at this outpost of the New York–based steakhouse in Planet Hollywood on the Strip; the à la carte menu boasts lusty dishes like beefy porterhouses and goose-fat potatoes, while stiff drinks make the steep tabs go down easier.

Let your voice be heard - visit ZAGAT.com/vote

DINING

	FOOD	DECOR	SERVICE	COST

StripSteak *Steak* — 25 | 23 | 24 | $91

Strip | Mandalay Bay Resort | 3950 Las Vegas Blvd. S. (Mandalay Bay Rd.) | 702-632-7414 | www.mandalaybay.com

"Imaginative" chef Michael Mina offers a "unique" chophouse experience at this "pricey" Mandalay Bay "gem" where the all-natural beef is slow-poached in butter before it's grilled, yielding "luscious" steaks complemented by "addictive sides", "world-class wines" and a "one-of-a-kind single-malt scotch list"; service is generally "excellent", though while some dig the "modern" setting with "classic rock" on the speakers, others find it "too noisy", even if they appreciate the "casual" ambiance with potential for "celebrity" sightings.

Sushi Roku *Japanese* — 24 | 22 | 21 | $57

Strip | Forum Shops at Caesars Palace | 3500 Las Vegas Blvd. S. (Flamingo Rd.) | 702-733-7373 | www.innovativedining.com

This LA import delivers "amazing sushi" in the Forum Shops at Caesars, where you can "back away" from the mall mania and "drop your jaw" at one of "the most fabulous views of the Strip"; rolls and slices ranging from the "typical to the innovative" pair well with "potent specialty cocktails" for a "delicious", "relaxing" break from the "busy" stores, even if sometimes "slow" service "leaves something to be desired."

NEW SushiSamba *Eclectic* — - | - | - | M

Strip | Palazzo Hotel | 3325 Las Vegas Blvd. S. (Sands Ave.) | 702-607-0700 | www.palazzolasvegas.com

A Mondrian-inspired glass facade marks the entranceway of this sceney boîte housed within the Palazzo on the Strip; the atmosphere and staff are as energetic as the menu, which features jalapeño- and fruit-spiked sushi rolls, robata selections and a number of entrees fusing Brazilian, Peruvian and Japanese flavors.

SW Steakhouse *Steak* — 26 | 26 | 25 | $90

Strip | Wynn Las Vegas | 3131 Las Vegas Blvd. S. (bet. Desert Inn & Spring Mountain Rds.) | 888-352-3463 | www.wynnlasvegas.com

"SW stands for 'swanky'" at this Wynn steakhouse "splurge" offering up "fabulous" food and bottles from a "dazzling wine list"; it may not be "as hip as other spots in town", but "incredible views" of the nightly fountain shows plus "expert" service keep it "crowded", just beware of occasional "waits, even with reservations."

NEW Table 10 *American* — - | - | - | E

Strip | Palazzo Hotel | 3327 Las Vegas Blvd. S. (Sands Ave.) | 702-607-6363 | www.emerils.com

The wrought-iron gates at Emeril's New American at the Palazzo on the Strip immediately transport diners from Venice-in-Vegas to New Orleans; crowd-pleasers from other Lagasse outposts – like pasta jambalaya and a hamachi-and-butter lettuce wrap – make an appearance on the expensive menu, as do regional classics like lobster pot pie.

Z Tableau *American* — 27 | 25 | 27 | $82

Strip | Wynn Las Vegas | 3131 Las Vegas Blvd. S. (bet. Desert Inn & Spring Mountain Rds.) | 888-352-3463 | www.wynnlasvegas.com

"Exceptional breakfasts", "civilized lunches" and "delectable" dinners await at this French-influenced New American whose "exclusive"

DINING

| | FOOD | DECOR | SERVICE | COST |

south tower location in the Wynn makes it feel like an "elegant" "private dining room", with poolside views and "flawless service" adding to the "appeal"; diehards decree that it "deserves more attention", though insiders insist the fact that it's "not so well known" is exactly what makes it "special."

Table 34 ⑤ *American* | - | - | - | M |

S of Strip | 600 E. Warm Springs Rd. (bet. Bermuda & Paradise Rds.) | 702-263-0034

The streamlined decor complements the New American fare at this south-of-the-Strip eatery (in the space of the former Wild Sage Café and under the same ownership), where wood floors and earth tones create a casual atmosphere; menu holdovers such as macaroni-and-cheese gratinée are joined by newer options like grilled rack of pork with chipotle mashed potatoes.

Tamba Indian Cuisine *Indian* | ▽ 21 | 19 | 18 | $30 |

Strip | Hawaiian Mktpl. | 3743 Las Vegas Blvd. S. (Harmon Ave.) | 702-798-7889 | www.tambalounge.com

Though oddly located in the Strip's Hawaiian Marketplace, masala mavens hail this "surprisingly complex" Indian for its "well-seasoned" dishes with "assertive, yet subtle flavors"; while the fare is "spicy", budget-minded types take comfort that the bill is relatively "mild"; P.S. there's also a "bargain buffet lunch."

NEW T&T (Tacos & Tequila) *Mexican* | - | - | - | M |

Strip | Luxor Hotel | 3900 Las Vegas Blvd. S. (Mandalay Bay Rd.) | 702-262-5225 | www.luxor.com

The Luxor continues its high-style makeover with this trendy new cantina catering to a young crowd that digs its flashy Adam Tihany-designed interior and soundtrack of rock 'n' roll; its midpriced menu from chef Richard Sandoval features twin flights of ceviche and tequila as well as comfort-zone classics like enchiladas and burritos backed by top-shelf margaritas.

Tao ● *Pan-Asian* | 23 | 27 | 21 | $63 |

Strip | Venetian Hotel | 3355 Las Vegas Blvd. S. (bet. Flamingo & Spring Mountain Rds.) | 702-388-8588 | www.taolasvegas.com

Even "ordinary Joes" will "feel like a rock star" at this "stylish beyond belief" Venetian megacomplex that merges restaurant, nightclub and lounge into one "cavernous", "action-packed" space "mobbed" with "beautiful people" yet presided over by a "peaceful" 20-ft.-tall Buddha hovering above a koi pond; "so-so" service and "tasty" Pan-Asian cuisine play second fiddle to the "earsplitting" scene, though partygoers praise the "drinks and apps", especially the Kobe shabu-shabu and "awesome Chilean sea bass."

Taqueria Cañonita *Mexican* | 20 | 18 | 18 | $33 |

Strip | Venetian Hotel | 3355 Las Vegas Blvd. S. (bet. Flamingo & Spring Mountain Rds.) | 702-414-3773 | www.canonita.net

"Mexican food on the canals of Venice?" - the "mismatched cultural cues" might leave you "not sure whether to order a margarita or Chianti" at this Venetian cantina, but it works well for a "quick", "informal" lunch; "unwind" while "singing gondoliers" float by, and enjoy this "strange" but "welcome respite from the high-priced restaurants of the Strip."

DINING

| | FOOD | DECOR | SERVICE | COST |

☑ T-Bones Chophouse Steak — 25 | 27 | 23 | $74
NW | Red Rock Casino | 11011 W. Charleston Blvd. (Hwy. 215) | 702-797-7576 | www.stationcasinos.com

"Live piano" enhances already "excellent" food at this "solid" steakhouse in the Red Rock Casino set in "beautiful" quarters with red-velvet booths and glittery chandeliers; a smattering of reviewers reports it's "a bit inconsistent" (especially the "hit-or-miss service") but the majority says it would "take it any day over similar places on the Strip" even if prices can feel "expensive for what you get."

Terra Verde Italian — - | - | - | M
Henderson | Green Valley Ranch | 2300 Paseo Verde Pkwy. (Green Valley Pkwy.) | 702-617-7075 | www.greenvalleyranchresort.com

This sunny Italian in Henderson's Green Valley Ranch presents a broad midpriced menu of rustic dishes like wood-fired pizzas, homemade pastas and herb-crusted veal chops that pair well with vintages from the 1,500-bottle strong collection; the elegant, Tuscan-styled space features white tablecloths and a pleasant patio area.

T.G.I. Friday's ● American — 15 | 15 | 16 | $21
E Side | 1800 E. Flamingo Rd. (Spencer St.) | 702-732-9905
Henderson | 4330 E. Sunset Rd. (Green Valley Pkwy.) | 702-990-8443
W of Strip | Orleans Hotel | 4500 W. Tropicana Ave. (Arville St.) | 702-873-1801
W Side | 4570 W. Sahara Ave. (bet. Arville St. & Decatur Blvd.) | 702-889-1866
www.tgifridays.com

Hooch hounds have it that the "Jack Daniel's flavoring is very good on the steaks and ribs", and it ain't bad in the glass either at this "after-work" "meat market" quartet that's part of the chain of "assembly-line" American eateries; "if you're not adventurous or maybe lazy" or "drunk", "this will work", although the majority claims "you can do better."

Thai Spice ⑧ Thai — ∇ 21 | 13 | 17 | $26
W Side | Flamingo & Arville Plaza | 4433 W. Flamingo Rd. (Arville St.) | 702-362-5308

"Locals" laud this West Side "diamond in the rough" for its "tasty" Thai fare served up in varying degrees of "spiciness" in a bare-bones, but "relaxing" strip-mall setting; service is "sometimes slow", but prices are a "bargain" making it a "dependable" bet for "everyday dining."

Tillerman, The Seafood/Steak — 23 | 22 | 21 | $58
E Side | 2245 E. Flamingo Rd. (west of Eastern Ave.) | 702-731-4036 | www.tillerman.com

"Lots of locals" will tell you that a "nice place to go off the Strip" is this "old-time" "standby", a "solid performer" for "great fish" and meat "grilled over hardwood"; the "professional waiters" make this East Side steak-and-seafood house "very comfortable", and the "trees growing through the middle" of the interior add to the "tranquil" ambiance.

Tinoco's Bistro ⑧ Continental — ∇ 23 | 20 | 21 | $38
Downtown | 103 E. Charleston Blvd. (Casino Center Blvd.) | 702-464-5008 | www.tinocos.net

An "understated" "find" tucked away in Downtown's Arts District, this "cozy" Continental is "worth the trip" for noteworthy crab cakes and

---

80 40,000 places to eat, drink, stay & play – free at ZAGAT.com

DINING

| | FOOD | DECOR | SERVICE | COST |

"excellent" pastas and entrees all at "reasonable" prices; wood floors, palette-shaped tables and paintings on the wall give it a funky vibe that "fits in with the neighborhood."

Tintoretto Bakery & Café ● *Bakery/Italian* — 20 | 17 | 18 | $22

Strip | Venetian Hotel | 3355 Las Vegas Blvd. S. (bet. Flamingo & Spring Mountain Rds.) | 702-414-3400 | www.venetian.com

For a "first choice for breakfast" in the "real" Italian style, check out this "charming" bakery in the Venetian where the "best espresso and cappuccino" is paired with "amazing pastries and decent breads"; at lunchtime, enjoy lasagna or a "creative sandwich" while "watching the gondoliers march by on their way to the canal", and 'round midnight, "pick up a sweet on the way to your room."

Todai *Japanese* — 18 | 11 | 15 | $31

Strip | Miracle Mile Shops | 3663 Las Vegas Blvd. S. (Harmon Ave.) | 702-892-0021

"All-you-can-eat buffets are common in this town, but there aren't many Asian ones", so if you're hankering to pig out "without spending a fortune", this "cafeteria-style" chain offering "sushi galore" is your "economy" ticket at the Miracle Mile Shops; "it's great for kids" – "and people with no taste buds" crab critics of the "average" fare.

☒ Todd's Unique Dining ☒ *Eclectic* — 28 | 16 | 25 | $47

Henderson | 4350 E. Sunset Rd. (Green Valley Pkwy.) | 702-259-8633 | www.toddsunique.com

One of Henderson's "best-kept secrets", chef-owner Todd Clore's "valley favorite" "shines" with "serious", "sophisticated" seasonal Eclectic dishes plus a wine list with "phenomenal values" (and no pouring charge on Wednesdays should you decide to bring your own); factor in "accommodating service" and enthusiasts appraise it's "as good as any on the Strip", but at "half the price"; even if the decor "could use sprucing up", everything else "just keeps getting better."

Togoshi Ramen *Japanese* — - | - | - | I

E Side | Twain Ctr. | 855 E. Twain Ave. (Swenson St.) | 702-737-7003

"Busloads of Japanese conventioneers can't be wrong" say slurpers stopping in to this inexpensive Japanese noodle house in the Twain Center east of the Strip, where "authentic" ramen is the star of a menu that also includes gyoza with plenty of beer, wine and sake to wash it down; service is swift, while the strip-mall setting is as no-frills as it gets.

NEW Tommy Bahama's Tropical Café *Caribbean/Pacific Rim* — - | - | - | M

S of Strip | Town Square | 6605 Las Vegas Blvd. S. (bet. I-215 & Sunset Rd.) | 702-948-8006 | www.tommybahama.com

You just might feel like you're in the islands, mon, at this tropical-themed chain outpost at Town Square; while the paddle fans spin lazily overhead, diners sip rum drinks and munch on moderately priced Caribbean-Pacific Rim fare like coconut shrimp and scallop sliders; N.B. there's also an attached retail store.

Tony Roma's *BBQ* — 16 | 13 | 17 | $29

Central | 620 E. Sahara Ave. (Kendale St.) | 702-733-9914

(continued)

DINING

(continued)

Tony Roma's

Downtown | Fremont Hotel | 200 E. Fremont St. (Casino Center Blvd.) | 702-385-3232
Henderson | 555 N. Stephanie St. (Sunset Rd.) | 702-436-2227
NW | 2040 N. Rainbow Blvd. (Lake Mead Blvd.) | 702-638-2100
www.tonyromas.com

The mood is "down to earth", but the "ribs are out of this world" at these links of the national barbecue chain offering "good" babybacks, "decent sides" and a "great-tasting", "greasy mess of an onion loaf"; the approval isn't universal, however: "indifferent service" and "high-school canteen" decor have critics shrugging "there are better BBQ places in the city."

Top of the World *American*   20 | 26 | 21 | $66

Strip | Stratosphere Hotel | 2000 Las Vegas Blvd. S., 106th fl. (north of Sahara Ave.) | 702-380-7711 | www.stratospherehotel.com

"The panoramic views take your breath away" at this "romantic" rotating restaurant 800 feet up in the Stratosphere where the "ordinary" New American fare, while "decent", is not as "spectacular" as the "jaw-dropping" vistas when the "nighttime glitz" lights up the Strip; considering prices that make some as "dizzy" as the setting, some reviewers recommend "drinks at the bar" as a "cheaper" alternative.

Trader Vic's ☻ *Polynesian*   - | - | - | M

Strip | Miracle Mile Shops | 3663 Las Vegas Blvd. S. (Harmon Ave.) | 702-405-4700 | www.tradervicslv.com

Set in Planet Hollywood's Miracle Mile Shops on the Strip, this branch of the Polynesian-themed worldwide chain (dating back to 1936) boasts all the tiki-style decor one would expect, in a bi-level space with an indoor dining room, outdoor patio and bar and second-floor lounge; fans can find those famous bracing mai tais (said to have originated in the San Francisco location in 1944) along with updated dishes like miso orange sea bass.

Trattoria del Lupo *Italian*   21 | 18 | 21 | $49

Strip | Mandalay Bay Resort | 3950 Las Vegas Blvd. S. (Mandalay Bay Rd.) | 702-632-7410 | www.wolfgangpuck.com

"Pizza, red wine and watching the talent hit the Mandalay Bay clubs" are three reasons to pop into this "solid" Wolfgang Puckster where "a touch of American style and flavor" stoke the wood-burning flame, adding "tantalizing tastes" to an otherwise "ordinary Italian" menu; the "noisy" setting may "feel like you're eating in a mall", but at least this is "one of the most reasonably priced eateries" in the hotel.

Trevi *Italian*   20 | 20 | 20 | $34

Strip | Forum Shops at Caesars Palace | 3500 Las Vegas Blvd. S. (Flamingo Rd.) | 702-735-4663 | www.trevi-italian.com

"Watch the indoor sky change colors from day to night" from your mezzanine seat "in the middle of the mall at Caesars Palace" at this "fast, friendly" Strip Italian serving a "generous", if "run-of-the-mill" meal; it's "noisy if you're close to the fountain", but it's a "great place to people-watch" – "for a quieter dinner, try inside" where the decor was dramatically designed by the David Rockwell Group.

DINING

| | FOOD | DECOR | SERVICE | COST |

Triple George Grill 🆉 *Seafood* — 22 | 23 | 22 | $34
Downtown | 201 N. Third St. (Ogden Ave.) | 702-384-2761 | www.triplegeorgegrill.com
Downtown "power-lunchers" praise this "gentlemanly" San Francisco-style seafooder serving up chowder, chops and classic cocktails in a "fabulous clubby atmosphere" "that feels like it's been here a comfortably long time"; fair prices increase the appeal – no wonder it's so "popular."

Triple 7 Restaurant & Brewery ☺ *American* — 21 | 20 | 19 | $19
Downtown | Main Street Station Hotel | 200 N. Main St. (Ogden Ave.) | 702-387-1896 | www.mainstreetcasino.com
Those who "want to watch a game" while they eat say that Main Street Station's "great microbrewery" is "probably your best bet for Downtown"; sure, the American menu (plus sushi) is your "typical pub stuff" and the vibe is standard "sports bar", but some "hot, hot wings" and a "nice sampler" of "handcrafted suds" are just the ticket if you're "looking to fill your inner grease receptical" and "stagger home" afterwards.

Valentino *Italian* — 23 | 21 | 23 | $73
Strip | Venetian Hotel | 3355 Las Vegas Blvd. S. (bet. Flamingo & Spring Mountain Rds.) | 702-414-3000 | www.welovewine.com
This is "food to live for" laud loyalists of Piero Selvaggio's "sleek" Italian in the Venetian where chef Luciano Pellegrini's "fantastic" "twists on the expected" and a "mind-boggling" wine list the "size of a phone book" add up to a much-appreciated sibling of the Santa Monica flagship; still, those put off by the "pretentious" service and "noisy grill" insist there are "better places in town for this kind of cash."

Ventano ☺ *Italian* — 20 | 21 | 19 | $36
Henderson | 191 S. Arroyo Grande (Horizon Ridge Pkwy.) | 702-944-4848 | www.ventanoitalian.com
You'll be "sitting on top of the hill" at chef-owner Arnauld Briand's Henderson Northern Italian with such "spectacular views" of the valley through its "wall of windows" that the "food seems even better than it is"; but a few feel that's the problem: it "never lives up to its reputation" (or its location), and "sometimes the service takes away from what could otherwise be a great experience."

Verandah, The *American/Italian* — 23 | 24 | 25 | $52
Strip | Four Seasons Hotel | 3960 Las Vegas Blvd. S. (Four Seasons Dr.) | 702-632-5121 | www.fourseasons.com
An "enchanting" "hideaway" nestled inside the Four Seasons, this "civilized" New American-Italian feels like an "instant vacation" sigh surveyors "lingering" over "wonderful" meals (including a "fabulous brunch") set down in the "elegant" dining room or on the poolside patio that's "an absolute dream"; a "solicitous" staff keeps it all "quite pleasant", in spite of prices that fall on the "high" side.

Vic & Anthony's Steakhouse *Steak* — 25 | 23 | 23 | $73
Downtown | Golden Nugget Hotel | 129 E. Fremont St. (Main St.) | 702-386-8399 | www.goldennugget.com
A "great addition to the Golden Nugget", this "surprisingly good" steakhouse Downtown is known for its "high-level" beef, lobsters and blue-

Let your voice be heard – visit ZAGAT.com/vote

DINING

point oysters; "it ain't cheap", but "outstanding service", late hours and softly draped, subdued decor help it "rank with the best in the city."

Vintner Grill American   - | - | - | M
NW | 10100 W. Charleston Blvd. (bet. Hualapai Way & Town Center Dr.) | 702-214-5590 | www.vglasvegas.com

Although an office park may seem an unlikely location for an innovative New American, this Northwest spot hits its marks with a seasonal, daily changing menu of Mediterranean-influenced dishes (think lamb osso buco with laurel leaf orzo) followed by truffles from Vosges Haut-Chocolat; the modern space includes a wood-floored dining room and a dramatic outdoor patio with two large canopies and custom-made couches and drapery.

Viva Mercado's Mexican   ▽ 22 | 13 | 19 | $22
W Side | 3553 S. Rainbow Blvd. (Spring Mountain Rd.) | 702-871-8826 | www.vivamercadoslv.com

It's "absolutely worth the trip off the Strip" for "authentic Mexican" food (fried in canola oil, not lard) at this "usually crowded", family-owned eatery where the "pride in the product shows"; "they know how to make salsa spicy", and there are lots of varieties here, along with 52 types of tequila, "wonderful service" and a casual setting.

NEW V Thai Cuisine, The Thai   - | - | - | I
W Side | Sahara Pavillion Shopping Ctr. | 4750 W. Sahara Ave. (Decatur Blvd.) | 702-870-8432 | www.thevthaicuisine.com/

Tucked inside a West Side shopping center, this Thai newcomer proffers well-spiced curries and zippy salads in sleek, serene surroundings; although service and decor are a step up from others in the genre, thankfully prices remain appealingly down-to-earth.

NEW White Chocolate Grill American   - | - | - | M
Henderson | 9510 S. Eastern Ave. (bet. Hardin Dr. & Richman Ave.) | 702-436-7100 | www.whitechocolategrill.com

Though it appears in many of the desserts, the namesake sweet isn't the only thing featured on the menu at this New American in western Henderson – an offshoot of the Phoenix original, whose specialties include tomato-gin soup, prime rib and burgers made with house-ground beef; the softly lit dining room is reminiscent of Frank Lloyd Wright with its streamlined wood, stone and leather design.

'wichcraft Sandwiches   20 | 12 | 16 | $16
Strip | MGM Grand Hotel | 3799 Las Vegas Blvd. S. (Tropicana Ave.) | 702-891-3166 | www.mgmgrand.com

If you're hankering for an "out-of-the-ordinary" sandwich "on the fly", this "fast and fabulous" offshoot of Tom Colicchio's NYC original in the MGM Grand earns an "A+" from "budget gourmets" for its "innovative" options and "modern" look; to the few who say "no big deal", others retort it's "no big price, either."

Wing Lei Chinese   25 | 25 | 24 | $76
Strip | Wynn Las Vegas | 3131 Las Vegas Blvd. S. (bet. Desert Inn & Spring Mountain Rds.) | 702-770-9966 | www.wynnlasvegas.com

Chinese cuisine is taken to "another level" at this "gourmet" Sino "splurge" in the Wynn where "authentic" Cantonese specialties and a five-course Peking duck meal stand out among other "well-crafted"

DINING

| | FOOD | DECOR | SERVICE | COST |

dishes; "white-glove" service is tapped as "tops", while some liken the experience – with its "lavish" decor with velvet and gold details and an onyx bar – to dining "inside of a Ming vase."

Wolfgang Puck Bar & Grill *American* | 21 | 17 | 19 | $41 |
Strip | MGM Grand Hotel | 3799 Las Vegas Blvd. S. (Tropicana Ave.) | 702-891-3000 | www.wolfgangpuck.com
Since when can you eat at a bar and grill and claim "every bite is an experience"? – since Wolfgang Puck "reinvented" his "backyard-y" MGM Grand New American with "delicious" twists on "comfort food as the guiding principle"; it's "in the center of the casino", so you might "have to struggle to hear your companion when granny hits the slots."

NEW Woo *Pan-Asian* | – | – | – | E |
Strip | Palazzo Hotel | 3325 Las Vegas Blvd. S. (Sands Ave.) | 702-699-8966 | www.woorestaurant.com
The family behind the late longtime favorite Mayflower Cuisinier has moved its talents to the Strip for this eponymous Pan-Asian showcase at the Palazzo; its muted colors are reminiscent of its predecessor's, creating a tranquil setting for expensive fare like Mongolian grilled lamb chops with a macadamia crust and wok-seared salmon.

NEW Yellowtail Sushi Restaurant & Bar *Japanese* | – | – | – | E |
Strip | Bellagio Hotel | 3600 Las Vegas Blvd. S. (Flamingo Rd.) | 702-730-3900 | www.bellagio.com
A mammoth bronze fish stationed above the entryway hints at the seafood-centric focus of this tony new Japanese at the Bellagio on the Strip turning out sushi and hand rolls as well as shared plates of lobster carpaccio and big-eye tuna pizza; sweeping views of the fountains drive the aquatic theme home.

Yolie's Brazilian Steakhouse *Brazilian/Steak* | 21 | 15 | 20 | $43 |
E of Strip | Citibank Park Plaza | 3900 Paradise Rd. (bet. Flamingo Rd. & Twain Ave.) | 702-794-0700
"Not for the faint of heart" or "stomach", this Brazilian "house o' meat" east of the Strip is a "great concept", if you're angling to "eat until you explode"; the "kind servers" "keep coming and coming" with "various flame-broiled meats" and "great caipirinhas", so "bring your appetite" and "your conventioneer's badge, and you'll fit right in" at this "tourist" "fleshfest"; N.B. the Decor score may not reflect a recent remodel.

NEW Yolos *Mexican* | – | – | – | E |
Strip | Planet Hollywood Resort | 3667 Las Vegas Blvd. S. (Harmon Ave.) | 702-785-0122 | www.planethollywoodresort.com
A hot-pink beam of light shooting from the entrance through the bar to the dining room sets a high-energy mood at this Jeffrey Beers–designed Mexican hot spot in the Strip's Planet Hollywood hotel; while the menu (and pricing) can be equally invigorating, there are still enough familiar dishes to appease traditionalists.

Zeffirino ☻ *Italian* | 21 | 21 | 21 | $58 |
Strip | Venetian Hotel | 3355 Las Vegas Blvd. S. (bet. Flamingo & Spring Mountain Rds.) | 702-414-3500 | www.zeffirinolasvegas.com
With a "fabulous view" from the patio "overlooking the Grand Canal and gondoliers", "you may as well be in Italy" at this "romantic

DINING

FOOD | DECOR | SERVICE | COST

Northern Italian" in the Venetian offering "excellent" dishes that reflect the chef's Genoese heritage; though "wandering musicians" add ambiance as you "watch the boats go by", less "inconsistent" service and "larger portions would be nice for the price."

NEW Zine Noodles | - | - | - | M |
Dim Sum ● *Chinese/Vietnamese*
Strip | Palazzo Hotel | 3325 Las Vegas Blvd. S. (Sands Ave.) | 702-607-2220 | www.palazzolasvegas.com

A wall of pebbled glass leads up to this new midpriced Asian set right off the casino at the Palazzo on the Strip; the contemporary space complements the modern menu showcasing a mix of Vietnamese dishes like filet mignon pho alongside Cantonese favorites like congee, roast meats and dim sum.

NIGHTLIFE

Most Popular

1. Tao
2. PURE
3. rumjungle
4. Tryst
5. House of Blues
6. miX Lounge
7. Red Square*
8. Studio 54
9. ghostbar
10. Coyote Ugly
11. ESPN Zone
12. JET
13. Bar at Times Square
14. Playboy Club
15. Body English
16. Beatles Revolution
17. Caramel
18. Rain
19. Nine Fine
20. Cleopatra's

KEY NEWCOMERS

Our editors' take on the year's top arrivals. See page 189 for a full list.

Bank, The
CatHouse
Christian Audigier
Gold Diggers
McFadden's

Penthouse
Privé
Rok
Sugarcane
Wasted Space

---

* Indicates a tie with place above

Top Appeal Ratings

Excludes places with low votes.

27	miX Lounge		Rehab
	Tryst		Red Square
26	Playboy Club		Peppermill Fireside
	Tao		ghostbar
25	PURE		VooDoo Lounge

Top Decor Ratings

27	Tryst		Beatles Revolution
	Playboy Club	24	Red Square
	Tao		ghostbar
26	miX Lounge		Peppermill Fireside
25	PURE		Caramel

Top Service Ratings

24	La Scena		Double Down
22	Playboy Club		Moon
	Petrossian	21	Red Square
	Tryst		V Bar
	Peppermill Fireside		Sapphire

BY CATEGORY

In order of Appeal ranking.

DANCING

27	Tryst
26	Tao
25	PURE
24	Body English
23	JET

DRINK SPECIALISTS

27	miX Lounge
	Tryst
26	Playboy Club
25	ghostbar
	VooDoo Lounge

HOTEL BARS

25	Red Square (Mandalay Bay)
	ghostbar (Palms)
	VooDoo Lounge (Rio)
23	Caramel (Bellagio)
	Tabú (MGM)

LOUNGES

27	miX Lounge
	Tryst
26	Playboy Club
25	Peppermill Fireside
	ghostbar

OPEN 24 HOURS

25	Peppermill Fireside
24	Double Down
	Petrossian
	Spearmint Rhino
23	Olympic Garden

STRIP CLUBS

24	Spearmint Rhino
23	Olympic Garden
	Sapphire
22	Cheetah's
21	Club Paradise

Let your voice be heard - visit ZAGAT.com/vote

APPEAL | DECOR | SERVICE | COST

Nightlife

Ratings & Symbols

Appeal, Decor and **Service** are rated on the Zagat 0 to 30 scale.

Cost reflects surveyors' estimated price of a typical single drink. For places listed without ratings, the price range is as follows:

| below $5
M| $5 to $10
E| $11 to $14
VE| $15 or more

Artisan Lounge   - | - | - | M
W of Strip | Artisan Hotel | 1501 W. Sahara Ave. (I-15) | 702-214-4000 | www.theartisanhotel.com

Set in the boutique Artisan Hotel – a casino-free oasis west of the Strip – this "beautiful" lounge decked out with black leather couches and rich polished woods provides the perfect "after-work" environment with two-for-one drinks (5–7 PM) poured by "friendly bartenders" and stellar "people-watching" to boot; things take a "trendy" turn on weekends, when DJs take control of the sound system and spin lounge, samba and house.

Bahama Breeze   19 | 20 | 18 | $11
E Side | 375 Hughes Center Dr. (bet. Flamingo & Paradise Rds.) | 702-731-3252 | www.bahamabreeze.com

There's "nothing better than sitting out on the deck and working your way through the menu" of "fruity" frozen specialty cocktails at this "laid-back" Caribbean-themed East Side chain outpost featuring "reasonable" prices and solid, if somewhat "generic" eats; live reggae music adds to the island atmosphere, although "after the novelty wears off", a few detractors find the "cheesy" decor a tropical turnoff.

NEW Bank Nightclub, The   - | - | - | VE
(fka Light)

Strip | Bellagio Hotel | 3600 Las Vegas Blvd. S. (Flamingo Rd.) | 702-693-8300 | www.bellagio.com

Get ready to deposit plenty of change at this A-list nightspot, which replaced celebrity magnet Light at the Bellagio; as golden-hued as Fort Knox itself, the shimmering, multilevel space sports a dance floor enveloped in frosted glass, two bars and an eye-popping entryway lined with dozens of bottles of Cristal; not surprisingly, a night here should be preceded by a visit to a real bank.

Bar at Times Square   22 | 18 | 18 | $11
Strip | New York-New York Hotel | 3790 Las Vegas Blvd. S. (Tropicana Ave.) | 702-740-6969 | www.nynyhotelcasino.com

Great White Way wannabes, "sing your hearts out" at New York-New York's "party" crossroads, where "dueling pianos rock" a "corny" songfest and the ambiance is as "noisy, crowded and fun" as the Big Apple itself; the "standing-room-only" attendees advise "get there early", order drink refills "two at a time" and "leave late (and a little hoarse)."

NIGHTLIFE

| | APPEAL | DECOR | SERVICE | COST |

Bare
- | - | - | E

Strip | Mirage Hotel | 3400 Las Vegas Blvd. S. (Spring Mountain Rd.) | 702-791-7111 | www.barepool.com

The bodies are hard but the reserved daybeds are anything but at this posh poolside lounge at the Mirage, an exclusive swimming hole bordered by palm trees where sun-worshipers can catch rays Euro-style (sans tops, if you choose) or take a semi-skinny dip; laid-back DJ jams, mojitos and specialty bites all figure among the bare essentials.

Beatles REVOLUTION Lounge
24 | 25 | 21 | $13

Strip | Mirage Hotel | 3400 Las Vegas Blvd. S. (Spring Mountain Rd.) | 702-692-8383 | www.thebeatlesrevolutionlounge.com

"Part *Austin Powers*, part *Yellow Submarine*", this "ultragroovy" "Beatles fan's dream" in the Mirage "perfectly complements" the Cirque de Soleil's 'Love' extravaganza with its "positively fab soundtrack" and "colorful" "'60s psychedelic" setup complete with "touch-screen" tables for "cool" "visual effects"; for a hard day's night of "kitschy fun", it's a "spendy" "treat" ("all you need is love and some cash").

Beauty Bar
22 | 22 | 19 | $9

Downtown | 517 Fremont St. (bet. Las Vegas Blvd. & 6th St.) | 702-598-1965 | www.beautybar.com

"Hip" types convene to curl a few at this bi-coastally bred Downtown theme bar, a replica of a beehive-era beauty salon featuring chair-mounted hairdryers and nail polishing on Fridays; with DJs spinning "indie dance rock" spritzed with alt-ish live acts on the patio, it's a "cute concept" that's extra "refreshing" "if you're under 25."

Bill's Gamblin' Hall
∇ 13 | 9 | 13 | $10

Strip | Bill's Gamblin' Hall | 3595 Las Vegas Blvd. S. (Flamingo Rd.) | 702-737-2100 | www.billslasvegas.com

There's "no better place to see a 400 lb. Elvis" than this "old Vegas" lounge in Bill's Gamblin' Hall on the Strip, where "gargantuan" impersonator Pete Vallee unleashes his "immense" voice at free weekday shows; but beyond the King's court, suspicious minds say the cheap hooch and run-down decor signal "a dive."

Blush
- | - | - | E

Strip | Wynn Las Vegas | 3131 Las Vegas Blvd. S. (bet. Desert Inn & Spring Mountain Rds.) | 702-770-3633 | www.wynnlasvegas.com

Clubgoers blush to their boots at this snug ultralounge in the Wynn, which graces the former Lure space with 270 silk lanterns overhead, plush couches for bottle buyers and bathrooms with shimmery walls like a king-sized disco ball; the mirrored patio is a literal breath of fresh air, and the illuminated onyx dance floor is a sure cure for late-night boogie fever.

Body English
24 | 22 | 20 | $14

E of Strip | Hard Rock Hotel | 4455 Paradise Rd. (bet. Flamingo Rd. & Harmon Ave.) | 702-693-4000 | www.bodyenglish.com

"Hardbodies" "pack in" to the Hard Rock's "dark" downstairs club, a chandeliered class act that's "poppin'" with "sexy" "celebs and wannabes" "looking to move it" on the "wild" sublevel dance floor or "pay for real estate" at the bottle-buyers' tables; turn a stiff upper lip to the "high" cost and "zoo at the door" and it's bound to be "memorable."

Let your voice be heard - visit ZAGAT.com/vote

NIGHTLIFE

| | APPEAL | DECOR | SERVICE | COST |

Brass Lounge, The — | — | — | I
Downtown | 425 Fremont St. (bet. Las Vegas Blvd. & Main St.) | 702-382-1182 | www.hennesseyslasvegas.com

Pint-sized takes on fresh meaning at this Downtowner, a homey bar tucked behind the inviting facade of an 85-ft. pint of Bass; it hosts DJs, rock bands and funky jazz troupes, and the balcony affords a bird's-eye view of the bustling Fremont Street Experience.

Breeze Bar 19 | 21 | 20 | $13
Strip | Treasure Island Hotel | 3300 Las Vegas Blvd. S. (Spring Mountain Rd.) | 702-894-7111 | www.treasureisland.com

The sun never sets on this Treasure Island lounge, making it a "convenient" locale to breeze by for a "cool one" and "courteous service" at any hour; castaways "taking a break" from the table games nearby can blow a few coconuts "chasing a video poker progressive."

Brendan's Irish Pub ▽ 16 | 17 | 17 | $12
W of Strip | Orleans Hotel | 4500 W. Tropicana Ave. (Arville St.) | 702-365-7111 | www.orleanscasino.com

If Irish whiskey makes you frisky, this "relaxed" midsize pub sited west of the Strip in the Orleans Casino is an affordable place to put a jig in your step; "friendly barkeeps", a strong selection of imported brews and "live music" of a Celtic stripe complete the mahogany-hued picture.

Bunkhouse Saloon — | — | — | I
Downtown | 124 S. 11th St. (bet. Carson Ave. & Fremont St.) | 702-384-4536 | www.bunkhouselv.com

Wrangle up some "inexpensive" sauce at this divey Downtowner with a cowpoke theme, where a tattooed staff rides herd 24/7; walls lined with antlers and pics of John Wayne confirm "it's the real thing", and the free live bands and open-mike comedy earn an extra tip of the Stetson.

NEW Canyon Club — | — | — | M
Downtown | Four Queens Hotel | 202 Fremont St. (Casino Centre Blvd.) | 702-387-5175 | www.fourqueens.com

Classic rockers and tribute acts headline this new midsize concert venue in the Four Queens Downtown also playing host to a nightly murder mystery dinner show; well-appointed in dark drapery with plenty of couches for lounging, it also boasts modestly priced drinks that won't leave a crater in your wallet.

Caramel Bar & Lounge 23 | 24 | 21 | $15
Strip | Bellagio Hotel | 3600 Las Vegas Blvd. S. (Flamingo Rd.) | 702-693-8300 | www.lightgroup.com

A "luxuriously yummy" bonbon, this "intimate lounge" at the heart of the Bellagio is a "seductive" "alternative" to the Strip's high-watt spots, drawing a "classy" crowd with its "wonderful" martini menu and "socialite" vibes; it's "pricey" and "hipper than thou", but it's still appealing as a "trendy" "start or finish" to "a night of clubbing."

Carnaval Court 22 | 16 | 20 | $8
Strip | Harrah's Las Vegas | 3475 Las Vegas Blvd. S. (Flamingo Rd.) | 702-369-5000 | www.harrahs.com

"Party down" at Harrah's "open-air" "mid-Strip" "jam", a "brightly colored" sideshow known for "cranking" live bands and "must-see" "flair

NIGHTLIFE

| | APPEAL | DECOR | SERVICE | COST |

bartenders" whose "bottle-flipping" antics deserve "a role in *Cocktail*"; with weekend blackjack and sets by lounge legend Cook E. Jarr to up the "cheesy" "entertainment value", revelers report it's "a riot for cheap."

NEW CatHouse | - | - | - | E |
Strip | Luxor Hotel | 3900 Las Vegas Blvd. S. (bet. Mandalay Bay Rd. & Reno Ave.) | 702-262-4228 | www.cathouselv.com

This lounge/eatery at the Luxor is modeled after a 19th-century bordello, complete with lingerie-clad vixens and classic erotica films viewed through peepholes; the 10,000-sq.-ft. interior features a chandelier-adorned dining room with American plates from chef Kerry Simon, while late-night drinking and debauchery is best suited to the adjacent Loungerie, which is checkered with banquettes and tables to dance on.

Champagnes Cafe ∉ | - | - | - | I |
E Side | 3557 S. Maryland Pkwy. (Dumont Blvd.) | 702-737-1699

"Faded" walls of "burnt velvet brocade" and general down-and-dirty atmosphere qualify this "low-class" "low-key" "locals' joint" on the East Side as a "definite must-see"; Frankie rules an "eclectic" jukebox, the drinking's dirt-cheap and the mixologists "pour it on strong", but don't ask for Dom Perignon – this is "a dive bar, people."

Cheetah's | 22 | 15 | 20 | $13 |
W of Strip | 2112 Western Ave. (bet. Sahara & Wyoming Aves.) | 702-384-0074

"When you just want to get your freak on", this all-hours "gentlemen's palace" west of the Strip is "purrrfect"; the "beautiful" gals "put extra effort into making you smile", and a "polite refusal of a lap dance is not met with scorn" here; though the "chairs make it hard to bounce multiple ladies" on your knee, attempting it is still a "great" workout – "just don't be shocked if the morning sun is blasting when you leave."

Cherry | ∇ 23 | 24 | 21 | $12 |
NW | Red Rock Casino | 11011 W. Charleston Blvd. (Hwy. 215) | 702-797-7777 | www.redrocklasvegas.com

This red "hot" spot in the Northwest's Red Rock Resort boasts a "stunning" interior bathed in shades of scarlet, with a hovering dance floor and "perks" like curtained couches "for the bottle-service crowd"; add an "awesome" poolside patio and it's a "go-to for locals" who never miss "the hassle of the Strip."

NEW Christian Audigier The Nightclub | - | - | - | E |
Strip | Treasure Island Hotel | 3300 Las Vegas Blvd. S. (Spring Mountain Rd.) | 702-894-7580 | www.audigierlv.com

Clothing designer Christian Audigier makes his first foray into nightlife with this Treasure Island club festooned with enough skulls and roses to make it look like one of his $250 T-shirts; red drapery, shiny black couches and a pair of 1,000 gallon tanks filled with jellyfish complete the eye-popping decor, which is set to a soundtrack of progressive house.

Chrome Showroom | - | - | - | M |
N Las Vegas | Santa Fe Station Hotel | 4949 N. Rancho Dr. (bet. Lone Mountain Rd. & Rainbow Blvd.) | North Las Vegas | 702-658-4900 | www.stationcasinos.com

Polish up your music appreciation at this live venue in the North Side's Santa Fe Station, which presents classic rockers, high-

NIGHTLIFE

| | APPEAL | DECOR | SERVICE | COST |

caliber cover bands and contemporary country artists up close in a midsize room; for boot scootin' fun on a budget, check out the Southern-style supergroup Big as Texas, who play free shows on Friday and Saturday nights.

Cleopatra's Barge   19 | 18 | 18 | $12

Strip | Caesars Palace | 3570 Las Vegas Blvd. S. (Flamingo Rd.) | 702-731-7110 | www.caesarspalace.com

A "funky cross between a Liz Taylor movie and a Vegas lounge", this "old-school" "schmaltz" ship run aground "in the middle of an aisle" in Caesars Palace "is not a place to see the pretty people", but it is a "standby for the LV veterans"; even the saltiest sinners "look seasick", though, when this "cheeseball" boat rocks – the hydraulics-and-hooch combination might lead you to ask "is this thing moving, or did I have one too many?"

Club, The   - | - | - | M

N Las Vegas | Cannery Hotel | 2121 E. Craig Rd. (Losee Rd.) | North Las Vegas | 702-507-5700 | www.cannerycasinos.com

The siren song of vintage AM radio lures "oldie" enthusiasts to the Cannery's North Las Vegas music hall, where the ripened likes of Little Anthony and the Imperials and Beach Boy Brian Wilson channel the '60s, '70s and '80s; it can morph into an amphitheater thanks to a detachable back wall, guaranteeing fresh air if not the freshest of sounds.

Club Paradise   21 | 18 | 18 | $15

E of Strip | 4416 Paradise Rd. (bet. Flamingo Rd. & Harmon Ave.) | 702-734-7990 | www.clubparadise.net

"Zealous" natives "circulate constantly", which probably is what keeps them in such "very good shape" at this east-of-the-Strip club, a "nice place" to get a load of the "hottest" "naked girls dancing around for your money"; its "pretty talent" and "easy access to the Hard Rock" lead to "standing-room-only weekend nights" in the "cramped main room", so if you're looking to spread out, "splurge on the outrageously marked-up champagne and get into the larger VIP area."

Coyote Ugly   17 | 15 | 15 | $11

Strip | New York-New York Hotel | 3790 Las Vegas Blvd. S. (Tropicana Ave.) | 702-740-6969 | www.nynyhotelcasino.com

"Fans of the movie" "leave their inhibitions at the door" at this "rowdy" saloon "knockoff" in New York-New York, a "catty" franchise famed for the "shenanigans" of "scantily clad" tapsterettes who "keep the shots flowing" when they're not "stomping" along the bar; still, the "stifling" "mosh pit" of "lady tourists" and "frat dudes" has hecklers yapping "tourist trap."

Crazy Armadillo   - | - | - | M

Strip | Stratosphere Hotel | 2000 Las Vegas Blvd. S. (north of Sahara Ave.) | 702-383-5230 | www.stratospherehotel.com

With "fun and sassy" staffers to dispense the margaritas and tequila shooters, this Friday–Sunday-night cantina in the Strip's Stratosphere mixes Mexican vibes with DJ madness; the spare setting gains *ojo* appeal when the cast of va-va-voom vampire revue *Bite* arrives to whet their fangs post-show, but cynics still shrug "nothing special."

NIGHTLIFE

| | APPEAL | DECOR | SERVICE | COST |

Diablo's Cantina   - | - | - | M

Strip | Monte Carlo Resort | 3770 Las Vegas Blvd. S. (bet. Harmon & Tropicana Aves.) | 702-730-7777 | www.lightgroup.com

Have a hell of a time at the Monte Carlo's causal indoor-outdoor fiesta, which updates old-world Mexico by pairing ceramics and rustic furniture with neon and plasmas TVs; the bi-level digs feature an upstairs stage for bands and DJs, and the sinfully vast tequila menu (32 varieties) will satiate even the most demonic margarita appetite.

Dino's Lounge ⌀   - | - | - | I

Downtown | 1516 Las Vegas Blvd. S. (Wyoming Ave.) | 702-382-3894 | www.dinoslv.com

In a city known for its turnover, this popular Downtown neighborhood dive has been a favorite watering hole 24 hours a day for more than 45 years; it offers up a laid-back, non-flashy vibe for anyone who wants to dress down, get down (to the jukebox or karaoke) and pound 'em down on the cheap, courtesy of the buy-four-get-one-free card.

Divebar   - | - | - | I

E of Strip | 3035 E. Tropicana Ave. (McLeod Dr.) | 702-435-7526 | www.vegasdivebar.com

Heavily inked regulars hail the "great decor" at this downscale haunt east of the Strip, which honors its name with beer lights, tacky wood grain and B movies on the tube; it can be "difficult to get in" when area rockers pack the back room's nightly shows, but otherwise it's perfect for plunging into a bender.

Double Down Saloon ⌀   24 | 18 | 22 | $7

E of Strip | 4640 Paradise Rd. (Naples Dr.) | 702-791-5775 | www.doubledownsaloon.com

"Those brave enough to enter" can "wallow" in the "grunge" at this 24/7 "punk dive" east of the Strip, a "subculture" "staple" where patrons flash "multiple piercings and tattoos" and no-cover "indie rock" shows compete with "unintelligible screaming" on the juke; "cheap", "strong" specialty drinks make it an "appealing" "escape from the Strip", though "not a place to bring a date."

Downtown Cocktail Room   - | - | - | M

Downtown | 111 Las Vegas Blvd. S. (Fremont St.) | 702-880-3696 | www.downtownlv.net

Helping the Fremont East District smooth over Downtown's gritty image, this svelte nightspot mixes classic cocktails in high bohemian-chic style defined by dark woods, rust-colored walls, leather chairs, and concrete countertops and flooring; the cool vibes – abetted by DJs spinning down-tempo sounds – keep spirits as high as the lights are low.

Drop Bar   21 | 22 | 18 | $12

Henderson | Green Valley Ranch | 2300 Paseo Verde Pkwy. (Green Valley Pkwy.) | 702-221-6560 | www.greenvalleyranchresort.com

Drop by day or night at this "relaxed" lounge in the round on the casino floor of Henderson's Green Valley Ranch, a "trendy" hub featuring constellations of lights overhead and "cool videos" on-screen; with extra "eye candy" courtesy of "smoking hot" waitresses in scanty outfits, most drop their resistance to the "expensive" tabs.

Let your voice be heard – visit ZAGAT.com/vote

NIGHTLIFE

| | APPEAL | DECOR | SERVICE | COST |

Ellis Island Lounge | 17 | 9 | 18 | $8

E of Strip | Ellis Island Casino & Brewery | 4178 Koval Ln. (Flamingo Rd.) | 702-733-8901 | www.ellisislandcasino.com

Karaoke is king at this "homey" lounge in the eponymous casino east of the Strip, where "cheap" house-brand brews inspire wannabe Sinatras to belt away nightly; the "funny" turns at the mike are "popular with the locals", though nonfans of "out-of-tune" crooning quip "if our great-grandparents arrived here first, they would've doubled back."

ESPN Zone | 20 | 19 | 18 | $10

Strip | New York-New York Hotel | 3790 Las Vegas Blvd. S. (Tropicana Ave.) | 702-933-3776 | www.espnzone.com

"Heaven" for jocks, New York-New York's "super-sized" chain sports bar fields "TVs everywhere" (including "in the men's room") so fans "never have to miss a single play"; it's "not much for socializing", but "guys" equipped with "cold beer", "appropriate" "grub" and a video arcade insist there's "plenty of action" when you're itching to "get away from the glitz."

eyecandy sound lounge & bar | - | - | - | VE

Strip | Mandalay Bay Resort | 3950 Las Vegas Blvd. S. (Mandalay Bay Rd.) | 877-632-7800 | www.mandalaybay.com

Equally a treat for the ears and the eyes, this high-tech ultralounge in Mandalay Bay features interactive tables that let patrons create and project visuals plus iPod-ready audio stations that allow them to soundtrack the action on the illuminated dance floor; the shiny, streamlined setup boasts circular VIP booths, two bars and an array of specialty cocktails.

Flight | - | - | - | M

Strip | Luxor Hotel | 3900 Las Vegas Blvd. S. (bet. Mandalay Bay Rd. & Reno Ave.) | 702-262-4000 | www.luxor.com

Upgrade to first class at this comfy lounge just outside LAX at the Luxor, which specializes in blending high-end hooch into drinks named for international destinations; the cushy blue-hued seating, blackjack tables and bartop video poker will ease any layover, and 24/7 availability makes it tempting to taxi in any time.

Flirt | - | - | - | M

W of Strip | Rio All-Suite Hotel | 3700 W. Flamingo Rd. (bet. I-15 & Valley View Blvd.) | 702-777-7777 | www.riovegasnights.com

Femmes out to ogle beefcake at the Rio All-Suites' Chippendales Theater can warm up or cool down at this nearby lounge, a modernistic fusion of purple hues and contoured furniture that's as well put together as the mannerly hunks serving the chic cocktails; featured dancers drop by after shows to get flirty with their heavy-breathing admirers.

NEW 4949 Lounge | - | - | - | M

N of Strip | Santa Fe Station Hotel | 4949 N. Rancho Dr. (bet. Lone Mountain Rd. & Rainbow Blvd.) | 702-658-4900 | www.santafestationlasvegas.com

High rollers can take a break from the tables at this swank circular bar smack in the middle of the gaming pit at the Santa Fe Station casino north of the Strip; a shimmering crystal facade and comfy lounge

NIGHTLIFE

| | APPEAL | DECOR | SERVICE | COST |

chairs create an inviting atmosphere perfect for sipping brightly colored cocktails; N.B. on Sunday mornings you can nurse your hangover in style at their make-your-own Bloody Mary bar.

Freakin' Frog ▽ 25 | 14 | 24 | $9
E of Strip | 4700 S. Maryland Pkwy. (Tropicana Ave.) | 702-597-3237 | www.freakinfrog.com

"Don't order a domestic if you can't take the ridicule" at this "hoppin'" pub east of the Strip, a "lovable dive" where up to 700 brands pad out the "unbelievable" suds selection and the "super-friendly" barkeeps "know more about beer than you know about your mother"; for a little more kick, the upstairs Whiskey Attic features a 500-label liquor lineup.

Z ghostbar 25 | 24 | 19 | $14
W of Strip | Palms Casino Hotel | 4321 W. Flamingo Rd., 55th fl. (Arville St.) | 702-942-7777 | www.n9negroup.com

"Sweeping views of the Strip" and a crowd torn "from the pages of *People*" are "something to behold" at this literally "high-end" "ultra-lounge" on the Palms' 55th floor, a "hip" haunt known for its "pretty" patrons, "awesome" DJs and "freaky" see-through deck with a fearsome drop underfoot; in keeping with the "trendy" spirit, it'll "cost you" and "line issues" may materialize.

Gipsy - | - | - | I
E of Strip | 4605 Paradise Rd. (Naples Dr.) | 702-731-1919 | www.gipsylv.net

This big, booming gay bar east of the Strip is a "must-go" for the common man given its "genuinely joyful" vibes, though the feisty drag shows and go-go boys don't hurt either; its rock-hard rep attracts the masses, but if you can "handle the crowds" it's the least pretentious "game in town."

Girls of Glitter Gulch 14 | 9 | 13 | $14
Downtown | 20 Fremont St. (Main St.) | 702-385-4774

An "oldie but goodie", this vintage Downtown strip club "entices" prurient prospectors with free entry to eyeball "just ok" dancers in a setting that's "rougher than a stucco bathtub"; but "beware" of "usurious drink charges" and a show that's disappointingly "clean" unless you're a "tourist" "from Utah."

Gold Coast Lounge ⌀ - | - | - | M
W of Strip | Gold Coast Hotel | 4000 W. Flamingo Rd. (bet. Valley View Blvd. & Wynn Rd.) | 702-367-7111 | www.goldcoastcasino.com

The Gold Coast goes Gulf Coast weekday afternoons as the foot-stompin' Royal Dixie Jazz Band kicks up Crescent City jams at this no-frills music bar west of the Strip; cover groups gig after dark, and "happening karaoke" nights bring out "old-timers" who ensure the classic lounge sound "lives on."

NEW Gold Diggers - | - | - | M
Downtown | Golden Nugget Hotel | 129 E. Fremont St. (Main St.) | 702-385-7111 | www.goldennugget.com

A rare upscale entry amid the budget-minded Downtown casino circuit, this glittery lair inside the Golden Nugget is best known for its patio, which offers eye-level views of the high-watt Fremont Street Experience; it also boasts a crowd-pleasing soundtrack of top 40 hits that makes the sizable dance floor all the more appealing.

Let your voice be heard - visit ZAGAT.com/vote

NIGHTLIFE

| | APPEAL | DECOR | SERVICE | COST |

Gordon Biersch | 18 | 16 | 18 | $10

E of Strip | 3987 Paradise Rd. (Flamingo Rd.) | 702-312-5249 | www.gordonbiersch.com

"Strippers and porn stars mingle with post-convention businessmen" at this "super-sized version of a San Fran brewpub" that offers "more beer than a frat-house basement" along with burgers and "reliable garlic fries"; this "yuppie hangout" "tends to close un-Vegas-ly early", but it's a popular "after-work" scene for "upscale Midwestern singles", so "dress well if you want to get lucky here."

Griffin, The | - | - | - | I

Downtown | 511 Fremont St. (Las Vegas Blvd.) | 702-382-0577 | www.thegriffinlounge.com

Exposed-brick walls, alluring leather booths and a pair of fireplaces furnish a warmly Gothic feel at this dusky hideaway in Downtown's Fremont East District; the Pabst is cheap and the unbeatable jukebox spans classic rock to indie pop, making it an instant fave among hip locals and tourists looking to recover from a neon hangover.

Hofbrauhaus Las Vegas | 20 | 22 | 19 | $12

E of Strip | 4510 Paradise Rd. (Harmon Ave.) | 702-256-5500 | www.hofbrauhauslasvegas.com

Hoisting "huge steins" of imported suds, merrymakers "toast" this "authentic" east-of-the-Strip facsimile of the famed Munich beer hall, a "really fun" "place to get raucous", "chow down" and groove to "an oompah band"; some say *nicht* to the "kitsch" and "tourists", but why quibble when it's "Oktoberfest all nights of the week"?

Hogs & Heifers | 21 | 19 | 18 | $9

Downtown | 201 N. Third St. (Ogden Ave.) | 702-676-1457 | www.hogsandheifers.com

"Don't let the bikers and hogs parked outside scare you away" from this scruffy Downtown saloon, which mimics the "original NYC outpost" and its infamous formula of "cool barmaids" "dancing on the bar" and "rowdy crowds" of "locals and tourists"; the going "can be crude", but "if you feel downmarket" it's "guaranteed" to get your motor runnin'.

⚡ House of Blues | 22 | 21 | 19 | $13

Strip | Mandalay Bay Resort | 3950 Las Vegas Blvd. S. (Mandalay Bay Rd.) | 702-632-7600 | www.hob.com

"The show's the thing" at this "first-rate" concert venue in the Mandalay Bay, which "grabs the best headliners" (plus tribute acts and "live-band karaoke") for "upbeat" gigs in an "up-close" setting; if "you're lucky", a member's invite to the top-floor Foundation Room yields "spectacular drinks" and "stunning" views, and carousers can exorcise the previous night at Sunday's "exciting" gospel brunch.

NEW I-Bar | - | - | - | M

W of Strip | Rio All-Suite Hotel | 3700 W. Flamingo Rd. (bet. I-15 & Valley View Blvd.) | 702-777-6869 | www.riovegasnights.com

Inspired by the flesh frenzy of Rio de Janeiro's Ipanema beach, this circular bar just off the gaming pit at the Rio boasts a curvy serving staff that bares about as much as allowed outside a gentleman's club; the luminous space is awash in high-tech flourishes, like interactive tables

NIGHTLIFE

| | APPEAL | DECOR | SERVICE | COST |

that enable customers to communicate with other clubgoers and play games while imbibing an array of specialty cocktails.

Images Lounge — | — | — | M
Strip | Stratosphere Hotel | 2000 Las Vegas Blvd. S. (north of Sahara Ave.) | 702-380-7777 | www.stratospherehotel.com

Starry-eyed "impersonators abound" in the cover bands that rattle the rafters at this lively lounge in the Stratosphere at the top of the Strip, which delivers a mix of Top 40, rock and R&B late into the night.

Indigo Lounge — | — | — | M
Strip | Bally's Las Vegas | 3645 Las Vegas Blvd. S. (Flamingo Rd.) | 702-967-4111 | www.ballyslasvegas.com

Awash in sapphire hues, this lounge adjoining the Bally's casino floor flashes back to vintage Vegas with a pianist, velvety seating and classy cocktails; "good bands" serving up "'70s and '80s party music" get nostalgists moving on the "small dance floor", though skeptics sense the scene's "in need of a certain something."

Ivan Kane's Forty Deuce 23 | 20 | 17 | $13
Strip | Mandalay Bay Resort | 3930 Las Vegas Blvd. S. (Mandalay Bay Rd.) | 702-632-9442 | www.fortydeuce.com

"Naughty" but "classy", the "ultrachic" late-night burlesque sets at this LA import in Mandalay Bay showcase "amazing dancers" merging "saucy" striptease with "Cirque du Soleil-like moves" into an "art form" that's "not for the faint of heart"; spectators keep the "funky little cabaret" "crowded", though stageside seats at the bar give a "lucky few" more jiggle room.

J. C. Wooloughan's ▽ 18 | 20 | 22 | $10
NW | JW Marriott | 221 N. Rampart Blvd. (Summerlin Pkwy.) | 702-869-7725 | www.jwlasvegasresort.com

"Irish to the core", this made-in-Dublin pub grafted onto the Northwest's JW Marriott does right by its roots with imported bevies, old-country grub and "lots of craic" (meaning good times, laddies); live Celtic music and "sing-alongs" with the harmonica-blowin' "John Windsor every Wednesday and Thursday" lure in locals looking to "share a pint."

JET Nightclub 23 | 21 | 19 | $15
Strip | Mirage Hotel | 3400 Las Vegas Blvd. S. (Spring Mountain Rd.) | 702-693-8300 | www.lightgroup.com

Prepare for takeoff at this "over-the-top" megaclub at the Mirage, where jet-setters in "skimpy" attire land to "hobnob with celebrities" in a "dark and sexy" multiroomed space complete with "stripper poles" ("a nice touch") and "fantastic" DJs pumping a "great mix"; players with "deep pockets" who can pilot "past the rope" call it a "premier" place to "get your groove on."

Jillian's 19 | 19 | 19 | $10
Downtown | Neonopolis Entertainment Complex | 450 Fremont St. (Las Vegas Blvd.) | 702-759-0450 | www.jillianslasvegas.com

"The entire family" can enjoy "a casual night out" at this Downtown amusement multiplex, a "neon"-lit jumble of "fun and games" that includes a sports bar and eatery, video arcade, pool hall and bowling alley; there's also an "eclectic" all-ages concert club, but given this

Let your voice be heard - visit ZAGAT.com/vote

NIGHTLIFE

| | APPEAL | DECOR | SERVICE | COST |

town's fast-lane attractions, some grumble it's "like going to Paris and having dinner at McDonald's."

Joint, The | 20 | 17 | 15 | $14

E of Strip | Hard Rock Hotel | 4455 Paradise Rd. (bet. Flamingo Rd. & Harmon Ave.) | 702-693-5000 | www.hardrockhotel.com

A "cool" crowd of "rock 'n' rollers" ranging from your average "wild child" to "thirtysomething hipsters" hails this "jam-packed" Hard Rock hangout as an "exciting place" to get "up-close and personal" with "top-drawer" talent in a "relatively intimate space"; factor in two "awesome bars" and "great people-watching", and it's no wonder some feel the "only issue" is that it's "too far from the Strip."

J-POP Sushi Bar and Lounge | 20 | 20 | 18 | $12

Strip | Mandalay Bay Resort | 3950 Las Vegas Blvd. S. (Mandalay Bay Rd.) | 877-632-7800 | www.mandalaybay.com

This sushi bar/"casino lounge" combo "in the center of all the action" at Mandalay Bay remains an "easy" spot to pop in for a "casual" bite or belt; service may run "slow", but pop and rock music and "a large dance floor" make it a popular "place to hang" ("what's not to like?").

Kahunaville | 19 | 18 | 20 | $10

Strip | Treasure Island Hotel | 3300 Las Vegas Blvd. S. (Spring Mountain Rd.) | 702-894-7390 | www.kahunaville.com

"Come in a bad mood" and you'll "leave with a grin and a buzz" say supporters of the "strong drinks" and "great entertainment" provided by "fantastic" barkeeps at this "friendly" Treasure Islander; still, the "unimpressed" proclaim that its "fair fare" and "corny" tropical decor make it a merely "decent option", "rather than a destination" in its own right.

Krave | 20 | 17 | 17 | $11

Strip | 3663 Las Vegas Blvd. S. (Harmon Ave.) | 702-836-0830 | www.kravelasvegas.com

There's "a place for everyone" at this "exciting" polysexual playground on the Strip next to Planet Hollywood, a gay club/lounge that draws a "young", "diversified" clientele craving "hot" sounds and "entertaining" theme nights; fleet-footed folks add if you intend to hit the dance floor, "you'd better mean it."

La Scena Lounge | 23 | 22 | 24 | $14

Strip | Venetian Hotel | 3355 Las Vegas Blvd. S. (bet. Flamingo & Spring Mountain Rds.) | 702-414-1000 | www.venetian.com

"Nonstop great music" powers the jumpin' scene at this "beautiful lounge" "on the gaming floor" at the Venetian featuring cool "cover bands" ("oh, yeah"); with some of "the best bartenders in Vegas" to do the honors (earning it the No. 1 score for Service), it's "definitely worth" "taking a break from the tables" for "a drink and a tune."

LAX | - | - | - | E

Strip | Luxor Hotel | 3900 Las Vegas Blvd. S. (bet. Mandalay Bay Rd. & Reno Ave.) | 702-262-4000 | www.laxthenightclub.com

Freshly touched down via Hollywood, the Luxor's mammoth, two-tiered celeb hub (part-owned by Christina Aguilera and DJ AM) recalls an ornate opera house with its crimson drapery, black marble floors, tufted red-leather walls and multiple chandeliers; the skyboxes and jumbo dance floor signal clear skies for clubbing, but

NIGHTLIFE

| | APPEAL | DECOR | SERVICE | COST |

long lines and a discriminating door mean it's the high fliers being cleared for takeoff.

NEW McFadden's — | — | — | M

W of Strip | Rio All-Suite Hotel | 3700 W. Flamingo Rd. (bet. I-15 & Valley View Blvd.) | 702-545-6777

Dueling pianos, damsels dancing on the bar and 90-oz. cocktails fuel the rowdy atmosphere at this self-proclaimed 'Wildest Irish pub on Earth' at the Rio west of the Strip – and it gets even wilder with rock bands on Wednesdays and beer pong competitions on Thursdays; for those in need of sustenance, they also offer a mix of standard bar fare and traditional plates like shepherd's pie.

Mermaid Restaurant and Lounge — | — | — | M

S of Strip | Silverton Casino & Lodge | 3333 Blue Diamond Rd. (I-15) | 702-263-7777 | www.silvertoncasino.com

Another kind of dive bar, this watery grotto at the Silverton south of the Strip is surrounded by a giant tank stocked with thousands of tropical fish; wavy walls, overhead lights resembling marine life and aqua illumination enhance the atmo, while specialty drinks like the King Neptune and Blue Mermaid shore up the crowd.

Mist 19 | 19 | 16 | $11

Strip | Treasure Island Hotel | 3300 Las Vegas Blvd. S. (Spring Mountain Rd.) | 702-894-7330 | www.lightgroup.com

This "small" but "swanky" enclave in TI is favored by "attractive young" things who appreciate the auburn interior or go misty-eyed over the "beautiful barmaids"; though critics steam it's a "snobbish" upstart "masquerading as an ultralounge", defenders find it "cooler" than most.

☑ miX Lounge 27 | 26 | 21 | $14

Strip | Mandalay Bay Resort | 3950 Las Vegas Blvd. S., 64th fl. (Mandalay Bay Rd.) | 702-632-7777 | www.mandalaybay.com

With "million-dollar" "views over Vegas" ("even from the bathrooms"), this "chichi" lounge crowning THEhotel at Mandalay Bay – ranked No. 1 for Appeal in the Las Vegas Nightlife Survey – is where "pretty people" "in-the-know" mix in a "mod" space featuring floor-to-ceiling windows and a "stunning" balcony "overlooking the Strip"; given the "can't-miss" "sex appeal" and "platinum-card" pricing, "you'll feel you've made it, if only for the night."

Moon 24 | 23 | 22 | $13

W of Strip | Palms Casino Hotel | 4321 W. Flamingo Rd., 53rd fl. (Arville St.) | 702-942-6832 | www.n9negroup.com

The "amazing" "retractable roof" and "celebrity sightings" offer ample opportunity to "stargaze" at this "lively" club-cum-"ultralounge" atop the Palms, where heavenly bodies gravitate for "pure dancing" on the "hot" floor; with "go-go" gals in space-age garb, multicolored floor tiles flashing a "light show" and a "gorgeous" patio high above the Strip, it's a refreshingly "friendly" satellite to ghostbar.

Napoleon's Champagne Bar 22 | 21 | 20 | $12

Strip | Paris Las Vegas | 3655 Las Vegas Blvd. S. (bet. Flamingo Rd. & Harmon Ave.) | 702-946-7000 | www.parislasvegas.com

"Jazz and more jazz" used to make the scene here, but dueling pianos have displaced the combos and transformed the mood at this "swanky

NIGHTLIFE

| | APPEAL | DECOR | SERVICE | COST |

cigar bar" in the Paris; it's still an "amazing place" where patrons "kick back" and enjoy a drink amid "upscale European" decor, though some say its "stereotypically French" service is its "weakest aspect."

Nine Fine Irishmen   22 | 23 | 20 | $8

Strip | New York-New York Hotel | 3790 Las Vegas Blvd. S. (Tropicana Ave.) | 702-740-6969 | www.ninefineirishmen.com

"There's not a leprechaun in sight", but patrons proclaiming "another pint of Guinness, please!" assert the "authenticity" of this Irish pub, which was moved piecemeal from its original location on the Emerald Isle to New York-New York; some say it "lost a little in the translation", but those who "love it" insist that "good food", "good music and a good vibe" make it a "great place."

Noir Bar   - | - | - | VE

Strip | Luxor Hotel | 3900 Las Vegas Blvd. S. (bet. Mandalay Bay Rd. & Reno Ave.) | 702-262-4000 | www.purelv.com

Meet the elite at this super-exclusive neighbor of the Luxor's LAX, a shadowy celebrity speakeasy that's accessible only through a private entrance; it's flush with crystal and fine leather and specializes in cocktails custom-made to your taste, but commoners be forewarned: though reservations are required, unless you're George Clooney they're not necessarily honored.

Olympic Garden   23 | 13 | 19 | $14
(aka OG)

Strip | 1531 Las Vegas Blvd. S. (Wyoming Ave.) | 702-385-8987 | www.ogvegas.com

"It doesn't get more Olympian in size" than this "monstrous" "coed strip club" on the Strip, a "sleazy" "Greek-themed" "garden of delights" offering "something for everyone" on "multiple stages": "luscious ladies" on the "large floor downstairs" and "hot" hunks upstairs in the "male revue" (Wednesday–Sunday); "everyone goes home broke and happy" after this "quintessential sybaritic" experience, since "the only thing missing is a machine to turn you over and shake the money out of you."

Ovation   - | - | - | M

Henderson | Green Valley Ranch | 2300 Paseo Verde Pkwy. (Green Valley Pkwy.) | 702-617-7777 | www.greenvalleyranchresort.com

Music lovers cheer this "great addition" to Henderson's Green Valley Ranch, a midsize live showroom that wins bravos for its souped-up sound system and handsome three-tiered setup; national acts like Macy Gray top the bill, and hard-rock satirists Steel Panther bring big hair and big riffs to Friday nights.

Palomino Club   ∇ 17 | 9 | 13 | $17

N Las Vegas | 1848 Las Vegas Blvd. N. (bet. Lake Mead Blvd. & St. Louis Ave.) | North Las Vegas | 702-642-2984 | www.palominolv.com

Allegedly "the only club in town that's fully nude and serves alcohol", this warhorse bareback joint in North Las Vegas steers buckaroos "far off the Strip" to pony up prices that strike some as "a bit extreme"; a "decline in talent" may render the entertainment "more humorous than alluring", but for a truly tawdry "bachelor party" "this is your place."

NIGHTLIFE

| | APPEAL | DECOR | SERVICE | COST |

Pearl, The — | — | — | E

W of Strip | Palms Casino Hotel | 4321 W. Flamingo Rd. (Arville St.) | 702-944-3200 | www.palms.com

Music fans, the world's your oyster at this stylish concert hall at The Palms, which presents arena-caliber shows in a 2,500-capacity setting with multi-tiered seating, crystalline sound and a mammoth lighting system worthy of *CE3K*; a multitude of bars and a steady lineup of A-list acts bolster its rep as a true gem.

ɴᴇᴡ Penthouse Club — | — | — | E

W of Strip | 3525 W. Russell Rd. (bet. Polaris Ave. & Valley View Blvd.) | 702-673-1700 | www.penthouselv.com

Your bankroll needs to be as big as the bust lines at this high-end gentleman's joint west of the Strip, where access to the V.I.P. area will set you back a membership fee of $1,500; housed in the former Sin space, this remodeled pleasure palace is spread over 46,000 sq. ft. and features three separate dancing areas, including one for locals only.

❷ Peppermill Fireside Lounge 25 | 24 | 22 | $11

Strip | 2985 Las Vegas Blvd. S. (bet. Convention Center Dr. & Riviera Blvd.) | 702-735-7635 | www.peppermilllasvegas.com

"Don't go changin'" implore admirers of this "iconic" 24-hour "retro lounge" on the Strip, where "fabulous vintage" touches like "velvet booths" and "shag carpeting" are as "atmospheric" as "a Rat Pack movie"; for a "late-night or early-morning" "rendezvous" "cuddled up by the fire pit" with "colorful tropical drinks" delivered by "servers in black gowns", it's the ultimate "campy" "throwback."

Petrossian Bar 24 | 22 | 22 | $17

Strip | Bellagio Hotel | 3600 Las Vegas Blvd. S. (Flamingo Rd.) | 702-693-7111 | www.bellagio.com

"A taste of the good life" awaits at this oh-so-"sophisticated" lounge off the Bellagio lobby, a "classy" retreat where the well-to-do "indulge" in afternoon tea service, "a bit of bubbly", premium vodkas or "caviar ecstasy"; a piano man helps the room "unwind", and the "priceless" "people-watching" offers a close-up look at "winners" on a "splurge."

❷ Playboy Club 26 | 27 | 22 | $14

W of Strip | Palms Casino Hotel | 4321 W. Flamingo Rd. (Arville St.) | 702-942-6832 | www.n9negroup.com

"Hef's dream" lives on at this "upscale" lounge on the Palms' 52nd floor, a "time warp" back to the swinging "'60s heyday" of the men's mag featuring crystal chandeliers, floor-to-ceiling windows, a fireplace and restroom walls papered with Playmates; with "super-friendly bunnies" slinging drinks and running "high-limit tables", it's bound to be "dude central" but "you won't want to leave."

Poetry — | — | — | E

Strip | Caesars Palace | 3500 Las Vegas Blvd. S. (Flamingo Rd.) | 702-369-4998 | www.poetrynightclub.com

The writing is on the wall at this hip-hop hot spot in the Forum Shops at Caesars Palace, where rhymes from rap greats and celebrated poets adorn just about every flat surface; top-shelf DJs and MCs manage a verse-atile mix of urban music, and playas and wordsmiths alike can look to the snazzy dance floor and VIP rooms for inspiration.

Let your voice be heard – visit ZAGAT.com/vote

NIGHTLIFE

| | APPEAL | DECOR | SERVICE | COST |

Polly Esthers — 22 | 19 | 15 | $13
Strip | Stratosphere Hotel | 2000 Las Vegas Blvd. S. (north of Sahara Ave.) | 702-380-7777 | www.pollyestherslv.com

Break out the "leg warmers and rubber bracelets" at this "cheesy" "nostalgia" trip in the Strip's Stratosphere, a "big, loud" "disco city" "spotlighting the '70s, '80s, '90s and '00s" with decade-specific memorabilia and musical "highlights"; whether you'd rather "reminisce" over the Partridge Family bus or a silver DeLorean, it's paradise "for trivia buffs" and "a guilty pleasure" for all.

NEW Privé — - | - | - | E
Strip | Planet Hollywood Resort | 3667 Las Vegas Blvd. S. (Harmon Ave.) | 702-523-6002 | www.planethollywoodresort.com

Big names like Bruce Willis and Pamela Anderson have been known to party at this mammoth South Beach transplant at Planet Hollywood, where towering crystal chandeliers and a 26-ft. ceiling add to the larger-than-life feel; top-flight DJs spin on the weekends, when the lines are long and cover tabs can be steep ($30 for women, $40 for men).

ⓩ PURE — 25 | 25 | 18 | $15
Strip | Caesars Palace | 3570 Las Vegas Blvd. S. (Flamingo Rd.) | 702-731-7873 | www.purethenightclub.com

"A-list celebs and those wishing they were" find "pure bliss" at this "phenomenal" "high-end" club in Caesars Palace, a "multiroom" expanse of "clean white" with a "packed dance floor" and a "fabulous" terrace boasting "breathtaking views"; the "insane" lines and "restrictive" door are "quite the ordeal", but if you "plan on spending" here's where to "go all out" ("believe the hype").

Pussycat Dolls Lounge — 24 | 22 | 18 | $14
Strip | Caesars Palace | 3570 Las Vegas Blvd. S. (Flamingo Rd.) | 702-731-7873 | www.pcdlounge.com

"Glamorous sex kittens" "swing from the ceiling", bathe "in a giant cocktail glass" and "vamp and camp" across the stage at this "swanky lounge" inside PURE in Caesars Palace, where the "entertaining shows" are "a throwback to an earlier era" of "fun burlesque"; occasional "celebrity guests" are another reason supporters "love the venue", but some "hot-blooded males" craving "more action" complain that the "brief" performances "should last longer."

Railhead, The — - | - | - | M
E Side | Boulder Station Hotel | 4111 Boulder Hwy. (Lamb Blvd.) | 702-432-7777 | www.stationcasinos.com

It's all aboard for "great concerts" at this roomy East Side music venue in Boulder Station, which has fans chugging over for genre-spanning shows headed up by major names; cover-band wizzes Yellow Brick Road bring the classic riffs for free on Friday and Saturday nights.

Rain Nightclub — 21 | 21 | 18 | $14
W of Strip | Palms Casino Hotel | 4321 W. Flamingo Rd. (Arville St.) | 702-942-7777 | www.n9negroup.com

"Water, fog and pyro effects" "thrill" the "trendy" "young" hordes at this "steamy" megaclub at the Palms west of the Strip, a "super-cool" multilevel party that pours on attractions like VIP "skyboxes" and "fireballs" lighting up the dance floor; but citing the "long wait" for en-

NIGHTLIFE

| | APPEAL | DECOR | SERVICE | COST |

try and a crowd "overrun" with "senior prom" refugees, some thunder "the appeal has dropped."

☑ Red Square — 25 | 24 | 21 | $13

Strip | Mandalay Bay Resort | 3950 Las Vegas Blvd. S. (Mandalay Bay Rd.) | 702-632-7407 | www.mandalaybay.com

"Drink up, comrade!" at this "Soviet-inspired" barski in Mandalay Bay, which goes back "behind the Iron Curtain" with its "overwhelming selection of vodkas" and "decadent" interior replete with red-velvet booths, an "über-cool" "frozen" bartop ("put your cares on ice") and a "freezer room" for subzero shots; though a "splurge" with frosty service "from Siberia", it's a "favorite for chilling."

☑ Rehab — 25 | 22 | 19 | $13

E of Strip | Hard Rock Hotel | 4455 Paradise Rd. (bet. Flamingo Rd. & Harmon Ave.) | 702-693-5000 | www.rehablv.com

Nobody's drying out at this "raunchy" "gold standard of pool parties", which makes a splash Sunday afternoons as "ripped" dudes and "hoochies" in "dental-floss bikinis" descend on the Hard Rock's expansive watering hole to "let it all hang out"; DJs and "enormous margaritas" fuel "hedonism all the way", but it's "just packed" and the "line is forever long."

Rick's Cabaret — 20 | 21 | 18 | $11
(fka Scores)

W of Strip | 3355 Procyon (Desert Inn Rd.) | 702-367-4000 | www.ricks.com

Fellas live "large" at this mammarian mecca west of the Strip, which showcases "great-looking" dancers and racy revues in a super-sized bi-level spread flaunting a sports lounge, VIP skyboxes and a piano bar; then again, charges that it's "pushy", "crowded" and "overpriced" suggest its playbook doesn't score with everyone.

Risqué — 19 | 20 | 19 | $14

Strip | Paris Las Vegas | 3655 Las Vegas Blvd. S. (bet. Flamingo Rd. & Harmon Ave.) | 702-946-4589 | www.parislasvegas.com

A "sexy" setup merging a contempo look with "19th-century" accents makes this club/lounge in the Paris an "awesome find" for a flirty "younger crowd" cavorting on the comfy seating or "the coolest" of VIP balconies; aside from beaucoup "mingling", "pumping" DJs boost its cachet as a "little-known place to dance."

NEW Rok — - | - | - | M

Strip | New York-New York Hotel | 3790 Las Vegas Blvd. S. (Tropicana Ave.) | 702-740-6765 | www.rokvegasnightclub.com

A mammoth video screen encircles the interior of this rock 'n' roll-themed nightspot at New York-New York, also featuring an enclosed patio boasting one of the best views of the Strip; since it's one of the few nightspots in Vegas to offer half-bottle service, this is the place to be for clubgoers on a budget.

Romance at the Top of the World — - | - | - | E

Strip | Stratosphere Hotel | 2000 Las Vegas Blvd. S., 107th fl. (north of Sahara Ave.) | 702-380-7777 | www.stratospherehotel.com

Given the 360-degree panorama from the Stratosphere's 107th floor, you may have a hard time gazing into your date's eyes at this lounge,

NIGHTLIFE

| | APPEAL | DECOR | SERVICE | COST |

even with rich appointments and low lighting to set a seductive mood; the Willie Moran Jazz trio bops by every night, while the champagne list allows for suitably stratospheric tabs.

NEW Rox — - | - | - | I

W of Strip | 5285 Dean Martin Dr. (Hacienda Ave.) | 702-804-7699 | www.myspace.com/roxclubvegas

Bikers and their hogs fill the parking lot of this former topless-joint-turned-roaring-rock-hang west of the Strip; though a stripper's pole still lingers from the club's past, it's now adorned with autographed guitars and albums, setting the scene for local and smaller national touring bands and a rowdy crowd downing cheap brews.

⊠ rumjungle — 22 | 23 | 19 | $13

Strip | Mandalay Bay Resort | 3950 Las Vegas Blvd. S. (Mandalay Bay Rd.) | 702-632-7408 | www.chinagrillmgt.com

"Cage dancers" and "heavy beats" ensure this "flashy" club in the Mandalay Bay "throbs with energy" as "par-tay" people prowling a "faux jungle" framed by "fire and water" lap up a "never-ending selection of rums" ("sip with caution"); tabs are "steep", but with a "banging" "elevated dance floor", it's "definitely a scene."

Sand Dollar Blues — - | - | - | I

W of Strip | 3355 Spring Mountain Rd. (Polaris Ave.) | 702-871-6651 | www.sanddollarblues.com

If "keepin' the blues alive" "is your thing", this 24/7 juke joint west of the Strip hosts nearly nightly gigs from "some of the best" sidemen in the biz, not to mention impromptu sets from the likes of Ted Nugent and Taylor Dane; otherwise it's low-cost, low-down and low-frills, but hey, you "come for the music."

Sapphire — 23 | 20 | 21 | $11

W of Strip | 3025 S. Industrial Rd. (Desert Inn Rd.) | 702-796-6000 | www.sapphirelasvegas.com

"Wow!" gasp onlookers at this "cavernous" gentlemen's club west of the Strip, billed as "the world's largest" boob bonanza and staffed with "beautiful" sirens "you just can't beat" for "down-to-earth" hospitality; but the layout's dimensions are as "disorienting" as those displayed onstage, and equally inflated pricing means it "packs them in and milks them dry."

Seahorse Lounge — 18 | 20 | 17 | $12

Strip | Caesars Palace | 3570 Las Vegas Blvd. S. (Flamingo Rd.) | 702-731-7110 | www.caesarspalace.com

A "floor-to-ceiling aquarium" stocked with "live seahorses" buoys this watering hole in Caesars Palace, a "pleasant" port of call rigged with pearly white columns and mermaid statues where castaways drown their sorrows via a maritime martini list or 20-label champagne lineup; given the "quiet" atmo, livelier crews use it to "meet up" then "move on."

Seamless — - | - | - | M

W of Strip | 4740 S. Arville St. (bet. Flamingo Rd. & Tropicana Ave.) | 702-227-5200 | www.seamlessclub.com

The "beautiful lady playing" in a bathtub-sized martini glass "reminds you what Sin City is all about" at this "premier" skin joint west of the

NIGHTLIFE

| | APPEAL | DECOR | SERVICE | COST |

Strip, a stylish "treat" with loungey decor and buxom belles seamlessly strutting the catwalk; strippers yield to hipsters at 4 AM as it morphs into an after-hours dance club where "female patrons" too are treated "like gold."

Sedona | - | - | - | M |

W Side | 9580 W. Flamingo Rd. (I-215) | 702-320-4700 | www.suburbanlv.com

"Loved by locals", this Andre Agassi–owned West Side lounge serves up an ace with a classy but comfy setting sporting plush red seats, flattering illumination and an outdoor patio equipped with sofas and a fire pit; meanwhile, foes volley it's "pricey" for what amounts to a "glammed-up video poker bar."

Shadow | 22 | 20 | 18 | $12 |

Strip | Caesars Palace | 3570 Las Vegas Blvd. S. (Flamingo Rd.) | 702-731-7110 | www.caesarspalace.com

The "only thing hotter" than the talent writhing in silhouette behind screens are the "hot girls inside the bar itself" – but even women "can hang out" and "not feel like pieces of meat" at this "sexy but not trashy" Caesars casino lounge; "world-class flair" mixologists getting "over the top" on the bartop and an easy door "without the commitment of a cover charge" "don't hurt either."

Sidebar | ∇ 22 | 21 | 23 | $8 |

Downtown | 201 N. Third St. (Ogden Ave.) | 702-259-9700 | www.sidebarlv.com

Tuned to a "lower key than the Strip", this "true gem" of a lounge is ranked among Downtown's "classiest cocktail spots" by the hipoisie who corner its plush white booths and "relaxing" patio; insiders say amenities like the "artfully prepared" specialty drinks and primo cigar selection are best appreciated "if you're over 30."

Spearmint Rhino | 24 | 17 | 20 | $13 |

W of Strip | 3340 Highland Dr. S. (Spring Mountain Rd.) | 702-796-3600 | www.spearmintrhinolv.com

"Drop-dead gorgeous girls" push "the hotness" "through the roof" at this "quality" skin safari west of the Strip, an "eye-candy" horn of plenty thanks to "classy" Dark Continent decor and a "preponderance of silicone"; a few fume it's "overcrowded" and "overpriced", but "hit it at the right time" and "this is the one to beat."

NEW Stoney's Rockin' Country | - | - | - | I |

S of Strip | 9151 Las Vegas Blvd. S. (bet. Agate & Serene Aves.) | 702-435-2855 | www.stoneysrockincountry.com

Lasso up some cheap beers at this new honky-tonk south of the Strip showcasing country acts on a sizable stage plus plenty of other entertainment, from two-step lessons to pool tournaments; Thursdays–Sundays there's a $20 all-you-can-drink beer special when bikini-clad patrons take turns riding the club's mechanical bull for a $500 prize.

Studio 54 | 21 | 20 | 18 | $14 |

Strip | MGM Grand Hotel | 3799 Las Vegas Blvd. S. (Tropicana Ave.) | 702-891-7254 | www.studio54lv.com

"A classic reborn", the MGM Grand's multi-tiered update of the disco-era flashpoint is a chance to "boogie oogie oogie" to "great

NIGHTLIFE

| | APPEAL | DECOR | SERVICE | COST |

'70s and '80s" sounds as "go-go dancers and acrobats" cavort under the mirror ball; if the "slightly older" clientele's "lacking", it's "easier to get in" than other Strip hot spots and it's got "staying power" like it's "still 1977."

NEW Sugarcane   - | - | - | E

Strip | Palazzo Hotel | 3325 Las Vegas Blvd. S. (Sands Ave.) | 702-789-4141 | www.sushisamba.com/top.html

A super-sweet adjunct to SushiSamba at the Palazzo, this luxe lounge's decor is eye-catching even by Vegas standards, with a main area illuminated by 4,000 sugarcane-shaped lights that dangle from the ceiling; it plays up its Japanese/Peruvian/Brazilian pedigree with samba dancers and taiko drummers on hand to entertain, while its drink menu offers caipirinhas, pisco sours and a 'cocktail tree', which lets you sample 12 delectable libations for $70.

Tabú   23 | 22 | 21 | $13

Strip | MGM Grand Hotel | 3799 Las Vegas Blvd. S. (Tropicana Ave.) | 702-891-7183 | www.tabulv.com

"Not too big, not too small, but just right" say club-going Goldilocks of this "sleek and sexy" ultraden in the MGM Grand, where the ubiquitous "awesome visual displays" even beam from the "sooo cool interactive tables"; "loungey" and "saucy" all at once, it draws so many "chic tourists and high-rollin' celebs" that it can be "difficult to get into unless you know someone who can get you on the list."

☑ Tao   26 | 27 | 20 | $15

Strip | Venetian Hotel | 3355 Las Vegas Blvd. S. (bet. Flamingo & Spring Mountain Rds.) | 702-388-8588

☑ Tao Beach

Strip | Venetian Hotel | 3355 Las Vegas Blvd. S. (bet. Flamingo & Spring Mountain Rds.) | 702-388-8338
www.taolasvegas.com

"East meets West" at the Venetian's "dark and exotic" "New York transplant", an "extravagant" sanctuary that bundles Buddhist "temple" statuary, "kinky" "models bathing", "killer DJs" and "celeb sightings" into "A-list" "allure" (it's voted Most Popular in the Las Vegas Nightlife Survey); the "'it'" scene makes for "very selective" entry, but acolytes with "cash to throw around" have no taobt it's "worth it"; N.B. Tao Beach, set inside the hotel's posh pool area, is open every day until sunset for lounging on daybeds or carousing in one of seven private cabanas outfitted with minibars and plasma TVs.

32 degrees   22 | 19 | 17 | $15

Strip | MGM Grand Hotel | 3799 Las Vegas Blvd. S. (Tropicana Ave.) | 702-891-1111

"Icy sticky drinks" keep things cool at this "fab" and fruity fill-'er-upper in the MGM Studio Walk where an "eclectic crowd" sucks down adult-oriented slurpees (and beer) before a meal at adjacent Pearl or Seablue; though some melt over the brightly hued modernist decor, the service isn't so hot: "32 degrees describes the cold shoulder the staff gives customers parched from the desert sun" who are "just trying to get a drink."

NIGHTLIFE

	APPEAL	DECOR	SERVICE	COST

Toby Keith's I Love This Bar & Grill 18 | 18 | 19 | $10
Strip | Harrah's Las Vegas | 3475 Las Vegas Blvd. S. (Flamingo Rd.) | 702-369-5000 | www.harrahs.com

"If you're into line dancing, pickup trucks" and good ol' "country music", Nashville star Keith's "redneck hangout" at Harrah's on the Strip is an all-American place to "mingle" as "C&W bands, flair bartenders" and "drinks served in mason jars" "keep the energy alive"; snobs shrug "tacky", but it's a "down-home" reminder that "Nevada's a red state."

Tommy Rocker's Rock 'n' Roll Topless Club - | - | - | I
W of Strip | 4275 Dean Martin Dr. (bet. Flamingo Rd. & Tropicana Ave.) | 702-261-6688 | www.tommyrocker.com

This 24/7 den of decadence west of the Strip is a dark hideaway where the fireplace and stone walls offer minimal distraction from the buxom displays onstage; the namesake rocker still regularly delivers humor-heavy, Jimmy Buffet-esque sets, but pole dancing's what pleases the crowd.

NEW Torrid - | - | - | M
Strip | Miracle Mile Shops | 3663 Las Vegas Blvd. S. (Harmon Ave.) | 702-731-4858 | www.hawaiiantropiczone.com

An offshoot of the Hawaiian Tropic Zone restaurant inside the Miracle Mile Shops on the Strip, this patio bar showcases notable DJs and fruity cocktails; best of all, unlike most, the cover charge is manageable (free for ladies, $10 for men) and drink prices won't leave you feeling burned.

Triq - | - | - | E
Strip | Miracle Mile Shops | 3667 Las Vegas Blvd. S. (Harmon Ave.) | 702-650-5081

Abracadabra!: this luxe ultralounge in Planet Hollywood's Miracle Mile is part of illusionist Steve Wyrick's entertainment complex; tricked out with an illuminated red bar, on special nights it merges with the adjacent theater to become a four-story DJ domain with the stage transformed into a dance floor and go-go girls conjuring up dazzling late-night action.

Z Tryst 27 | 27 | 22 | $15
Strip | Wynn Las Vegas | 3131 Las Vegas Blvd. S. (bet. Desert Inn & Spring Mountain Rds.) | 702-770-3375 | www.trystlasvegas.com

Tryst the night away in "stunning" style at this swanketorium in the Wynn, where "star-seekers" and "serious hotties" roam "the poshest" of velvet-lined interiors (it's rated No. 1 for Decor in the Las Vegas Nightlife Survey), having "a blast" on the indoor/outdoor dance floor or "cooling off" on the loungey patio alongside an "awesome" 90-ft. waterfall; despite a "brutal" door and "over-the-top" tabs, it'll "impress even the most traveled and jaded clubber."

V Bar 23 | 21 | 21 | $15
Strip | Venetian Hotel | 3355 Las Vegas Blvd. S. (bet. Flamingo & Spring Mountain Rds.) | 702-414-3200 | www.arkvegas.com

"Hard to define", this "classy" lounge in the Venetian "can go from a laid-back" "place to relax" to a "dance party in the blink of an eye"; the "DJ spins a good beat" in a "stylish, dark room", making it a "great way to start off the evening" with "cocktails and conversation" or "wind down after a night of debauchery."

Let your voice be heard – visit ZAGAT.com/vote

NIGHTLIFE

| | APPEAL | DECOR | SERVICE | COST |

ⓩ VooDoo Lounge | 25 | 21 | 20 | $12 |

W of Strip | Rio All-Suite Hotel | 3700 W. Flamingo Rd., 51st fl. (bet. I-15 & Valley View Blvd.) | 702-777-6875 | www.riovegasnights.com

Set in a "nice location" on the 51st floor of the Rio, this "fun and funky lounge" with an "incredible" two-story outdoor patio "overlooking the entire Strip" boasts the "ghostbar view without the wannabes" (or "the wait"); "less hype" makes for an "interesting crowd" that's "a little mellower", at least till they sample the sounds of the "talented house band" or the flair bartenders' "unbelievable cocktails" – "beware the Witch Doctor."

NEW Wasted Space | - | - | - | M |

E of Strip | Hard Rock Hotel | 4455 Paradise Rd. (bet. Flamingo Rd. & Harmon Ave.) | 702-693-4040 | www.hartswastedspace.com

Owned in part by pro biker Carey Hart, this shadowy 'anti club' in the Hard Rock is just as raucous as your average motorcross rally with national touring bands and boldname DJs providing the soundtrack; for those willing to risk life and limb, try the Hart Attack, an eye-watering mix of Jägermeister, Jameson's, Red Bull and cranberry juice sure to get your motor running.

Zuri | ∇ 20 | 20 | 20 | $12 |

Strip | MGM Grand Hotel | 3799 Las Vegas Blvd. S. (Tropicana Ave.) | 702-891-1111 | www.mgmgrandhotel.com

"They call it a lobby bar", but this soothing 24/7 refuge at the MGM Grand "is much more than that" to aficionados of designer drinks poured by pros, specializing in infused vodkas, unusual beers and "great house martinis"; the humidor's well-stocked with stogies, and its 'liquid brunch' concoctions are a lifesaver for nursing a hangover in style.

SHOPPING

Most Popular

1. Nordstrom
2. Neiman Marcus
3. Sephora
4. Tiffany & Co.
5. Saks Fifth Avenue
6. Brooks Bros.
7. Chanel
8. Prada
9. A/X
10. BOSS
11. Z Gallerie*
12. Harry Winston
13. Kiehl's
14. Niketown*
15. Bass Pro Shops
16. Art of Shaving
17. John Varvatos*
18. Kenneth Cole*
19. Manolo Blahnik*
20. Dior

KEY NEWCOMERS

Our editors' take on the year's top arrivals. See page 202 for a full list.

Annie Creamcheese
Barneys New York
Canali
Chloé
Christian Louboutin
Michael Kors

---

* Indicates a tie with store above

Top Quality Ratings

Excludes places with low votes.

29) Brioni
Oscar de la Renta
Harry Winston
Hermès*
Cartier

Chanel
Mikimoto
Baccarat

28) Bulgari
Giorgio Armani

Top Display Ratings

29) Bass Pro Shops
28) Leiber
27) Cartier
Harry Winston
Agent Provocateur

26) Tiffany & Co.
Giorgio Armani
Bulgari
Manolo Blahnik
Oscar de la Renta

Top Service Ratings

27) Oscar de la Renta
26) Art of Shaving
Nordstrom
25) Kiehl's
Fred Leighton

Harry Winston
St. John
Cartier
Brioni
Tiffany & Co.

BY CATEGORY

In order of Quality ranking.

ACCESSORIES
29) Hermès
28) Bottega Veneta
Leiber
27) Montblanc
24) Kate Spade

MENS/WOMENSWEAR
26) Bass Pro Shops
Brooks Bros.
24) Kenneth Cole
23) Lacoste
22) A/X

GIFTS/NOVELTIES
29) Baccarat
25) Ferrari

24) West of Santa Fe
23) Field of Dreams
21) Secret Garden

JEWELRY
29) Harry Winston
Cartier
Mikimoto
28) Bulgari
Chopard

SHOES
28) Manolo Blahnik
27) Bally
Donald J Pliner
Jimmy Choo
25) Taryn Rose

QUALITY | DISPLAY | SERVICE | COST

Shopping

Ratings & Symbols

Quality, Display and **Service** are rated on the Zagat 0 to 30 scale.

Cost reflects our surveyors' estimate of each store's price range:

| I | Inexpensive | E | Expensive |
| M | Moderate | VE | Very Expensive |

- ☽ usually open after 9 PM Ⓜ closed on Monday
- ⊠ closed on Sunday

Agent Provocateur ☽ — 26 | 27 | 23 | E

Strip | Forum Shops at Caesars Palace | 3500 Las Vegas Blvd. S. (Flamingo Rd.) | 702-696-7174 | www.agentprovocateur.com

"If Victoria's Secret had a kinky sister" it would be this "wild", "high-end" lingerie lair in the Forum Shops at Caesars Palace full of "lacy, seductive" bras, briefs and corsets and where the "great" staff "makes buying the sluttiest underwear a lot less embarrassing"; in addition to the *Desperate Housewives*-style unmentionables, there are plenty of "enticing" perfumes, candles and lotions; "it's worth a visit just for the drama" of the "sexy" store alone.

Along Came a Spider — 25 | 24 | 20 | M

Henderson | District at Green Valley Ranch | 2260 Village Walk Dr. (off Green Valley Pkwy.) | 702-341-5437

Moms scouting for "absolutely adorable" childrenswear and "one-of-a-kind gifts" flock to this "eclectic" store in the District in Henderson stocking a "good variety" of "darling" styles from brands like Diesel and Juicy; "you may pay a high price", but rest assured "you'll come home with something exclusive."

Anne Fontaine ☽ — 25 | 19 | 20 | E

Strip | Forum Shops at Caesars Palace | 3500 Las Vegas Blvd. S. (Flamingo Rd.) | 702-733-6205 | www.annefontaine.com

A "niche store" that elevates the "classic" white blouse to high art, this French import in the Forum Shops at Caesars Palace specializes in absolutely "amazing shirts" with some jackets and fragrances rounding out the slim offerings; "it may be the euro's fault", but some find the wares "ridiculously overpriced" so wallet-watchers keep their eyes out for "sales" when you can "clean up on the best styles in town."

NEW Annie Creamcheese ☽ — - | - | - | E

Strip | Palazzo Hotel | 3325 Las Vegas Blvd. S. (Sands Ave.) | 702-452-9600 | www.anniecreamcheese.com

Celebs and fashionistas flock to this high-end boutique at the Palazzo on the Strip specializing in vintage couture womenswear from the likes of Pucci, Diane von Furstenberg and Lanvin plus jewelry and accessories from a bevy of up-and-coming designers; its chic setup features pink walls, groovy tunes and a parachute-style ceiling made of colorful Parisian silks.

SHOPPING

| | QUALITY | DISPLAY | SERVICE | COST |

NEW Anya Hindmarch ●   - | - | - | E
Strip | Palazzo Hotel | 3325 Las Vegas Blvd. S. (Sands Ave.) | 702-566-8900 | www.anyahindmarch.com

Bags, bags and more bags (plus some women's shoes and accessories) are the raison d'être of this British leather specialist in the Palazzo on the Strip showcasing timeless pieces big on details like hidden compartments and geometric clasps; service is refreshingly unobtrusive, while bright walls and a black-and-white-tiled floor create a spare, uncluttered setting that doesn't detract from the goods.

Z Art of Shaving, The   27 | 24 | 26 | M
Strip | Fashion Show Mall | 3200 Las Vegas Blvd. S. (Spring Mountain Rd.) | 702-733-9509
Strip | Mandalay Place | 3930 Las Vegas Blvd. S. (Mandalay Bay Rd.) | 702-632-9356 ●
www.theartofshaving.com

"High-end" grooming gear and potions that "bring enjoyment to an otherwise dull morning" make these "wonderful" shops on the Strip a "frivolous" favorite for "gentlemen"; an "impeccable" level of service means there's "no pressure to buy" though some patrons can't help but indulge in a "hot towel shave" or haircut on the premises (Mandalay Place only) – what better way to "pamper yourself for an hour"?

a. testoni ●   ▽ 24 | 24 | 21 | VE
Strip | Forum Shops at Caesars Palace | 3500 Las Vegas Blvd. S. (Flamingo Rd.) | 702-735-7732 | www.testoni.com

"Amazing quality" is invested in the "wonderful" Italian leather goods at this "high-end" cobbler in the Forum Shops at Caesars Palace offering "conservative" footwear for men and women; prices are extremely high, but a "warm staff" and a sleek, "beautiful setting" make it an appealing place to unload some winnings.

Attic, The ☒   20 | 20 | 19 | M
Downtown | 1018 S. Main St. (bet. Boulder & Coolidge Aves.) | 702-388-4088 | www.theatticlasvegas.com

This mammoth vintage emporium Downtown boasts an "outstanding selection" of "cool" clothes from the 1940s–70s plus their own line of reproduction merchandise, furniture and lighting all "artfully displayed" in a "funky" atmosphere with cacophonous caged parrots; some find it "overpriced", but it's a "fun place to shop" where "you can find the best stuff" as long as you're willing to dig.

A/X Armani Exchange ●   22 | 20 | 19 | M
NEW **S of Strip** | Town Square | 6605 Las Vegas Blvd. S. (bet. I-215 & Sunset Rd.) | 702-263-3393
Strip | Forum Shops at Caesars Palace | 3500 Las Vegas Blvd. S. (Flamingo Rd.) | 702-733-1666
www.armaniexchange.com

"A mix of stylish and functional" clothes for the "under-30" set defines these "hip" chain outposts in the Forum Shops at Caesars Palace and Town Square offering "more affordable" (though still moderately "expensive") men's and women's lines from designer Giorgio Armani; as long as you can deal with a little "attitude from salespeople", they make a solid option for "fab" pieces "for going out on the town or if you've left anything at home."

Let your voice be heard – visit ZAGAT.com/vote

SHOPPING

	QUALITY	DISPLAY	SERVICE	COST

Baccarat ⓓ   29 | 26 | 24 | VE

Strip | Forum Shops at Caesars Palace | 3500 Las Vegas Blvd. S. (Flamingo Rd.) | 702-693-6877 | www.baccarat.fr

"Admire the crystal art form" at this "teeny" boutique in the Forum Shops at Caesars Palace touting "extraordinary" examples of imported French stemware, vases and tabletop knickknacks that connoisseurs claim are among "the most beautiful in the world"; multilingual personnel are available should you need assistance, and though it's "hardly affordable for the average person", it's "worth the time to go in", even if it's just to browse.

Bally of Switzerland   27 | 22 | 21 | VE

Strip | Fashion Show Mall | 3200 Las Vegas Blvd. S. (Spring Mountain Rd.) | 702-737-1968 | www.bally.com

"Luxurious leather shoes and bags" as well as "quality" keychains and wallets and a selection of clothing are in generous supply at this Eurochic "classic" for men and women in the Fashion Show Mall on the Strip; though some shoppers are daunted by "expensive" prices, others insist they offer "good value" since the gear comes in "classic styles" and "lasts for years."

NEW Barneys New York ⓓ   26 | 25 | 20 | VE

Strip | Palazzo Hotel | 3325 Las Vegas Blvd. S. (Sands Ave.) | 702-629-4200 | www.barneys.com

Those with "money to burn" live it up at this new Palazzo branch of the "luxury mecca" known for "up-to-the-minute styles" from "the hippest" "established and new designers"; "only the truly skinny" can fit into the "size-two" clothing, but the "fabulous shoes, accessories" and cosmetics "provide the flourish for any wardrobe", and the "artfully displayed" home furnishings make it "wonderful for browsing", even if some have encountered "snooty" staff.

☒ Bass Pro Shops ⓓ   26 | 29 | 23 | M

S of Strip | 8200 Dean Martin Dr. (Blue Diamond Rd.) | 702-730-5200 | www.basspro.com

"If you want to catch it, kill it or grill it", "sportsmen" swear by this "outdoor" megastore south of the Strip that offers a "nice selection" of "everything you could imagine" for hunting, camping and golfing as well as full lines of outerwear that will make you "the envy of others" in inclement weather; a "friendly staff" seems to "have never met a question it didn't like" and prices are reasonable, so the only drawback is that it's so "huge" you "may need a map and a compass to get around."

NEW Bauman Rare Books ⓓ   - | - | - | VE

Strip | Palazzo Hotel | 3325 Las Vegas Blvd. S. (Sands Ave.) | 702-948-1617 | www.baumanrarebooks.com

If you're looking for a signed, limited first edition of Hemingway's *A Farewell to Arms* complete with a scarce original slipcase, it can be yours – for a mere $20,000 – at this Vegas-based offshoot of a New York City rare-books dealer in the Palazzo on the Strip; appropriately done up in dark woods, it has the hushed atmosphere of a library (and a staff to match); it's also open for lingering till midnight on weekends.

SHOPPING

	QUALITY	DISPLAY	SERVICE	COST

Bonanza Gifts ⦿ — 16 | 19 | 18 | I
Strip | 2440 Las Vegas Blvd. S. (Sahara Ave.) | 702-385-7359 | www.worldslargestgiftshop.com

"The holy grail of trinket stores", this souvenir shop on the Strip is the ultimate source for Vegas "kitsch" with a "mind-boggling" array of T-shirts, magnets, keychains, gaming items, gag gifts and more "fuzzy dice" than you'll know what to do with; "the selection is endless" and prices are cheap, meaning it's a "must-see" for visitors who'll likely "shop to [their] heart's content" to find something for the "folks back home."

BOSS Hugo Boss ⦿ — 25 | 22 | 21 | E
Strip | Forum Shops at Caesars Palace | 3500 Las Vegas Blvd. S. (Flamingo Rd.) | 702-696-9444 | www.hugoboss.com

"Classic clothing" fit for a "classic man" defines the selection at this "attractive" menswear emporium at the Forum Shops at Caesars Palace offering jeans, shirts, suits and sport coats from "the legendary German design house"; in spite of "extravagant prices", it's a "pleasant experience", thanks to "helpful employees" who provide hands-on assistance.

Bottega Veneta ⦿ — 28 | 25 | 23 | VE
NEW Strip | Palazzo Hotel | 3325 Las Vegas Blvd. S. (Sands Ave.) | 702-369-0747
Strip | Bellagio Hotel | 3600 Las Vegas Blvd. S. (Flamingo Rd.) | 702-369-2944
www.bottegaveneta.com

Fashionistas fawn over the "drop-dead" "gorgeous" leather goods at these "stylish" boutiques at the Bellagio and the Palazzo on the Strip with an "amazing array of "fine" Italian luggage and accessories as well as some of "the best bags on the planet"; the staff is "warm", but as for prices – "if you have to ask" chances are "you can't afford them."

☑ Brioni ⦿ — 29 | 26 | 25 | VE
Strip | Wynn Las Vegas | 3131 Las Vegas Blvd. S. (bet. Desert Inn & Spring Mountain Rds.) | 702-770-3440 | www.brioni.com

"Elegant tailoring" is the hallmark of this "excellent" Italian retailer in the Wynn (rated No. 1 for Quality in the Las Vegas Survey) offering "custom-made" suits for "men of distinction" and a "fine" line of ready-to-wear items for women; it's a "beautiful store" with lots of woodwork and high ceilings making shopping here "a pleasure", so long as you're not fazed by the "stratospheric prices."

Brooks Brothers ⦿ — 26 | 23 | 24 | E
Strip | Forum Shops at Caesars Palace | 3500 Las Vegas Blvd. S. (Flamingo Rd.) | 702-369-0705 | 800-274-1815 | www.brooksbrothers.com

"A perennial favorite" for "preppy" types, this "conservative" "staple" at the Forum Shops at Caesars Palace "can't be beat" for "classically tailored" attire for both men and women – ranging from suits to "business casual" wear – that "lasts for decades" and "never looks dated"; it's "dependable" all around, from the "helpful staff" to the prices that, while "high", are entirely "fair", given that "they don't skimp on quality."

Buffalo Exchange — 19 | 15 | 16 | I
E of Strip | Pioneer Plaza | 4110 S. Maryland Pkwy. (Flamingo Rd.) | 702-791-3960 | 866-235-8255 | www.buffaloexchange.com

"Some of the finds can be wild" at this strip-mall secondhand shop east of the Strip where customers trade in their used clothing for cash

Let your voice be heard – visit ZAGAT.com/vote   117

SHOPPING

| | QUALITY | DISPLAY | SERVICE | COST |

or credit, making for an ever-changing selection that yields some "great bargains" "if you're willing to go through the racks"; it appeals mostly to "students" and "thirtysomething" hipsters who hail the "mint" quality selection; N.B. those with a sharp eye should keep a lookout for overstock available from the likes of America Apparel.

Bulgari ●   28 | 26 | 24 | VE
Strip | Forum Shops at Caesars Palace | 3500 Las Vegas Blvd. S. (Flamingo Rd.) | 702-734-2001 | www.bulgari.com

"The sparkle of these baubles will knock you over" (as will the hefty prices) at this jewel box of a store in the Forum Shops at Caesars Palace where a "warm, professional" staff proffers "wonderful" Italian gold and gemstone jewelry as well as a "nice selection" of leather goods and fragrances; given that the "products last a lifetime", the only complaint is that "Las Vegas could use another" of these "wonderful" shops.

NEW Burberry ●   27 | 23 | 22 | VE
Strip | Palazzo Hotel | 3325 Las Vegas Blvd. S. (Sands Ave.) | 702-382-1911 | www.burberry.com

"A Burberry trench coat is your friend for life" aver admirers of this "timeless" British brand that's "world-famous" for its "signature plaid merchandise", which includes "conservatively cut, well-made clothing and accessories" ("beautiful scarves") as well as a more "contemporary" and "upscale Prorsum line"; set in the new Palazzo, the "gorgeous displays" take the edge off occasionally "snooty service", and while prices are "high", know that your purchase "will never go out of style."

NEW Canali ●   - | - | - | VE
Strip | Palazzo Hotel | 3325 Las Vegas Blvd. S. (Sands Ave.) | 702-607-7777 | www.canali.it

Everything from classic suits to modern separates – plus shoes and accessories – are showcased at this marble-floored Italian menswear specialist at the Palazzo on the Strip; service is smooth, and though the pieces fit like a glove, a master tailor is also on-hand for alterations.

Z Cartier ●   29 | 27 | 25 | VE
Strip | Wynn Las Vegas | 3131 Las Vegas Blvd. S. (bet. Desert Inn & Spring Mountain Rds.) | 702-696-0146 | 800-227-8437
Strip | Appian Way Shops at Caesars Palace | 3570 Las Vegas Blvd. S. (Flamingo Rd.) | 702-733-6652
www.cartier.com

"Who cares about little blue boxes when you can have red ones?" muse admirers of this "classic" jeweler with outposts in the Appian Way Shops and the Wynn offering "beautifully designed" baubles and "stunning" accessories that are the stuff of "every girls' dream"; it's "unaffordable for the average person" (they "don't even display prices"), but a "friendly" staff means there's no reason you can't still "window shop."

NEW Catherine Malandrino ●   ▽ 26 | 24 | 19 | VE
Strip | Palazzo Hotel | 3325 Las Vegas Blvd. S. (Sands Ave.) | 702-369-7300 | www.catherinemalandrino.com

"Delivering flattering [styles] season after season", this French designer with a new Palazzo outpost offers "flirty, feminine clothing" that's been seen on the likes of Demi Moore; loyalists "love the cut-out designs that have become her signature", but less-than-model-thin

SHOPPING

| | QUALITY | DISPLAY | SERVICE | COST |

mavens say the "fabulous" frocks can "sometimes look more beautiful on the rack" – and are always "expensive."

Chanel ● | 29 | 26 | 24 | VE |
Strip | Wynn Las Vegas | 3131 Las Vegas Blvd. S. (bet. Desert Inn & Spring Mountain Rds.) | 702-765-5055
Strip | Bellagio Hotel | 3600 Las Vegas Blvd. S. (Flamingo Rd.) | 702-765-5505
www.chanel.com

"You can't go wrong" at these "classic" havens of haute couture at the Bellagio and the Wynn where once you get past the "standoffish" sales help you'll be enticed by "gorgeous" quilted bags and "collectable" accessories as well as "entrance-making ensembles" that are the picture of "elegance"; it's all "displayed so brilliantly" that even if the "expensive" prices are "out of your range", it's still a great place to "dream."

CH Carolina Herrera ● | 27 | 24 | 21 | VE |
Strip | Forum Shops at Caesars Palace | 3500 Las Vegas Blvd. S. (Flamingo Rd.) | 702-894-5242 | www.carolinaherrera.com

"Elegance at its finest" attest admirers who flock to the Venezuelan legend's boutique – perhaps the "prettiest" in the Forum Shops at Caesars – to peruse the "large selection" of womenswear, menswear and accessories from the designer's luxury-for-less (but still expensive) spin-off line; CH's trademark white blouses are all in evidence, along with logo-heavy handbags and chunky jewelry, nevertheless, a handful sigh "wish they carried her formalwear" and bridal collection.

NEW Chloé ● | - | - | - | VE |
Strip | Palazzo Hotel | 3325 Las Vegas Blvd. S. (Sands Ave.) | 702-266-8122 | www.chloe.com

Inside the Palazzo dwells this youthful French label's first Vegas outpost showcasing separates, shoes and handbags for the moneyed boho set; the wares are set in wood-framed displays and also modeled by staffers who walk softly and carry a big sense of style.

Chopard ● | 28 | 25 | 22 | VE |
Strip | Forum Shops at Caesars Palace | 3500 Las Vegas Blvd. S. (Flamingo Rd.) | 702-862-4440 | www.chopard.com

It's "all diamonds" all the time at this jeweler in the Forum Shops at Caesars where timepieces dazzle as much as the big sparklers and signature pieces featuring 'floating' gemstones; with such fine merch and a celebrity clientele, "haute" prices should come as no surprise.

NEW Christian Louboutin ● | - | - | - | VE |
Strip | Palazzo Hotel | 3325 Las Vegas Blvd. S. (Sands Ave.) | 702-818-1650 | www.christianlouboutin.com

Red is the word at this high-end boutique at the Palazzo on the Strip where the crimson displays, walls and carpet match the signature soles of this much-loved French brand of sexy shoes; the elegant space has a quiet feel, all the better for peaceful indulgences by footwear fanatics.

C Level | - | - | - | E |
NW | Fashion Village at Boca Park | 750 S. Rampart Blvd. (Charleston Blvd.) | 702-933-6867 | www.clevel-lv.com

Savvy shoppers seek out this loungey bi-level boutique in the Northwest's Fashion Village at Boca Park, which stocks a well-edited collection of indie and boldface designer clothing for women – like

Let your voice be heard – visit ZAGAT.com/vote

SHOPPING

wares from Catherine Malandrino, LAMB and Kooba - and plenty of denim and T-shirts for men; the cutting-edge wares don't come cheap, but it's chock-full of original pieces you won't see elsewhere; N.B. a second location closer to the Strip is reportedly in the works.

De Beers ❷   26 | 24 | 24 | E

Strip | Forum Shops at Caesars Palace | 3500 Las Vegas Blvd. S. (Flamingo Rd.) | 702-650-9559 | www.debeers.com

Whether you're searching for a tennis bracelet or wedding band, this is "one of the best places to go" declare diamond devotees who "love the idea of buying straight from the manufacturer" at this outpost in the Forum Shops at Caesars Palace; raised counters permit easy viewing, and the pieces are arranged by carat size, which range in price from up in the millions to more earth-bound offerings in the hundreds of dollars.

NEW Diane von Furstenberg ❷   24 | 21 | 19 | E

Strip | Palazzo Hotel | 3325 Las Vegas Blvd. S. (Sands Ave.) | 702-818-2294 | www.dvf.com

"She knows how to make a woman feel sexy" aver acolytes of this designer whose "classic wrap dresses" and other "flattering" and "functional" frocks are on offer at this outpost in the Palazzo hotel; while a few believe the brand has "truly lost its way", most "grown-ups and professional" types jump on the opportunity to purchase "timeless pieces" at prices that are "pretty impressive compared to the competition."

Dior ❷   27 | 25 | 21 | VE

Strip | Wynn Las Vegas | 3131 Las Vegas Blvd. S. (bet. Desert Inn & Spring Mountain Rds.) | 702-770-7000
Strip | Forum Shops at Caesars Palace | 3500 Las Vegas Blvd. S. (Flamingo Rd.) | 702-737-9777
Strip | Bellagio Hotel | 3600 Las Vegas Blvd. S. (Flamingo Rd.) | 702-731-1334
www.dior.com

John Galliano's "opulent", "edgy" designs woo women with "small bodies and big budgets" to these posh boutiques where the "fantastic selection" of "top-quality" apparel and "handbags to die for" are made all the more alluring by the "funky" displays; "despite the appearance of being snobby", "pretty salespeople" are "quick to assist" and "always ready to make suggestions", whether you're shopping for yourself or your "girlfriend"; N.B. menswear is available at the Wynn branch.

Dolce & Gabbana ❷   25 | 24 | 20 | VE

Strip | Forum Shops at Caesars Palace | 3500 Las Vegas Blvd. S. (Flamingo Rd.) | 702-892-0880 | www.dolcegabbana.it

Perhaps a "bit too 'out there' for the average person", "trendsetters" still treasure the sexy, quintessentially "Vegas" duds from Domenico Dolce and Stefano Gabbana at this flashy outpost in the Forum Shops at Caesars Palace; clothing is "displayed in an easy-to-find format", so sticker shock proves to be the only deterrent; N.B. insiders insist you visit their store in the Las Vegas Premium Outlets for great deals.

Donald J Pliner ❷   27 | 24 | 22 | E

Strip | Forum Shops at Caesars Palace | 3500 Las Vegas Blvd. S. (Flamingo Rd.) | 702-796-0900 | www.donaldjpliner.com

"Nothing could be finer than to have your feet in Pliner" chorus fans of this "quality" cobbler in the Forum Shops with "funky" men's and

SHOPPING

| | QUALITY | DISPLAY | SERVICE | COST |

women's shoes as well as leather wear and seasonal jackets; "you can get some real finds" if your "timing" is right, otherwise the "friendly staff" helps soften the blow of usually "unfriendly prices."

Escada ◐ — 27 | 23 | 23 | VE
Strip | Forum Shops at Caesars Palace | 3500 Las Vegas Blvd. S. (Flamingo Rd.) | 702-791-2300 | www.escada.com

"Adventurous" couture gowns designed "with a real woman's figure" in mind lure sexy socialite types to this airy boutique in the Forum Shops at Caesars Palace; a few find the line "less relevant than it was 10 years ago", but connoisseurs confess they "always enjoy" shopping here, though they wish the "sales clerks" lived up to the products and prices.

FAO Schwarz ◐ — - | - | - | M
Strip | Forum Shops at Caesars Palace | 3500 Las Vegas Blvd. S. (Flamingo Rd.) | 702-796-6500 | www.fao.com

Toys come to life at this 55,000-sq.-ft., three-floor Strip outpost of the specialty retail chain, where a gigantic trojan horse and a live toy soldier guard the entrance, customers can play a huge floor piano with their feet and life-size stuffed animals abound; located in the Forum Shops at Caesars, it offers lots of branded merchandise (i.e. Harry Potter, Barbie) and more movie collectibles than one can imagine.

Fendi ◐ — 27 | 23 | 23 | VE
NEW **Strip** | Palazzo Hotel | 3325 Las Vegas Blvd. S. (Sands Ave.) | 702-369-0587
Strip | Forum Shops at Caesars Palace | 3500 Las Vegas Blvd. S. (Flamingo Rd.) | 702-732-9040
Strip | Bellagio Hotel | 3600 Las Vegas Blvd. S. (Flamingo Rd.) | 702-732-7766
www.fendi.com

"The home of the baguette and the spy bag – need you say more?" ask admirers of this venerable Italian brand peddling "the purse of choice for many ladies" as well as fabulous furs, luxe leather accessories and ready-to-wear garments designed by Karl Lagerfeld; the "beautiful" settings and attentive (if "slightly snooty") service may just encourage you to "scrape up the courage" and go ahead and "max out a charge card."

Ferrari Store ◐ — 25 | 23 | 19 | M
Strip | Wynn Las Vegas | 3131 Las Vegas Blvd. S. (bet. Desert Inn & Spring Mountain Rds.) | 702-770-7000 | www.wynnlasvegas.com

Unless you're "über-rich", you may want to "skip the car and get a keychain" at this "toy store" for "husbands" at the Wynn featuring memorabilia all in the Italian automotive brand's signature red; next door is a "gorgeous" Ferrari-Maserati showroom where "mere peasants can gawk" at the "phenomenally cool" vehicles for a $10 cover charge.

Field of Dreams ◐ — 23 | 22 | 19 | E
Strip | Forum Shops at Caesars Palace | 3500 Las Vegas Blvd. S. (Flamingo Rd.) | 702-792-8233
Strip | Smith & Wollensky | 3767 Las Vegas Blvd. S. (Tropicana Ave.) | 702-740-5401
W of Strip | Rio All-Suite Hotel | 3700 W. Flamingo Rd. (bet. I-15 & Valley View Blvd.) | 702-221-9144
www.fieldofdreams.com

Enthusiasts attest these chain outposts "crowded" full of autographed helmets, photographs, jerseys and equipment are the "perfect" places

SHOPPING

| | QUALITY | DISPLAY | SERVICE | COST |

to find "gifts" for "sports fans" and celeb-obsessed types "on your shopping list"; a "knowledgeable staff" will help guide you through the "great selection", and though some collectors claim they're "overpriced" and suggest you "check eBay" first, these spots are still worth a "browse"; as an added bonus, "there's often a signing going on", so check the website for the scheduled lineup.

Fred Leighton ☻   28 | 25 | 25 | VE
Strip | Bellagio Hotel | 3600 Las Vegas Blvd. S. (Flamingo Rd.) | 702-693-7050 | www.fredleighton.com

"Serious jewelry for those who want to impress the 'little people'" is in store for shoppers at this Bellagio boutique stocking a "beautiful array" of "awestriking vintage gems" and "to-die-for" "heirloom" jewels and reproductions that "leave everyone wishing they could walk the red carpet" in them; the "lovely" shop really "packs it in", meaning the whole experience feels a bit "like going through your grandmother's jewelry box – that is, if your grandmother had owned emeralds and rubies."

Giorgio Armani ☻   28 | 26 | 24 | VE
Strip | Bellagio Hotel | 3600 Las Vegas Blvd. S. (Flamingo Rd.) | 702-893-8327 | www.giorgioarmani.com

There's "nothing more classy" than the timeless, tailored suits and separates (like tuxes for him and "the best little dresses" for her) at the Italian designer's sleek, serene outpost in the Bellagio; an "experienced staff" helps novices navigate their way through the racks while additional special touches like "bottled water presented on a silver tray" help justify the "beyond very expensive" prices.

H&M ☻   - | - | - | I
NEW **S of Strip** | Town Square | 6605 Las Vegas Blvd. S. (bet. I-215 & Sunset Rd.) | 702-260-1481
Strip | Miracle Mile Shops | 3663 Las Vegas Blvd. S. (Harmon Ave.) | 702-369-1195
www.hm.com

These all-white outposts of the Swedish department store chain in the Miracle Mile Shops at Planet Hollywood and Town Square are a bargain-hunter's paradise filled with of-the-moment men's and women's fashions at low prices; expect neat displays (at least until the hordes descend) and one-off lines from top designers like Comme des Garçons.

☒ Harry Winston ☻   29 | 27 | 25 | VE
Strip | Forum Shops at Caesars Palace | 3500 Las Vegas Blvd. S. (Flamingo Rd.) | 702-933-7370 | www.harrywinston.com

"Wow" is the "only word to describe" the "large" and stratospherically priced jewels at this icon favored by "stars" in the Forum Shops at Caesars; some detractors dis the glass-walled decor ("who wants to shop in a fishbowl?"), while others are so mesmerized by "the good stuff" that they don't seem to mind.

☒ Hermès ☻   29 | 26 | 24 | VE
Strip | Bellagio Hotel | 3600 Las Vegas Blvd. S. (Flamingo Rd.) | 702-893-8900 | www.hermes.com

You don't need a "trip to Paris" to savor "French luxury at its best" claim connoisseurs of this "exclusive" Bellagio boutique that "packs a punch" with an "incredible selection of the best the brand has to of-

SHOPPING

| | QUALITY | DISPLAY | SERVICE | COST |

fer", from "breathtakingly beautiful scarves" and "sharp silk ties" to "divine" leather wallets and purses (however, "like everywhere else, don't expect to find a Birkin or Kelly bag here"); though a few feel snubbed by "rude" service, others insist a sip of "champagne on their balcony overlooking the fountains" should soften the sting of any "attitude" from the staff (as well as the "expensive" prices).

Intermix — — — E

Strip | Forum Shops at Caesars Palace | 3500 Las Vegas Blvd. S. (Flamingo Rd.) | 702-731-1922 | www.intermixonline.com

It doesn't take long to drop some major bucks at this NYC import in the Forum Shops at Caesars Palace featuring an incredible array of flirty outfits by the likes of Chloé, LaROK, Theory and Robert Rodriguez; the sleek, streamlined racks also feature loads of top-brand designer jeans and piles of purses and accessories all neatly organized by color and designer for easy perusal.

Jessica McClintock 22 20 21 M

Strip | Fashion Show Mall | 3200 Las Vegas Blvd. S. (Spring Mountain Rd.) | 702-733-4003 | www.jessicamcclintock.com

For "fancy" "last-minute" femme-finds "for a night on the town", this "youthful" standby in the Fashion Show Mall "is a sure bet" for all kinds of "cocktail dresses and gowns" (and even bridal wear) that "may not be the best quality, but is good enough for a wear-and-toss"; "bargains" abound in the English garden–style space, so take advantage of the "great service" and enlist an employee to help you choose.

Jimmy Choo ● 27 24 21 VE

NEW **Strip** | Palazzo Hotel | 3327 Las Vegas Blvd. S. (Sands Ave.) | 702-733-1802

Strip | Forum Shops at Caesars Palace | 3500 Las Vegas Blvd. S. (Flamingo Rd.) | 702-691-2097

www.jimmychoo.com

"Oh god" swoon supporters of the "sexy" shoes and "fabulous" boots and accessories at these shrines to stilettos on the Strip where the "outrageously priced" wares leave some wishing they'd "done better at the craps table"; views vary on the service ("lethargic" vs. "willing to assist") while the boudoir-style design creates the ultimate environment to "try on"; it's hard to leave without "multiple bags"; N.B. the Grand Canal Shoppes branch recently relocated to the Palazzo.

Johnston & Murphy 26 22 23 M

Strip | Fashion Show Mall | 3200 Las Vegas Blvd. S. (Spring Mountain Rd.) | 702-737-0114 | www.johnstonmurphy.com

"Quality" kicks and leather jackets and luggage "to die for" characterize this "conservative" men's shop in the Fashion Show Mall tended to by a "knowledgeable staff"; "prices are better than most", and while admirers assure the shoes "will last", re-soling is also available through the manufacturer; N.B. they now offer footwear and handbags for women as well.

John Varvatos ● 25 22 21 VE

Strip | Forum Shops at Caesars Palace | 3500 Las Vegas Blvd. S. (Flamingo Rd.) | 702-939-0922 | www.johnvarvatos.com

"Too cool for school" duds (and sales staff) define this "fashionable" men's store in the Forum Shops at Caesars offering a "great selection"

SHOPPING

<small>QUALITY | DISPLAY | SERVICE | COST</small>

of understated sportswear and suits so appealing you'll see "ladies dragging their gents in there"; a few find it "overpriced", though it's worth the splurge for those who don't "have these kinds of options at home."

Juicy Couture ◐ — 23 | 23 | 20 | E

NEW **S of Strip** | Town Square | 6605 Las Vegas Blvd. S. (bet. I-215 & Sunset Rd.) | 702-269-3199
Strip | Forum Shops at Caesars Palace | 3500 Las Vegas Blvd. S. (Flamingo Rd.) | 702-365-5600
www.juicycouture.com

An endless array of "teenybopper-esque" velour sweatsuits in "lollipop colors" await at these "cute" candy-colored boutiques in the Forum Shops at Caesars Palace and at Town Square where "you can't go wrong" with the "comfortable" duds and "funky" bags and accessories and "they even have matching outfits for your dog"; the "friendly staff" keeps the mood upbeat and "happy" in spite of prices that some find "expensive."

Kate Spade ◐ — 24 | 23 | 21 | E

Strip | Forum Shops at Caesars Palace | 3500 Las Vegas Blvd. S. (Flamingo Rd.) | 702-515-6075 | www.katespade.com

Accessories addicts are charmed by the "stylish purses" and "trendy shoes" at this "lovely" locale in the Forum Shops at Caesars Palace where "nicely made totes", clothing, jewelry and hand-engraved stationery round out the offerings from the quirky NYC designer; a "perky staff makes you feel welcome" – "a plus when you are spending over $300 on a handbag."

Kenneth Cole ◐ — 24 | 22 | 20 | M

Strip | Grand Canal Shoppes | 3377 Las Vegas Blvd. S. (bet. Flamingo & Spring Mountain Rds.) | 702-836-1916 | www.kennethcole.com

"Hip" yet "wearable" clothes and "fantastic" shoes made from "quality leathers" are the hallmarks of this "trendy" shop on the Strip where both men and women "can always find something stylish", "as long as you're 25 and thin"; "service runs anywhere from hot to cold", but reviewers report that "once you get past that, you can find some great pieces" that are a "good value" too.

Kiehl's ◐ — 27 | 24 | 25 | M

Strip | Forum Shops at Caesars Palace | 3500 Las Vegas Blvd. S. (Flamingo Rd.) | 702-784-0025 | www.kiehls.com

Loads of "free samples" proffered by "extremely knowledgeable" employees make this "terrific" old-fashioned toiletries import in the Forum Shops at Caesars Palace a "favorite" place to stock up on everything you need to "treat your skin" right, from "amazing lip balm" to scrubs, sunscreens and moisturizers (and psst – "guys, the shaving cream is terrific!"); yes, "it's pricey", but with "so much to offer", supporters swear it's totally "worth it."

Lacoste — 23 | 20 | 20 | M

Strip | Fashion Show Mall | 3200 Las Vegas Blvd. S. (Spring Mountain Rd.) | 702-796-6676
Strip | Forum Shops at Caesars Palace | 3500 Las Vegas Blvd. S. (Flamingo Rd.) | 702-791-7616 ◐
www.lacoste.com

"Nostalgia reigns" at these "preppy" purveyors of "classic" polos on the Strip where the "bright-colored" men's and women's sportswear

SHOPPING

| | QUALITY | DISPLAY | SERVICE | COST |

stands in contrast to the airy, white stores staffed with energetic employees; "the quality is there" and you'll surely "wear the clothes for a long time", but some find fault with prices that are "not cheap" – "is the alligator really that expensive to sew on?"

La Perla ● 27 | 24 | 22 | VE

Strip | Forum Shops at Caesars Palace | 3500 Las Vegas Blvd. S. (Flamingo Rd.) | 702-732-9820 | www.laperla.com

"Luxurious" lingerie lures fans to this "pearl" in the Forum Shops at Caesars Palace proffering "the prettiest undies around" as well as other "classy, not trashy" unmentionables ranging from "elegant" camis and robes to more "risqué" bustiers and garter belts; it's "a bit overpriced", but gratified gift-givers maintain "when you see your lady" in these "exquisite" designs, "how much you paid won't be at the top of your mind"; P.S. there's also a "nice sitting area" where "ladies can model their potential purchases."

Las Vegas Golf & Tennis 25 | 23 | 23 | M

E of Strip | 4211 Paradise Rd. (bet. Flamingo Rd. & Harmon Ave.) | 702-892-9999

Henderson | 140 S. Green Valley Pkwy. (Paseo Verde Pkwy.) | 702-878-4653 www.saintandrewsgolfshop.com

These area mainstays are "favorites" for stocking up on "the latest and greatest" gear and activewear for golfers and tennis enthusiasts all "at a decent price" (keep an eye out for "great sales" too); "there's never a problem finding what you want" thanks to "helpful" employees who also offer full club repair and racquet stringing.

Las Vegas Premium Outlets - | - | - | M

W Side | 875 S. Grand Central Pkwy. (Bonneville St.) | 702-474-7500 | www.premiumoutlets.com

An unending parade of tourists descends on this outdoor West Side outlet center where deals abound on over 120 high-end brands like Coach, Dolce & Gabbana, Kate Spade and Ted Baker; located a mere five minutes from the Strip, it's easily accessible by taxi, trolley or bus.

Leiber ● 28 | 28 | 25 | VE
(fka Judith Leiber)

Strip | Forum Shops at Caesars Palace | 3500 Las Vegas Blvd. S. (Flamingo Rd.) | 702-792-0661 | www.judithleiber.com

Loyalists liken the "gorgeous" animal-shaped, crystal-encrusted evening bags to "works of art" at this "museum"-like boutique in the Forum Shops where the "glittery" "treasures" are worth "gazing at in awe", even if you can't afford to "splurge" on one; sure they're "impractical", but fans still fawn – "if I could have one evening bag for a lifetime, this would be it."

Manolo Blahnik ● 28 | 26 | 24 | VE

Strip | Wynn Las Vegas | 3131 Las Vegas Blvd. S. (bet. Desert Inn & Spring Mountain Rds.) | 702-770-3477 | www.manoloblahnik.com

"Carrie Bradshaw had it right – these shoes are to die for" declare "obsessed" fans who "love love love" this "treasure trove" in the Wynn loaded with "tons" of "gorgeous" stilettos, flats and boots that are "very much worth" the exorbitant prices; the "phenomenal" staff and luxurious setting come together to create a "tremendous shopping experience"; "however the top of the line is defined, this is above it."

Let your voice be heard – visit ZAGAT.com/vote

SHOPPING

| | QUALITY | DISPLAY | SERVICE | COST |

Marc Jacobs ⓥ 27 | 25 | 22 | VE
Strip | Forum Shops at Caesars Palace | 3500 Las Vegas Blvd. S. (Flamingo Rd.) | 702-369-2007 | www.marcjacobs.com

"NYC" fashionistas proclaim Marc Jacobs' tiny eponymous boutique in the Forum Shops "the place to go" for "great handbags" as well as men's and women's basics with a cool, casual feel; the "staff is eager to help", though a disappointed few say the "limited" selection leaves them wondering if they may be "better off going to a department store" instead.

NEW Michael Kors Collection ⓥ - | - | - | E
Strip | Palazzo Hotel | 3325 Las Vegas Blvd. S. (Sands Ave.) | 702-731-2510 | www.michaelkors.com

Runway shows looping on flat-screen TVs create a high-energy atmosphere at this bright, white boutique at the Palazzo on the Strip showcasing the New York designer's chic, but understated, separates, shoes and bags; although everything is primly displayed on floating shelves and behind metal-chain curtains, high foot traffic and a sizable staff ensure the air is always buzzing.

Mikimoto ⓥ 29 | 26 | 25 | VE
Strip | Grand Canal Shoppes | 3377 Las Vegas Blvd. S. (bet. Flamingo & Spring Mountain Rds.) | 702-414-3900 | www.mikimotoamerica.com

"Truly cultured" types tout the "exquisite pearls of every shape and color" at this "superb quality" boutique in the Grand Canal Shoppes at the Venetian where the "spectacular" strands are displayed in elegant pear wood cases; the "friendly staff" is happy to "spend time with you", even if "steep prices" mean all you can afford to do is "look and dream."

Montblanc ⓥ 27 | 25 | 23 | VE
NEW Strip | Palazzo Hotel | 3325 Las Vegas Blvd. S. (Sands Ave.) | 702-696-0185
Strip | Forum Shops at Caesars Palace | 3500 Las Vegas Blvd. S. (Flamingo Rd.) | 702-732-0569
www.montblanc.com

"A fine array" of "exceptional writing implements" fit for "serious professionals" fill these "top-brand" boutiques in the Forum Shops and the Palazzo with watches and leather goods among other "classy" offerings; "connoisseurs" "can't say enough about the caliber of sales people" who go "above and beyond" to "satisfy" customers, ensuring a "great shopping experience" for all.

Nanette Lepore ⓥ 26 | 24 | 23 | E
Strip | Forum Shops at Caesars Palace | 3500 Las Vegas Blvd. S. (Flamingo Rd.) | 702-893-9704 | www.nanettelepore.com

Groupies gush over the "adorable" "feminine" togs with a "Parisian" feel at this "girlie" girl boutique in the Forum Shops at Caesars Palace with a "feel-good" vibe thanks to oodles of "wearable" blouses, skirts and pants and a "helpful" staff; prices can feel a bit "extreme", but frugal sorts say there's often a "great selection of sale items."

☒ Neiman Marcus 28 | 25 | 24 | VE
Strip | Fashion Show Mall | 3200 Las Vegas Blvd. S. (Spring Mountain Rd.) | 702-731-3636 | www.neimanmarcus.com

"A perennial favorite" for "one-stop designer shopping", this "upscale" emporium anchoring the Fashion Show Mall offers a "fabulous

SHOPPING

| | QUALITY | DISPLAY | SERVICE | COST |

selection" of "splurge"-worthy clothing (for both men and women), cosmetics, handbags, shoes and jewelry plus their "famous chocolate chip cookies" at the on-premises cafe; with such "beautiful" displays and "impeccable service" some shoppers can't understand why anyone would "bother going elsewhere."

Niketown ⓿ — 24 | 24 | 19 | M

Strip | Forum Shops at Caesars Palace | 3500 Las Vegas Blvd. S. (Flamingo Rd.) | 702-650-8888 | www.nike.com

"Sports fanatics" say they could spend hours getting "lost in" this "large" athletic emporium where they "have everything" – from the classic Air Force 1 sneaks to an "excellent" array of gear and clothing for men and women – "all in one place" in the Forum Shops; a few find the goods "overpriced" and the service "slack", but the "visuals" and "displays" are so "incredible" it's "worth a stroll", even if you don't drop any cash.

☑ Nordstrom — 26 | 24 | 26 | M

Strip | Fashion Show Mall | 3200 Las Vegas Blvd. S. (Spring Mountain Rd.) | 702-862-2525 | www.nordstrom.com

"Service is king" at this "high-end, but not snooty" department store in the Fashion Show Mall where the "superb" sales people "really take care of you" and "elegant" extras like "live piano" and "valet parking" make it "a pleasure to shop here"; "strappy heel divas give high ratings to the shoe department", but loyalists laud the "wonderful selection" in all areas, noting that it's "well laid out" too; P.S. there's also a cafe and espresso bar offering "delicious" noshes for a quick pick-me-up.

☑ Oscar de la Renta ⓿ — 29 | 26 | 27 | VE

Strip | Wynn Las Vegas | 3131 Las Vegas Blvd. S. (bet. Desert Inn & Spring Mountain Rds.) | 702-770-3488 | www.oscardelarenta.com

"Stunning" womenswear that represents "the pinnacle of American design" makes this Wynn boutique showcasing the lines of the couturier "*the* place to get a dress for a night on the town"; "tasteful" suits and accessories are also available in the "charming" shop, all adding up to a "fabulous experience" so long as you're on an "unlimited budget."

NEW Piaget ⓿ — - | - | - | VE

Strip | Palazzo Hotel | 3325 Las Vegas Blvd. S. (Sands Ave.) | 702-418-3033 | www.piaget.com

Fine jewelry and timepieces come together at this Swiss luxury goods specialist at the Palazzo on the Strip known as much for its signature bracelet-style Polo watch as for its extremely upscale pricing (up to $2 million for some items); the store is done up in muted grays – even the staff is dressed in dark, neutral tones – all the better to show off the sparkle of the dazzling goods scattered in glass boxes and set in display windows trimmed in silver and black.

Prada ⓿ — 27 | 24 | 23 | VE

Strip | Bellagio Hotel | 3600 Las Vegas Blvd. S. (Flamingo Rd.) | 702-866-6886 | www.prada.com

"A must-stop for any shopaholic", this "museumlike" masterpiece in the Bellagio showcases Italian designer Miuccia Prada's "gorgeous", "minimalist" apparel and "magnificent leather goods" and shoes in

SHOPPING

"clean and neat displays" that are "lovely" to browse and require "bags of money" to buy; while most maintain the staff's at least "helpful", some suggest that if you don't "flaunt it when you walk in", you will be "so so ignored."

Roberto Cavalli ☻ | 26 | 23 | 20 | VE

Strip | Forum Shops at Caesars Palace | 3500 Las Vegas Blvd. S. (Flamingo Rd.) | 702-893-0369 | www.robertocavalli.com

"If you've got the bod", this Italian designer in the Forum Shops at Caesars Palace turns out "edgy" apparel in leathers and signature animal prints that can be "*très chic*" for a night on the town; a "nice selection" of "ready-to-wear suits" and shoes are good for guys, though beware of prices that befit the high-end service and merchandise.

☑ Saks Fifth Avenue | 27 | 24 | 22 | M

Strip | Fashion Show Mall | 3200 Las Vegas Blvd. S. (Spring Mountain Rd.) | 702-733-8300 | www.saksfifthavenue.com

"A well-balanced selection" of "top designer goods" and more "moderately priced" "staples" characterize this Fashion Show Mall department store full of clothing and accessories and boasting an "accommodating" staff and "easy to navigate" layout; non-shopping companions should make note of the "living room" on the first floor where Internet service and magazines make it a nice place to "take a load off."

NEW Scoop | - | - | - | E

Strip | Forum Shops at Caesars Palace | 3500 Las Vegas Blvd. (Flamingo Rd.) | (702) 734-0026 | www.scoopnyc.com

A veritable mecca for trend-conscious types with money to burn, this outpost of the NYC-based clothing boutique in the Forum Shops at Caesars Palace features the latest high-end designs for guys and gals; its white, streamlined space is chock-full of pieces from popular lines like Marc Jacobs and 7 for all Mankind, all grouped by color and trend on island displays and modeled by an energetic young staff; N.B. it's open till midnight on weekends.

Secret Garden Store | 21 | 22 | 18 | M

Strip | Mirage Hotel | 3400 Las Vegas Blvd. S. (Spring Mountain Rd.) | 702-791-7768 | 800-888-2522 | www.mirage.com

"Filled with the magic of Siegfried & Roy's animals", this emporium in the Mirage impresses fans with "full displays" of exclusive plush toys and "wonderful tropical gifts", so "if you love white tigers" – on playing cards, towels and tees – "this is the store for you"; since it's inside the Secret Garden and Dolphin Habitat, guests must pay to enter the complex.

☑ Sephora ☻ | 26 | 25 | 21 | M

Strip | Grand Hotel Shoppes | 3377 Las Vegas Blvd. S. (bet. Flamingo & Spring Mountain Rds.) | 702-735-3896
Strip | Miracle Mile Shops | 3663 Las Vegas Blvd. S. (Harmon Ave.) | 702-737-0550
www.sephora.com

Cosmetics coveters find a "makeup wonderland" offering "just about every brand you'd want" at the Miracle Mile Shops at Planet Hollywood and at the Grand Hotel Shoppes at the Venetian where the "quality" products are showcased in a "high-energy environment"

SHOPPING

QUALITY | DISPLAY | SERVICE | COST

with a "clean alphabetical arrangement" that makes browsing "a pleasure"; add in a "helpful staff" that's "generous with samples", and some ask "how can you not love it?"

Shark Reef Aquarium Gift Shop ⏺ 20 | 21 | 19 | M

Strip | Mandalay Place | 3930 Las Vegas Blvd. S. (Mandalay Bay Rd.) | 702-632-7777 | www.sharkreef.com

Toe-dippers say this sea-themed store at Mandalay Bay is "good for the kids" because the "really cute souvenirs" and other items are "everything you'd ever want in a hotel gift shop"; although some complain that it's "crowded", "too gimmicky" and "needs more educational items", most agree it's "better" than the "trashy" alternatives found around town.

St. John ⏺ 28 | 23 | 25 | VE

Strip | Grand Canal Shoppes | 3377 Las Vegas Blvd. S. (bet. Flamingo & Spring Mountain Rds.) | 702-731-3330
Strip | Forum Shops at Caesars Palace | 3500 Las Vegas Blvd. S. (Flamingo Rd.) | 702-893-0044
www.stjohnknits.com

"Classy, conservative, well-made clothes" are the signature of these stores at the Forum Shops at Caesars Palace and the Grand Canal Shoppes at the Venetian that largely cater to moneyed "middle-aged to older women"; the "terrific selection" of the company's iconic knits, plus shoes and handbags, includes "more stylish choices" than are found in many department stores, and is sold by a "very nice" staff.

Taryn Rose ⏺ 25 | 22 | 21 | VE

Strip | Forum Shops at Caesars Palace | 3500 Las Vegas Blvd. S. (Flamingo Rd.) | 702-732-2712 | www.tarynrose.com

"You simply cannot beat the quality and style" of these "high-priced", "seductive" women's and men's shoes according to customers who call them the "most comfortable you'll ever wear" (even if that means "dowdy" to some); its location at the Forum Shops at Caesars Palace has something of a "Zen-nightclub" feel, with a streamlined modern look matched by polished service.

Z Tiffany & Co. ⏺ 28 | 26 | 25 | VE

Strip | Forum Shops at Caesars Palace | 3500 Las Vegas Blvd. S. (Flamingo Rd.) | 702-644-3065
Strip | Bellagio Hotel | 3600 Las Vegas Blvd. S. (Flamingo Rd.) | 702-697-5400
800-843-3269 | www.tiffany.com

"When you crave a gift from the little blue box", head to this jewelry "icon" in the Bellagio and the Forum Shops known for its "breathtaking diamonds" ("an amazing array of engagement rings for big winners") and more "affordable" silver pieces; the "lovely staff" works to "make sure you're happy in every respect", so it's "equal to the NYC experience" for many, even if a few wish it were less "ubiquitous" these days.

NEW Tommy Bahama's Emporium ⏺ - | - | - | M

S of Strip | Town Square | 6605 Las Vegas Blvd. S. (bet. I-215 & Sunset Rd.) | 702-948-6828 | 866-986-8282 | www.tommybahama.com

Island ease with a touch of panache describes the goods at this laid-back shop at Town Square south of the Strip peddling tropics-inspired mens- and womenswear plus home furnishings and personal accessories; whirring paddle fans and bamboo accents set a relaxed mood,

SHOPPING

QUALITY | DISPLAY | SERVICE | COST

and for a post-shopping lift, you can visit the adjacent restaurant for a bite and a fruity cocktail.

NEW Tory Burch ● — | — | — | E
Strip | Palazzo Hotel | 3325 Las Vegas Blvd. S. (Sands Ave.) | 702-369-0541 | www.toryburch.com

Bold prints and brassy accents are the hallmarks of NYC designer/socialite Tory Burch's eponymous line showcased at this new boutique at the Palazzo on the Strip; while the resortwear-inspired looks are reminiscent of 1960s St. Tropez, the shop itself conjures up a glamorous 1970s rec room with jade-green carpet, orange showcases and mirrored walls.

Truefitt & Hill ● ▽ 28 | 24 | 26 | E
Strip | Forum Shops at Caesars Palace | 3500 Las Vegas Blvd. S. (Flamingo Rd.) | 702-735-7428 | www.truefittandhill.com

"A branch of the London specialty store with the most wonderful shaving equipment, creams" and colognes is nestled among the boutiques at the Forum Shops at Caesars Palace; in addition to offering a line that's "luxe and worth every cent", it also serves as a classic barber shop, so "while the girls are off shopping", the guys can get "a little pampering too."

Versace ● 25 | 25 | 20 | VE
Strip | Forum Shops at Caesars Palace | 3500 Las Vegas Blvd. S. (Flamingo Rd.) | 702-796-7222 | www.versace.com

What could be more Vegas than this "loud, lavish" landmark in the Forum Shops at Caesars Palace overrun with flashy fashionistas, *Showgirls* fanatics and the occasional "highly paid hooker" all "craving" the brand's sexy silhouettes, snug-fitting menswear and outrageously patterned home accessories; "service can be aloof" and prices only befitting the "fattest of wallets", but mere mortals shrug both off, asking – "does anyone actually wear this stuff" anyway?

West of Santa Fe ● 24 | 23 | 22 | E
Strip | Forum Shops at Caesars Palace | 3500 Las Vegas Blvd. S. (Flamingo Rd.) | 702-737-1993 | www.westofsantafe.com

"If you love silver and Western paraphernalia", you'll find it in spades at this rustic-looking store at the Forum Shops at Caesars Palace, which some consider "the only place to buy turquoise with confidence" outside of "New Mexico or Arizona"; the staff provides "lots of individual attention", and even those who balk at the cost are "pleasantly surprised to find some moderately priced, well-made items."

Z Gallerie 22 | 24 | 20 | M
Strip | Fashion Show Mall | 3200 Las Vegas Blvd. S. (Spring Mountain Rd.) | 702-696-9733 | www.zgallerie.com

"Pottery Barn meets the Bombay Company" quip customers of this home decor store at the Fashion Show Mall, which provides "beautiful", "unique" furnishings, accessories and gifts, and "do an exceptional job with seasonal decorations"; since the prices are "moderate" too, fans find it "impossible to leave with nothing bought!" N.B. the branch at Planet Hollywood's Miracle Mile Shops has closed.

SITES & ATTRACTIONS DIRECTORY

APPEAL | FACIL. | SERVICE | COST

Sites & Attractions

Ratings & Symbols

Appeal, Facilities and **Service** are rated on the Zagat 0 to 30 scale.

Cost reflects the attraction's high-season price range for one adult admission, indicated as follows:

$0 Free
I $10 and below
M $11 to $25
E $26 to $40
VE $41 or more

MOST POPULAR
1. Fountains of Bellagio
2. Bellagio Conservatory/Gardens
3. Fremont St. Experience
4. Hoover Dam
5. Red Rock Canyon

TOP APPEAL
28 Fountains of Bellagio
   Red Rock Canyon
   Valley of Fire State Park
26 Hoover Dam
   Bellagio Conservatory/Gardens

Adventuredome, The   17 | 16 | 13 | M

Strip | Circus Circus | 2880 Las Vegas Blvd. S. (bet. Desert Inn Rd. & Sahara Ave.) | 702-734-0410 | 800-424-7287 | www.circuscircus.com

"It's no Disneyland", but this "noisy" indoor amusement park under the pink Plexiglas dome at Circus Circus can be "lots of fun" for "families" with the double-loop Canyon Blaster coaster appealing to "teens", while a carousel and carnival games are "good for little ones"; critics complain that the attractions are "getting old", but it's still an "ok diversion", especially if you need to "get out of the heat."

A Little White Wedding Chapel   - | - | - | M

Strip | 1301 Las Vegas Blvd. S. (bet. Charleston Blvd. & St. Louis Ave.) | 702-382-5943 | 800-545-8111 | www.alittlewhitechapel.com

From the Chapel of Promises to the Tunnel of Love Drive Thru, this wedding complex in the north end of the Strip offers five separate settings in which to tie the knot; made famous by uniting couples Frank Sinatra/Mia Farrow and Bruce Willis/Demi Moore - not to mention Britney Spears' first ill-fated union - it offers all the needed accoutrements from flowers to gowns for ceremonies from 7 AM to midnight (later on weekends).

Atomic Testing Museum, The   - | - | - | M

E Side | 755 E. Flamingo Rd. (Swenson St.) | 702-794-5161 | www.atomictestingmuseum.org

Visitors are greeted by a life-sized photo of "Miss Atomic Bomb 1957" at this offbeat East Side museum recounting the 50-year history of nuclear testing in Nevada; tour guides in lab coats lead you through multimedia exhibits, computer simulations and artifacts (like a replica fallout shelter) while the gift shop stocks plenty of kitschy Cold War curiosities.

Auto Collections at the Imperial Palace   22 | 17 | 17 | I

Strip | Imperial Palace | 3535 Las Vegas Blvd. S. (bet. Flamingo & Spring Mountain Rds.) | 702-794-3174 | www.autocollections.com

"A car buff's dream come true", this informal display of more than 250 antique vehicles at the Imperial Palace on the Strip includes "wonder-

SITES & ATTRACTIONS

| | APPEAL | FACIL. | SERVICE | COST |

ful one-of-a-kind" showpieces like Johnny Carson's 1939 Chrysler Royal Sedan among the "ever-changing" collection of Bentleys, Ferraris and Aston Martins all available for sale; those with budgets for Buicks rather than BMWs may want to note that "free coupons" for admission are often available, so check their website or "ask your concierge."

ⓩ Bellagio Conservatory & Botanical Gardens | 26 | 27 | 21 | $0 |

Strip | Bellagio Hotel | 3600 Las Vegas Blvd. S. (Flamingo Rd.) | 702-693-7111 | www.bellagio.com

"A literal breath of fresh air in smoky Las Vegas", this "lush", "tranquil respite" within the Bellagio is a "joy to behold" for its "jaw-dropping topiaries", "spectacular" flowers and "stunning" seasonal displays that make for a stellar "photo op"; in spite of occasional "crowds", it's a "must-visit", "even for a quick walk-through", and best of all, it's free.

Eiffel Tower Experience | 23 | 21 | 20 | M |

Strip | Paris Las Vegas | 3655 Las Vegas Blvd. S. (bet. Flamingo Rd. & Harmon Ave.) | 877-603-4386 | www.parislasvegas.com

"First-time visitors" to this half-scale replica of *la Tour Eiffel* towering over Paris Las Vegas come for the "spectacular views" and glimpses of the Bellagio fountains; it's "a little expensive", but even fans insist you only need to "do it once."

Floyd Lamb Park | - | - | - | I |

N Las Vegas | 9200 Tule Springs Rd. (off Maggie Ave.) | North Las Vegas | 702-229-8100

This Northwest open-air oasis shows a side of Las Vegas few visitors ever experience with grassy fields, bike paths, picnic areas, lakes and wildlife (including peacocks); back in the day, it was known as Tule Springs Ranch where would-be divorcées cooled their heels while waiting for their splits to become legal; it's also an archaeological site that's listed on the National Register of Historic Places.

ⓩ Fountains of Bellagio | 28 | 25 | 18 | $0 |

Strip | Bellagio Hotel | 3600 Las Vegas Blvd. S. (Flamingo Rd.) | 702-693-7111 | www.bellagio.com

Conjuring up the quintessential "Las Vegas image" is this Bellagio "spectacle" (rated Most Popular and No. 1 for Appeal among Las Vegas Attractions) where onlookers "ooh and ahh" at the "mesmerizing" water show synchronized to "thunderous" music that's best enjoyed with your "arms wrapped around your special someone"; there's "ample room" to appreciate it from "out on the boulevard", though diehards declare it's most "memorable" "from a lakefront room in the hotel"; either way, it's truly "awe-inspiring", "and it's free!"

ⓩ Fremont Street Experience | 22 | 18 | 15 | $0 |

Downtown | 425 Fremont St. (bet. Las Vegas Blvd. & Main St.) | 702-678-5777 | 800-249-3559 | www.vegasexperience.com

Downtown "sparkles" "brighter" than it did back when it was known as 'Glitter Gulch' thanks to this "touristy" attention-getter – a pedestrian mall where "light shows" are projected onto an LED display canopy and "free concerts", a "hodgepodge" of entertainers and a collection of refurbished historic neon signs provide additional draws; the vibe's a bit "seedy" (think "lowbrow carnival"), so those seeking the "golden

SITES & ATTRACTIONS

APPEAL | FACIL. | SERVICE | COST

years" of "old Vegas" would do best to skip the street "scene" and duck into one of the vintage casinos.

GameWorks — 17 | 17 | 13 | I

Strip | 3785 Las Vegas Blvd. S. (Tropicana Ave.) | 702-432-4263 | www.gameworks.com

Gamers gravitate to this "awesome arcade" on the Strip with "tons of" amusements including the latest releases from Sega, Sammy and Nintendo as well as billiards, classic pinball and a bar area and restaurant featuring basic burgers and wings; your "money goes fast" and some say it "could use more staff", but most maintain, it's a fine place to "hang out" and "pass a few hours" so long as you don't mind the "noise."

Gondola Adventures — - | - | - | M

Lake LV | 41 Casa di Lago (off Lake Mead Pkwy.) | Henderson | 877-446-6365 | www.gondola.com

It may be a surprise to see the Ponte Vecchio in the middle of the desert – and in typical fashion, the Lake Las Vegas version houses rooms in the Ritz-Carlton hotel – but cruise under it in an authentic gondola and you'll likely think you're in Italy; lovebirds can opt for a package that includes champagne and chocolates while pricier picks include a three-course meal under the stars.

Gondola Rides at the Ventian — 22 | 23 | 22 | M

Strip | Venetian Hotel | 3355 Las Vegas Blvd. S. (bet. Flamingo & Spring Mountain Rds.) | 702-414-4300 | www.venetian.com

"Cheesy? you bet", but plenty of "romantics" "still love" gliding through the Venetian's Grand Canal to the strains of "singing gondoliers", even if the whole experience essentially adds up to "a pricey boat ride through a mall"; enthusiasts advise you make a "reservation" to bypass "waits" and be prepared for "everyone" to "gawk" "as you go by."

Graceland Wedding Chapel — - | - | - | M

Downtown | 619 Las Vegas Blvd. S. (Bonneville Ave.) | 702-382-0091 | www.gracelandchapel.com

This Downtown wedding chapel is about as "only-in-Vegas" as it gets with various Elvis impersonators on-hand to escort you and your sweetie down the aisle and belt out a few post-ceremony tunes; betrotheds can opt to add on limousine service, photography and flowers or splurge for the deluxe package that includes not one, but two versions of the King dueling it out in song.

☑ Hoover Dam — 26 | 23 | 21 | I

Boulder City | US Hwy. 93, SE of Las Vegas | 702-597-5970 | 866-291-8687 | www.usbr.gov/lc/hooverdam

"A marvel of Depression-era engineering", this "true man-made wonder" straddling the Arizona-Nevada border near Boulder City is "an absolute must-see" rave reviewers who say it's best appreciated via one of the tours led by "personable guides" who make it all the more "exciting" and "educational"; "traffic" and "summer temperatures" may be a deterrent to some, but the majority insists it'd be "ridiculous to miss it" – this is the "one thing the Strip can't replicate."

SITES & ATTRACTIONS

APPEAL | FACIL. | SERVICE | COST

Imax Theatre
22 | 23 | 18 | M

Strip | Luxor Hotel | 3900 Las Vegas Blvd. S. (bet. Mandalay Bay Rd. & Reno Ave.) | 702-262-4000

This big-as-life movie theater in the Luxor's atrium puts you "right into the action" with a seven-story screen and 3D imaging making the ever-changing rotation of films an "incredible experience"; some shrug it off, saying that one could find the same "in any mall these days", but "after a lot of walking" in the summer heat, most find it a welcome "inexpensive" place to "cool-off."

Las Vegas Mini Grand Prix
▽ 18 | 18 | 17 | I

NW | 1401 N. Rainbow Blvd. (bet. Vegas Dr. & Washington Ave.) | 702-259-7000 | 888-259-7223 | www.lvmgp.com

Go-Carts, rides and video games provide plenty of "entertainment" at this Northwest speedway; "adrenalin junkies" complain the thrills don't live up to the hype, but it's "great for families" (hence the "crowds") with pizza and snacks available for those who decide to make a day of it.

Las Vegas Natural History Museum
▽ 19 | 21 | 17 | I

N of Strip | 900 Las Vegas Blvd. N. (Washington Ave.) | 702-384-3466 | www.lvnhm.org

This "fine museum" north of the Strip will "entertain" the family "for about an hour or so" with rotating educational exhibits, animatronic dinosaurs, examples of marine life and various "stuffed" animal species as well as hands-on areas where kids can dig for fossils; big-screen films boost the appeals for teens, while adults will appreciate the two-for-one coupons available on the website.

Liberace Museum
23 | 21 | 21 | M

E Side | 1775 E. Tropicana Ave. (Spencer St.) | 702-798-5595 | www.liberace.org

"As gaudy as it gets", this "glittery" tribute to the "larger than life" performer showcases "the cars, the clothes, the pianos" (and one of "the world's largest rhinestones") all in one "kitschy", "quintessentially" Vegas attraction east of the Strip; "it's worth checking out, whether you're a fan or not" if only as a "sight to see", or to answer the question: how on earth did he "tickle the ivories" with all those "giant rings" on?

Lied Discovery Children's Museum
▽ 21 | 18 | 16 | I

Downtown | 833 Las Vegas Blvd. N. (bet. Bonanza Rd. & Washington Ave.) | 702-382-3445 | www.ldcm.org

Though it "caters specifically to smaller children", "kids of all ages" will enjoy this interactive museum Downtown featuring temporary and permanent hands-on exhibits exploring the arts, sciences and humanities; additional draws include a Baby Oasis with crawling ramps for tots and the Parent Resource Room where families can relax and read books.

Lion Habitat
21 | 19 | 16 | $0

Strip | MGM Grand Hotel | 3799 Las Vegas Blvd. S. (Tropicana Ave.) | 702-891-1111 | www.mgmgrand.com

"Quite a thrill" if you catch them "at feeding time", otherwise these "casino kitties" holding court outside the MGM Grand on the Strip "are a lot more mellow than most of Vegas" (read: they "lie around" a

SITES & ATTRACTIONS

APPEAL | FACIL. | SERVICE | COST

lot); still, the area is often "overrun with people" clamoring for "close-up views" or waiting for a "photo op" or "souvenir."

Little Church of the West, The | - | - | - | M |
Strip | 4617 Las Vegas Blvd. S. (Russell Rd.) | 702-739-7971 | 800-821-2452 | www.littlechurchlv.com

The scene of more celebrity marriages than any chapel in the world, from Betty Grable/Harry James to Angelina Jolie/Billy Bob Thornton, this replica of an old mining town church (complete with a cedar exterior and California redwood interior) is the only Strip spot listed on the National Register of Historic Places; knot-tyers can get the works – from flowers, to photos to organists – to complement their 20-minute ceremony.

Madame Tussauds | 23 | 23 | 19 | M |
Strip | Venetian Hotel | 3355 Las Vegas Blvd. S. (bet. Flamingo & Spring Mountain Rds.) | 702-862-7800 | www.mtvegas.com

"Eerily realistic" wax replicas of film, music and sports icons are the draw at this "kitschy" chain exhibit in the Venetian favored by "tourists" for "great Kodak moments" (employees "encourage posing" with your favorite star, so feel free to throw "J-Lo" some "bunny ears"); admission prices are "expensive", though enthusiasts insist you can often find "two-for-one coupons" online or in a "visitor's publication"; N.B. hard-core devotees may want to check out the on-site Chapel of the Dreams where you can get married alongside facsimiles of Brad and Angelina.

Mystic Falls Park | 19 | 19 | 18 | $0 |
E Side | Sam's Town Hotel | 5111 Boulder Hwy. (Nellis Blvd.) | 702-456-7777 | 800-897-8696 | www.samstownlv.com

There's "a lot going on" at this skylit indoor park at Sam's Town on the East Side where a babbling brook and animatronic wildlife simulate a wooded glen that makes for "a relaxing break from the noise and crowds"; it's a little "cheesy", but it's free, and "kids love" the laser light show that runs in the evenings.

Neon Museum, The | - | - | - | M |
Downtown | 821 Las Vegas Blvd. N. (Washington Ave.) | 702-387-6366 | www.neonmuseum.org

The iconic swooping lobby from the 1960s-era La Concha Motel is set to be restored as the visitors' center of this fledgling museum dedicated to the preservation of Las Vegas' neon history; although the doors don't open until 2009, in the meantime, design and architecture aficionados can take guided tours through a graveyard of retired landmarks including the original signs that graced the Stardust and Golden Nugget hotels; N.B. by advance appointment only, check website for details.

Nevada State Museum Las Vegas | - | - | - | I |
W Side | 700 Twin Lakes Dr. (bet. I-95 & Washington Aves.) | 702-486-5205 | www.nevadaculture.org

Ichthyosaurs meet the Old West in this West Side museum that officially depicts the state's history, pre-history and natural history but touches on casino life and lore as well; its current condition "is old and run-down" to some, but optimists opine that "perhaps we'll see an improvement when it moves to its new location at the Springs Preserve" in 2010.

SITES & ATTRACTIONS

| | APPEAL | FACIL. | SERVICE | COST |

ⓩ Red Rock Canyon National Conservation Area 28 | 22 | 20 | I

W Side | 1000 Scenic Loop Dr. (off Hwy. 159) | 702-515-5350 | www.redrockcanyonlv.org

Surrounded by "spectacular", "rugged" red rocks, this "stunning" West Side "respite" offers "terrific hiking", biking and rock climbing, as well as a 13-mile scenic drive, making it a "no-brainer" for a "delightful excursion" that's "a wonderful antidote to the neon and plastic of Las Vegas"; it's only about 20 minutes away so surveyors suggest you "rent a car", bring a "camera" (and water) and get ready to "commune with nature"; N.B. admission to the park is free, but there's a $5 charge per vehicle.

Roller Coaster at New York-New York 23 | 20 | 17 | M

Strip | New York-New York Hotel | 3790 Las Vegas Blvd. S. (Tropicana Ave.) | 702-740-6969 | www.nynyhotelcasino.com

"Thrill-seekers" who haven't gotten enough "excitement" at the tables head to this "awesome roller coaster" that plummets down a 144-ft. drop and then twists and dives around New York-New York offering "great views" of the Statue of Liberty (as long as you can "keep your eyes open"); "long lines" and "expensive" tickets may seem daunting, but "even the most jaded" overlook both for what they say is one of "the best rides in Vegas"; P.S. "try it at night!"

Shark Reef 25 | 24 | 20 | M

Strip | Mandalay Bay Resort | 3950 Las Vegas Blvd. S. (Mandalay Bay Rd.) | 702-632-4580 | www.mandalaybay.com

"Considering you're nowhere near the ocean", this "neat, but small" aquarium in Mandalay Bay is quite a "surprise", "enticing both parents and kids" with "beautifully laid out" tanks of piranha, sea turtles and, of course, sharks, as well as "interactive feeding displays" and a "petting" area that's pretty "amazing" too; a few complain of "predatory" pricing, but fin fans find it a "fascinating" experience nonetheless, abetted by "helpful" guides – "it's hard to believe this is in a casino!"

Show in the Sky 21 | 22 | 17 | $0

W of Strip | Rio All-Suite Hotel | 3700 W. Flamingo Rd. (bet. I-15 & Valley View Blvd.) | 702-777-7776 | www.harrahs.com

There's "plenty of flash, color and buzz" at this "entertaining spectacle" in the Rio west of the Strip that simulates Brazil's Carnivale parade with "dance numbers", "faux-glam" costumes and a festive atmosphere; though intended for adults, it's still "kid-friendly" (meaning revelers "catch beads" while keeping "their shirt on"), but the majority insists that while it's "a nice freebie if you happen to be there", "it's not really worth a special trip"; N.B. for an extra charge you can ride the floats.

Siegfried & Roy's Secret Garden & Dolphin Habitat 24 | 24 | 21 | M

Strip | Mirage Hotel | 3400 Las Vegas Blvd. S. (Spring Mountain Rd.) | 702-791-7111 | www.miragehabitat.com

A "lush tropical escape", this "mini-zoo" at the Mirage founded by Siegfried & Roy houses an "amazing" array of Royal White Tigers, lions, panthers and leopards all "lovingly cared for" in a "natural setting"; adjoining the garden is a marine "research facility" where you

Let your voice be heard – visit ZAGAT.com/vote

SITES & ATTRACTIONS

APPEAL | FACIL. | SERVICE | COST

can see dolphins "at play" in an "educational" context ("don't go expecting a show"); both areas are "well organized and guided."

Springs Preserve | - | - | - | I |

W Side | 333 S. Valley View Blvd. (bet. I-95 & Meadows Ln.) | 702-822-7700 | www.springspreserve.org

This 180-acre site on the West Side – home of the springs that begat the meadows for which Las Vegas was named – is a combination nature preserve, botanical garden, museum and performance venue offering rotating exhibits, walking trails, yoga classes, tai chi and live music for both locals and tourists; light bites from Wolfgang Puck are available at the on-site cafe, and in 2010 the Nevada State Museum will reopen in its new home here.

Stratosphere Tower & Rides | 24 | 20 | 17 | I |

Strip | Stratosphere Hotel | 2000 Las Vegas Blvd. S. (north of Sahara Ave.) | 702-380-7777 | 800-998-6937 | www.stratospherehotel.com

"Sin City looks heavenly" when seen from the top of the Stratosphere over 800 feet above the Strip where timid types can visit the observation deck for "breathtaking views" and "adventure-seekers" can choose from any of the three "heart-pounding", "scare-your-pants-off" rides; either way, it's an "original way to see all of Vegas" with a "courteous staff" doing its best to control the sometimes "frustrating" lines.

☑ Valley of Fire State Park | 28 | 19 | 15 | I |

Overton | I-15 at Hwy. 169 (I-15) | 702-397-2088 | parks.nv.gov/vf.htm

"When you want a break from the glitz" trek out to this "beautiful [Mojave] desert destination" for hiking, camping or a simple "drive on a Sunday afternoon", where natural wonders include areas of petrified wood and miles of red sandstone formations for which the site is named; facilities are a little "sparse", and its location 55 miles northeast of the Strip makes it "a bit of a drive", but it's "well worth" either inconvenience, especially if you decide to "make a whole day of it."

Vegas Indoor Skydiving | ▽ 26 | 21 | 23 | E |

E of Strip | 200 Convention Center Dr. (Las Vegas Blvd.) | 702-731-4768 | 877-293-0639 | www.vegasindoorskydiving.com

Those "who always wanted to try skydiving" seek out this "thrilling" east of the Strip substitute that simulates the real thing with a "vertical wind tunnel with air speeds up to 120 mph" that, "son of a gun, actually works!" as visitors are "borne aloft" in their "special flight suits" following a short training period; "expensive" prices are worth noting, though converts claim it's "worth it" for this "much fun."

Wildlife Habitat at the Flamingo | 20 | 20 | 15 | $0 |

Strip | Flamingo Las Vegas | 3555 Las Vegas Blvd. S. (Flamingo Rd.) | 702-733-3111 | 800-732-2111 | www.flamingolasvegas.com

"It's no South African safari", but this "nice little diversion" at the Flamingo on the Strip boasts a "cute" collection of flamingos, ducks, swans, koi and turtles that appeals to "children" and "animal lovers"; though longtimers lament it's "not the same since the penguins left" (they're now living at the Dallas Zoo), it's still "free" and "lovely to stroll through", though the less-enchanted maintain they "wouldn't go out of [their] way for it."

GOLF DIRECTORY

Golf

> COURSE | FACIL. | SERVICE | VALUE | COST

Ratings & Symbols

Course, Facilities, Service and **Value** are rated on the Zagat 0 to 30 scale.

Cost reflects the price per non-member or non-guest to play 18 holes on a weekend in high season, i.e. the highest price of play. Yardage, USGA Rating and Slope are listed after each address.

⛳ caddies/forecaddies   o⇥ guests only
🛒 carts only

MOST POPULAR
1. Reflection Bay/Lake Las Vegas
2. Shadow Creek
3. Las Vegas Paiute/Wolf
4. Rio Secco
5. Falls/Lake Las Vegas

TOP-RATED COURSES
29 | Cascata
 * | Shadow Creek
27 | Falls/Lake Las Vegas
    | Rio Secco
    | Las Vegas Paiute/Wolf

Angel Park, Mountain 🛒 | 19 | 18 | 19 | 21 | $155 |
Las Vegas | 100 S. Rampart Blvd. | 702-254-4653 | 888-446-5358 | www.angelpark.com | 6722/5150; 71.1/69.1; 130/114

"One of the busiest courses in Las Vegas for a reason", this often "overcrowded" Arnold Palmer/Ed Seay design is "challenging and fun to play" with a "friendly staff" and "beautiful views" of the valley to deter critics who claim it's merely "ordinary"; a few feel there are "better [options] in the area", but perhaps not at such "bargain" prices - "you won't need a high-rolling bank account to play here."

Angel Park, Palm 🛒 | 18 | 21 | 21 | 19 | $155 |
Las Vegas | 100 S. Rampart Blvd. | 702-254-4653 | 888-446-5358 | www.angelpark.com | 6525/4570; 70.9/66.2; 129/111

"Not for the low-handicapper", this "interesting", "decent" design offers just enough challenge - "lots of water, some forced carries and big, undulating greens" - to make it "great for a fun outing with friends" and "very woman-friendly"; the "scenic" spread is enhanced by "beautiful desert landscaping", a "nice pro shop" and a "friendly staff", but some suggest "you get what you pay for in Vegas" - which in this case, may be an "unmemorable" experience.

Bali Hai ⛳ | 22 | 22 | 23 | 13 | $325 |
Las Vegas | 5160 Las Vegas Blvd. S. | 702-450-8000 | 888-427-6678 | www.balihaigolfclub.com | 7002/5535; 73/71.5; 130/121

The "exotic beaches, marvelous palms", "water hazards" and black volcanic rock are all "nice touches" at this "South Pacific-themed" spread that's "forgiving" due to "generous", "funnel-shaped fairways" and "loud" courtesy of a "convenient location" "next to McCarran Airport"; though it's also "pricey" for a place with "no driving range", it has an "excellent pro shop" and, besides, "it could charge $400 and people would still pay because of its proximity to the Strip."

GOLF

	COURSE	FACIL.	SERVICE	VALUE	COST

Bear's Best Las Vegas
25 | 24 | 24 | 18 | $275

Las Vegas | 11111 W. Flamingo Rd. | 702-804-8500 | 866-385-8500 | www.bearsbestlasvegas.com | 7194/5043; 74/68.7; 147/116

Bringing together "Jack's best holes" from his "greatest hits", this "impressive" "collection" is "a lot of fun" but can be "tricky"; plus, it's "only beginning to be developed", although "as houses are added", the "spectacular views of the red rock landscape" may "be less inviting"; the only hitch: "all courses in Vegas are overpriced – and this is no exception."

☑ Cascata
29 | 29 | 29 | 17 | $500

Boulder City | 1 Cascata Dr. | 702-294-2000 | www.golfcascata.com | 7137/5591; 74.6/67.2; 143/117

"Vegas tourists must play this course at least twice in their life", as Rees Jones' "absolutely amazing" resort spread southeast of Henderson is "every bit the experience of Shadow Creek" – and is also Nevada's top-rated Course; while the "immaculately maintained greens" and "stunning scenery" "wow" club-wielders, it's the "world-class clubhouse" (where "a running waterfall welcomes you") and "fantastic service" that make this "rare treat" worth its "hefty fees": "they treat you very well – but for that kind of money, they ought to."

☑ Falls at Lake Las Vegas Resort
27 | 24 | 25 | 20 | $275

Henderson | 101 Via Vin Santo | 702-740-5258 | 877-698-4653 | www.lakelasvegas.com | 7250/5021; 74.7/68.3; 136/118

"Extremely tough but worth the whupping", this "desert oasis" winds "through the mountains" near Henderson with "significant elevation changes", particularly on a "spectacular back nine"; although the design delivers "dramatic views of Downtown Vegas", the "challenging" layout has already caught "the disease many nice courses get" – "condo-itis" – so while you should be sure to "play it, try not to pay full price."

Las Vegas Paiute Resort, Snow Mountain
25 | 24 | 24 | 22 | $169

Las Vegas | 10325 Nu Wav Kaiv Blvd. | 702-658-1400 | 866-284-2833 | www.lvpaiutegolf.com | 7146/5341; 73.3/70.4; 125/117

Golfers "can't go wrong with any of the three courses" at the Paiute Resort, so head "northwest to the reservation" to play the facility's "outstanding" original design, this "beautiful" Pete Dye piece that's "always in pristine condition"; offering mountain views plus "quality and service that continue to set the standard", the "fun", "reasonably priced" option proves "well worth the 30-minute" "trip from the Strip" – "now if only they could turn down that wind."

Las Vegas Paiute Resort, Sun Mountain
26 | 24 | 23 | 21 | $169

Las Vegas | 10325 Nu Wav Kaiv Blvd. | 702-658-1400 | 866-284-2833 | www.lvpaiutegolf.com | 7112/5465; 73.3/71; 130/123

"You won't believe this oasis could exist" "just a short drive from the Strip", but this "beautifully kept" resort course "pops out of the desert to provide an incredible experience for the avid golfer" on a "tough" but "playable" Pete Dye design that remains "faithful to the local topography" – meaning it can "get very windy in the PM"; although some find it "pricey", most "love" the "quality course" for its "amazing mountain views", grass driving range and "courteous, friendly staff."

GOLF

	COURSE	FACIL.	SERVICE	VALUE	COST

🆉 Las Vegas Paiute Resort, Wolf ⛳   27 | 24 | 23 | 23 | $199
Las Vegas | 10325 Nu Wav Kaiv Blvd. | 702-658-1400 | 866-284-2833 | www.lvpaiutegolf.com | 7604/5130; 76.3/68.8; 149/116

"Fall asleep for a second and the Wolf will bite you in the butt" bemoan boosters of "the hardest of the Paiute courses", this "tough but fair" Pete Dye creation that's an "utterly superb" "long ball hitter's delight" delivering "incredible views of the desert and mountains"; "get out early to beat the breezes", but "rest assured" that the AM tee time and "drive is worth it" for a "top-notch" experience that can be summed up in four simple words: "golf, clubhouse, nature, period."

Legacy, The ⛳   20 | 20 | 21 | 19 | $155
Henderson | 130 Par Excellence Dr. | 702-897-2187 | 888-446-5358 | www.thelegacygc.com | 7233/5340; 74.5/71; 137/120

Proving you "don't need to break the piggy bank to play a decent course" "in the land of the casinos", this "solid" Arthur Hills design is "great fun" and a "good selection for your day of departure", as it's "close to the airport" in Henderson; although it's an "older course", most maintain it's "a cut above a muni" and downright "wonderful when it's in shape"; N.B. the scores do not reflect a summer 2008 renovation.

🆉 Reflection Bay at   27 | 25 | 24 | 17 | $275
Lake Las Vegas Resort ⛳
Henderson | 75 Montelago Blvd. | 702-740-4653 | 877-698-4653 | www.lakelasvegas.com | 7261/5166; 74.8/70; 138/127

Is this "feast for the eyes" "really in Nevada"? ask swingers surprised to find "mountains, desert and water all in one" "beautiful course" routed "along Lake Las Vegas" in Henderson; though "fairly flat", the "fantastic" Jack Nicklaus resort design features "a few really tough holes", especially on the "more difficult back"; be sure, however, to "watch out for the coyotes" and "freakishly expensive" fees – "forgive me Jack", for though "the lakeside holes are great, they don't justify the price."

Revere, Concord ⛳   23 | 24 | 23 | 21 | $195
Henderson | 2600 Hampton Rd. | 702-259-4653 | 877-273-8373 | www.reveregolf.com | 7069/5171; 72.8/69.7; 126/118

"Take your mind off the casino tables" at this "forgiving, forgiving, forgiving" layout that's the newer of the two tracks at this Paul Revere-themed facility in Henderson; "a mid-handicapper's delight", the "wide-open" "mountain course" offers "amazing terrain changes", "huge greens" and "rough that slopes back to the fairway"; "gorgeous scenery" and a location "within 20 minutes of the Strip" are two more reasons it's a "secret jewel."

Revere, Lexington ⛳   24 | 23 | 21 | 20 | $235
Henderson | 2600 Hampton Rd. | 702-259-4653 | 877-273-8373 | www.reveregolf.com | 7143/5305; 73.5/69.9; 138/116

"You'll need to play it a couple of times" or "bring your A-game" to this "tough" track that serves up "sloped lies", "small greens", "blind shots" and "lots of hills" on a "tight" layout that, "unlike the Concord, doesn't funnel wayward shots back to the fairway"; all in all, the "magnificent" "mountain course" is "really nifty" with "some great views and awesome lighting at dusk", but given a "beautiful" location so near to Vegas, "it tends to get crowded."

GOLF

	COURSE	FACIL.	SERVICE	VALUE	COST

⚡ Rio Secco ⛳   27 | 23 | 21 | 18 | $285

Henderson | 2851 Grand Hills Dr. | 702-889-2400 | 888-867-3226 | www.riosecco.net | 7314/5760; 75.7/70; 142/127

It's "hard to believe such a rustic course is 20 minutes from the craps tables", but this "long, challenging" Rees Jones design is nestled in the Vegas foothills; "play the back tees" only "if you have masochistic tendencies", as the desert track "runs through canyons" and valleys with "forced carries" and "heavy winds"; still, though "faithful to the terrain", the layout is "surrounded by million-dollar homes" – with "expensive" greens fees to match; N.B. it's home to the Butch Harmon School of Golf.

Royal Links ⛳   22 | 21 | 23 | 16 | $275

Las Vegas | 5995 Vegas Valley Dr. | 702-450-8123 | 888-446-5385 | www.royallinksgolfclub.com | 7029/5142; 73.7/69.8; 135/115

"If you can't get to the U.K.", head to this collection of "the best holes from the great British Open courses" that's "wonderfully fun" with its "huge pot bunkers", "unusual rough" and "traditionally garbed caddies"; though the "enjoyable experience" comes with a castlelike clubhouse and English tavern, a few commoners claim you "can't get a real links feel without an ocean", which makes this the type of "faux reality" you find "only in Vegas."

⚡ Shadow Creek ⛳   29 | 28 | 28 | 20 | $500

North Las Vegas | 3 Shadow Creek Dr. | 702-791-7161 | 866-260-0069 | www.shadowcreek.com | 7239/6701

"Somehow, they managed to build a North Carolina course in the middle of Vegas", so enjoy a "top-shelf day" at this "insanely beautiful" "feat of engineering" that pairs its "amazing" stream-filled setting with "to-die-for views" and "superlative service"; "you might well bump into Tiger" or get a "locker next to Michael Jordan's" at this "expensive, exclusive" MGM Mirage retreat, so though you'd "never guess you were in the desert", you'll know you're getting "a once-in-a-lifetime opportunity"; N.B. the course will be remodeled in late 2008.

Siena ⛳   22 | 21 | 22 | 22 | $189

Las Vegas | 10575 Siena Monte Ave. | 702-341-9200 | 888-689-6469 | www.sienagolfclub.com | 6843/4978; 71.7/68; 131/112

"Traps, traps, traps" make it "tough to avoid the beach at this sporty" track that's "worth the drive from the Strip" to "the outskirts of Vegas"; a "nice course" "all the way around" with its "breathtaking vistas of the desert and mountain terrain", "great clubhouse", "good upkeep" and greens fees that are "not prohibitively expensive", this "beautiful" "hidden gem" "sure beats four hours at the craps table."

Wynn Las Vegas ⛳   25 | 25 | 26 | 12 | $500

Las Vegas | 3131 Las Vegas Blvd. S. | 702-770-3575 | 888-320-9966 | www.wynnlasvegas.com | 7042/6464

"Like being taken to a golf oasis in the middle of a slot-machine desert", this guests-only Tom Fazio/Steve Wynn "wonder" "has the advantage of a fabulous location" on the Strip; while "well-manicured conditions" and "the best service available" make it "a helluva place to play", some say the "decent" design is "not nearly as challenging" as the "ridiculously priced" greens fees and the "shockingly snooty" vibe; N.B. the layout has not yet been rated by the USGA.

HOTEL, RESORT & SPA DIRECTORY

Hotels

Ratings & Symbols

Rooms, **Service**, **Dining** and **Facilities** are rated on the Zagat 0 to 30 scale.

Cost reflects the hotel's high-season rate for a standard double room. It does not reflect seasonal changes.

- 🛉 children's programs
- ✗ exceptional restaurant
- ⌒ kitchens
- ✌ allow pets
- 👓 views
- ⌄ 18-hole golf course
- Ⓢ notable spa facilities
- ≋ swimming pools
- ⚲ tennis

MOST POPULAR
1. Bellagio
2. Wynn
3. Venetian
4. Mandalay Bay
5. Caesars

TOP OVERALL
- 27 Wynn
- Four Seasons
- 26 Bellagio
- Ritz-Carlton
- 25 Palazzo

Alexis Park Resort ≋ | 15 | 14 | 15 | 15 | $99

E of Strip | 375 E. Harmon Ave. | 702-796-3300 | 800-582-2228 | www.alexispark.com | 500 suites

This "spread-out", "family-friendly hotel" is three miles from the convention center and "a $5 cab ride" east of the Strip ("the Hard Rock Hotel is across the street"); the "spacious" bungalow suites (with "small kitchenettes" and a living room) are a "good value" for Vegas, but many require a walk upstairs and are "worn and outdated", with "relatively thin walls"; "curt clerks" and frequent airplanes passing overhead are further buzzkills.

Bally's Las Vegas Ⓢ≋⚲ | 16 | 16 | 14 | 17 | $89

Strip | 3645 Las Vegas Blvd. S. | 702-967-4111 | fax 702-967-4405 | 888-742-9248 | www.ballyslv.com | 2549 rooms, 265 suites

It's "not luxury personified", but the "spacious rooms" and a "good location" "in the middle of the Strip action" easily "justify a trip" to this "slightly-smaller-than-the-Pentagon" "old-timer"; "service is hit-or-miss", "none of the many dining options stands out" and the "old-school Vegas decor - neon, low ceilings and endless gambling floors" - is "cheesy" or classic, depending on one's taste; but if this '70s vet is "not nearly as fancy as the top-drawer resorts", it's "not as expensive" either.

🅩 Bellagio Hotel ✗👓Ⓢ≋ | 26 | 23 | 27 | 27 | $169

Strip | 3600 Las Vegas Blvd. S. | 702-693-7111 | fax 702-693-8546 | 888-987-6667 | www.bellagio.com | 3421 rooms, 512 suites

"Top-of-the-line in every respect", this landmark is "as close to tasteful as one gets in Las Vegas", offering guests a "classic rather than plastic" experience at a true resort, "not a casino with rooms"; "plush" accommodations - the fountain views are "well

HOTELS

| | ROOMS | SERVICE | DINING | FACIL. | COST |

worth the extra cost" – add to the "va-va-voom" factor, as do the "outstanding" public areas with "spectacular" flowers, a collection of "first-class" restaurants, "fantastic shopping" and a "phenomenal" 55,000-sq.-ft. spa.

☑ Caesars Palace ✕ⓈⓈ≋

| 22 | 21 | 24 | 25 | $250 |

Strip | 3570 Las Vegas Blvd. S. | 702-731-7110 | fax 702-866-1700 | 866-227-5938 | www.caesarspalace.com | 3452 rooms, 245 suites

"There may be more sparkle at other spots", but the majority agrees this "immense" staple of the Strip still "exudes elegance"; "rooms vary from classic" with "round beds" and "mirrored ceilings" to "state-of-the-art refurbished" in "the newer upscale towers"; boosters report the staff is "attentive", the on-site Forum Shops are a "shopaholic's dream come true" and the restaurants are "amazing", but detractors liken this "way too big" "zoo" to a "haggard '50s cocktail waitress trapped in the '70s"; N.B. the Forum Tower is undergoing renovations, and a new Octavius Tower is set for 2009.

Flamingo Las Vegas Ⓢ≋✑

| 13 | 14 | 13 | 16 | $130 |

Strip | 3555 Las Vegas Blvd. S. | 702-733-3111 | 800-225-4882 | www.flamingolasvegas.com | 3545 rooms

Back in the '40s, "Bugsy Siegel started it all here" at what's now an "old Strip standard", still known for the "flamingos, penguins and fish ponds" dotting the grounds; while it's a "classic" with history, it's only recent renovations that elevate this beyond what some describe as a "'60s-era third-world hostel", so make sure you get one of the redone rooms with liberal splashes of pink, cutting-edge baths and 42-inch, flat-panel TVs, then head to the new topless pool (ladies get in free, men pay a cover charge).

☑ Four Seasons ✕❀♨Ⓢ≋

| 27 | 27 | 25 | 27 | $390 |

Strip | 3960 Las Vegas Blvd. S. | 702-632-5000 | fax 702-632-5195 | 877-632-5000 | www.fourseasons.com | 338 rooms, 86 suites

"In the midst of the bustling Las Vegas pulse", this "calming, luxurious" "no-casino hotel" offers the best of both worlds on the Strip with "its own entrance and all of its own facilities" as well as "easy access to the Mandalay Bay grounds and casino" located next door; fans rave about "the top-notch service" ("about as close to perfect as one can expect"), the "high-class" accommodations, the "delicious food", the "celebrity-filled private swimming pool" and – "thank goodness" – "the quiet."

Golden Nugget Hotel ♨Ⓢ≋

| 22 | 21 | 18 | 21 | $199 |

Downtown | 129 E. Fremont St. | 702-385-7111 | fax 702-386-8362 | 800-634-3454 | www.goldennugget.com | 1876 rooms, 34 suites, 5 penthouses

Major renovations have "much improved" this Downtown "standard of old Las Vegas" that's now run by Landry's Restaurants; "large" rooms, some with views of the Spring Mountain range, are "fabulous", the staff is "efficient" and there's a refurbished spa, salon and fitness center, a revamped showroom and a $30-million, three-story pool with a 200,000-gallon shark tank; though "away from the noise of the Strip", there's still "plenty to do" from the "fun" Fremont Street to the on-site dining, plus comedian Don Rickles signed an exclusive contract to perform here.

Let your voice be heard – visit ZAGAT.com/vote

HOTELS

	ROOMS	SERVICE	DINING	FACIL.	COST

Green Valley Ranch — 24 | 22 | 21 | 25 | $400
Resort & Spa
Henderson | 2300 Paseo Verde Pkwy. | 702-617-7777 | fax 702-617-7738 | 866-782-9487 | www.greenvalleyranchresort.com | 423 rooms, 73 suites
Just "a short drive" from the "cha-ching of the slots" on the Strip, this "luxurious-without-being-pretentious" resort in Henderson is an "oasis in the land of neon"; with "big fluffy beds", a "pool out of a Chanel No. 5 commercial" and plenty of "Mediterranean flair", it has "all you'll ever need", including "beautiful public spaces", plus a "fantastic" spa and "restaurants, grounds and shopping much nicer than expected"; although critics say "service tries, but misses the mark", the majority has a "relaxing" time.

Hard Rock Hotel & Casino — 20 | 18 | 20 | 23 | $299
E of Strip | 4455 Paradise Rd. | 702-693-5000 | fax 702-693-5010 | 800-473-7625 | www.hardrockhotel.com | 648 rooms, 96 suites
While it's "not as trendy as it once was", this "sexy" hotel is still the place to "party like a rock star" with a "fun, young crowd" in a "festive atmosphere"; guests say "the rooms are modern" ("try to get a renovated" one), ditto the restaurants (the newest is Ago, via chef Agostino Sciandri and partner Robert De Niro), "the small gaming floor is inviting" and the pool "is the reason to stay"; but while some surveyors "like its intimacy", others warn it's "far from the Strip" and there's "nonstop music."

Hooters Casino Hotel — 14 | 15 | 14 | 13 | $209
S of Strip | 115 E. Tropicana Ave. | 702-739-9000 | 866-584-6687 | www.hooterscasinohotel.com | 691 rooms, 5 suites
Whether you consider this lodging "within walking distance of the Strip" "good, clean fun", with a "smaller, cozier and friendlier" vibe than Vegas' mega-resorts, or you knock the "garish" "pine-and-surf decor" and "cheap furnishings and fixtures", most agree it's not exactly a "good environment for married couples" or families; for many guests, "spacious" rooms and a "nice pool area" aren't enough to compensate for "dingy and dilapidated" facilities.

Imperial Palace — 11 | 14 | 12 | 12 | $149
Strip | 3535 Las Vegas Blvd. S. | 702-731-3311 | 800-634-6441 | www.imperialpalace.com | 1100 rooms
Faint praise for "one of the few remaining" "old-school" casino-hotels "in the middle of the Strip" include a nod to "very attentive service" and an appreciation of the "ample parking space" and "easy monorail access"; critics, however, grumble about the "run-down appearance" and "tacky" rooms that "smell like smoke" and contain "inferior" towels and linens.

JW Marriott Resort & Spa — 27 | 22 | 18 | 25 | $289
NW | 221 N. Rampart Blvd. | 702-869-7777 | fax 702-869-7771 | 877-869-8777 | www.jwlasvegasresort.com | 471 rooms, 77 suites
Surrounded by championship golf courses and "impeccable grounds" in upscale Summerlin, this "great escape from hectic Downtown" (yet just a "shuttle to the Strip") boasts a "romantic", full-service spa, rooms with "magnificent bathrooms" (rainfall showerheads, Jacuzzi tubs) and an "excellent pool area"; the dining leaves something to be desired, however, and you'd best pack some walking shoes since it's all "a bit sprawling."

HOTELS

	ROOMS	SERVICE	DINING	FACIL.	COST

Las Vegas Hilton — — — — $159
E of Strip | 3000 Paradise Rd. | 702-732-5111 | fax 702-732-5778 | 800-732-7117 | www.hilton.com | 2473 rooms, 500 suites
Ongoing renovations are breathing new life into this 45-year-old legend where the plethora of activities and amenities includes tennis courts, a pool, a spa, a salon, a video arcade and lots of shopping in addition to the casino's jangling slots and quieter card tables; dining options run the gamut from the classic buffet to sushi to Benihana, and if you're lucky you'll catch a performance by Paul Anka, Barry Manilow or Tony Bennett.

Loews 22 23 20 24 $369
Lake Las Vegas Resort
Henderson | 101 Montelago Blvd. | 702-567-6000 | fax 702-567-6067 | 877-285-6397 | www.loewshotels.com | 454 rooms, 46 suites
"The ultimate man-made environment, including a huge lake in the middle of the desert", can be found at this "lovely", "low-key" "Mediterranean village" offering "a fun family escape" about a half-hour from "the insanity of the Strip"; while there's "no gambling on-site" and some balk at "cramped" accommodations and "food that's not nearly as good as it should be", advocates assert that the recreational facilities – which include a "pool, boating" and "golf" at two Jack Nicklaus–designed courses – and "excellent service" help make for a "relaxing" "respite."

Luxor Las Vegas 17 16 15 18 $170
Strip | 3900 Las Vegas Blvd. S. | 702-262-4000 | fax 702-262-4404 | 888-777-0188 | www.luxor.com | 3852 rooms, 555 suites, 1 penthouse
Located "far down the Strip", this "Egyptian-themed" establishment is "arguably one of Vegas' most impressive hotels", with "slanted-wall rooms" (in the pyramid section), "funky diagonally inclined elevators" and a "light that shines from the top" at night; alas, all the other amenities are "rather average" (except for the "impressive spa") and service is "nothing special", so most say it's "amusing for a one-night stay" only, unless you're traveling *en famille* (pricewise, it's a "pretty good deal").

Z Mandalay Bay Resort 24 21 24 26 $229
Strip | 3950 Las Vegas Blvd. S. | 702-632-7777 | fax 702-632-7328 | 877-632-7000 | www.mandalaybay.com | 2662 rooms, 1553 suites
Popular with the "twenty- to thirtysomething crowd", this "classy" spot with a "tropical" feel is "right up there with the best of them"; kudos go to the "best pools in town" (a three-story complex), miX Lounge (voted the No. 1 in overall Appeal in our *Las Vegas Nightlife* Survey), the "spacious" rooms, the "awesome spa" and "food that does not disappoint" (from Michael Mina's StripSteak to Rick Moonen's RM Seafood); but if you want a "really special" experience, head to its separate "best-kept-secret rooms in the country" – THEhotel tower suites with flat-screen TVs, wet bars and stylish lobby areas.

Marriott Las Vegas Suites 22 22 20 21 $199
E of Strip | 325 Convention Center Dr. | 702-650-2000 | fax 702-650-9466 | 800-228-9290 | www.marriott.com | 278 suites
"Just enough off the Strip that you can get in and out easily", this "great hotel" "if you're not in town to gamble" is a true "break from the over-

HOTELS

| | ROOMS | SERVICE | DINING | FACIL. | COST |

stimulation"; rooms are surprisingly "plush" and "modern", the staff is "happy" and you can "walk to the convention center", so the only drawback is being in an area that's "not friendly" for late-night strolls.

MGM Grand ✕ 👯 ⓢ ≋ | 19 | 18 | 22 | 22 | $109

Strip | 3799 Las Vegas Blvd. S. | 702-891-7777 | fax 702-891-1030 | 877-880-0880 | www.mgmgrand.com | 4216 rooms, 2527 suites, 29 villas

"If size matters to you", this "sprawling", "mall-like" property with a "freshly renovated" interior "delivers big", with "a dizzying array of amenities" that "makes its less than central location on the Strip worthwhile"; fans say the dining – "from coffee shop to ultra-high end" (L'Atelier de Joël Robuchon "is without equal" and was voted No. 1 for Food in our *Las Vegas Restaurants* Survey) – impresses, "the gaming floor is out of this world" and the remodeled rooms are "modern", but given the "crowds", service can be "impersonal"; N.B. the all-suite Signature (with three towers) is the newest addition.

Mirage Hotel ✕ 👯 ⓢ ≋ | 19 | 19 | 21 | 22 | $159

Strip | 3400 Las Vegas Blvd. S. | 702-791-7111 | fax 702-891-1030 | 800-374-9000 | www.mirage.com | 2763 rooms, 281 suites

This "quintessential grande dame of Las Vegas" "remains one of the best mega-resorts" thanks to "a staff that's eager to serve", an interesting "restaurant lineup" and "newly remodeled rooms" boasting "all the comforts"; with "great entertainment" for all ages (a "hot nightclub" for adults, a "kid-friendly" dolphin habitat), it's no wonder that despite some gripes, the majority maintains this "original gem still shines"; N.B. a $25-million upgrade is in store for its iconic erupting faux volcano, including 120 new fireball-throwing devices.

Monte Carlo Resort & Casino 👯 ⓢ ≋ | 18 | 19 | 17 | 20 | $149

Strip | 3770 Las Vegas Blvd. S. | 702-730-7777 | fax 702-730-7250 | 800-311-8999 | www.montecarlo.com | 2743 rooms, 259 suites

"Calmer than most casino hotels", this "oasis on the Strip" doesn't hit you over the head with a theme concept, so offers an "unpretentious experience" for many; it's an "excellent buy for the location" with "tasteful" decor (though walls are "paper-thin") and an "inexpensive spa"; but it's "middle-of-the-road" "vanilla" to those who consider it "just an upgraded Holiday Inn" with a "plain-Jane" lobby and a "poor choice of restaurants."

New York-New York Hotel & Casino 👯 ⓢ ≋ | 17 | 17 | 17 | 20 | $219

Strip | 3790 Las Vegas Blvd. S. | 702-740-6969 | fax 702-740-6700 | 888-696-9887 | www.nynyhotelcasino.com | 1909 rooms, 115 suites

"If you need a quick" Gotham "fix", this "overwhelming" NYC-themed hotel-cum–amusement park is "just like visiting the Big Apple" ("love the steam coming from the sewer vents"), but "with slot machines"; critics carp about the "bizarrely designed corridors", "some of the smallest standard rooms on the Strip" and the staff ("was there service?"), but most must find it a "cool concept" since all the attractions are perpetually "bombarded with tourists"; P.S. unless you're a Coney Island fan, better "avoid rooms near the roller coaster."

HOTELS

	ROOMS	SERVICE	DINING	FACIL.	COST

Orleans Hotel & Casino 🚻Ⓢ🏊 | 18 | 18 | 17 | 18 | $175

W of Strip | 4500 W. Tropicana Ave. | 702-365-7111 | fax 702-365-7500 | 800-675-3267 | www.orleanscasino.com | 1811 rooms, 75 suites

"Off the Strip" and "off the chart in value", given its "spacious rooms" and "friendly staff", this hotel "away from the bustle and congestion" has a "family-friendly" "gorgeous pool", 70-lane bowling center, video arcade and 18-screen movie theater; it may be an "average" spot overall with "nondescript" food options, but the "really good rates" save the day.

NEW Palazzo Resort, Hotel, & Casino ✕🚻Ⓢ🏊 | 28 | 22 | 26 | 25 | $199

Strip | 3325 Las Vegas Blvd. S. | 702-414-1000 | fax 702-414-4884 | 877-883-6423 | www.palazzolasvegas.com | 3066 suites

"Mama mia" – there are "no bachelorette parties, buffet-seekers or fraternity bashes" at this new "gem on the Strip", a "ridiculously opulent" "all-suite property" that's "still finding its legs", but "promises to be a worthy younger sister to the Venetian" next door (the two share amenities, including "the world-famous" Canyon Ranch Spa); guests rave about the "pristine rooms" with "large baths", "impeccable service", "outstanding restaurant selection", "super shopping" and "beautiful casinos" that exemplify "how Vegas should be."

Palms Casino Resort 🚻🍸Ⓢ🏊 | 20 | 18 | 20 | 21 | $599

W of Strip | 4321 W. Flamingo Rd. | 702-942-7777 | fax 702-942-7001 | 866-942-7777 | www.palms.com | 552 rooms, 150 suites

"Though off-Strip", this "trendy hotel" that "caters to a cooler, younger crowd" is "the ultimate party scene" where "the casino is abuzz with activity at all hours, and the glitterati stay awake and dressed to the nines for most of the night"; while our respondents report the rooms "are nothing to write home about", the "service is average" and the pool is "small", enthusiasts claim there's absolutely "no substitute for the nightlife" or "the eye candy" here.

Paris Las Vegas Ⓢ🏊 | 20 | 19 | 21 | 20 | $109

Strip | 3655 Las Vegas Blvd. S. | 702-946-7000 | fax 702-946-4405 | 877-603-4386 | www.parislasvegas.com | 2621 rooms, 295 suites

With a "center-of-the-action" location and a casino that "isn't as hectic as most", this older property may not be "in the same league as Bellagio" but you can appreciate "French character without the attitude"; given the "average" rooms and facilities where "nothing stands out" ("other than the faux Eiffel Tower"), many are "not impressed."

Planet Hollywood Resort & Casino Ⓢ🏊 | 18 | 16 | 18 | 18 | $199

Strip | 3667 Las Vegas Blvd. S. | 702-785-5555 | fax 702-785-9450 | 866-517-3263 | www.planethollywood.com | 2300 rooms, 300 suites

"They certainly rubbed the lamp right when they renovated the former Aladdin" into this "flashy" hotel that "provides good value for the Strip" with "basic", "comfortable" rooms ("above-average baths") and "varied food choices" (including Koi from LA and Strip House from NYC); "they have everything you need", from a "shiny redone casino" with "dancing girls on the tables" to "a variety of stores", though the required "march through the labyrinth of shops" to enter the hotel is a minus.

HOTELS

	ROOMS	SERVICE	DINING	FACIL.	COST

Platinum Hotel & Spa ✕🐾♨️Ⓢ🏊 | - | - | - | - | $359

E of Strip | 211 E. Flamingo Rd. | 702-365-5000 | fax 702-365-5001 | 877-211-9211 | www.theplatinumhotel.com | 255 suites

Ok, there's no gaming or smoking at this all-suite boutique hotel east of the Strip, but you will find "great rooms" that include gourmet kitchens, whirlpool tubs and private balconies with views, "good but expensive food", a "nice upper-level pool" and the rejuvenating WELL spa; just "plan for a hike" to get to the heart of Sin City action.

Red Rock Casino Resort & Spa 🍴♨️Ⓢ🏊 | 27 | 22 | 21 | 26 | $199

NW | 11011 W. Charleston Blvd. | 702-797-7777 | fax 702-797-7771 | 866-767-7773 | www.redrocklasvegas.com | 816 rooms

"What's not to enjoy?" at this "breathtakingly beautiful" resort from Station Casinos that's "away from the insanity of the Strip", with "comfortable rooms" boasting "gorgeous views of Red Rock Park" (just a "short drive" away) and amenities that "rival anything" near the action (and "at a lower cost"); "the pool is a high point", as is the "gaming" and the "eye-catching cocktail lounges", most notably Cherry; N.B. a recently completed tower almost doubles its capacity.

Renaissance ♨️🏊 | ▽ 26 | 25 | 22 | 20 | $139

E of Strip | 3400 Paradise Rd. | 702-784-5700 | fax 702-735-3130 | 800-750-0980 | www.renaissancelasvegas.com | 518 rooms, 30 suites

Accommodations at this "incredibly convenient" business hotel within "walking distance to the Convention Center" boast flat-panel TVs and "chic", "'50s-retro" "Rat Pack" decor; "excellent" business services, an "attentive" staff and the lack of a casino ("yay!") give it a "less touristy", professional ambiance, and regulars say Envy steakhouse is both a "must for dinner" and a "cozy" spot for drinks; a pool with "no afternoon sun" is a small trade-off for those who "don't want to be on the Strip" and appreciate being around others who are "appropriate in attire and mannerism."

Rio All-Suite Hotel & Casino ♨️Ⓢ🏊 | 20 | 18 | 19 | 20 | $120

W of Strip | 3700 W. Flamingo Rd. | 702-777-7777 | fax 702-777-2360 | 866-746-7671 | www.playrio.com | 2551 suites

The views are decidedly mixed on this off-Strip, Brazilian-themed, all-suiter; fans dig the "fun", "24/7 carnival atmosphere", the lively clubs, the buffet and the "huge" accommodations, but foes frown over a "once shining star that's now a black hole", citing "marginal dining", "large rooms passed off as suites" and the "cheesy" vibe that "needs some work."

Z Ritz-Carlton Lake Las Vegas 🎾🍴♨️⛷Ⓢ🏊 | 27 | 26 | 24 | 27 | $299

Henderson | 1610 Lake Las Vegas Pkwy. | 702-567-4700 | fax 702-567-4777 | 800-241-3333 | www.ritzcarlton.com | 314 rooms, 35 suites

"A calming alternative to the noise and glitz of the Strip", this "practically perfect" Henderson resort offers "typically wonderful Ritz-Carlton service", "special rooms" and "nice spa facilities" in a "beautiful desert setting"; for "pure luxury", the "club-level" suites on a Tuscan-inspired bridge over the lake "are the way to go" ("awesome

HOTELS

| | ROOMS | SERVICE | DINING | FACIL. | COST |

service"), while a "great" Jack Nicklaus–designed golf course awaits duffers; still, some say it's "way too far" from the Vegas action.

Riviera Hotel & Casino ⑤≋ | - | 13 | 12 | 13 | $250

E Side | 2901 Las Vegas Blvd. S. | 702-734-5110 | fax 702-794-9451 | 800-634-6753 | www.rivierahotel.com | 1942 rooms, 158 suites

One of the oldest major hotels in Las Vegas, this "down-to-earth" 50-plus-year-old veteran still manages to please some who like the "well-priced", "spacious" rooms; and critics who cited "dated" digs may be pleased to hear that a major remodeling was completed in '08, thus outdating our Rooms score.

Signature at MGM Grand 🐕♨⑤≋ | 27 | 24 | 18 | 22 | $159

Strip | 145 E. Harmon Ave. | 702-891-7777 | fax 702-891-1275 | 877-612-2121 | www.signaturemgmgrand.com | 1728 suites

For "a quiet oasis away from the Strip", this "beautiful" three-tower "escape" with a separate entrance on the MGM Grand property offers "everything you can imagine" – "spacious", "smoke-free" suites with "top-notch facilities", "royal" treatment from an "excellent" staff and a "relaxing pool area"; if you want more action, though, "put on your walking shoes" and "trek" via "indoor walkways" to the main hotel's casino, restaurants and nightclubs.

Skylofts at MGM Grand ♨≋ | - | - | - | - | $600

Strip | 3799 Las Vegas Blvd. | 702-891-3832 | fax 702-891-1030 | 877-646-5638 | www.skyloftsmgmgrand.com | 51 loft rooms

Atop the MGM Grand, this swanky boutique hotel offers luxurious one- to three-bedroom lofts with expansive views of the skyline; furnishings include HDTV entertainment systems, bathrooms with spa tubs and steam rooms, plus amenities like espresso machines, free beverages and fresh fruit; guests also receive preferred seating at MGM restaurants and shows, airport limo service and their own personal butlers.

South Point ⑤≋ | 21 | 19 | 18 | 20 | $85

SW | 9777 Las Vegas Blvd. | 702-796-7111 | fax 702-272-3266 | 866-796-7111 | www.southpointcasino.com | 1296 rooms, 54 suites

"Large", "beautiful" rooms with "gorgeous baths" are a highlight of this hotel in the "southern part of the Las Vegas valley" that's "a ways off the Strip" and probably requires "getting a rental car" (or paying "very expensive taxi fees") to visit the bigger casinos; there's a kids' pool, a bowling alley, gaming and a "customer-focused staff", but the "on-site restaurants are marginal."

Treasure Island ♨⑤≋ | - | - | - | - | $99

Strip | 3300 Las Vegas Blvd. S. | 702-894-7111 | fax 702-894-7414 | 800-288-7206 | www.treasureisland.com | 2665 rooms, 218 suites, 2 penthouses

A complete refurbishment a few years back, along with renovations in 2008, have made this veteran property at the end of the Strip a "pleasant surprise" for most guests; accommodations sport modern decor, "comfortable" signature beds, iPod alarm clocks and flat-panel TVs, the swimming pool has "heavenly cabanas", the aquatic-themed Wet spa features unique water-based treatments and service is "prompt"; the "happening" atmosphere includes the "best sports betting area", Cirque

Let your voice be heard – visit ZAGAT.com/vote

HOTELS

| | ROOMS | SERVICE | DINING | FACIL. | COST |

du Soleil's *Mystère*, the scantily clad Sirens (performed several times daily at the hotel entrance) and a new Christian Audigier nightclub.

NEW Trump International Hotel & Tower

▽ 21 | 22 | 18 | 19 | $199

Strip | 3128 Las Vegas Blvd. S. | 702-982-0000 | fax 702-476-8450 | 866-939-8786 | www.trumplv.com | 1282 suites

Fans of this new 64-floor Trump property minutes from the Strip action find it "an oasis" for the "ego-driven, jet-set crowd" with "unobtrusive service", a spa and accommodations that include 50 penthouse suites with floor-to-ceiling windows and European-style kitchens; on-site eateries include DJT, serving New American fare, and the poolside H2(Eau).

☒ Venetian Hotel

27 | 22 | 25 | 26 | $379

Strip | 3355 Las Vegas Blvd. S. | 702-414-1000 | fax 702-414-1100 | 877-883-6423 | www.venetian.com | 4027 suites

"Get swept away" at this "true Italian gem in the desert", a "huge", "all-suite" "city under one roof" in the "center of the Strip", touting "luxurious rooms", "endless quality dining options" (from top toques like Mario Batali and David Burke), a "friendly, attentive staff" (its La Scena Lounge was voted the No. 1 spot for Service in our *Las Vegas Nightlife* Survey), plus an on-site Canyon Ranch Spa and "great shopping" opportunities along the Grand Canal "mall" ("take a gondola ride"); though some bemoan the "maze"-like design, admirers ask "why would you ever leave?"; N.B. it shares amenities with its sister, Palazzo.

Westin Casuarina Hotel, Casino & Spa

19 | 18 | 11 | 15 | $155

E of Strip | 160 E. Flamingo Rd. | 702-836-9775 | fax 702-836-9776 | 866-837-4215 | www.westin.com | 816 rooms, 10 suites

"Not your typical resort", this "no-frills" spot is "good for an in 'n' out trip" "for business travelers" or "non-gamblers who want to stay one step removed from the Strip's hurly-burly" (it's located a block east); however, skeptics snap that "small" is the operative word here, from the "postage stamp–size rooms" to the "undistinguished restaurant" to the "boring casino", and though service can be "gracious", this one is definitely "below average for a Westin."

☒ Wynn Las Vegas Casino Resort

28 | 25 | 27 | 27 | $300

Strip | 3131 Las Vegas Blvd. S. | 702-770-7100 | fax 702-770-1571 | 888-320-9966 | www.wynnlasvegas.com | 2108 rooms, 608 suites

There's "no need to stay anywhere else" cheer champions of this overthe-top piece of "eye candy", especially if you "get a room on the upper floors facing the Strip" for "incredible" night views; there are "dining choices for every taste", "winning nightlife", decor that's "top-notch" (the velvet-lined Tryst club was voted No. 1 for Decor in the *Las Vegas Nightlife* Survey) and a "breathtaking" golf course ("the only in-town links left"); still, sour sorts "can't figure out what all the fuss is about."

INDEXES

Dining Cuisines 156
Dining Locations 162
Dining Special Features 168
Nightlife Locations 187
Nightlife Special Appeals 189
Shopping Merchandise 198
Shopping Locations 200
Shopping Special Features 202
Sites & Attractions Types 205
Sites & Attractions Locations 206
Golf Features 207
Hotel Locations 209
Hotel Special Features 210

Dining Cuisines

Includes restaurant names, locations and Food ratings.

AMERICAN (NEW)

🇿 Aureole | **Strip**	25
🇿 Bradley Ogden | **Strip**	26
Café Bellagio | **Strip**	20
Canyon Ranch | **Strip**	21
NEW CatHouse | **Strip**	–
NEW Company Bistro | **Strip**	–
David Burke | **Strip**	24
NEW DJT | **Strip**	–
NEW Hawaiian Tropic | **Strip**	–
Kona Grill | **NW**	18
Medici Café | **Lake LV**	22
🇿 miX | **Strip**	23
Postrio | **Strip**	24
Potato Valley | **Downtown**	–
🇿 Rosemary's | **W Side**	28
Spago | **Strip**	23
NEW Table 10 | **Strip**	–
🇿 Tableau | **Strip**	27
Table 34 | **S of Strip**	–
Top of the World | **Strip**	20
Verandah | **Strip**	23
Vintner Grill | **NW**	–
NEW White Chocolate | **Henderson**	–
Wolfgang Puck | **Strip**	21

AMERICAN (TRADITIONAL)

All-American B&G | **W of Strip**	20
America | **Strip**	15
Applebee's | **multi.**	13
Big Dog's | **multi.**	17
Buffet (Golden Nugget) | **Downtown**	17
Cafe, The | **Strip**	19
Cafe Lago | **Strip**	17
Caribe Café | **Strip**	17
Cheesecake Factory | **multi.**	20
Chicago Brew. | **multi.**	17
Chili's | **multi.**	16
Claim Jumper | **multi.**	–
Dick's | **Strip**	–
Egg & I | **W Side**	21
Fix | **Strip**	23
Hard Rock Cafe | **E of Strip**	15
Harley-Davidson | **Strip**	15
Hash House | **W Side**	20
Jimmy Buffett's | **Strip**	17
Lake Mead Cruises | **Boulder City**	–
Martinis | **NW**	–
MGM Buffet | **Strip**	17
Mr. Lucky's | **E of Strip**	19
Planet Hollywood | **Strip**	13
Raffles Café | **Strip**	16
Red, White/Blue | **Strip**	15
NEW Simon | **W of Strip**	–
TGI Friday's | **multi.**	15
Triple 7 | **Downtown**	21

ASIAN

Café Wasabi | **W Side**	21
China Grill | **Strip**	23
Chinois | **Strip**	22
Fusia | **Strip**	21
Little Buddha | **W of Strip**	24
Sensi | **Strip**	25

BAKERIES

Jean Philippe | **Strip**	26
Tintoretto | **Strip**	20

BARBECUE

Famous Dave's | **multi.**	20
Lucille's | **Henderson**	22
Memphis BBQ | **multi.**	21
NEW RUB | **W of Strip**	–
Salt Lick | **NW**	15
Tony Roma's | **multi.**	16

BRAZILIAN

Pampas | **Strip**	22
Samba | **Strip**	20
Yolie's | **E of Strip**	21

BRITISH

Crown & Anchor | **E Side**	16

156   40,000 places to eat, drink, stay & play – free at ZAGAT.com

BURGERS

All-American B&G	W of Strip	20
Big Dog's	multi.	17
NEW BLT Burger	Strip	-
Burger Bar	Strip	23
Fatburger	multi.	21
Hard Rock Cafe	E of Strip	15
In-N-Out	multi.	24

CAJUN

Big Al's	W of Strip	19
Z Emeril's	Strip	23
NEW New Orleans Connection	E Side	-

CALIFORNIAN

Nobhill Tavern	Strip	26

CARIBBEAN

NEW Tommy Bahama's	S of Strip	-

CHINESE

(* dim sum specialist)

Ah Sin*	Strip	20
Cathay Hse.*	W Side	21
Chang's*	multi.	21
Chin Chin*	Strip	20
Dragon Noodle	Strip	18
Empress Court*	Strip	22
Fin	Strip	25
Jasmine	Strip	23
Joyful House	W Side	21
Noodles*	Strip	22
Noodle Shop	Strip	19
Pearl	Strip	23
P.F. Chang's	multi.	21
Ping Pang Pong*	W Side	21
Sam Woo	W Side	20
Shanghai Lilly	Strip	22
Wing Lei	Strip	25
NEW Zine	Strip	-

COFFEE SHOPS/DINERS

Café Bellagio	Strip	20
Caribe Café	Strip	17
Coffee Pub	W of Strip	19
Mr. Lucky's	E of Strip	19
Raffles Café	Strip	16
Roxy's	Strip	16

CONTINENTAL

Z Hugo's Cellar	Downtown	26
Z Michael's	S of Strip	26
Pahrump Valley	Pahrump	21
Tinoco's	Downtown	23

CREOLE

Big Al's	W of Strip	19
Z Emeril's	Strip	23
NEW New Orleans Connection	E Side	-

CUBAN

Florida Café	Central	19
Rincon Criollo	Downtown	-

DELIS

Cafe Heidelberg	E of Strip	22
Canter's	Strip	18
Carnegie Deli	Strip	21
Stage Deli	Strip	20

DESSERT

Chocolate Swan	Strip	23
Ethel's	multi.	21
Giorgio	Strip	20
Jean Philippe	Strip	26
NEW Payard	Strip	-
Red, White/Blue	Strip	15
Tintoretto	Strip	20

ECLECTIC

Bay Side	Strip	19
Z Bellagio Buffet	Strip	24
Big Kitchen	Strip	16
Black Mtn.	Henderson	17
Buffet (Wynn)	Strip	-
Buffet (Hilton)	E of Strip	17
Cafe Lago	Strip	17
Carnival World	W of Strip	20
Carson St.	Downtown	17
Cravings	Strip	22
Elephant Bar	Henderson	17
Feast, The	multi.	18
Feast Around/World	multi.	18

Let your voice be heard – visit ZAGAT.com/vote

Festival	multi.	14
Firelight	E Side	15
Flavors	Strip	18
French Mkt.	W of Strip	19
Garden Ct.	Downtown	19
Grand Lux	Strip	20
Spice Mkt.	Strip	22
Sterling Brunch	Strip	26
NEW SushiSamba	Strip	–
Z Todd's	Henderson	28

FONDUE

| Melting Pot | multi. | 21 |

FRENCH

Alizé	W of Strip	26
Z André's	multi.	26
Eiffel Tower	Strip	22
Le Village	Strip	23
Pamplemousse	E Side	25

FRENCH (BISTRO)

Z Bouchon	Strip	25
Le Provençal	Strip	22
Marché Bacchus	NW	24
Z Mon Ami Gabi	Strip	23
NEW Morels	Strip	–
NEW Payard	Strip	–
Pinot	Strip	22

FRENCH (NEW)

Z Alex	Strip	27
Z Daniel Boulud	Strip	26
Fleur de Lys	Strip	25
Z Guy Savoy	Strip	28
Z Joël Robuchon	Strip	28
Z L'Atelier/Robuchon	Strip	28
Z Le Cirque	Strip	26
Les Artistes	Strip	22
Z miX	Strip	23
Z Picasso	Strip	27

GERMAN

| Cafe Heidelberg | E of Strip | 22 |

HAWAIIAN

| Kona Grill | NW | 18 |
| Roy's | multi. | 24 |

HEALTH FOOD

(See also Vegetarian)

| Canyon Ranch | Strip | 21 |

INDIAN

Gandhi	E of Strip	21
Gaylord's	W of Strip	20
India Palace	E of Strip	24
Origin	E of Strip	26
Tamba	Strip	21

IRISH

| Auld Dubliner | Lake LV | 20 |
| Nine Fine Irish | Strip | 17 |

ITALIAN

(N=Northern; S=Southern)

NEW Ago	E of Strip	–
al Dente	N	Strip	19
Antonio's	W of Strip	25
Z B&B	Strip	26
Bartolotta	Strip	24
Battista's	E of Strip	17
Bootlegger	S	S of Strip	19
NEW Brio	S of Strip	–
Cafe Martorano	W of Strip	25
Canaletto	N	Strip	21
Carluccio's	E Side	21
NEW Carnevino	Strip	–
Casa Nicola	N	E of Strip	20
Chicago Joe's	Downtown	21
Circo	N	Strip	25
NEW Dal Toro	Strip	–
Enoteca/Marco	Strip	21
Fellini's	Strip	24
Ferraro's	W Side	26
Fiamma Trattoria	Strip	22
Gaetano's	N	Henderson	23
Giorgio	Strip	20
Il Fornaio	Strip	20
Il Mulino NY	Strip	26
NEW Le Golosita	Henderson	–
Le Provençal	Strip	22
Lombardi's	N	Strip	20
NEW Lucio	W Side	–
Luna Rossa	Lake LV	20
Maggiano's	Strip	20

Market City	**Strip**	18
Metro Pizza	**Henderson**	24
Montesano's	**Henderson**	20
Nora's	**multi.**	24
Nove	**W of Strip**	27
Onda	**Strip**	22
Panevino	**S of Strip**	21
Pasta Mia	**N	W Side**	23
Pasta Shop	**E Side**	24
Penazzi	**Strip**	22
Piero's	**N	E of Strip**	24
Rao's	**S	Strip**	23
Romano's	**multi.**	17
Sensi	**Strip**	25
Spiedini	**NW**	21
NEW Stratta	**Strip**	–
Terra Verde	**Henderson**	–
Tintoretto	**Strip**	20
Trattoria del Lupo	**Strip**	21
Trevi	**Strip**	20
Valentino	**Strip**	23
Ventano	**Henderson**	20
Verandah	**Strip**	23
Zeffirino	**N	Strip**	21

JAPANESE

(* sushi specialist)

Ah Sin*	**Strip**	20
Benihana	**E of Strip**	19
Hamada*	**multi.**	19
Hyakumi*	**Strip**	24
I Love Sushi*	**Henderson**	24
Japonais	**Strip**	23
NEW Kabuki	**S of Strip**	–
NEW Koi	**Strip**	–
Makino*	**multi.**	21
Z Nobu*	**E of Strip**	28
Z Okada*	**Strip**	25
Osaka Bistro*	**multi.**	22
Osaka Cuisine*	**NW**	20
Sapporo*	**W Side**	21
Sen*	**W Side**	27
Shibuya*	**Strip**	25
Sushi Roku*	**Strip**	24
Todai*	**Strip**	18
Togoshi Ramen	**E Side**	–
NEW Yellowtail*	**Strip**	–

MEDITERRANEAN

Casa Nicola	**E of Strip**	20
Grape St.	**NW**	23
NEW Lavo	**Strip**	–
MiraLago	**Lake LV**	21
Z Olives	**Strip**	23
Paymon's	**multi.**	23
Postrio	**Strip**	24

MEXICAN

Agave	**NW**	18
Baja Fresh	**multi.**	19
Border Grill	**Strip**	22
NEW Caminos de Morelia	**W Side**	–
Chevys	**Henderson**	14
Chipotle	**multi.**	20
Diablo's	**Strip**	–
Diego	**Strip**	21
Doña Maria	**multi.**	19
Don Miguel's	**W of Strip**	19
NEW Dos Caminos	**Strip**	–
El Jefe's	**Henderson**	17
El Sombrero	**Downtown**	–
NEW Galerias	**NW**	–
Garduño's	**multi.**	20
Guadalajara	**multi.**	19
Isla	**Strip**	23
NEW La Madonna	**SW**	–
La Salsa	**multi.**	15
Lindo Michoacan	**multi.**	–
Pink Taco	**E of Strip**	19
Rubio's	**multi.**	18
NEW T&T	**Strip**	–
Taqueria Cañonita	**Strip**	20
Viva Mercado's	**W Side**	22
NEW Yolos	**Strip**	–

MIDDLE EASTERN

Paymon's	**multi.**	23
Spice Mkt.	**Strip**	22

MOROCCAN

Marrakech	**E of Strip**	20

Let your voice be heard – visit ZAGAT.com/vote

NOODLE SHOPS

Noodles	Strip	22
Noodle Shop	**Strip**	19
Togoshi Ramen	**E Side**	–

PACIFIC RIM

Café Wasabi	**W Side**	21
Sapporo	**W Side**	21
Second St.	**Downtown**	24
NEW Tommy Bahama's	**S of Strip**	–

PAN-ASIAN

Ah Sin	**Strip**	20
NEW Jade	**Strip**	–
Noodles	**Strip**	22
Red 8	**Strip**	23
Social Hse.	**Strip**	25
Tao	**Strip**	23
NEW Woo	**Strip**	–

PIZZA

Bootlegger	**S of Strip**	19
Cal. Pizza	**multi.**	18
Canaletto	**Strip**	21
Le Provençal	**Strip**	22
Metro Pizza	**multi.**	24
NEW Pie Town	**Henderson**	–
Sammy's	**multi.**	21
Settebello	**Henderson**	–
Spago	**Strip**	23
Trattoria del Lupo	**Strip**	21

POLYNESIAN

Trader Vic's	**Strip**	–

PUB FOOD

Auld Dubliner	**Lake LV**	20
Chicago Brew.	**multi.**	17
Crown & Anchor	**E Side**	16
Nine Fine Irish	**Strip**	17

RUSSIAN

Artem	**W Side**	21

SANDWICHES

Canter's	**Strip**	18
Capriotti's	**multi.**	23
Carnegie Deli	**Strip**	21
Stage Deli	**Strip**	20
'wichcraft	**Strip**	20

SEAFOOD

AquaKnox	**Strip**	23
Bartolotta	**Strip**	24
Big Al's	**W of Strip**	19
Billy Bob's	**E Side**	24
Bonefish	**Henderson**	21
Broiler	**multi.**	21
Buzio's	**W of Strip**	24
Canal St.	**W of Strip**	22
Craftsteak	**Strip**	25
Z Emeril's	**Strip**	23
Empress Court	**Strip**	22
Fin	**Strip**	25
Hush Puppy	**multi.**	22
Joe's	**Strip**	25
Joyful House	**W Side**	21
King's	**Henderson**	23
Makino	**multi.**	21
McCormick/Schmick	**E of Strip**	21
Z Michael Mina	**Strip**	27
Morton's Steak	**E of Strip**	25
Palm, The	**Strip**	25
Piero's	**E of Strip**	24
Range	**Strip**	23
Redwood	**Downtown**	24
NEW Rest. Charlie	**Strip**	–
Rick Moonen's	**Strip**	24
Rosewood	**Strip**	23
Seablue	**Strip**	24
Sensi	**Strip**	25
Tillerman	**E Side**	23
Triple George	**Downtown**	22

SMALL PLATES

(See also Spanish tapas specialist)

NEW Company Bistro	Amer.	**Strip**	–
NEW CUT	Steak	**Strip**	–
Enoteca/Marco	Italian	**Strip**	21
Fix	Amer.	**Strip**	23
Grape St.	Med.	**NW**	23
Z L'Atelier/Robuchon	French	**Strip**	28

Nora's | Italian | **multi.**	24
🏆 Rosemary's | Amer. | **W Side**	28
Social Hse. | Pan-Asian | **Strip**	25
Stack | Steak | **Strip**	24
Tao | Pan-Asian | **Strip**	23
Terra Verde | Italian | **Henderson**	–

SOUL FOOD

Kathy's | **Henderson**	24
Lucille's | **Henderson**	22

SOUTHERN

Hush Puppy | **multi.**	22
Kathy's | **Henderson**	24
NEW Louis's LV | **S of Strip**	–

SOUTHWESTERN

Garduño's | **multi.**	20
🏆 Mesa Grill | **Strip**	25
Roadrunner | **multi.**	16

SPANISH

(* tapas specialist)

Cafe/Reeba!* | **Strip**	22
Firefly* | **E of Strip**	24

STEAKHOUSES

AJ's | **E of Strip**	23
Alan Albert's | **Strip**	22
Austins Steak | **N Las Vegas**	24
Bally's | **Strip**	22
Billy Bob's | **E Side**	24
Binion's | **Downtown**	24
Boa | **Strip**	24
Bob Taylor's | **NW**	20
NEW Brand Steak | **Strip**	–
Broiler | **multi.**	21
Canal St. | **W of Strip**	22
Capital Grille | **Strip**	26
NEW Carnevino | **Strip**	–
Charlie Palmer | **Strip**	25
Craftsteak | **Strip**	25
NEW CUT | **Strip**	–
🏆 Del Frisco's | **E of Strip**	26
🏆 Delmonico | **Strip**	26
Envy | **E of Strip**	21
Fleming's | **W Side**	25
Gallagher's | **Strip**	24
Golden Steer | **W of Strip**	22
Hank's | **Henderson**	23
Joe's | **Strip**	25
Lawry's | **E of Strip**	25
Les Artistes | **Strip**	22
🏆 Mon Ami Gabi | **Strip**	23
Morton's Steak | **E of Strip**	25
Neros | **Strip**	24
N9ne | **W of Strip**	25
Outback | **multi.**	18
Palm, The | **Strip**	25
Pampas | **Strip**	22
🏆 Prime | **Strip**	26
Pullman Grille | **Downtown**	24
Range | **Strip**	23
Redwood | **Downtown**	24
Rosewood | **Strip**	23
Ruth's Chris | **multi.**	24
Samba | **Strip**	20
Smith & Wollensky | **Strip**	23
Stack | **Strip**	24
Steak Hse. (Circus) | **Strip**	25
Steak Hse. (Treasure Is.) | **Strip**	23
Steakhouse46 | **Strip**	26
Strip Hse. | **Strip**	–
StripSteak | **Strip**	25
SW Steak | **Strip**	26
🏆 T-Bones | **NW**	25
Tillerman | **E Side**	23
Vic & Anthony's | **Downtown**	25
Yolie's | **E of Strip**	21

TEX-MEX

Chili's | **multi.**	16

THAI

Archi's | **W Side**	24
🏆 Lotus of Siam | **E Side**	27
Thai Spice | **W Side**	21
NEW V Thai | **W Side**	–

VEGETARIAN

Origin | **E of Strip**	26

VIETNAMESE

NEW Zine | **Strip**	–

Dining Locations

Includes restaurant names, cuisines and Food ratings.

CENTRAL

Doña Maria	*Mex.*	19
Florida Café	*Cuban*	19
Tony Roma's	*BBQ*	16

DOWNTOWN

🛿 André's	*French*	26
Binion's	*Steak*	24
Buffet (Golden Nugget)	*Amer.*	17
Carson St.	*Eclectic*	17
Chicago Brew.	*Amer.*	17
Chicago Joe's	*Italian*	21
El Sombrero	*Mex.*	–
Garden Ct.	*Eclectic*	19
🛿 Hugo's Cellar	*Continental*	26
Makino	*Japanese*	21
Potato Valley	*Amer.*	–
Pullman Grille	*Steak*	24
Redwood	*Seafood/Steak*	24
Rincon Criollo	*Cuban*	–
Second St.	*Pac. Rim*	24
Tinoco's	*Continental*	23
Tony Roma's	*BBQ*	16
Triple George	*Seafood*	22
Triple 7	*Amer.*	21
Vic & Anthony's	*Steak*	25

EAST OF STRIP

NEW Ago	*Italian*	–
AJ's	*Steak*	23
Battista's	*Italian*	17
Benihana	*Japanese*	19
Buffet (Hilton)	*Eclectic*	17
Cafe Heidelberg	*German*	22
Casa Nicola	*Italian/Med.*	20
🛿 Del Frisco's	*Steak*	26
Envy	*Steak*	21
Firefly	*Spanish*	24
Gandhi	*Indian*	21
Hamada	*Japanese*	19
Hard Rock Cafe	*Amer.*	15
India Palace	*Indian*	24
Lawry's	*Steak*	25
Marrakech	*Moroccan*	20
McCormick/Schmick	*Seafood*	21
Metro Pizza	*Pizza*	24
Morton's Steak	*Steak*	25
Mr. Lucky's	*Diner*	19
🛿 Nobu	*Japanese*	28
Origin	*Indian*	26
P.F. Chang's	*Chinese*	21
Piero's	*Italian/Seafood*	24
Pink Taco	*Mex.*	19
Roy's	*Hawaiian*	24
Ruth's Chris	*Steak*	24
Yolie's	*Brazilian/Steak*	21

EAST SIDE

Applebee's	*Amer.*	13
Baja Fresh	*Mex.*	19
Big Dog's	*Amer.*	17
Billy Bob's	*Seafood/Steak*	24
Broiler	*Seafood/Steak*	21
Capriotti's	*Sandwiches*	23
Carluccio's	*Italian*	21
Chili's	*Amer./Tex-Mex*	16
Chipotle	*Mex.*	20
Crown & Anchor	*British*	16
Fatburger	*Burgers*	21
Feast, The	*Eclectic*	18
Firelight	*Eclectic*	15
Guadalajara	*Mex.*	19
Hush Puppy	*Seafood/Southern*	22
In-N-Out	*Burgers*	24
La Salsa	*Mex.*	15
Lindo Michoacan	*Mex.*	–
🛿 Lotus of Siam	*Thai*	27
Memphis BBQ	*BBQ*	21
Metro Pizza	*Pizza*	24
NEW New Orleans Connection	*Cajun/Creole*	–
Outback	*Steak*	18
Pamplemousse	*French*	25

Pasta Shop	*Italian*	24	
Paymon's	*Med./Mideastern*	23	
Roadrunner	*SW*	16	
TGI Friday's	*Amer.*	15	
Tillerman	*Seafood/Steak*	23	
Togoshi Ramen	*Japanese*	–	

Terra Verde	*Italian*	–
TGI Friday's	*Amer.*	15
🅉 Todd's	*Eclectic*	28
Tony Roma's	*BBQ*	16
Ventano	*Italian*	20
🆕 White Chocolate	*Amer.*	–

HENDERSON

Applebee's	*Amer.*	13
Black Mtn.	*Eclectic*	17
Bonefish	*Seafood*	21
Cheesecake Factory	*Amer.*	20
Chevys	*Mex.*	14
Chili's	*Amer./Tex-Mex*	16
Chipotle	*Mex.*	20
Claim Jumper	*Amer.*	–
Elephant Bar	*Eclectic*	17
El Jefe's	*Mex.*	17
Ethel's	*Dessert*	21
Fatburger	*Burgers*	21
Feast, The	*Eclectic*	18
Feast Around/World	*Eclectic*	18
Festival	*Eclectic*	14
Gaetano's	*Italian*	23
Guadalajara	*Mex.*	19
Hank's	*Steak*	23
I Love Sushi	*Japanese*	24
In-N-Out	*Burgers*	24
Kathy's	*Southern*	24
King's	*Seafood*	23
La Salsa	*Mex.*	15
🆕 Le Golosita	*Italian*	–
Lucille's	*BBQ*	22
Makino	*Japanese*	21
Melting Pot	*Fondue*	21
Metro Pizza	*Pizza*	24
Montesano's	*Italian*	20
Osaka Bistro	*Japanese*	22
Outback	*Steak*	18
P.F. Chang's	*Chinese*	21
🆕 Pie Town	*Pizza*	–
Romano's	*Italian*	17
Rubio's	*Mex.*	18
Sammy's	*Pizza*	21
Settebello	*Pizza*	–

LAKE LAS VEGAS

Auld Dubliner	*Irish*	20
Luna Rossa	*Italian*	20
Medici Café	*Amer.*	22
MiraLago	*Med.*	21

NORTH LAS VEGAS

Austins Steak	*Steak*	24
Feast Around/World	*Eclectic*	18
Memphis BBQ	*BBQ*	21
Outback	*Steak*	18

NORTHWEST

Agave	*Mex.*	18
Applebee's	*Amer.*	13
Baja Fresh	*Mex.*	19
Bob Taylor's	*Steak*	20
Capriotti's	*Sandwiches*	23
Cheesecake Factory	*Amer.*	20
Chili's	*Amer./Tex-Mex*	16
Chipotle	*Mex.*	20
Claim Jumper	*Amer.*	–
Doña Maria	*Mex.*	19
Famous Dave's	*BBQ*	20
Fatburger	*Burgers*	21
Feast, The	*Eclectic*	18
Festival	*Eclectic*	14
🆕 Galerias	*Mex.*	–
Garduño's	*Mex./SW*	20
Grape St.	*Med.*	23
In-N-Out	*Burgers*	24
Kona Grill	*Amer.*	18
Marché Bacchus	*French*	24
Martinis	*Amer.*	–
Melting Pot	*Fondue*	21
Nora's	*Italian*	24
Osaka Cuisine	*Japanese*	20
Outback	*Steak*	18
P.F. Chang's	*Chinese*	21

Let your voice be heard – visit ZAGAT.com/vote

Roadrunner | SW	16
Romano's | Italian	17
Roy's | Hawaiian	24
Rubio's | Mex.	18
Salt Lick | BBQ	15
Sammy's | Pizza	21
Spiedini | Italian	21
☑ T-Bones | Steak	25
Tony Roma's | BBQ	16
Vintner Grill | Amer.	-

OUT OF TOWN

Lake Mead Cruises | Amer.	-
Pahrump Valley | Continental	21

SOUTH OF STRIP

Applebee's | Amer.	13
Bootlegger | Italian	19
NEW Brio | Italian	-
Cal. Pizza | Pizza	18
Capriotti's | Sandwiches	23
Chili's | Amer./Tex-Mex	16
Claim Jumper | Amer.	-
Famous Dave's | BBQ	20
In-N-Out | Burgers	24
NEW Kabuki | Japanese	-
NEW Louis's LV | Southern	-
☑ Michael's | Continental	26
Outback | Steak	18
Panevino | Italian	21
Roadrunner | SW	16
Table 34 | Amer.	-
NEW Tommy Bahama's | Carib./Pacific Rim	-

SOUTHWEST

Applebee's | Amer.	13
Baja Fresh | Mex.	19
Capriotti's | Sandwiches	23
NEW La Madonna | Mex.	-
Roadrunner | SW	16

STRIP

Ah Sin | Pan-Asian	20
Alan Albert's | Steak	22
al Dente | Italian	19
☑ Alex | French	27
America | Amer.	15
☑ André's | French	26
AquaKnox | Seafood	23
☑ Aureole | Amer.	25
Bally's | Steak	22
☑ B&B | Italian	26
Bartolotta | Italian/Seafood	24
Bay Side | Eclectic	19
☑ Bellagio Buffet | Eclectic	24
Big Kitchen | Eclectic	16
NEW BLT Burger | Burgers	-
Boa | Steak	24
Border Grill | Mex.	22
☑ Bouchon | French	25
☑ Bradley Ogden | Amer.	26
NEW Brand Steak | Steak	-
Buffet (Wynn) | Eclectic	-
Burger Bar | Burgers	23
Cafe, The | Amer.	19
Cafe/Reeba! | Spanish	22
Café Bellagio | Amer.	20
Cafe Lago | Eclectic	17
Cal. Pizza | Pizza	18
Canaletto | Italian	21
Canter's | Deli	18
Canyon Ranch | Amer./Health	21
Capital Grille | Steak	26
Caribe Café | Amer.	17
Carnegie Deli | Deli	21
NEW Carnevino | Italian/Steak	-
NEW CatHouse | American	-
Charlie Palmer | Steak	25
Cheesecake Factory | Amer.	20
China Grill | Asian	23
Chin Chin | Chinese	20
Chinois | Asian	22
Chipotle | Mex.	20
Chocolate Swan | Dessert	23
Circo | Italian	25
NEW Company Bistro | Amer.	-
Craftsteak | Seafood/Steak	25
Cravings | Eclectic	22
NEW CUT | Steak	-
NEW Dal Toro | Italian	-
☑ Daniel Boulud | French	26

David Burke	Amer.	24	Le Provençal	French/Italian	22
🆉 Delmonico	Steak	26	Les Artistes	French/Steak	22
Diablo's	Mex.	–	Le Village	French	23
Dick's	American	–	Lombardi's	Italian	20
Diego	Mex.	21	Maggiano's	Italian	20
NEW DJT	Amer.	–	Market City	Italian	18
NEW Dos Caminos	Mex.	–	🆉 Mesa Grill	SW	25
Dragon Noodle	Chinese	18	MGM Buffet	Amer.	17
Eiffel Tower	French	22	🆉 Michael Mina	Seafood	27
🆉 Emeril's	Seafood	23	🆉 miX	Amer./French	23
Empress Court	Chinese	22	🆉 Mon Ami Gabi	French	23
Enoteca/Marco	Italian	21	NEW Morels	French/Steak	–
Ethel's	Dessert	21	Neros	Steak	24
Fatburger	Burgers	21	Nine Fine Irish	Irish	17
Fellini's	Italian	24	Nobhill Tavern	Calif.	26
Fiamma Trattoria	Italian	22	Noodles	Pan-Asian	22
Fin	Chinese	25	Noodle Shop	Chinese	19
Fix	Amer.	23	🆉 Okada	Japanese	25
Flavors	Eclectic	18	🆉 Olives	Med.	23
Fleur de Lys	French	25	Onda	Italian	22
Fusia	Asian	21	Outback	Steak	18
Gallagher's	Steak	24	Palm, The	Seafood/Steak	25
Giorgio	Italian	20	Pampas	Brazilian/Steak	22
Grand Lux	Eclectic	20	NEW Payard	French	–
🆉 Guy Savoy	French	28	Pearl	Chinese	23
Hamada	Japanese	19	Penazzi	Italian	22
Harley-Davidson	Amer.	15	P.F. Chang's	Chinese	21
NEW Hawaiian Tropic	Amer.	–	🆉 Picasso	French	27
Hyakumi	Japanese	24	Pinot	French	22
Il Fornaio	Italian	20	Planet Hollywood	Amer.	13
Il Mulino NY	Italian	26	Postrio	Amer./Med.	24
Isla	Mex.	23	🆉 Prime	Steak	26
NEW Jade	Pan-Asian	–	Raffles Café	Diner	16
Japonais	Japanese	23	Range	Seafood/Steak	23
Jasmine	Chinese	23	Rao's	Italian	23
Jean Philippe	Dessert	26	Red 8	Pan-Asian	23
Jimmy Buffett's	Amer.	17	Red, White/Blue	Amer.	15
🆉 Joël Robuchon	French	28	NEW Rest. Charlie	Seafood	–
Joe's	Seafood/Steak	25	Rick Moonen's	Seafood	24
NEW Koi	Japanese	–	Rosewood	Seafood/Steak	23
La Salsa	Mex.	15	Roxy's	Diner	16
🆉 L'Atelier/Robuchon	French	28	Rubio's	Mex.	18
NEW Lavo	Med.	–	Samba	Brazilian/Steak	20
🆉 Le Cirque	French	26	Seablue	Seafood	24

Let your voice be heard – visit ZAGAT.com/vote

Sensi	Asian/Italian	25
Shanghai Lilly	Chinese	22
Shibuya	Japanese	25
Smith & Wollensky	Steak	23
Social Hse.	Pan-Asian	25
Spago	Amer.	23
Spice Mkt.	Eclectic	22
Stack	Steak	24
Stage Deli	Deli	20
Steak Hse. (Circus)	Steak	25
Steak Hse. (Treasure Is.)	Steak	23
Steakhouse46	Steak	26
Sterling Brunch	Eclectic	26
NEW Stratta	Italian	–
Strip Hse.	Steak	–
StripSteak	Steak	25
Sushi Roku	Japanese	24
NEW SushiSamba	Eclectic	–
SW Steak	Steak	26
NEW Table 10	Amer.	–
Z Tableau	Amer.	27
Tamba	Indian	21
NEW T&T	Mex.	–
Tao	Pan-Asian	23
Taqueria Cañonita	Mex.	20
Tintoretto	Bakery/Italian	20
Todai	Japanese	18
Top of the World	Amer.	20
Trader Vic's	Polynesian	–
Trattoria del Lupo	Italian	21
Trevi	Italian	20
Valentino	Italian	23
Verandah	Amer./Italian	23
'wichcraft	Sandwiches	20
Wing Lei	Chinese	25
Wolfgang Puck	Amer.	21
NEW Woo	Pan-Asian	–
NEW Yellowtail	Jap.	–
NEW Yolos	Mex.	–
Zeffirino	Italian	21
NEW Zine	Chinese/Viet.	–

WEST OF STRIP

Alizé	French	26
All-American B&G	Amer.	20
Antonio's	Italian	25
Big Al's	Seafood	19
Broiler	Seafood/Steak	21
Buzio's	Seafood	24
Cafe Martorano	Italian	25
Canal St.	Seafood/Steak	22
Capriotti's	Sandwiches	23
Carnival World	Eclectic	20
Chang's	Chinese	21
Coffee Pub	Diner	19
Don Miguel's	Mex.	19
Feast, The	Eclectic	18
French Mkt.	Eclectic	19
Garduño's	Mex./SW	20
Gaylord's	Indian	20
Golden Steer	Steak	22
Hamada	Japanese	19
In-N-Out	Burgers	24
Little Buddha	Asian	24
N9ne	Steak	25
Nove	Italian	27
Romano's	Italian	17
NEW RUB	BBQ	–
NEW Simon	Amer.	–
TGI Friday's	Amer.	15

WEST SIDE

Applebee's	Amer.	13
Archi's	Thai	24
Artem	Russian	21
Baja Fresh	Mex.	19
Big Dog's	Amer.	17
Café Wasabi	Pac. Rim	21
NEW Caminos de Morelia	Mex.	–
Capriotti's	Sandwiches	23
Cathay Hse.	Chinese	21
Chang's	Chinese	21
Chicago Brew.	Amer.	17
Chili's	Amer./Tex-Mex	16
Egg & I	Amer.	21
Famous Dave's		20
Fatburger	Burgers	21
Ferraro's	Italian	26
Fleming's	Steak	25
Hash House	Amer.	20

Hush Puppy	Seafood/Southern	22	Ping Pang Pong	Chinese	21
Joyful House	Chinese	21	🆉 Rosemary's	Amer.	28
Lindo Michoacan	Mex.	-	Rubio's	Mex.	18
🆕 Lucio	Italian	-	Ruth's Chris	Steak	24
Makino	Japanese	21	Sammy's	Pizza	21
Memphis BBQ	BBQ	21	Sam Woo	Chinese	20
Metro Pizza	Pizza	24	Sapporo	Japanese/Pac. Rim	21
Nora's	Italian	24	Sen	Japanese	27
Osaka Bistro	Japanese	22	TGI Friday's	Amer.	15
Outback	Steak	18	Thai Spice	Thai	21
Pasta Mia	Italian	23	Viva Mercado's	Mex.	22
Paymon's	Med./Mideastern	23	🆕 V Thai	Thai	-

Dining Special Features

Listings cover the best in each category and include names, locations and Food ratings. Multi-location restaurants' features may vary by branch.

ADDITIONS

(Properties added since the last edition of the book)

Ago	**E of Strip**	-
BLT Burger	**Strip**	-
Brand Steak	**Strip**	-
Brio	**S of Strip**	-
Caminos de Morelia	**W Side**	-
Carnevino	**Strip**	-
CatHouse	**Strip**	-
Claim Jumper	**multi.**	-
Company Bistro	**Strip**	-
CUT	**Strip**	-
Dal Toro	**Strip**	-
DJT	**Strip**	-
Dos Caminos	**Strip**	-
Galerias	**NW**	-
Hawaiian Tropic	**Strip**	-
Jade	**Strip**	-
Kabuki	**S of Strip**	-
Koi	**Strip**	-
La Madonna	**SW**	-
Lavo	**Strip**	-
Le Golosita	**Henderson**	-
Louis's LV	**S of Strip**	-
Lucio	**W Side**	-
Morels	**Strip**	-
New Orleans Connection	**E Side**	-
Payard	**Strip**	-
Pie Town	**Henderson**	-
Rest. Charlie	**Strip**	-
RUB	**W of Strip**	-
Simon	**W of Strip**	-
Stratta	**Strip**	-
SushiSamba	**Strip**	-
Table 10	**Strip**	-
T&T	**Strip**	-
Tommy Bahama's	**S of Strip**	-
V Thai	**W Side**	-
White Chocolate	**Henderson**	-
Woo	**Strip**	-
Yellowtail	**Strip**	-
Yolos	**Strip**	-
Zine	**Strip**	-

BREAKFAST

(See also Hotel Dining)

Big Dog's	**multi.**	17
Black Mtn.	**Henderson**	17
Bootlegger	**S of Strip**	19
Coffee Pub	**W of Strip**	19
Crown & Anchor	**E Side**	16
Egg & I	**W Side**	21
Fatburger	**multi.**	21
Martinis	**NW**	-
Roadrunner	**multi.**	16

BRUNCH

☑ Bellagio Buffet	**Strip**	24
☑ Bouchon	**Strip**	25
Cheesecake Factory	**NW**	20
Feast, The	**multi.**	18
Le Village	**Strip**	23
☑ Mesa Grill	**Strip**	25
Steak Hse. (Circus)	**Strip**	25
Sterling Brunch	**Strip**	26
☑ Tableau	**Strip**	27
Zeffirino	**Strip**	21

BUFFET

(Check availability)

Bay Side	**Strip**	19
☑ Bellagio Buffet	**Strip**	24
Big Kitchen	**Strip**	16
Buffet (Wynn)	**Strip**	-
Buffet (Golden Nugget)	**Downtown**	17
Buffet (Hilton)	**E of Strip**	17
Cafe Lago	**Strip**	17
Carnival World	**W of Strip**	20
Cravings	**Strip**	22
Feast, The	**multi.**	18
Feast Around/World	**multi.**	18

168   40,000 places to eat, drink, stay & play – free at ZAGAT.com

Festival	multi.	14	Gaetano's	Henderson	23
Firelight	E Side	15	NEW Galerias	NW	–
Flavors	Strip	18	Grand Lux	Strip	20
French Mkt.	W of Strip	19	NEW Jade	Strip	–
Gandhi	E of Strip	21	Joe's	Strip	25
Garden Ct.	Downtown	19	NEW La Madonna	SW	–
Gaylord's	W of Strip	20	Lawry's	E of Strip	25
India Palace	E of Strip	24	NEW Le Golosita	Henderson	–
Joyful House	W Side	21	NEW Louis's LV	S of Strip	–
Lake Mead Cruises	Boulder City	–	NEW Lucio	W Side	–
Le Village	Strip	23	Martinis	NW	–
Z Lotus of Siam	E Side	27	Z Michael's	S of Strip	26
Makino	multi.	21	NEW Morels	Strip	–
MGM Buffet	Strip	17	Morton's Steak	E of Strip	25
MiraLago	Lake LV	21	Neros	Strip	24
Spice Mkt.	Strip	22	Palm, The	Strip	25
Steak Hse. (Circus)	Strip	25	Pearl	Strip	23
Sterling Brunch	Strip	26	Piero's	E of Strip	24
Tamba	Strip	21	Postrio	Strip	24
Todai	Strip	18	Z Prime	Strip	26
Verandah	Strip	23	Rao's	Strip	23
Zeffirino	Strip	21	NEW Rest. Charlie	Strip	–
		Rick Moonen's	Strip	24

BUSINESS DINING

NEW Ago	E of Strip	–	Z Rosemary's	W Side	28
Alan Albert's	Strip	22	Roy's	multi.	24
Z Aureole	Strip	25	NEW RUB	W of Strip	–
Z B&B	Strip	26	Ruth's Chris	multi.	24
NEW BLT Burger	Strip	–	NEW Simon	W of Strip	–
Z Bouchon	Strip	25	Smith & Wollensky	Strip	23
Z Bradley Ogden	Strip	26	Spago	Strip	23
NEW Brand Steak	Strip	–	Spiedini	NW	21
NEW Brio	S of Strip	–	Steak Hse. (Treasure Is.)	Strip	23
Capital Grille	Strip	26	NEW Stratta	Strip	–
NEW Carnevino	Strip	–	Strip Hse.	Strip	–
Charlie Palmer	Strip	25	NEW SushiSamba	Strip	–
Craftsteak	Strip	25	SW Steak	Strip	26
NEW CUT	Strip	–	NEW Table 10	Strip	–
NEW Dal Toro	Strip	–	Table 34	S of Strip	–
David Burke	Strip	24	Terra Verde	Henderson	–
Z Delmonico	Strip	26	Z Todd's	Henderson	28
Diablo's	Strip	–	NEW Tommy Bahama's	S of Strip	–
NEW DJT	Strip	–	Triple George	Downtown	22
NEW Dos Caminos	Strip	–	Valentino	Strip	23
Fleming's	W Side	25		

Let your voice be heard - visit ZAGAT.com/vote

Verandah	**Strip**	23
Vintner Grill	**NW**	–
NEW V Thai	**W Side**	–
NEW White Chocolate	Henderson	–
NEW Woo	**Strip**	–
NEW Yolos	**Strip**	–

CATERING

Charlie Palmer	**Strip**	25
Chocolate Swan	**Strip**	23
Firefly	**E of Strip**	24
Grape St.	**NW**	23
Hamada	**E of Strip**	19
Marché Bacchus	**NW**	24
☑ Nobu	**E of Strip**	28
Paymon's	**E Side**	23
Piero's	**E of Strip**	24
Postrio	**Strip**	24
☑ Rosemary's	**W Side**	28
Roy's	**multi.**	24
Sensi	**Strip**	25
Spago	**Strip**	23
Spiedini	**NW**	21
'wichcraft	**Strip**	20

CELEBRITY CHEFS

☑ Alex	*Alex Stratta*	**Strip**	27
☑ Aureole	*Charlie Palmer*	**Strip**	25
☑ B&B	*Mario Batali*	**Strip**	26
Bartolotta	*Paul Bartolotta*	**Strip**	24
NEW BLT Burger	*Laurent Tourondel*	**Strip**	–
☑ Bouchon	*Thomas Keller*	**Strip**	25
☑ Bradley Ogden	*Bradley Ogden*	**Strip**	26
Burger Bar	*Hubert Keller*	**Strip**	23
NEW Carnevino	*Mario Batali*	**Strip**	–
NEW CatHouse	*Kerry Simon*	**Strip**	–
Charlie Palmer	*Charlie Palmer*	**Strip**	25
Chinois	*Wolfgang Puck*	**Strip**	22
Craftsteak	*Tom Colicchio*	**Strip**	25
NEW CUT	*Wolfgang Puck*	**Strip**	–
☑ Daniel Boulud	*Daniel Boulud*	**Strip**	26
David Burke	*David Burke*	**Strip**	24
☑ Delmonico	*Emeril Lagasse*	**Strip**	26
☑ Emeril's	*Emeril Lagasse*	**Strip**	23
Enoteca/Marco	*Mario Batali*	**Strip**	21
Fleur de Lys	*Hubert Keller*	**Strip**	25
Giorgio	*Piero Selvaggio*	**Strip**	20
☑ Guy Savoy	*Guy Savoy*	**Strip**	28
NEW Hawaiian Tropic	*David Burke*	**Strip**	–
Isla	*Richard Sandoval*	**Strip**	23
☑ Joël Robuchon	*Joël Robuchon*	**Strip**	28
☑ L'Atelier/Robuchon	*Joël Robuchon*	**Strip**	28
NEW Louis's LV	*Louis Osteen*	**S of Strip**	–
☑ Mesa Grill	*Bobby Flay*	**Strip**	25
☑ Michael Mina	*Michael Mina*	**Strip**	27
☑ miX	*Alain Ducasse*	**Strip**	23
Nobhill Tavern	*Michael Mina*	**Strip**	26
☑ Nobu	*Nobu Matsuhisa*	**E of Strip**	28
☑ Olives	*Todd English*	**Strip**	23
NEW Payard	*François Payard*	**Strip**	–
☑ Picasso	*Julian Serrano*	**Strip**	27
Pinot	*Joachim Splichal*	**Strip**	22
Postrio	*Wolfgang Puck*	**Strip**	24
☑ Prime	*J.-G. Vongerichten*	**Strip**	26
NEW Rest. Charlie	*Charlie Trotter*	**Strip**	–
Rick Moonen's	*Rick Moonen*	**Strip**	24
Seablue	*Michael Mina*	**Strip**	24
Spago	*Wolfgang Puck*	**Strip**	23
NEW Stratta	*Alex Stratta*	**Strip**	–
StripSteak	*Michael Mina*	**Strip**	25
NEW Table 10	*Emeril Lagasse*	**Strip**	–
NEW T&T	*Richard Sandoval*	**Strip**	–

Trattoria del Lupo | *Wolfgang Puck* | **Strip** — 21
Valentino | *Piero Selvaggio* | **Strip** — 23
'wichcraft | *Tom Colicchio* | **Strip** — 20
Wolfgang Puck | *Wolfgang Puck* | **Strip** — 21

CHEESE TRAYS

🆉 Alex	**Strip**	27
Alizé	**W of Strip**	26
🆉 André's	**multi.**	26
🆉 Aureole	**Strip**	25
🆉 B&B	**Strip**	26
🆉 Bouchon	**Strip**	25
🆉 Bradley Ogden	**Strip**	26
🆉 Daniel Boulud	**Strip**	26
Enoteca/Marco	**Strip**	21
Fleur de Lys	**Strip**	25
Garden Ct.	**Downtown**	19
Giorgio	**Strip**	20
🆉 Joël Robuchon	**Strip**	28
🆉 L'Atelier/Robuchon	**Strip**	28
NEW Louis's LV	**S of Strip**	–
Marché Bacchus	**NW**	24
Market City	**Strip**	18
NEW Morels	**Strip**	–
Onda	**Strip**	22
Pahrump Valley	**Pahrump**	21
🆉 Tableau	**Strip**	27

CHEF'S TABLE

🆉 Alex	**Strip**	27
AquaKnox	**Strip**	23
NEW Dal Toro	**Strip**	–
🆉 Delmonico	**Strip**	26
🆉 Emeril's	**Strip**	23
Fleur de Lys	**Strip**	25
Medici Café	**Lake LV**	22
🆉 miX	**Strip**	23
Nobhill Tavern	**Strip**	26
🆉 Olives	**Strip**	23
NEW Rest. Charlie	**Strip**	–
Rick Moonen's	**Strip**	24
NEW Simon	**W of Strip**	–
Smith & Wollensky	**Strip**	23

NEW Table 10 | **Strip** — –
Valentino | **Strip** — 23

CHILD-FRIENDLY

(Alternatives to the usual fast-food places; * children's menu available)

America*	**Strip**	15
Applebee's*	**multi.**	13
Bay Side	**Strip**	19
🆉 Bellagio Buffet	**Strip**	24
Black Mtn.*	**Henderson**	17
Bootlegger*	**S of Strip**	19
Border Grill*	**Strip**	22
🆉 Bouchon*	**Strip**	25
Burger Bar*	**Strip**	23
Cafe Heidelberg*	**E of Strip**	22
Cafe Lago*	**Strip**	17
Cal. Pizza*	**Strip**	18
Capriotti's*	**multi.**	23
Caribe Café	**Strip**	17
Cheesecake Factory*	**multi.**	20
Chicago Brew.*	**W Side**	17
Chili's*	**multi.**	16
Chipotle*	**multi.**	20
Chocolate Swan	**Strip**	23
Coffee Pub*	**W of Strip**	19
Cravings	**Strip**	22
Dick's	**Strip**	–
Doña Maria*	**multi.**	19
Don Miguel's	**W of Strip**	19
Egg & I*	**W Side**	21
Feast, The	**W of Strip**	18
Festival	**NW**	14
Firelight*	**E Side**	15
Flavors*	**Strip**	18
Florida Café*	**Central**	19
Garden Ct.	**Downtown**	19
Garduño's*	**W of Strip**	20
Grape St.	**NW**	23
Guadalajara	**E Side**	19
Hard Rock Cafe*	**E of Strip**	15
Harley-Davidson*	**Strip**	15
Hush Puppy*	**multi.**	22
In-N-Out*	**multi.**	24
Jimmy Buffett's*	**Strip**	17

Kathy's* | **Henderson**	24
King's* | **Henderson**	23
Kona Grill* | **NW**	18
La Salsa* | **multi.**	15
Lombardi's | **Strip**	20
🆉 Lotus of Siam | **E Side**	27
Market City | **Strip**	18
Medici Café* | **Lake LV**	22
Memphis BBQ* | **multi.**	21
🆉 Mesa Grill | **Strip**	25
Metro Pizza* | **multi.**	24
MGM Buffet* | **Strip**	17
MiraLago* | **Lake LV**	21
Mr. Lucky's* | **E of Strip**	19
Neros | **Strip**	24
Nora's | **W Side**	24
Outback* | **multi.**	18
Pasta Mia | **W Side**	23
Pasta Shop* | **E Side**	24
Paymon's* | **E Side**	23
Pearl | **Strip**	23
P.F. Chang's | **multi.**	21
Planet Hollywood* | **Strip**	13
Raffles Café | **Strip**	16
Red, White/Blue* | **Strip**	15
Roadrunner* | **multi.**	16
Romano's* | **multi.**	17
🆉 Rosemary's | **W Side**	28
Roxy's* | **Strip**	16
Roy's* | **multi.**	24
Rubio's* | **multi.**	18
Salt Lick* | **NW**	15
Sammy's* | **multi.**	21
Second St. | **Downtown**	24
Terra Verde | **Henderson**	-
TGI Friday's* | **multi.**	15
Tony Roma's* | **multi.**	16
Ventano* | **Henderson**	20
Viva Mercado's* | **W Side**	22

CHILDREN NOT ALLOWED

🆉 Alex | **Strip**	27
Alizé | **W of Strip**	26
🆉 André's | **Downtown**	26
Bartolotta | **Strip**	24
Chicago Brew. | **Downtown**	17
Circo | **Strip**	25
🆉 Daniel Boulud | **Strip**	26
Fin | **Strip**	25
Fix | **Strip**	23
Il Mulino NY | **Strip**	26
Japonais | **Strip**	23
🆉 Joël Robuchon | **Strip**	28
🆉 Le Cirque | **Strip**	26
🆉 Michael Mina | **Strip**	27
🆉 Okada | **Strip**	25
Onda | **Strip**	22
🆉 Prime | **Strip**	26
Samba | **Strip**	20
Sensi | **Strip**	25
Stack | **Strip**	24
Steak Hse. (Treasure Is.) | **Strip**	23

CIGARS WELCOME

Chicago Brew. | **multi.**	17
Crown & Anchor | **E Side**	16
Ruth's Chris | **E of Strip**	24

DELIVERY/TAKEOUT

(D=delivery, T=takeout)

Alizé | T | **W of Strip**	26
Austins Steak | T | **N Las Vegas**	24
Bootlegger | D | **S of Strip**	19
Burger Bar | T | **Strip**	23
Cafe/Reeba! | T | **Strip**	22
Capriotti's | D | **multi.**	23
Chocolate Swan | D | **Strip**	23
Ferraro's | T | **W Side**	26
Fiamma Trattoria | T | **Strip**	22
Firefly | T | **E of Strip**	24
Fix | T | **Strip**	23
Gaetano's | T | **Henderson**	23
Grape St. | T | **NW**	23
Jean Philippe | T | **Strip**	26
Joe's | T | **Strip**	25
King's | T | **Henderson**	23
Lawry's | T | **E of Strip**	25
🆉 Lotus of Siam | T | **E Side**	27
Makino | T | **multi.**	21

Metro Pizza	D	**multi.**	24	Bob Taylor's	**NW**	20
☑ Mon Ami Gabi	T	**Strip**	23	Canal St.	**W of Strip**	22
Osaka Bistro	D	**Henderson**	22	Chicago Brew.	**W Side**	17
Palm, The	T	**Strip**	25	Claim Jumper	**Summerlin**	–
Piero's	T	**E of Strip**	24	Fiamma Trattoria	**Strip**	22
☑ Rosemary's	T	**W Side**	28	☑ Guy Savoy	**Strip**	28
Roy's	T	**multi.**	24	☑ Joël Robuchon	**Strip**	28
Sam Woo	T	**W Side**	20	Lawry's	**E of Strip**	25
Shanghai Lilly	T	**Strip**	22	McCormick/Schmick	**E of Strip**	21
Smith & Wollensky	T	**Strip**	23	Memphis BBQ	**multi.**	21
☑ Todd's	T	**Henderson**	28	Nobhill Tavern	**Strip**	26
Valentino	T	**Strip**	23	Pahrump Valley	**Pahrump**	21

ENTERTAINMENT

(Call for days and times of performances)

Bootlegger	blues/jazz	**S of Strip**	19
Charlie Palmer	piano	**Strip**	25
Crown & Anchor	bands	**E Side**	16
☑ Del Frisco's	piano/vocals	**E of Strip**	26
☑ Delmonico	piano	**Strip**	26
Egg & I	dinner theater	**W Side**	21
Ferraro's	varies	**W Side**	26
Firefly	DJ	**E of Strip**	24
Golden Steer	piano	**W of Strip**	22
Hank's	piano	**Henderson**	23
Jimmy Buffett's	reggae/top '40s	**Strip**	17
Le Provençal	singing waiters	**Strip**	22
Little Buddha	DJ	**W of Strip**	24
Lucille's	blues	**Henderson**	22
Nine Fine Irish	Irish	**Strip**	17
Nora's	jazz	**W Side**	24
Osaka Bistro	jazz	**Henderson**	22
Piero's	piano	**E of Strip**	24
Range	jazz/piano	**Strip**	23
Redwood	piano	**Downtown**	24
Ruth's Chris	jazz	**multi.**	24
Yolie's	piano	**E of Strip**	21
Zeffirino	guitar/piano	**Strip**	21

FIREPLACES

☑ André's	**multi.**	26
Black Mtn.	**Henderson**	17

Pamplemousse	**E Side**	25
Panevino	**S of Strip**	21
Roadrunner	**multi.**	16
Ruth's Chris	**W Side**	24

GAME IN SEASON

NEW Ago	**E of Strip**	–
☑ Alex	**Strip**	27
Alizé	**W of Strip**	26
☑ Aureole	**Strip**	25
☑ B&B	**Strip**	26
☑ Bouchon	**Strip**	25
NEW Carnevino	**Strip**	–
NEW Company Bistro	**Strip**	–
Craftsteak	**Strip**	25
☑ Daniel Boulud	**Strip**	26
☑ Delmonico	**Strip**	26
☑ Joël Robuchon	**Strip**	28
☑ L'Atelier/Robuchon	**Strip**	28
☑ Le Cirque	**Strip**	26
NEW Louis's LV	**S of Strip**	–
Nobhill Tavern	**Strip**	26
☑ Picasso	**Strip**	27
Pinot	**Strip**	22
Postrio	**Strip**	24
☑ Rosemary's	**W Side**	28
Valentino	**Strip**	23

HISTORIC PLACES

(Year opened; * building)

1930	André's*	**Downtown**	26
1933	Chicago Joe's*	**Downtown**	21
1934	El Sombrero*	**Downtown**	–

Let your voice be heard – visit ZAGAT.com/vote

1952	Fatburger	**multi.**	21
1955	Bob Taylor's	**NW**	20
1958	Golden Steer	**W of Strip**	22

HOTEL DINING

Bally's Las Vegas
al Dente	Strip	19
Bally's	Strip	22
Big Kitchen	Strip	16
Sterling Brunch	Strip	26

Bellagio Hotel
🏆 Bellagio Buffet	Strip	24
Café Bellagio	Strip	20
Circo	Strip	25
Fix	Strip	23
Jasmine	Strip	23
Jean Philippe	Strip	26
🏆 Le Cirque	Strip	26
🏆 Michael Mina	Strip	27
Noodles	Strip	22
🏆 Olives	Strip	23
🏆 Picasso	Strip	27
🏆 Prime	Strip	26
Sensi	Strip	25
NEW Yellowtail	Strip	–

Binion's Hotel
| Binion's | Downtown | 24 |

Boulder Station Hotel
Broiler	E Side	21
Feast, The	E Side	18
Guadalajara	E Side	19
Metro Pizza	E Side	24

Caesars Palace
🏆 Bradley Ogden	Strip	26
Cafe Lago	Strip	17
Empress Court	Strip	22
🏆 Guy Savoy	Strip	28
Hyakumi	Strip	24
Joe's	Strip	25
🏆 Mesa Grill	Strip	25
Neros	Strip	24
NEW Payard	Strip	–
Rao's	Strip	23

California Hotel
| Redwood | Downtown | 24 |

Casino Royale Hotel
| Outback | Strip | 18 |

Circus Circus
| Steak Hse. (Circus) | Strip | 25 |

Ellis Island Casino & Brewery
| Metro Pizza | E of Strip | 24 |

Excalibur Hotel
| Dick's | Strip | – |

Fiesta Henderson Hotel
| Festival | Henderson | 14 |

Fiesta Rancho Hotel
| Festival | NW | 14 |
| Garduño's | NW | 20 |

Flamingo Las Vegas
Hamada	Strip	19
Jimmy Buffett's	Strip	17
Steakhouse46	Strip	26

Forum Shops at Caesars Palace
Boa	Strip	24
Cheesecake Factory	Strip	20
Chinois	Strip	22
Il Mulino NY	Strip	26
La Salsa	Strip	15
Palm, The	Strip	25
Planet Hollywood	Strip	13
Spago	Strip	23
Sushi Roku	Strip	24
Trevi	Strip	20

Four Queens Hotel
| Chicago Brew. | Downtown | 17 |
| 🏆 Hugo's Cellar | Downtown | 26 |

Four Seasons Hotel
| Charlie Palmer | Strip | 25 |
| Verandah | Strip | 23 |

Fremont Hotel
| Second St. | Downtown | 24 |
| Tony Roma's | Downtown | 16 |

Gold Coast Hotel
| Ping Pang Pong | W Side | 21 |

Golden Nugget Hotel
Buffet (Golden Nugget)	Downtown	17
Carson St.	Downtown	17
Vic & Anthony's	Downtown	25

Green Valley Ranch
- Fatburger | **Henderson** — 21
- Feast Around/World | **Henderson** — 18
- Hank's | **Henderson** — 23

Hard Rock Hotel
- NEW Ago | **E of Strip** — –
- AJ's | **E of Strip** — 23
- Mr. Lucky's | **E of Strip** — 19
- ☒ Nobu | **E of Strip** — 28
- Pink Taco | **E of Strip** — 19

Harrah's Las Vegas
- Penazzi | **Strip** — 22
- Range | **Strip** — 23

Howard Johnson Hotel
- Florida Café | **Central** — 19

JW Marriott
- Spiedini | **NW** — 21

Las Vegas Hilton
- Benihana | **E of Strip** — 19
- Buffet (Hilton) | **E of Strip** — 17
- Casa Nicola | **E of Strip** — 20

Luxor Hotel
- NEW CatHouse | **Strip** — –
- NEW Company Bistro | **Strip** — –
- Fusia | **Strip** — 21
- NEW T&T | **Strip** — –

Main Street Station Hotel
- Garden Ct. | **Downtown** — 19
- Pullman Grille | **Downtown** — 24
- Triple 7 | **Downtown** — 21

Mandalay Bay Resort
- ☒ Aureole | **Strip** — 25
- Bay Side | **Strip** — 19
- Border Grill | **Strip** — 22
- Cafe, The | **Strip** — 19
- China Grill | **Strip** — 23
- Fleur de Lys | **Strip** — 25
- ☒ miX | **Strip** — 23
- Raffles Café | **Strip** — 16
- Red, White/Blue | **Strip** — 15
- Shanghai Lilly | **Strip** — 22
- StripSteak | **Strip** — 25
- Trattoria del Lupo | **Strip** — 21

Mandalay Place
- Burger Bar | **Strip** — 23
- Chocolate Swan | **Strip** — 23
- Giorgio | **Strip** — 20
- Rick Moonen's | **Strip** — 24

MGM Grand Hotel
- Craftsteak | **Strip** — 25
- Diego | **Strip** — 21
- ☒ Emeril's | **Strip** — 23
- Fiamma Trattoria | **Strip** — 22
- ☒ Joël Robuchon | **Strip** — 28
- ☒ L'Atelier/Robuchon | **Strip** — 28
- MGM Buffet | **Strip** — 17
- Nobhill Tavern | **Strip** — 26
- Pearl | **Strip** — 23
- Seablue | **Strip** — 24
- Shibuya | **Strip** — 25
- Stage Deli | **Strip** — 20
- 'wichcraft | **Strip** — 20
- Wolfgang Puck | **Strip** — 21

Miracle Mile Shops
- NEW Hawaiian Tropic | **Strip** — –
- La Salsa | **Strip** — 15
- Lombardi's | **Strip** — 20
- Pampas | **Strip** — 22
- Todai | **Strip** — 18
- Trader Vic's | **Strip** — –

Mirage Hotel
- NEW BLT Burger | **Strip** — –
- Cal. Pizza | **Strip** — 18
- Caribe Café | **Strip** — 17
- Carnegie Deli | **Strip** — 21
- Cravings | **Strip** — 22
- Fin | **Strip** — 25
- Japonais | **Strip** — 23
- Onda | **Strip** — 22
- Samba | **Strip** — 20
- Stack | **Strip** — 24

Monte Carlo Resort
- ☒ André's | **Strip** — 26
- NEW Brand Steak | **Strip** — –
- Diablo's | **Strip** — –
- Dragon Noodle | **Strip** — 18
- Market City | **Strip** — 18

New York-New York Hotel
- America | **Strip** | 15
- Chin Chin | **Strip** | 20
- Gallagher's | **Strip** | 24
- Il Fornaio | **Strip** | 20
- Nine Fine Irish | **Strip** | 17

Orleans Hotel
- Big Al's | **W of Strip** | 19
- Canal St. | **W of Strip** | 22
- Don Miguel's | **W of Strip** | 19
- French Mkt. | **W of Strip** | 19
- TGI Friday's | **W of Strip** | 15

Palace Station Hotel
- Broiler | **W of Strip** | 21
- Chang's | **W of Strip** | 21
- Feast, The | **W of Strip** | 18

Palazzo Hotel
- NEW Canyon Ranch | **Strip** | 21
- NEW Carnevino | **Strip** | –
- NEW CUT | **Strip** | –
- NEW Dal Toro | **Strip** | –
- NEW Dos Caminos | **Strip** | –
- NEW Grand Lux | **Strip** | 20
- NEW Jade | **Strip** | –
- NEW Lavo | **Strip** | –
- NEW Morels | **Strip** | –
- NEW Rest. Charlie | **Strip** | –
- NEW SushiSamba | **Strip** | –
- NEW Table 10 | **Strip** | –
- NEW Woo | **Strip** | –
- NEW Zine | **Strip** | –

Palms Casino Hotel
- Alizé | **W of Strip** | 26
- Garduño's | **W of Strip** | 20
- Little Buddha | **W of Strip** | 24
- N9ne | **W of Strip** | 25
- Nove | **W of Strip** | 27

Palms Place
- NEW Simon | **W of Strip** | –

Paris Las Vegas
- Ah Sin | **Strip** | 20
- Eiffel Tower | **Strip** | 22
- Le Provençal | **Strip** | 22
- Les Artistes | **Strip** | 22
- Le Village | **Strip** | 23
- ☑ Mon Ami Gabi | **Strip** | 23

Planet Hollywood Resort
- NEW Koi | **Strip** | –
- P.F. Chang's | **Strip** | 21
- Spice Mkt. | **Strip** | 22
- Strip Hse. | **Strip** | –
- NEW Yolos | **Strip** | –

Red Rock Casino
- Feast, The | **NW** | 18
- Rubio's | **NW** | 18
- Salt Lick | **NW** | 15
- ☑ T-Bones | **NW** | 25

Renaissance Las Vegas Hotel
- Envy | **E of Strip** | 21

Rio All-Suite Hotel
- All-American B&G | **W of Strip** | 20
- Antonio's | **W of Strip** | 25
- Buzio's | **W of Strip** | 24
- Cafe Martorano | **W of Strip** | 25
- Carnival World | **W of Strip** | 20
- Gaylord's | **W of Strip** | 20
- Hamada | **W of Strip** | 19
- NEW RUB | **W of Strip** | –

Ritz-Carlton, Lake Las Vegas
- Medici Café | **Lake LV** | 22

Sam's Town Hotel
- Billy Bob's | **E Side** | 24
- Firelight | **E Side** | 15

Santa Fe Station Hotel
- Fatburger | **NW** | 21

South Point Hotel
- ☑ Michael's | **S of Strip** | 26

Stratosphere Hotel
- Fellini's | **Strip** | 24
- Roxy's | **Strip** | 16
- Top of the World | **Strip** | 20

Sunset Station Hotel
- Fatburger | **Henderson** | 21
- Feast, The | **Henderson** | 18
- Guadalajara | **Henderson** | 19

Texas Station Hotel
- Austins Steak | **N Las Vegas** | 24

Restaurant	Rating
Feast Around/World | N Las Vegas	18

Treasure Island Hotel

Restaurant	Rating
Canter's | Strip	18
Isla | Strip	23
Social Hse. | Strip	25
Steak Hse. (Treasure Is.) | Strip	23

Trump International Hotel

Restaurant	Rating
NEW DJT | Strip	–

Venetian Hotel

Restaurant	Rating
AquaKnox | Strip	23
Z B&B | Strip	26
Z Bouchon | Strip	25
Canaletto | Strip	21
Canyon Ranch | Strip	21
David Burke | Strip	24
Z Delmonico | Strip	26
Enoteca/Marco | Strip	21
Grand Lux | Strip	20
Pinot | Strip	22
Postrio | Strip	24
Tao | Strip	23
Taqueria Cañonita | Strip	20
Tintoretto | Strip	20
Valentino | Strip	23
Zeffirino | Strip	21

Wynn Las Vegas

Restaurant	Rating
Z Alex | Strip	27
Bartolotta | Strip	24
Buffet (Wynn) | Strip	–
Z Daniel Boulud | Strip	26
Z Okada | Strip	25
Red 8 | Strip	23
NEW Stratta | Strip	–
SW Steak | Strip	26
Z Tableau | Strip	27
Wing Lei | Strip	25

LATE DINING

(Weekday closing hour)

Restaurant	Rating
Agave | 2 AM | NW	18
All-American B&G | 6 AM | W of Strip	20
America | 24 hrs. | Strip	15
Artem | 1 AM | W Side	21
Big Dog's | 24 hrs. | multi.	17
Black Mtn. | 24 hrs. | Henderson	17
NEW BLT Burger | varies | Strip	–
Bootlegger | 24 hrs. | S of Strip	19
Café Bellagio | 24 hrs. | Strip	20
Cafe Martorano | 2 AM | W of Strip	25
Cal. Pizza | 12 AM | Strip	18
Canter's | 12 AM | Strip	18
Caribe Café | 24 hrs. | Strip	17
Carnegie Deli | 2 AM | Strip	21
Carson St. | 24 hrs. | Downtown	17
Chang's | varies | W of Strip	21
Chicago Brew. | varies | multi.	17
Chipotle | 12 AM | Strip	20
Crown & Anchor | 24 hrs. | E Side	16
NEW Dal Toro | varies | Strip	–
Diablo's | 12 AM | Strip	–
Dick's | 12 AM | Strip	–
Fatburger | varies | multi.	21
Firefly | 3 AM | E of Strip	24
Fix | 12 AM | Strip	23
Grand Lux | 24 hrs. | Strip	20
Hamada | varies | E of Strip	19
Hard Rock Cafe | 12 AM | E of Strip	15
NEW Hawaiian Tropic | 12 AM | Strip	–
Il Fornaio | varies | Strip	20
In-N-Out | varies | multi.	24
Isla | 4 AM | Strip	23
NEW Jade | 12 AM | Strip	–
Jimmy Buffett's | 1 AM | Strip	17
Joyful House | 3 AM | W Side	21
NEW Lavo | varies | Strip	–
Martinis | 24 hrs. | NW	–
Metro Pizza | varies | E of Strip	24
Mr. Lucky's | 24 hrs. | E of Strip	19
Noodles | 2 AM | Strip	22
Osaka Bistro | varies | multi.	22
Outback | varies | Strip	18
Paymon's | 1 AM | multi.	23
P.F. Chang's | varies | Strip	21
Ping Pang Pong | 3 AM | W Side	21
Raffles Café | 24 hrs. | Strip	16

Let your voice be heard – visit ZAGAT.com/vote

Roadrunner	24 hrs.	multi.	16
Rubio's	varies	Strip	18
Ruth's Chris	varies	W Side	24
Sapporo	1 AM	W Side	21
Smith & Wollensky	3 AM	Strip	23
Social Hse.	varies	Strip	25
NEW SushiSamba	4 AM	Strip	-|
Tao	12 AM	Strip	23
TGI Friday's	varies	multi.	15
Tintoretto	12:30 AM	Strip	20
Trader Vic's	4 AM	Strip	-|
Ventano	varies	Henderson	20
Zeffirino	12 AM	Strip	21
NEW Zine	12:30 AM	Strip	-|

MEET FOR A DRINK

Agave	NW	18
AJ's	E of Strip	23
Z Aureole	Strip	25
Z B&B	Strip	26
NEW BLT Burger	Strip	-|
Boa	Strip	24
NEW Brand Steak	Strip	-|
NEW Brio	S of Strip	-|
Cafe/Reeba!	Strip	22
Cafe Martorano	W of Strip	25
Capital Grille	Strip	26
NEW Carnevino	Strip	-|
NEW CatHouse	Strip	-|
Charlie Palmer	Strip	25
Chicago Brew.	W Side	17
Chinois	Strip	22
Claim Jumper	S of Strip	-|
NEW Company Bistro	Strip	-|
Craftsteak	Strip	25
Crown & Anchor	E Side	16
NEW CUT	Strip	-|
NEW Dal Toro	Strip	-|
David Burke	Strip	24
Z Del Frisco's	E of Strip	26
Z Delmonico	Strip	26
Diablo's	Strip	-|
Dick's	Strip	-|
NEW DJT	Strip	-|
NEW Dos Caminos	Strip	-|
Eiffel Tower	Strip	22
Elephant Bar	Henderson	17
Enoteca/Marco	Strip	21
Envy	E of Strip	21
Fleming's	W Side	25
NEW Hawaiian Tropic	Strip	-|
Joe's	Strip	25
NEW Kabuki	S of Strip	-|
NEW Lavo	Strip	-|
Z Le Cirque	Strip	26
NEW Le Golosita	Henderson	-|
Martinis	NW	-|
Z Michael Mina	Strip	27
Z miX	Strip	23
NEW Morels	Strip	-|
Z Nobu	E of Strip	28
Z Olives	Strip	23
Palm, The	Strip	25
Z Picasso	Strip	27
Piero's	E of Strip	24
Postrio	Strip	24
Z Prime	Strip	26
Rao's	Strip	23
NEW Rest. Charlie	Strip	-|
Roadrunner	S of Strip	16
Roy's	multi.	24
NEW Simon	W of Strip	-|
Spago	Strip	23
Spiedini	NW	21
NEW Stratta	Strip	-|
Strip Hse.	Strip	-|
NEW SushiSamba	Strip	-|
NEW Table 10	Strip	-|
Table 34	S of Strip	-|
NEW T&T	Strip	-|
Taqueria Cañonita	Strip	20
Terra Verde	Henderson	-|
TGI Friday's	multi.	15
NEW Tommy Bahama's	S of Strip	-|
Trader Vic's	Strip	-|
Trevi	Strip	20
Valentino	Strip	23
Vintner Grill	NW	-|

🆕 White Chocolate | Henderson	⊥
🆕 Woo | Strip	⊥
🆕 Yellowtail | Strip	⊥
🆕 Yolos | Strip	⊥
🆕 Zine | Strip	⊥

OUTDOOR DINING

(G=garden; P=patio; S=sidewalk; T=terrace; W=waterside)

Agave | P | NW	18
Ah Sin | P | Strip	20
🟆 Alex | G, W | Strip	27
🟆 André's | P | Downtown	26
Bartolotta | P, W | Strip	24
Black Mtn. | P | Henderson	17
Boa | P | Strip	24
Border Grill | P | Strip	22
🟆 Bouchon | P | Strip	25
Cafe/Reeba! | P | Strip	22
Cafe Lago | P | Strip	17
Canaletto | P | Strip	21
Chicago Brew. | P | W Side	17
Chocolate Swan | P | Strip	23
Coffee Pub | P | W of Strip	19
🟆 Daniel Boulud | P, W | Strip	26
Elephant Bar | P | Henderson	17
Empress Court | P | Strip	22
Firefly | P | E of Strip	24
Garduño's | P | W of Strip	20
Grape St. | P | NW	23
Harley-Davidson | P | Strip	15
Il Mulino NY | P | Strip	26
Jimmy Buffett's | P | Strip	17
🟆 Joël Robuchon | G, T | Strip	28
King's | P | Henderson	23
Kona Grill | P | NW	18
Le Provençal | P | Strip	22
Little Buddha | P | W of Strip	24
Lucille's | P | Henderson	22
Luna Rossa | P | Lake LV	20
Maggiano's | P | Strip	20
Marché Bacchus | T, W | NW	24
Medici Café | P | Lake LV	22
Memphis BBQ | P | E Side	21
Metro Pizza | P | E Side	24
MiraLago | P | Lake LV	21
🟆 miX | T | Strip	23
🟆 Mon Ami Gabi | P | Strip	23
Nine Fine Irish | P | Strip	17
🟆 Okada | G, W | Strip	25
🟆 Olives | P, W | Strip	23
Pahrump Valley | P | Pahrump	21
Pasta Mia | P | W Side	23
🟆 Picasso | P, W | Strip	27
Pink Taco | P, S | E of Strip	19
Postrio | P | Strip	24
Roy's | P | NW	24
Sammy's | P | Henderson	21
Smith & Wollensky | P | Strip	23
Spiedini | P | NW	21
SW Steak | P | Strip	26
🟆 Tableau | P | Strip	27
Taqueria Cañonita | P | Strip	20
🟆 T-Bones | P | NW	25
Trader Vic's | P | Strip	⊥
Ventano | P | Henderson	20
Verandah | P | Strip	23

PEOPLE-WATCHING

🆕 Ago | E of Strip	⊥
AJ's | E of Strip	23
🟆 Alex | Strip	27
🟆 Aureole | Strip	25
🟆 B&B | Strip	26
Bartolotta | Strip	24
Boa | Strip	24
Bootlegger | S of Strip	19
🆕 Carnevino | Strip	⊥
🆕 CatHouse | Strip	⊥
Charlie Palmer | Strip	25
Chinois | Strip	22
Circo | Strip	25
🆕 Company Bistro | Strip	⊥
Craftsteak | Strip	25
🆕 CUT | Strip	⊥
🆕 Dal Toro | Strip	⊥
🟆 Daniel Boulud | Strip	26
David Burke | Strip	24
🟆 Delmonico | Strip	26

Let your voice be heard – visit ZAGAT.com/vote

Diablo's	Strip	–	
NEW DJT	Strip	–	
Fiamma Trattoria	Strip	22	
NEW Hawaiian Tropic	Strip	–	
Joe's	Strip	25	
NEW Lavo	Strip	–	
Z Le Cirque	Strip	26	
Little Buddha	W of Strip	24	
Z Michael Mina	Strip	27	
Z Mon Ami Gabi	Strip	23	
NEW Morels	Strip	–	
Mr. Lucky's	E of Strip	19	
N9ne	W of Strip	25	
Z Nobu	E of Strip	28	
Z Olives	Strip	23	
Palm, The	Strip	25	
Pearl	Strip	23	
Z Picasso	Strip	27	
Piero's	E of Strip	24	
Pink Taco	E of Strip	19	
Postrio	Strip	24	
Rao's	Strip	23	
Red 8	Strip	23	
NEW Rest. Charlie	Strip	–	
Seablue	Strip	24	
Sensi	Strip	25	
NEW Simon	W of Strip	–	
Spago	Strip	23	
NEW Stratta	Strip	–	
Strip Hse.	Strip	–	
NEW SushiSamba	Strip	–	
SW Steak	Strip	26	
NEW Table 10	Strip	–	
Table 34	S of Strip	–	
Tao	Strip	23	
Tintoretto	Strip	20	
Trader Vic's	Strip	–	
Trevi	Strip	20	
Valentino	Strip	23	
NEW Yellowtail	Strip	–	

POWER SCENES

Z André's	Downtown	26
AquaKnox	Strip	23
Z Aureole	Strip	25
Z Bradley Ogden	Strip	26
Charlie Palmer	Strip	25
Chinois	Strip	22
Craftsteak	Strip	25
NEW CUT	Strip	–
NEW DJT	Strip	–
Eiffel Tower	Strip	22
Z Joël Robuchon	Strip	28
Z Le Cirque	Strip	26
Z Michael Mina	Strip	27
Z miX	Strip	23
Morton's Steak	E of Strip	25
Z Nobu	E of Strip	28
Z Olives	Strip	23
Palm, The	Strip	25
Pearl	Strip	23
Z Picasso	Strip	27
Piero's	E of Strip	24
Postrio	Strip	24
Z Prime	Strip	26
NEW Rest. Charlie	Strip	–
Z Rosemary's	W Side	28
Ruth's Chris	multi.	24
Spago	Strip	23
Spiedini	NW	21
SW Steak	Strip	26
Table 34	S of Strip	–
Tillerman	E Side	23
Trattoria del Lupo	Strip	21
Valentino	Strip	23
Vintner Grill	NW	–

QUIET CONVERSATION

Alizé	W of Strip	26
Z B&B	Strip	26
Bartolotta	Strip	24
NEW Brand Steak	Strip	–
NEW Brio	S of Strip	–
Capital Grille	Strip	26
Charlie Palmer	Strip	25
Claim Jumper	S of Strip	–
Craftsteak	Strip	25
NEW CUT	Strip	–
NEW DJT	Strip	–

Envy	**E of Strip**	21	
Gaetano's	**Henderson**	23	
🆕 Galerias	**NW**	–	
Golden Steer	**W of Strip**	22	
🔼 Guy Savoy	**Strip**	28	
🔼 Hugo's Cellar	**Downtown**	26	
Joe's	**Strip**	25	
King's	**Henderson**	23	
🆕 La Madonna	**SW**	–	
🔼 Le Cirque	**Strip**	26	
🆕 Le Golosita	**Henderson**	–	
🆕 Louis's LV	**S of Strip**	–	
🆕 Lucio	**W Side**	–	
Marché Bacchus	**NW**	24	
Martinis	**NW**	–	
🆕 Morels	**Strip**	–	
🆕 New Orleans Connection	**E Side**	–	
🔼 Okada	**Strip**	25	
🆕 Payard	**Strip**	–	
Pearl	**Strip**	23	
🆕 Pie Town	**Henderson**	–	
Red 8	**Strip**	23	
🆕 Rest. Charlie	**Strip**	–	
Second St.	**Downtown**	24	
Sensi	**Strip**	25	
Shibuya	**Strip**	25	
Steak Hse. (Circus)	**Strip**	25	
🆕 Stratta	**Strip**	–	
SW Steak	**Strip**	26	
Terra Verde	**Henderson**	–	
🔼 Todd's	**Henderson**	28	
🆕 Tommy Bahama's	**S of Strip**	–	
Verandah	**Strip**	23	
🆕 V Thai	**W Side**	–	
🆕 White Chocolate	**Henderson**	–	
Wing Lei	**Strip**	25	
🆕 Woo	**Strip**	–	

RAW BARS

Bartolotta	**Strip**	24
Big Al's	**W of Strip**	19
🔼 Bouchon	**Strip**	25
Broiler	**W of Strip**	21
Buzio's	**W of Strip**	24
Cravings	**Strip**	22
🔼 Daniel Boulud	**Strip**	26
🔼 Emeril's	**Strip**	23
Garduño's	**W of Strip**	20
King's	**Henderson**	23
🔼 Mon Ami Gabi	**Strip**	23
🆕 Morels	**Strip**	–
Penazzi	**Strip**	22
Seablue	**Strip**	24
Shibuya	**Strip**	25
Ventano	**Henderson**	20
Zeffirino	**Strip**	21

ROMANTIC PLACES

🔼 Alex	**Strip**	27
Alizé	**W of Strip**	26
🔼 André's	**multi.**	26
🔼 Aureole	**Strip**	25
🔼 B&B	**Strip**	26
Bartolotta	**Strip**	24
🆕 Brio	**S of Strip**	–
Canaletto	**Strip**	21
🆕 Carnevino	**Strip**	–
🆕 CatHouse	**Strip**	–
Chicago Joe's	**Downtown**	21
🔼 Daniel Boulud	**Strip**	26
Eiffel Tower	**Strip**	22
Fleur de Lys	**Strip**	25
🔼 Hugo's Cellar	**Downtown**	26
🔼 Joël Robuchon	**Strip**	28
🔼 Le Cirque	**Strip**	26
🆕 Le Golosita	**Henderson**	–
🆕 Louis's LV	**S of Strip**	–
🆕 Lucio	**W Side**	–
Marché Bacchus	**NW**	24
Melting Pot	**NW**	21
🔼 Michael's	**S of Strip**	26
🔼 miX	**Strip**	23
🆕 Morels	**Strip**	–
Nobhill Tavern	**Strip**	26
Pamplemousse	**E Side**	25
Panevino	**S of Strip**	21
Pearl	**Strip**	23

Let your voice be heard – visit ZAGAT.com/vote

🏆 Picasso | **Strip**	27
🏆 Prime | **Strip**	26
Rao's | **Strip**	23
Sensi | **Strip**	25
Settebello | **Henderson**	–
NEW Simon | **W of Strip**	–
Terra Verde | **Henderson**	–
Top of the World | **Strip**	20
Valentino | **Strip**	23
Wing Lei | **Strip**	25
NEW Woo | **Strip**	–
Zeffirino | **Strip**	21

SENIOR APPEAL

Applebee's | **W Side**	13
Bootlegger | **S of Strip**	19
Buffet (Wynn) | **Strip**	–
Cal. Pizza | **S of Strip**	18
Cheesecake Factory | **multi.**	20
Claim Jumper | **S of Strip**	–
Coffee Pub | **W of Strip**	19
Egg & I | **W Side**	21
Festival | **Henderson**	14
Fleming's | **W Side**	25
Florida Café | **Central**	19
Garden Ct. | **Downtown**	19
🏆 Hugo's Cellar | **Downtown**	26
Hush Puppy | **multi.**	22
Lindo Michoacan | **E Side**	–
Martinis | **NW**	–
Pasta Shop | **E Side**	24
Redwood | **Downtown**	24
Settebello | **Henderson**	–
Tintoretto | **Strip**	20
Todai | **Strip**	18
Tony Roma's | **multi.**	16
Verandah | **Strip**	23

SINGLES SCENES

AJ's | **E of Strip**	23
NEW Brand Steak | **Strip**	–
NEW CatHouse | **Strip**	–
NEW Company Bistro | **Strip**	–
NEW Dal Toro | **Strip**	–
🏆 Del Frisco's | **E of Strip**	26
Diablo's | **Strip**	–
Fiamma Trattoria | **Strip**	22
Fleming's | **W Side**	25
Gaetano's | **Henderson**	23
Hamada | **E of Strip**	19
Harley-Davidson | **Strip**	15
NEW Hawaiian Tropic | **Strip**	–
Jimmy Buffett's | **Strip**	17
NEW Kabuki | **S of Strip**	–
Kona Grill | **NW**	18
NEW Lavo | **Strip**	–
Little Buddha | **W of Strip**	24
Marrakech | **E of Strip**	20
Martinis | **NW**	–
Mr. Lucky's | **E of Strip**	19
N9ne | **W of Strip**	25
🏆 Nobu | **E of Strip**	28
Panevino | **S of Strip**	21
Paymon's | **E Side**	23
Pearl | **Strip**	23
P.F. Chang's | **multi.**	21
Pink Taco | **E of Strip**	19
Roadrunner | **S of Strip**	16
Roy's | **multi.**	24
Sapporo | **W Side**	21
Sensi | **Strip**	25
NEW Simon | **W of Strip**	–
Smith & Wollensky | **Strip**	23
Spago | **Strip**	23
NEW SushiSamba | **Strip**	–
NEW T&T | **Strip**	–
Taqueria Cañonita | **Strip**	20
TGI Friday's | **multi.**	15
Todai | **Strip**	18
Trader Vic's | **Strip**	–
Trattoria del Lupo | **Strip**	21
Triple 7 | **Downtown**	21
Viva Mercado's | **W Side**	22
NEW Yellowtail | **Strip**	–

SLEEPERS

(Good to excellent food, but little known)

AJ's | **E of Strip**	23
Alan Albert's | **Strip**	22

Antonio's | **W of Strip**	25	☑ B&B | **Strip**	26
Archi's | **W Side**	24	Border Grill | **Strip**	22
Austins Steak | **N Las Vegas**	24	Craftsteak | **Strip**	25
Billy Bob's | **E Side**	24	Eiffel Tower | **Strip**	22
Buzio's | **W of Strip**	24	☑ Emeril's | **Strip**	23
Cafe Heidelberg | **E of Strip**	22	Empress Court | **Strip**	22
Cafe Martorano | **W of Strip**	25	Fleur de Lys | **Strip**	25
Canal St. | **W of Strip**	22	☑ Guy Savoy | **Strip**	28
Empress Court | **Strip**	22	☑ Joël Robuchon | **Strip**	28
Fellini's | **Strip**	24	☑ L'Atelier/Robuchon | **Strip**	28
Ferraro's | **W Side**	26	☑ Le Cirque | **Strip**	26
Fin | **Strip**	25	Medici Café | **Lake LV**	22
Gaetano's | **Henderson**	23	☑ Michael Mina | **Strip**	27
Golden Steer | **W of Strip**	22	☑ miX | **Strip**	23
Grape St. | **NW**	23	Nobhill Tavern | **Strip**	26
Hush Puppy | **multi.**	22	☑ Nobu | **E of Strip**	28
I Love Sushi | **Henderson**	24	☑ Okada | **Strip**	25
India Palace | **E of Strip**	24	Pamplemousse | **E Side**	25
Kathy's | **Henderson**	24	☑ Picasso | **Strip**	27
Medici Café | **Lake LV**	22	Pinot | **Strip**	22
Nove | **W of Strip**	27	**NEW** Rest. Charlie | **Strip**	-
Origin | **E of Strip**	26	Rick Moonen's | **Strip**	24
Osaka Bistro | **multi.**	22	☑ Rosemary's | **W Side**	28
Pampas | **Strip**	22	Shibuya | **Strip**	25
Pasta Mia | **W Side**	23	☑ Tableau | **Strip**	27
Pasta Shop | **E Side**	24	Valentino | **Strip**	23
Pearl | **Strip**	23	Wing Lei | **Strip**	25
Penazzi | **Strip**	22		
Piero's | **E of Strip**	24	**TEEN APPEAL**	
Pullman Grille | **Downtown**	24	Benihana | **E of Strip**	19
Redwood | **Downtown**	24	Cheesecake Factory | **multi.**	20
Second St. | **Downtown**	24	Chevys | **Henderson**	14
Sen | **W Side**	27	Florida Café | **Central**	19
Steak Hse. (Treasure Is.) | **Strip**	23	Grand Lux | **Strip**	20
Steakhouse46 | **Strip**	26	Hard Rock Cafe | **E of Strip**	15
Tillerman | **E Side**	23	Harley-Davidson | **Strip**	15
Tinoco's | **Downtown**	23	In-N-Out | **multi.**	24
Triple George | **Downtown**	22	Jean Philippe | **Strip**	26
Vic & Anthony's | **Downtown**	25	La Salsa | **multi.**	15
Viva Mercado's | **W Side**	22	Melting Pot | **NW**	21
		Mr. Lucky's | **E of Strip**	19
TASTING MENUS		Osaka Bistro | **multi.**	22
☑ Alex | **Strip**	27	Planet Hollywood | **Strip**	13
☑ André's | **Downtown**	26	Roxy's | **Strip**	16
☑ Aureole | **Strip**	25	Tao | **Strip**	23

Let your voice be heard – visit ZAGAT.com/vote

Taqueria Cañonita	**Strip**	20	Postrio	**Strip**	24
Tintoretto	**Strip**	20	Seablue	**Strip**	24
Todai	**Strip**	18	Settebello	**Henderson**	–
Top of the World	**Strip**	20	**NEW** Simon	**W of Strip**	–
Viva Mercado's	**W Side**	22	Spago	**Strip**	23
Wolfgang Puck	**Strip**	21	**NEW** Stratta	**Strip**	–
		Strip Hse.	**Strip**	–

TRENDY

NEW Ago	**E of Strip**	–	**NEW** SushiSamba	**Strip**	–
Ah Sin	**Strip**	20	Table 34	**S of Strip**	–
AJ's	**E of Strip**	23	**NEW** T&T	**Strip**	–
⚡ Alex	**Strip**	27	Tao	**Strip**	23
AquaKnox	**Strip**	23	Trader Vic's	**Strip**	–
⚡ Aureole	**Strip**	25	Trattoria del Lupo	**Strip**	21
⚡ B&B	**Strip**	26	Vintner Grill	**NW**	–
NEW BLT Burger	**Strip**	–	**NEW** Yellowtail	**Strip**	–
Boa	**Strip**	24	**NEW** Yolos	**Strip**	–
⚡ Bradley Ogden	**Strip**	26	**NEW** Zine	**Strip**	–

VIEWS

NEW Brand Steak	**Strip**	–	⚡ Alex	**Strip**	27
Cafe Martorano	**W of Strip**	25	Alizé	**W of Strip**	26
NEW CatHouse	**Strip**	–	Binion's	**Downtown**	24
China Grill	**Strip**	23	⚡ Bouchon	**Strip**	25
Circo	**Strip**	25	Buzio's	**W of Strip**	24
NEW Company Bistro	**Strip**	–	Café Bellagio	**Strip**	20
NEW Dal Toro	**Strip**	–	Cafe Lago	**Strip**	17
⚡ Daniel Boulud	**Strip**	26	Canaletto	**Strip**	21
David Burke	**Strip**	24	Capital Grille	**Strip**	26
Diablo's	**Strip**	–	Carson St.	**Downtown**	17
Fiamma Trattoria	**Strip**	22	Circo	**Strip**	25
Firefly	**E of Strip**	24	⚡ Daniel Boulud	**Strip**	26
NEW Galerias	**NW**	–	Eiffel Tower	**Strip**	22
⚡ Guy Savoy	**Strip**	28	⚡ Guy Savoy	**Strip**	28
Joe's	**Strip**	25	Japonais	**Strip**	23
NEW Kabuki	**S of Strip**	–	Jasmine	**Strip**	23
Kona Grill	**NW**	18	Lake Mead Cruises	**Boulder City**	–
NEW Lavo	**Strip**	–	⚡ Le Cirque	**Strip**	26
Little Buddha	**W of Strip**	24	Marché Bacchus	**NW**	24
Martinis	**NW**	–	Medici Café	**Lake LV**	22
⚡ miX	**Strip**	23	⚡ Michael Mina	**Strip**	27
Mr. Lucky's	**E of Strip**	19	MiraLago	**Lake LV**	21
N9ne	**W of Strip**	25	⚡ miX	**Strip**	23
⚡ Nobu	**E of Strip**	28	**NEW** Morels	**Strip**	–
⚡ Olives	**Strip**	23	Nove	**W of Strip**	27
Pearl	**Strip**	23	⚡ Okada	**Strip**	25
Pink Taco	**E of Strip**	19		

🆉 Olives	**Strip**	23
Outback	**Strip**	18
Pahrump Valley	**Pahrump**	21
🆉 Picasso	**Strip**	27
🆉 Prime	**Strip**	26
Range	**Strip**	23
Rao's	**Strip**	23
NEW Simon	**W of Strip**	-
Smith & Wollensky	**Strip**	23
Social Hse.	**Strip**	25
🆉 Tableau	**Strip**	27
Taqueria Cañonita	**Strip**	20
Top of the World	**Strip**	20
Trevi	**Strip**	20
NEW Yellowtail	**Strip**	-

VISITORS ON EXPENSE ACCOUNT

NEW Ago	**E of Strip**	-
🆉 Alex	**Strip**	27
🆉 Aureole	**Strip**	25
🆉 B&B	**Strip**	26
Bartolotta	**Strip**	24
Boa	**Strip**	24
NEW Brand Steak	**Strip**	-
Capital Grille	**Strip**	26
NEW Carnevino	**Strip**	-
Charlie Palmer	**Strip**	25
Circo	**Strip**	25
NEW Company Bistro	**Strip**	-
Craftsteak	**Strip**	25
NEW CUT	**Strip**	-
🆉 Daniel Boulud	**Strip**	26
David Burke	**Strip**	24
🆉 Del Frisco's	**E of Strip**	26
🆉 Delmonico	**Strip**	26
NEW DJT	**Strip**	-
Eiffel Tower	**Strip**	22
Envy	**E of Strip**	21
🆉 Guy Savoy	**Strip**	28
NEW Hawaiian Tropic	**Strip**	-
🆉 Hugo's Cellar	**Downtown**	26
Il Mulino NY	**Strip**	26
Joe's	**Strip**	25
🆉 Le Cirque	**Strip**	26
NEW Louis's LV	**S of Strip**	-
🆉 Michael Mina	**Strip**	27
🆉 miX	**Strip**	23
NEW Morels	**Strip**	-
Morton's Steak	**E of Strip**	25
Neros	**Strip**	24
N9ne	**W of Strip**	25
🆉 Nobu	**E of Strip**	28
Nove	**W of Strip**	27
🆉 Okada	**Strip**	25
Palm, The	**Strip**	25
Piero's	**E of Strip**	24
🆉 Prime	**Strip**	26
Red 8	**Strip**	23
NEW Rest. Charlie	**Strip**	-
Rick Moonen's	**Strip**	24
🆉 Rosemary's	**W Side**	28
Rosewood	**Strip**	23
Roy's	**multi.**	24
Ruth's Chris	**multi.**	24
Sensi	**Strip**	25
Smith & Wollensky	**Strip**	23
Sterling Brunch	**Strip**	26
NEW Stratta	**Strip**	-
Strip Hse.	**Strip**	-
SW Steak	**Strip**	26
NEW Table 10	**Strip**	-
🆉 Tableau	**Strip**	27
Table 34	**S of Strip**	-
Tillerman	**E Side**	23
Top of the World	**Strip**	20
Wing Lei	**Strip**	25
Yolie's	**E of Strip**	21

WINNING WINE LISTS

Alan Albert's	**Strip**	22
🆉 Alex	**Strip**	27
Alizé	**W of Strip**	26
🆉 André's	**multi.**	26
🆉 Aureole	**Strip**	25
🆉 B&B	**Strip**	26
Bartolotta	**Strip**	24
Boa	**Strip**	24
NEW Brio	**S of Strip**	-

Let your voice be heard - visit ZAGAT.com/vote

Capital Grille	Strip	26	☑ miX	Strip	23
NEW Carnevino	Strip	–	Nora's	multi.	24
Charlie Palmer	Strip	25	☑ Picasso	Strip	27
Circo	Strip	25	Piero's	E of Strip	24
Craftsteak	Strip	25	Postrio	Strip	24
NEW CUT	Strip	–	NEW Rest. Charlie	Strip	–
☑ Daniel Boulud	Strip	26	Rick Moonen's	Strip	24
NEW DJT	Strip	–	Sensi	Strip	25
Enoteca/Marco	Strip	21	Smith & Wollensky	Strip	23
Envy	E of Strip	21	Spago	Strip	23
Grape St.	NW	23	SW Steak	Strip	26
☑ Guy Savoy	Strip	28	NEW Table 10	Strip	–
Joe's	Strip	25	☑ Tableau	Strip	27
☑ Le Cirque	Strip	26	Table 34	S of Strip	–
Marché Bacchus	NW	24	Valentino	Strip	23
☑ Michael Mina	Strip	27	Vic & Anthony's	Downtown	25

Nightife Locations

Includes venue names and Appeal ratings.

DOWNTOWN

Beauty Bar	22
Brass	-
Bunkhouse	-
NEW Canyon Club	-
Dino's	-
Downtown Cocktail Rm.	-
Girls of Glitter	14
NEW Gold Diggers	-
Griffin, The	-
Hogs & Heifers	21
Jillian's	19
Sidebar	22

EAST OF STRIP

Body English	24
Club Paradise	21
Divebar	-
Double Down	24
Ellis Island	17
Freakin' Frog	25
Gipsy	-
Gordon Biersch	18
Hofbrauhaus	20
Joint, The	20
☑ Rehab	25
NEW Wasted Space	-

EAST SIDE

Bahama Breeze	19
Champagnes	-
Railhead, The	-

HENDERSON

Drop Bar	21
Ovation	-

NORTH LAS VEGAS

Chrome	-
Club, The	-
NEW 4949	-
Palomino	17

NORTHWEST

Cherry	23
J. C. Woologhan's	18

SOUTH OF STRIP

Mermaid	-
NEW Stoney's	-

STRIP

NEW Bank	-
Bar at Times Sq.	22
Bare	-
Beatles	24
Bill's Gamblin' Hall	13
Blush	-
Breeze Bar	19
Caramel	23
Carnaval	22
NEW CatHouse	-
NEW Christian Audigier	-
Cleopatra's	19
Coyote Ugly	17
Crazy Armadillo	-
Diablo's Cantina	-
ESPN Zone	20
eyecandy	-
Flight	-
☑ House of Blues	22
Images	-
Indigo	-
Ivan Kane's	23
JET Nightclub	23
J-POP	20
Kahunaville	19
Krave	20
La Scena	23
LAX	-
Mist	19
☑ miX	27
Napoleon's	22
Nine Fine	22
Noir Bar	-

Let your voice be heard – visit ZAGAT.com/vote

Olympic Gdn.	23	**WEST OF STRIP**	
☑ Peppermill Fireside	25	Artisan	-
Petrossian	24	Brendan's	16
Poetry	-	Cheetah's	22
Polly Esthers	22	Flirt	-
NEW Privé	-	☑ ghostbar	25
☑ PURE	25	Gold Coast	-
Pussycat Dolls	24	NEW I-Bar	-
☑ Red Sq.	25	NEW McFadden's	-
Risqué	19	Moon	24
NEW Rok	-	Pearl, The	-
Romance	-	NEW Penthouse	-
☑ rumjungle	22	☑ Playboy	26
Seahorse	18	Rain	21
Shadow	22	Rick's Cabaret	20
Studio 54	21	NEW Rox	-
NEW Sugarcane	-	Sand Dollar Blues	-
Tabú	23	Sapphire	23
☑ Tao	26	Seamless	-
32 degrees	22	Spearmint Rhino	24
Toby Keith's	18	Tommy Rocker's	-
NEW Torrid	-	☑ VooDoo	25
Triq	-	**WEST SIDE**	
☑ Tryst	27	Sedona	-
V Bar	23		
Zuri	20		

Nightlife Special Appeals

Listings cover the best in each category and include venue names, locations and Appeal ratings. Multi-location nightspots' features may vary by branch.

ADDITIONS

Bank	**Strip**	-
Canyon Club	**Downtown**	-
CatHouse	**Strip**	-
Christian Audigier	**Strip**	-
4949	**N Las Vegas**	-
Gold Diggers	**Downtown**	-
I-Bar	**W of Strip**	-
McFadden's	**W of Strip**	-
Penthouse	**W of Strip**	-
Privé	**Strip**	-
Rok	**Strip**	-
Rox	**W of Strip**	-
Stoney's	**S of Strip**	-
Sugarcane	**Strip**	-
Torrid	**Strip**	-
Wasted Space	**E of Strip**	-

AFTER WORK

Artisan	**W of Strip**	-
Bahama Breeze	**E Side**	19
Bar at Times Sq.	**Strip**	22
Beauty Bar	**Downtown**	22
Cleopatra's	**Strip**	19
Dino's	**Downtown**	-
ESPN Zone	**Strip**	20
Gordon Biersch	**E of Strip**	18
Hogs & Heifers	**Downtown**	21
Images	**Strip**	-
Indigo	**Strip**	-
Kahunaville	**Strip**	19
☑ miX	**Strip**	27
Nine Fine	**Strip**	22
☑ Red Sq.	**Strip**	25
Rick's Cabaret	**W of Strip**	20
Seahorse	**Strip**	18

BACHELOR PARTIES

Body English	**E of Strip**	24
Cheetah's	**W of Strip**	22
Club Paradise	**E of Strip**	21
Girls of Glitter	**Downtown**	14
Hogs & Heifers	**Downtown**	21
Ivan Kane's	**Strip**	23
Olympic Gdn.	**Strip**	23
☑ PURE	**Strip**	25
Rick's Cabaret	**W of Strip**	20
Shadow	**Strip**	22
Spearmint Rhino	**W of Strip**	24
☑ Tao	**Strip**	26

BACHELORETTE PARTIES

Body English	**E of Strip**	24
Flirt	**W of Strip**	-
Hogs & Heifers	**Downtown**	21
Olympic Gdn.	**Strip**	23
☑ PURE	**Strip**	25
☑ Tao	**Strip**	26

BLUES

Chrome	**N Las Vegas**	-
Divebar	**E of Strip**	-
☑ House of Blues	**Strip**	22
Railhead, The	**E Side**	-
Sand Dollar Blues	**W of Strip**	-

BOTTLE SERVICE

(Bottle purchase sometimes required to secure a table)

NEW Bank	**Strip**	-
Beatles	**Strip**	24
Blush	**Strip**	-
Cherry	**NW**	23
NEW Christian Audigier	**Strip**	-
Downtown Cocktail Rm.	**Downtown**	-
eyecandy	**Strip**	-
NEW Gold Diggers	**Downtown**	-
Ivan Kane's	**Strip**	23
JET Nightclub	**Strip**	23
Krave	**Strip**	20
LAX	**Strip**	-

Let your voice be heard – visit ZAGAT.com/vote

189

☑ miX	**Strip**	27
Moon	**W of Strip**	24
Noir Bar	**Strip**	–
Ovation	**Henderson**	–
☑ Playboy	**W of Strip**	26
Poetry	**Strip**	–
☑ PURE	**Strip**	25
Pussycat Dolls	**Strip**	24
Rain	**W of Strip**	21
☑ Red Sq.	**Strip**	25
Rick's Cabaret	**W of Strip**	20
Risqué	**Strip**	19
NEW Rok	**Strip**	–
Romance	**Strip**	–
☑ rumjungle	**Strip**	22
Seamless	**W of Strip**	–
Sidebar	**Downtown**	22
NEW Stoney's	**S of Strip**	–
Studio 54	**Strip**	21
Tabú	**Strip**	23
☑ Tao	**Strip**	26
☑ Tryst	**Strip**	27
V Bar	**Strip**	23
☑ VooDoo	**W of Strip**	25

BURLESQUE

Ivan Kane's	**Strip**	23
Pussycat Dolls	**Strip**	24
Risqué	**Strip**	19
Shadow	**Strip**	22

CELEB-SIGHTINGS

NEW Bank	**Strip**	–
Body English	**E of Strip**	24
Ivan Kane's	**Strip**	23
JET Nightclub	**Strip**	23
LAX	**Strip**	–
Moon	**W of Strip**	24
☑ Playboy	**W of Strip**	26
NEW Privé	**Strip**	–
☑ PURE	**Strip**	25
Pussycat Dolls	**Strip**	24
☑ Rehab	**E of Strip**	25
☑ Tao	**Strip**	26
NEW Wasted Space	**E of Strip**	–

CIGAR-FRIENDLY

Bahama Breeze	**E Side**	19
Bill's Gamblin' Hall	**Strip**	13
Body English	**E of Strip**	24
Breeze Bar	**Strip**	19
Carnaval	**Strip**	22
Cheetah's	**W of Strip**	22
Coyote Ugly	**Strip**	17
☑ ghostbar	**W of Strip**	25
Girls of Glitter	**Downtown**	14
Hofbrauhaus	**E of Strip**	20
Hogs & Heifers	**Downtown**	21
Indigo	**Strip**	–
J. C. Woolloughan's	**NW**	18
Joint, The	**E of Strip**	20
Krave	**Strip**	20
La Scena	**Strip**	23
NEW McFadden's	**W of Strip**	–
Mist	**Strip**	19
☑ miX	**Strip**	27
Moon	**W of Strip**	24
Olympic Gdn.	**Strip**	23
☑ Peppermill Fireside	**Strip**	25
Petrossian	**Strip**	24
☑ Playboy	**W of Strip**	26
Rain	**W of Strip**	21
Rick's Cabaret	**W of Strip**	20
Risqué	**Strip**	19
Sand Dollar Blues	**W of Strip**	–
Sapphire	**W of Strip**	23
Shadow	**Strip**	22
Sidebar	**Downtown**	22
Spearmint Rhino	**W of Strip**	24
Studio 54	**Strip**	21
Tabú	**Strip**	23
32 degrees	**Strip**	22
☑ Tryst	**Strip**	27
Zuri	**Strip**	20

DANCING

NEW Bank	**Strip**	–
Blush	**Strip**	–
Body English	**E of Strip**	24
NEW Canyon Club	**Downtown**	–
Cherry	**NW**	23

Chrome | N Las Vegas	-]
Cleopatra's | Strip	19]
Club, The | N Las Vegas	-]
Crazy Armadillo | Strip	-]
Z ghostbar | W of Strip	25]
Gipsy | E of Strip	-]
NEW Gold Diggers | Downtown	-]
Gordon Biersch | E of Strip	18]
Griffin, The | Downtown	-]
Z House of Blues | Strip	22]
JET Nightclub | Strip	23]
Joint, The | E of Strip	20]
J-POP | Strip	20]
Kahunaville | Strip	19]
La Scena | Strip	23]
LAX | Strip	-]
NEW McFadden's | W of Strip	-]
Mist | Strip	19]
Moon | W of Strip	24]
Napoleon's | Strip	22]
Z Playboy | W of Strip	26]
Poetry | Strip	-]
Polly Esthers | Strip	22]
Z PURE | Strip	25]
Pussycat Dolls | Strip	24]
Railhead, The | E Side	-]
Rain | W of Strip	21]
Risqué | Strip	19]
NEW Rok | Strip	-]
Romance | Strip	-]
Z rumjungle | Strip	22]
Sand Dollar Blues | W of Strip	-]
Studio 54 | Strip	21]
Z Tao | Strip	26]
Tommy Rocker's | W of Strip	-]
Z Tryst | Strip	27]
V Bar | Strip	23]
Z VooDoo | W of Strip	25]

DIVES

Bill's Gamblin' Hall | Strip	13]
Champagnes | E Side	-]
Dino's | Downtown	-]
Divebar | E of Strip	-]
Double Down | E of Strip	24]
Palomino | N Las Vegas	17]
Sand Dollar Blues | W of Strip	-]

DRINK SPECIALISTS

BEER
(* Microbrewery)

Ellis Island* | E of Strip	17]
Freakin' Frog | E of Strip	25]
Gordon Biersch* | E of Strip	18]
Hofbrauhaus | E of Strip	20]
J. C. Woolougham's | NW	18]
NEW McFadden's | W of Strip	-]
Zuri | Strip	20]

CHAMPAGNE

NEW Bank | Strip	-]
Cherry | NW	23]
NEW Christian Audigier | Strip	-]
JET Nightclub | Strip	23]
Moon | W of Strip	24]
Napoleon's | Strip	22]
Petrossian | Strip	24]
Z Playboy | W of Strip	26]
NEW Privé | Strip	-]
Seahorse | Strip	18]
Z Tryst | Strip	27]

COCKTAILS

NEW Bank | Strip	-]
NEW CatHouse | Strip	-]
Cherry | NW	23]
Downtown Cocktail Rm. | Downtown	-]
NEW 4949 | N Las Vegas	-]
Z ghostbar | W of Strip	25]
NEW I-Bar | W of Strip	-]
JET Nightclub | Strip	23]
Z miX | Strip	27]
Moon | W of Strip	24]
Z Playboy | W of Strip	26]
NEW Privé | Strip	-]
NEW Rok | Strip	-]
Sidebar | Downtown	22]
NEW Sugarcane | Strip	-]
NEW Torrid | Strip	-]
Z Tryst | Strip	27]
Z VooDoo | W of Strip	25]

Let your voice be heard – visit ZAGAT.com/vote

191

MARTINIS
Beauty Bar	Downtown	22
Cherry	NW	23
JET Nightclub	Strip	23
Moon	W of Strip	24
☑ Playboy	W of Strip	26
☑ Red Sq.	Strip	25
Seahorse	Strip	18
NEW Torrid	Strip	-
☑ Tryst	Strip	27
Zuri	Strip	20

TEQUILA
Crazy Armadillo	Strip	-

VODKA
Petrossian	Strip	24
☑ Red Sq.	Strip	25
Zuri	Strip	20

WHISKEY
Brendan's	W of Strip	16
J. C. Wooloughan's	NW	18
Nine Fine	Strip	22

WINE BY THE GLASS
Artisan	W of Strip	-

FLAIR BARTENDERS
Carnaval	Strip	22
Coyote Ugly	Strip	17
Kahunaville	Strip	19
Shadow	Strip	22
☑ VooDoo	W of Strip	25

FRAT HOUSE
NEW Canyon Club	Downtown	-
Coyote Ugly	Strip	17
Double Down	E of Strip	24
ESPN Zone	Strip	20
Freakin' Frog	E of Strip	25
Hogs & Heifers	Downtown	21
☑ House of Blues	Strip	22
NEW McFadden's	W of Strip	-
NEW Rok	Strip	-
Seahorse	Strip	18
NEW Stoney's	S of Strip	-

GAY
Gipsy	E of Strip	-
Krave	Strip	20

HAPPY HOUR
Artisan	W of Strip	-
Beauty Bar	Downtown	22
Brass	Downtown	-
Divebar	E of Strip	-
Downtown Cocktail Rm.	Downtown	-
Ellis Island	E of Strip	17
Gordon Biersch	E of Strip	18
Griffin, The	Downtown	-
Napoleon's	Strip	22
Spearmint Rhino	W of Strip	24
Tommy Rocker's	W of Strip	-

HOTEL BARS
Artisan Hotel
Artisan	W of Strip	-

Bally's Las Vegas
Indigo	Strip	-

Bellagio Hotel
NEW Bank	Strip	-
Caramel	Strip	23
Petrossian	Strip	24

Bill's Gamblin' Hall
Bill's Gamblin' Hall	Strip	13

Boulder Station Hotel
Railhead, The	E Side	-

Caesars Palace
Cleopatra's	Strip	19
Poetry	Strip	-
☑ PURE	Strip	25
Pussycat Dolls	Strip	24
Seahorse	Strip	18
Shadow	Strip	22

Cannery Hotel
Club, The	N Las Vegas	-

Ellis Island Casino & Brewery
Ellis Island	E of Strip	17

Gold Coast Hotel
Gold Coast	W of Strip	-

Golden Nugget Hotel
NEW Gold Diggers	Downtown	-

Green Valley Ranch
Drop Bar	Henderson	21

NIGHTLIFE / SPECIAL APPEALS

Hard Rock Hotel
- Body English | **E of Strip** — 24
- Joint, The | **E of Strip** — 20
- ☑ Rehab | **E of Strip** — 25
- NEW Wasted Space | **E of Strip** — –

Harrah's Las Vegas
- Carnaval | **Strip** — 22
- Toby Keith's | **Strip** — 18

JW Marriott
- J. C. Wooloughan's | **NW** — 18

Luxor Hotel
- NEW CatHouse | **Strip** — –
- Flight | **Strip** — –
- LAX | **Strip** — –
- Noir Bar | **Strip** — –

Mandalay Bay Resort
- eyecandy | **Strip** — –
- ☑ House of Blues | **Strip** — 22
- Ivan Kane's | **Strip** — 23
- J-POP | **Strip** — 20
- ☑ miX | **Strip** — 27
- ☑ Red Sq. | **Strip** — 25
- ☑ rumjungle | **Strip** — 22

MGM Grand Hotel
- Studio 54 | **Strip** — 21
- Tabú | **Strip** — 23
- 32 degrees | **Strip** — 22
- Zuri | **Strip** — 20

Miracle Mile Shops
- NEW Torrid | **Strip** — –
- Triq | **Strip** — –

Mirage Hotel
- Bare | **Strip** — –
- Beatles | **Strip** — 24
- JET Nightclub | **Strip** — 23

Monte Carlo Resort
- Diablo's Cantina | **Strip** — –

New York-New York Hotel
- Bar at Times Sq. | **Strip** — 22
- Coyote Ugly | **Strip** — 17
- ESPN Zone | **Strip** — 20
- Nine Fine | **Strip** — 22
- NEW Rok | **Strip** — –

Orleans Hotel
- Brendan's | **W of Strip** — 16

Palazzo Hotel
- NEW Sugarcane | **Strip** — –

Palms Casino Hotel
- ☑ ghostbar | **W of Strip** — 25
- Moon | **W of Strip** — 24
- Pearl, The | **W of Strip** — –
- ☑ Playboy | **W of Strip** — 26
- Rain | **W of Strip** — 21

Paris Las Vegas
- Napoleon's | **Strip** — 22
- Risqué | **Strip** — 19

Planet Hollywood Resort
- NEW Privé | **Strip** — –

Red Rock Casino
- Cherry | **NW** — 23

Rio All-Suite Hotel
- Flirt | **W of Strip** — –
- NEW I-Bar | **W of Strip** — –
- NEW McFadden's | **W of Strip** — –
- ☑ VooDoo | **W of Strip** — 25

Santa Fe Station Hotel
- Chrome | **N Las Vegas** — –

Silverton Casino & Lodge
- Mermaid | **S of Strip** — –

Stratosphere Hotel
- Crazy Armadillo | **Strip** — –
- Images | **Strip** — –
- Polly Esthers | **Strip** — 22
- Romance | **Strip** — –

Treasure Island Hotel
- Breeze Bar | **Strip** — 19
- NEW Christian Audigier | **Strip** — –
- Kahunaville | **Strip** — 19
- Mist | **Strip** — 19

Venetian Hotel
- La Scena | **Strip** — 23
- ☑ Tao | **Strip** — 26
- V Bar | **Strip** — 23

Wynn Las Vegas
- Blush | **Strip** — –
- ☑ Tryst | **Strip** — 27

Let your voice be heard – visit ZAGAT.com/vote

LIVE ENTERTAINMENT

(See also Blues, Strip Clubs)

Bahama Breeze | reggae | **E Side**	19
Brendan's | bands | **W of Strip**	16
Carnaval | varies | **Strip**	22
Champagnes | karaoke | **E Side**	–
Cleopatra's | bands | **Strip**	19
Coyote Ugly | bartenders | **Strip**	17
Dino's | bands/karaoke | **Downtown**	–
Double Down | metal/punk/rock | **E of Strip**	24
Ellis Island | karaoke | **E of Strip**	17
Gold Coast | jazz | **W of Strip**	–
Hofbrauhaus | German | **E of Strip**	20
Hogs & Heifers | bartenders | **Downtown**	21
Images | R&B/rock | **Strip**	–
Indigo | R&B | **Strip**	–
J. C. Wooloughan's | varies | **NW**	18
J-POP | bands | **Strip**	20
Kahunaville | reggae | **Strip**	19
Krave | adult show | **Strip**	20
La Scena | rock | **Strip**	23
Mermaid | performers | **S of Strip**	–
Mist | varies | **Strip**	19
Napoleon's | jazz | **Strip**	22
Nine Fine | Irish | **Strip**	22
Rain | dancers | **W of Strip**	21
☑ rumjungle | dancers | **Strip**	22
Studio 54 | dancers | **Strip**	21
☑ Tao | performers | **Strip**	26
☑ VooDoo | jazz | **W of Strip**	25

MEAT MARKETS

Bahama Breeze | **E Side**	19
NEW Bank | **Strip**	–
NEW CatHouse | **Strip**	–
Cherry | **NW**	23
NEW Christian Audigier | **Strip**	–
Coyote Ugly | **Strip**	17
Downtown Cocktail Rm. | **Downtown**	–
☑ ghostbar | **W of Strip**	25
Gipsy | **E of Strip**	–
NEW Gold Diggers | **Downtown**	–
Gordon Biersch | **E of Strip**	18
Hogs & Heifers | **Downtown**	21
NEW I-Bar | **W of Strip**	–
JET Nightclub | **Strip**	23
NEW McFadden's | **W of Strip**	–
☑ miX | **Strip**	27
Moon | **W of Strip**	24
NEW Privé | **Strip**	–
Pussycat Dolls | **Strip**	24
Rain | **W of Strip**	21
NEW Rok | **Strip**	–
☑ rumjungle | **Strip**	22
Shadow | **Strip**	22
NEW Stoney's | **S of Strip**	–
Studio 54 | **Strip**	21
NEW Sugarcane | **Strip**	–
NEW Torrid | **Strip**	–
☑ Tryst | **Strip**	27
V Bar | **Strip**	23
☑ VooDoo | **W of Strip**	25
NEW Wasted Space | **E of Strip**	–

OPEN 24 HOURS

Artisan | **W of Strip**	–
Bill's Gamblin' Hall | **Strip**	13
Breeze Bar | **Strip**	19
Bunkhouse | **Downtown**	–
Champagnes | **E Side**	–
Cheetah's | **W of Strip**	22
Dino's | **Downtown**	–
Divebar | **E of Strip**	–
Double Down | **E of Strip**	24
Drop Bar | **Henderson**	21
Ellis Island | **E of Strip**	17
Flight | **Strip**	–
Gold Coast | **W of Strip**	–
J-POP | **Strip**	20
Olympic Gdn. | **Strip**	23
☑ Peppermill Fireside | **Strip**	25
Petrossian | **Strip**	24
Rick's Cabaret | **W of Strip**	20
Sand Dollar Blues | **W of Strip**	–
Sapphire | **W of Strip**	23
Seahorse | **Strip**	18

194   40,000 places to eat, drink, stay & play – free at ZAGAT.com

Seamless	W of Strip	–
Spearmint Rhino	W of Strip	24
Tommy Rocker's	W of Strip	–
Zuri	Strip	20

OUTDOOR SPACES

PATIO/TERRACE
Bahama Breeze	E Side	19
Beauty Bar	Downtown	22
Carnaval	Strip	22
Cherry	NW	23
NEW Christian Audigier	Strip	–
Club, The	N Las Vegas	–
NEW Gold Diggers	Downtown	–
Gordon Biersch	E of Strip	18
J. C. Wooloughan's	NW	18
Z miX	Strip	27
Moon	W of Strip	24
Nine Fine	Strip	22
NEW Rok	Strip	–
Sedona	W Side	–
Sidebar	Downtown	22
Z Tao	Strip	26
Tommy Rocker's	W of Strip	–
NEW Torrid	Strip	–
Z Tryst	Strip	27
Z VooDoo	W of Strip	25

ROOFTOP
Diablo's Cantina	Strip	–
Z ghostbar	W of Strip	25
Z VooDoo	W of Strip	25

SIDEWALK
| J. C. Wooloughan's | NW | 18 |

WATERSIDE
Bare	Strip	–
Kahunaville	Strip	19
Z Rehab	E of Strip	25
Z Tao	Strip	26
Z Tryst	Strip	27

PEOPLE-WATCHING
Bar at Times Sq.	Strip	22
Carnaval	Strip	22
Cleopatra's	Strip	19
Coyote Ugly	Strip	17
Double Down	E of Strip	24
Gipsy	E of Strip	–
Hogs & Heifers	Downtown	21
Z House of Blues	Strip	22
Ivan Kane's	Strip	23
Joint, The	E of Strip	20
Kahunaville	Strip	19
La Scena	Strip	23
Mermaid	S of Strip	–
Nine Fine	Strip	22
Z Peppermill Fireside	Strip	25
Pussycat Dolls	Strip	24
Z Red Sq.	Strip	25
Z Rehab	E of Strip	25
Seahorse	Strip	18
Studio 54	Strip	21
Z Tao	Strip	26
Z VooDoo	W of Strip	25

QUIET CONVERSATION
Artisan	W of Strip	–
NEW 4949	N Las Vegas	–
Mermaid	S of Strip	–
Napoleon's	Strip	22
Petrossian	Strip	24
Sidebar	Downtown	22

ROADHOUSES
Coyote Ugly	Strip	17
Double Down	E of Strip	24
Hogs & Heifers	Downtown	21
NEW Rox	W of Strip	–
Sand Dollar Blues	W of Strip	–
NEW Stoney's	S of Strip	–
Toby Keith's	Strip	18

ROMANTIC
Caramel	Strip	23
NEW CatHouse	Strip	–
Cherry	NW	23
JET Nightclub	Strip	23
Z miX	Strip	27
Z Peppermill Fireside	Strip	25
Sidebar	Downtown	22

🆉 Tryst | **Strip**	27	🆉 Tao | **Strip**	26
V Bar | **Strip**	23	**NEW** Torrid | **Strip**	–
🆉 VooDoo | **W of Strip**	25	🆉 Tryst | **Strip**	27

SPORTS BARS

ESPN Zone | **Strip**	20
Jillian's | **Downtown**	19
Rick's Cabaret | **W of Strip**	20

STRIP CLUBS

Cheetah's | **W of Strip**	22
Club Paradise | **E of Strip**	21
Girls of Glitter | **Downtown**	14
Olympic Gdn. | **Strip**	23
Palomino | **N Las Vegas**	17
Rick's Cabaret | **W of Strip**	20
Sapphire | **W of Strip**	23
Seamless | **W of Strip**	–
Spearmint Rhino | **W of Strip**	24
Tommy Rocker's | **W of Strip**	–

SWANKY

NEW Bank | **Strip**	–
NEW Canyon Club | **Downtown**	–
Caramel | **Strip**	23
NEW CatHouse | **Strip**	–
Cherry | **NW**	23
NEW Christian Audigier | **Strip**	–
Downtown Cocktail Rm. | **Downtown**	–
Drop Bar | **Henderson**	21
NEW 4949 | **N Las Vegas**	–
NEW Gold Diggers | **Downtown**	–
NEW I-Bar | **W of Strip**	–
JET Nightclub | **Strip**	23
Joint, The | **E of Strip**	20
🆉 miX | **Strip**	27
Moon | **W of Strip**	24
🆉 Playboy | **W of Strip**	26
NEW Privé | **Strip**	–
Rain | **W of Strip**	21
🆉 rumjungle | **Strip**	22
Seahorse | **Strip**	18
Sidebar | **Downtown**	22
Studio 54 | **Strip**	21
NEW Sugarcane | **Strip**	–

TRENDY

NEW Bank | **Strip**	–
Beauty Bar | **Downtown**	22
NEW CatHouse | **Strip**	–
Cherry | **NW**	23
NEW Christian Audigier | **Strip**	–
Coyote Ugly | **Strip**	17
Downtown Cocktail Rm. | **Downtown**	–
Drop Bar | **Henderson**	21
🆉 ghostbar | **W of Strip**	25
NEW Gold Diggers | **Downtown**	–
Hogs & Heifers | **Downtown**	21
JET Nightclub | **Strip**	23
LAX | **Strip**	–
🆉 miX | **Strip**	27
Moon | **W of Strip**	24
NEW Penthouse | **W of Strip**	–
🆉 Playboy | **W of Strip**	26
Poetry | **Strip**	–
NEW Privé | **Strip**	–
Pussycat Dolls | **Strip**	24
Rain | **W of Strip**	21
🆉 Rehab | **E of Strip**	25
NEW Rok | **Strip**	–
🆉 rumjungle | **Strip**	22
Shadow | **Strip**	22
Sidebar | **Downtown**	22
Studio 54 | **Strip**	21
NEW Sugarcane | **Strip**	–
🆉 Tao | **Strip**	26
NEW Torrid | **Strip**	–
🆉 Tryst | **Strip**	27
V Bar | **Strip**	23
NEW Wasted Space | **E of Strip**	–

VELVET ROPE

NEW Bank | **Strip**	–
Body English | **E of Strip**	24
Cherry | **NW**	23
NEW Christian Audigier | **Strip**	–
🆉 ghostbar | **W of Strip**	25

JET Nightclub	**Strip**	23	
LAX	**Strip**	–	
Moon	**W of Strip**	24	
🗹 Playboy	**W of Strip**	26	
NEW Privé	**Strip**	–	
🗹 PURE	**Strip**	25	
Pussycat Dolls	**Strip**	24	
Rain	**W of Strip**	21	
Studio 54	**Strip**	21	
NEW Sugarcane	**Strip**	–	
Tabú	**Strip**	23	
🗹 Tao	**Strip**	26	
🗹 Tryst	**Strip**	27	

VIEWS

Cherry	**NW**	23
🗹 ghostbar	**W of Strip**	25
NEW Gold Diggers	**Downtown**	–
Mermaid	**S of Strip**	–
🗹 miX	**Strip**	27
Moon	**W of Strip**	24
🗹 Playboy	**W of Strip**	26
NEW Rok	**Strip**	–
🗹 Tao	**Strip**	26
NEW Torrid	**Strip**	–
🗹 VooDoo	**W of Strip**	25

Shopping Merchandise

Includes store names, locations and Quality ratings.

ACCESSORIES

Bottega Veneta | **Strip**	28
Chanel | **Strip**	29
CH | **Strip**	27
Dior | **Strip**	27
Ferrari | **Strip**	25
Giorgio Armani | **Strip**	28
🆉 Hermès | **Strip**	29
Johnston/Murphy | **Strip**	26
Juicy Couture | **Strip**	23
Kate Spade | **Strip**	24
Leiber | **Strip**	28
Marc Jacobs | **Strip**	27
Montblanc | **Strip**	27
Prada | **Strip**	27
🆉 Saks | **Strip**	27

BRIDAL

Jessica McClintock | **Strip**	22

CLOTHING: DESIGNER

🆉 Brioni | **Strip**	29
NEW Burberry | **Strip**	27
NEW Catherine Malandrino | **Strip**	26
Chanel | **Strip**	29
CH | **Strip**	27
NEW Chloé | **Strip**	-
NEW Diane/Furstenberg | **Strip**	24
Dior | **Strip**	27
Dolce/Gabbana | **Strip**	25
Fendi | **Strip**	27
Giorgio Armani | **Strip**	28
John Varvatos | **Strip**	25
Marc Jacobs | **Strip**	27
NEW Michael Kors | **Strip**	-
Nanette Lepore | **Strip**	26
🆉 Oscar de la Renta | **Strip**	29
Prada | **Strip**	27
Roberto Cavalli | **Strip**	26
NEW Tory Burch | **Strip**	-
Versace | **Strip**	25

CLOTHING: MEN'S/WOMEN'S

(Stores carrying both)

Attic, The | **Downtown**	20
A/X | **Strip**	22
NEW Barneys New York | **Strip**	26
🆉 Bass Pro | **S of Strip**	26
Brooks Bros. | **Strip**	26
Buffalo | **E of Strip**	19
C Level | **NW**	-
H&M | **Strip**	-
Kenneth Cole | **Strip**	24
Lacoste | **Strip**	23
Las Vegas Outlets | **W Side**	-
NEW Scoop | **Strip**	-
NEW Tommy Bahama's | **S of Strip**	-

CLOTHING: MEN'S

BOSS | **Strip**	25
NEW Canali | **Strip**	-

CLOTHING: WOMEN'S

Anne Fontaine | **Strip**	25
NEW Annie Creamcheese | **Strip**	-
Escada | **Strip**	27
Intermix | **Strip**	-
Jessica McClintock | **Strip**	22
Juicy Couture | **Strip**	23
St. John | **Strip**	28

CONSIGNMENT/THRIFT/VINTAGE

Attic, The | **Downtown**	20
Buffalo | **E of Strip**	19

COSMETICS/TOILETRIES

🆉 Art/Shaving | **Strip**	27
Kiehl's | **Strip**	27
🆉 Sephora | **Strip**	26
Truefitt & Hill | **Strip**	28

DEPARTMENT STORES

NEW Barneys New York | **Strip**	26
🆉 Neiman Marcus | **Strip**	28

40,000 places to eat, drink, stay & play – free at ZAGAT.com

| Z Nordstrom | Strip | 26 |
| Z Saks | Strip | 27 |

GIFTS/NOVELTIES

Baccarat	Strip	29
Bonanza	Strip	16
Ferrari	Strip	25
Field/Dreams	multi.	23
Secret Gdn.	Strip	21
Shark Reef Gift	Strip	20
West/Santa Fe	Strip	24

HANDBAGS

NEW Anya Hindmarch	Strip	–
Bally	Strip	27
Bottega Veneta	Strip	28
Chanel	Strip	29
CH	Strip	27
Dior	Strip	27
Fendi	Strip	27
Juicy Couture	Strip	23
Kate Spade	Strip	24
Marc Jacobs	Strip	27
Prada	Strip	27
Roberto Cavalli	Strip	26
Taryn Rose	Strip	25

HOME

| Baccarat | Strip | 29 |
| Z Gallerie | Strip | 22 |

HOSIERY/LINGERIE

| Agent Provocateur | Strip | 26 |
| La Perla | Strip | 27 |

JEWELRY

COSTUME/SEMIPRECIOUS

| NEW Annie Creamcheese | Strip | – |
| West/Santa Fe | Strip | 24 |

FINE

Bulgari	Strip	28
Z Cartier	Strip	29
Chopard	Strip	28
De Beers	Strip	26
Dior	Strip	27
Fred Leighton	Strip	28
Z Harry Winston	Strip	29
Mikimoto	Strip	29
NEW Piaget	Strip	–
Z Tiffany	Strip	28

SHOES: MEN'S/WOMEN'S

a. testoni	Strip	24
Bally	Strip	27
CH	Strip	27
NEW Christian Louboutin	Strip	–
Dior	Strip	27
Donald J Pliner	Strip	27
Jimmy Choo	Strip	27
Johnston/Murphy	Strip	26
Manolo Blahnik	Strip	28
Marc Jacobs	Strip	27
Prada	Strip	27
Roberto Cavalli	Strip	26
Z Saks	Strip	27
Taryn Rose	Strip	25

SNEAKERS

| Niketown | Strip | 24 |

SPORTING GOODS

Z Bass Pro	S of Strip	26
Las Vegas Golf/Tennis	E of Strip	25
Niketown	Strip	24

WATCHES

Z Cartier	Strip	29
Chopard	Strip	28
Montblanc	Strip	27
NEW Piaget	Strip	–
Z Tiffany	Strip	28

Let your voice be heard – visit ZAGAT.com/vote

Shopping Locations

Includes store names, merchandise type (where necessary) and Quality ratings.

DOWNTOWN
Attic, The | *Vintage*	20

EAST OF STRIP
Buffalo | *Vintage*	19
Las Vegas Golf/Tennis | *Sports*	25

HENDERSON
Along/Spider | *Childrenswear*	25
Las Vegas Golf/Tennis | *Sports*	25

NORTHWEST
C Level | *Mens/Womenswear*	–

SOUTH OF STRIP
A/X | *Mens/Womenswear*	22
Z Bass Pro | *Sports*	26
H&M | *Mens/Womenswear*	–
Juicy Couture | *Womenswear*	23
NEW Tommy Bahama's | *Mens/Womenswear*	–

STRIP
Agent Provocateur | *Hose/Lingerie*	26
Anne Fontaine | *Womenswear*	25
NEW Annie Creamcheese | *Womenswear*	–
NEW Anya Hindmarch | *Handbags*	–
Z Art/Shaving | *Toiletries*	27
a. testoni | *Shoes*	24
A/X | *Mens/Womenswear*	22
Baccarat | *Home*	29
Bally | *Shoes*	27
NEW Barneys New York | *Dept. Store*	26
NEW Bauman Books | *Books*	–
Bonanza | *Gifts/Novelties*	16
BOSS | *Menswear*	25
Bottega Veneta | *Accessories*	28
Z Brioni | *Designer*	29
Brooks Bros. | *Menswear*	26
Bulgari | *Jewelry*	28
NEW Burberry | *Designer*	27
NEW Canali | *Menswear*	–
Z Cartier | *Jewelry*	29
NEW Catherine Malandrino | *Womenswear*	26
Chanel | *Designer*	29
CH | *Designer*	27
NEW Chloé | *Womenswear*	–
Chopard | *Jewelry*	28
NEW Christian Louboutin | *Shoes*	–
De Beers | *Jewelry*	26
NEW Diane/Furstenberg | *Designer*	24
Dior | *Designer*	27
Dolce/Gabbana | *Designer*	25
Donald J Pliner | *Shoes*	27
Escada | *Womenswear*	27
FAO | *Toys*	–
Fendi | *Designer*	27
Ferrari | *Gifts/Novelties*	25
Field/Dreams | *Gifts/Novelties*	23
Fred Leighton | *Jewelry*	28
Giorgio Armani | *Designer*	28
H&M | *Mens/Womenswear*	–
Z Harry Winston | *Jewelry*	29
Z Hermès | *Accessories*	29
Intermix | *Womenswear*	–
Jessica McClintock | *Womenswear*	22
Jimmy Choo | *Shoes*	27
Johnston/Murphy | *Shoes*	26
John Varvatos | *Designer*	25
Juicy Couture | *Womenswear*	23
Kate Spade | *Accessories*	24
Kenneth Cole | *Mens/Womenswear*	24
Kiehl's | *Toiletries*	27
Lacoste | *Mens/Womenswear*	23
La Perla | *Hose/Lingerie*	27
Leiber | *Handbags*	28
Manolo Blahnik | *Shoes*	28
Marc Jacobs | *Designer*	27
NEW Michael Kors | *Designer*	–

40,000 places to eat, drink, stay & play – free at ZAGAT.com

Mikimoto	*Jewelry*	29
Montblanc	*Accessories*	27
Nanette Lepore	*Designer*	26
☑ Neiman Marcus	*Dept. Store*	28
Niketown	*Sports*	24
☑ Nordstrom	*Dept. Store*	26
☑ Oscar de la Renta	*Designer*	29
NEW Piaget	*Jewelry*	–
Prada	*Designer*	27
Roberto Cavalli	*Designer*	26
☑ Saks	*Dept. Store*	27
NEW Scoop	*Mens/Womenswear*	–
Secret Gdn.	*Gifts/Novelties*	21
☑ Sephora	*Toiletries*	26
Shark Reef Gift	*Gifts/Novelties*	20
St. John	*Womenswear*	28
Taryn Rose	*Shoes*	25
☑ Tiffany	*Jewelry*	28
NEW Tory Burch	*Designer*	–
Truefitt & Hill	*Toiletries*	28
Versace	*Mens/Womenswear*	25
West/Santa Fe	*Gifts/Novelties*	24
Z Gallerie	*Home*	22

WEST OF STRIP

Field/Dreams | *Gifts/Novelties*   23

WEST SIDE

Las Vegas Outlets | *Mens/Womenswear*   –

Shopping Special Features

Listings cover the best in each category and include store names, locations and Quality ratings.

ADDITIONS
(Properties added since the last edition of the book)

Annie Creamcheese | **Strip**	-|
Anya Hindmarch | **Strip**	-|
Barneys New York | **Strip**	26|
Bauman Books | **Strip**	-|
Burberry | **Strip**	27|
Canali | **Strip**	-|
Catherine Malandrino | **Strip**	26|
Chloé | **Strip**	-|
Christian Louboutin | **Strip**	-|
Diane/Furstenberg | **Strip**	24|
Michael Kors | **Strip**	-|
Piaget | **Strip**	-|
Scoop | **Strip**	-|
Tommy Bahama's | **S of Strip**	-|
Tory Burch | **Strip**	-|

AVANT-GARDE

Agent Provocateur | **Strip**	26|
NEW Annie Creamcheese | **Strip**	-|
Attic, The | **Downtown**	20|
Buffalo | **E of Strip**	19|
Dolce/Gabbana | **Strip**	25|
Giorgio Armani | **Strip**	28|
Jimmy Choo | **Strip**	27|
Manolo Blahnik | **Strip**	28|
Marc Jacobs | **Strip**	27|
Roberto Cavalli | **Strip**	26|
Versace | **Strip**	25|

CELEBRITY CLIENTELE

Agent Provocateur | **Strip**	26|
NEW Annie Creamcheese | **Strip**	-|
NEW Anya Hindmarch | **Strip**	-|
a. testoni | **Strip**	24|
Baccarat | **Strip**	29|
NEW Barneys New York | **Strip**	26|
Bottega Veneta | **Strip**	28|
Z Brioni | **Strip**	29|
NEW Burberry | **Strip**	27|
NEW Canali | **Strip**	-|
Z Cartier | **Strip**	29|
NEW Catherine Malandrino | **Strip**	26|
Chanel | **Strip**	29|
CH | **Strip**	27|
NEW Chloé | **Strip**	-|
Chopard | **Strip**	28|
NEW Christian Louboutin | **Strip**	-|
De Beers | **Strip**	26|
NEW Diane/Furstenberg | **Strip**	24|
Dior | **Strip**	27|
Dolce/Gabbana | **Strip**	25|
Escada | **Strip**	27|
Fendi | **Strip**	27|
Ferrari | **Strip**	25|
Fred Leighton | **Strip**	28|
Giorgio Armani | **Strip**	28|
Z Harry Winston | **Strip**	29|
Z Hermès | **Strip**	29|
Jimmy Choo | **Strip**	27|
John Varvatos | **Strip**	25|
Juicy Couture | **multi.**	23|
Kate Spade | **Strip**	24|
Leiber | **Strip**	28|
Manolo Blahnik | **Strip**	28|
Marc Jacobs | **Strip**	27|
NEW Michael Kors | **Strip**	-|
Montblanc | **Strip**	27|
Nanette Lepore | **Strip**	26|
Z Oscar de la Renta | **Strip**	29|
NEW Piaget | **Strip**	-|
Prada | **Strip**	27|
Roberto Cavalli | **Strip**	26|
Z Tiffany | **Strip**	28|
NEW Tory Burch | **Strip**	-|
Versace | **Strip**	25|

CUSTOM-MADE GOODS

NEW Anya Hindmarch	Strip	–
a. testoni	Strip	24
Baccarat	Strip	29
Chanel	Strip	29
CH	Strip	27
Fendi	Strip	27
Fred Leighton	Strip	28
Z Harry Winston	Strip	29
Roberto Cavalli	Strip	26
Taryn Rose	Strip	25
Z Tiffany	Strip	28

HIP/HOT PLACES

Agent Provocateur	Strip	26
NEW Annie Creamcheese	Strip	–
Z Art/Shaving	Strip	27
a. testoni	Strip	24
Attic, The	Downtown	20
A/X	multi.	22
BOSS	Strip	25
Z Brioni	Strip	29
Buffalo	E of Strip	19
NEW Christian Louboutin	Strip	–
C Level	NW	–
Dolce/Gabbana	Strip	25
Giorgio Armani	Strip	28
Intermix	Strip	–
Jimmy Choo	Strip	27
Juicy Couture	Strip	23
Kiehl's	Strip	27
Manolo Blahnik	Strip	28
Marc Jacobs	Strip	27
Prada	Strip	27
Roberto Cavalli	Strip	26
NEW Scoop	Strip	–
NEW Tory Burch	Strip	–
Versace	Strip	25

ONLY IN LAS VEGAS

Attic, The	Downtown	20
Bonanza	Strip	16
Ferrari	Strip	25
Secret Gdn.	Strip	21
Shark Reef Gift	Strip	20
West/Santa Fe	Strip	24

REGISTRY: BRIDAL/GIFT

Baccarat	Strip	29
De Beers	Strip	26
Z Hermès	Strip	29
Montblanc	Strip	27
Z Saks	Strip	27
Z Tiffany	Strip	28
Z Gallerie	Strip	22

STATUS GOODS

Agent Provocateur	Strip	26
Anne Fontaine	Strip	25
NEW Anya Hindmarch	Strip	–
Z Art/Shaving	Strip	27
a. testoni	Strip	24
A/X	multi.	22
Baccarat	Strip	29
Bally	Strip	27
NEW Bauman Books	Strip	–
BOSS	Strip	25
Bottega Veneta	Strip	28
Z Brioni	Strip	29
Brooks Bros.	Strip	26
Bulgari	Strip	28
NEW Burberry	Strip	27
NEW Canali	Strip	–
Z Cartier	Strip	29
NEW Catherine Malandrino	Strip	26
Chanel	Strip	29
CH	Strip	27
NEW Chloé	Strip	–
Chopard	Strip	28
NEW Christian Louboutin	Strip	–
De Beers	Strip	26
NEW Diane/Furstenberg	Strip	24
Dior	Strip	27
Dolce/Gabbana	Strip	25
Donald J Pliner	Strip	27
Escada	Strip	27
Fendi	Strip	27

Let your voice be heard – visit ZAGAT.com/vote

Ferrari	**Strip**	25	Montblanc	**Strip**	27
Fred Leighton	**Strip**	28	Nanette Lepore	**Strip**	26
Giorgio Armani	**Strip**	28	☑ Neiman Marcus	**Strip**	28
☑ Harry Winston	**Strip**	29	☑ Oscar de la Renta	**Strip**	29
☑ Hermès	**Strip**	29	NEW Piaget	**Strip**	-
Jimmy Choo	**Strip**	27	Prada	**Strip**	27
Johnston/Murphy	**Strip**	26	Roberto Cavalli	**Strip**	26
John Varvatos	**Strip**	25	☑ Saks	**Strip**	27
Juicy Couture	**Strip**	23	NEW Scoop	**Strip**	-
Kate Spade	**Strip**	24	St. John	**Strip**	28
Kiehl's	**Strip**	27	Taryn Rose	**Strip**	25
Leiber	**Strip**	28	☑ Tiffany	**Strip**	28
Manolo Blahnik	**Strip**	28	NEW Tommy Bahama's	**S of Strip**	-
Marc Jacobs	**Strip**	27		
NEW Michael Kors	**Strip**	-	NEW Tory Burch	**Strip**	-
Mikimoto	**Strip**	29	Versace	**Strip**	25

Sites & Attractions Types

Includes attraction names, locations and Appeal ratings.

AMUSEMENT PARKS

Adventuredome	**Strip**	17
Las Vegas Mini Grand Prix	**NW**	18
Roller Coaster/NY-NY	**Strip**	23
Stratosphere	**Strip**	24
Vegas Indoor Skydiving	**E of Strip**	26

AQUARIUMS

Shark Reef | **Strip** — 25

ENTERTAINMENT COMPLEX

GameWorks | **Strip** — 17

FAMOUS SITES

A Little White/Chapel	**Strip**	–
Eiffel Tower	**Strip**	23
ⓩ Fountains/Bellagio	**Strip**	28
Graceland Chapel	**Downtown**	–
ⓩ Hoover Dam	**Boulder City**	26
Little Church	**Strip**	–
Stratosphere	**Strip**	24

GARDENS/ORCHARDS

ⓩ Bellagio Cons./Gdns.	**Strip**	26
Springs Preserve	**W Side**	–

HISTORIC LANDMARKS

ⓩ Hoover Dam | **Boulder City** — 26

HOTEL ATTRACTIONS

Eiffel Tower	**Strip**	23
Gondola Rides	**Strip**	22
Imax Theatre	**Strip**	22
Mystic Falls Park	**E Side**	19
Show in the Sky	**W of Strip**	21
Stratosphere	**Strip**	24

MUSEUMS

Atomic Testing Mus.	**E Side**	–
Auto Collections	**Strip**	22
Las Vegas Nat. History Mus.	**N of Strip**	19
Liberace Mus.	**E Side**	23
Lied/Children's Mus.	**Downtown**	21
Madame Tussauds	**Strip**	23
Neon Museum	**Downtown**	–
Nevada State Mus.	**W Side**	–

NATIONAL/STATE PARKS

Floyd Lamb Pk.	**N Las Vegas**	–
ⓩ Red Rock Canyon	**W Side**	28
Springs Preserve	**W Side**	–
ⓩ Valley of Fire	**Overton**	28

NEIGHBORHOODS/STREETS

ⓩ Fremont St. | **Downtown** — 22

ZOOS/ANIMAL PARKS

Lion Habitat	**Strip**	21
Shark Reef	**Strip**	25
Siegfried & Roy's Garden/Dolphin Habitat	**Strip**	24
Wildlife Habitat	**Strip**	20

Sites & Attractions Locations

Includes attraction names and Appeal ratings.

DOWNTOWN

⚡ Fremont St.	22
Graceland Chapel	-
Lied/Children's Mus.	21
Neon Museum	-

EAST OF STRIP

Vegas Indoor Skydiving	26

EAST SIDE

Atomic Testing Mus.	-
Liberace Mus.	23
Mystic Falls Park	19

LAKE LAS VEGAS

Gondola Adventures	-

NORTH LAS VEGAS

Floyd Lamb Pk.	-

NORTH OF STRIP

Las Vegas Nat. History Mus.	19

NORTHWEST

Las Vegas Mini Grand Prix	18

OUT OF TOWN

⚡ Hoover Dam	26
⚡ Valley of Fire	28

STRIP

Adventuredome	17
A Little White/Chapel	-
Auto Collections	22
⚡ Bellagio Cons./Gdns.	26
Eiffel Tower	23
⚡ Fountains/Bellagio	28
GameWorks	17
Gondola Rides	22
Imax Theatre	22
Lion Habitat	21
Little Church	-
Madame Tussauds	23
Roller Coaster/NY-NY	23
Shark Reef	25
Siegfried & Roy's Garden/ Dolphin Habitat	24
Stratosphere	24
Wildlife Habitat	20

WEST OF STRIP

Show in the Sky	21

WEST SIDE

Nevada State Mus.	-
⚡ Red Rock Canyon	28
Springs Preserve	-

40,000 places to eat, drink, stay & play – free at ZAGAT.com

Golf Features

Listings cover the best in each category and include names, locations and course ratings.

BUDGET

($175 and under)
- Angel Park, Mountain | **Las Vegas** 19
- Angel Park, Palm | **Las Vegas** 18
- Las Vegas Paiute Golf Resort, Snow Mountain | **Las Vegas** 25
- Las Vegas Paiute Golf Resort, Sun Mountain | **Las Vegas** 26
- Legacy | **Henderson** 20

BUNKERING

- 🏆 Shadow Creek | **North Las Vegas** 29

CELEBRITY DESIGNS

ARNOLD PALMER
Angel Park, Mountain | **Las Vegas** 19

ARTHUR HILLS
Legacy | **Henderson** 20

JACK NICKLAUS
- Bear's | **Las Vegas** 25
- 🏆 Reflection/Lake LV | **Henderson** 27

PETE DYE
- Las Vegas Paiute Golf Resort, Snow Mountain | **Las Vegas** 25
- Las Vegas Paiute Golf Resort, Sun Mountain | **Las Vegas** 26
- 🏆 Las Vegas Paiute Golf Resort, Wolf | **Las Vegas** 27
- Royal Links | **Las Vegas** 22

REES JONES
- 🏆 Cascata | **Boulder City** 29
- 🏆 Rio Secco | **Henderson** 27

TOM FAZIO
- 🏆 Shadow Creek | **North Las Vegas** 29
- Wynn | **Las Vegas** 25

CONDITIONING

- Bear's | **Las Vegas** 25
- 🏆 Cascata | **Boulder City** 29
- Las Vegas Paiute Golf Resort, Snow Mountain | **Las Vegas** 25
- Las Vegas Paiute Golf Resort, Sun Mountain | **Las Vegas** 26
- 🏆 Shadow Creek | **North Las Vegas** 29
- Wynn | **Las Vegas** 25

EASIEST

(Courses with the lowest slope ratings from the back tees)
- Las Vegas Paiute Golf Resort, Snow Mountain | **Las Vegas** 25

EXPENSE ACCOUNT

($300 and over)
- Bali Hai | **Las Vegas** 22
- 🏆 Cascata | **Boulder City** 29
- 🏆 Shadow Creek | **North Las Vegas** 29
- Wynn | **Las Vegas** 25

FINISHING HOLES

- 🏆 Cascata | **Boulder City** 29
- 🏆 Reflection/Lake LV | **Henderson** 27
- Wynn | **Las Vegas** 25

LINKS-STYLE

Royal Links | **Las Vegas** 22

PACE OF PLAY

🏆 Cascata | **Boulder City** 29

PAR-3 HOLES

- 🏆 Cascata | **Boulder City** 29
- Wynn | **Las Vegas** 25

PAR-4 HOLES

🏆 Falls/Lake LV | **Henderson** 27

PAR-5 HOLES

🏆 Falls/Lake LV | **Henderson** 27

REPLICAS

- Bear's | **Las Vegas** 25
- Royal Links | **Las Vegas** 22

Let your voice be heard – visit ZAGAT.com/vote

SCENIC

- ☑ Cascata | **Boulder City** — 29
- ☑ Falls/Lake LV | **Henderson** — 27
- ☑ Reflection/Lake LV | **Henderson** — 27
- ☑ Shadow Creek | **North Las Vegas** — 29
- Wynn | **Las Vegas** — 25

TOUGHEST

(Courses with the highest slope ratings from the back tees)

- Bear's | **Las Vegas** — 25
- ☑ Las Vegas Paiute Golf Resort, Wolf | **Las Vegas** — 27

WOMEN-FRIENDLY

- Angel Park, Palm | **Las Vegas** — 18
- ☑ Reflection/Lake LV | **Henderson** — 27

Hotel Locations

Includes hotel names and Room ratings.

DOWNTOWN
Golden Nugget	22

EAST OF STRIP
Alexis	15
Hard Rock	20
Las Vegas Hilton	-
Marriott	22
Platinum	-
Renaissance	26
Westin Casuarina	19

EAST SIDE
Riviera	12

HENDERSON
Green Valley	24
Loews	22
☑ Ritz-Carlton	27

NORTHWEST
JW Marriott	27
Red Rock	27

SOUTH OF STRIP
Hooters	14

SOUTHWEST
South Point	21

STRIP
Bally's	16
☑ Bellagio	26
☑ Caesars	22
Flamingo	13
☑ Four Seasons	27
Imperial Palace	11
Luxor	17
☑ Mandalay Bay	24
MGM Grand	19
Mirage	19
Monte Carlo	18
New York-NY	17
NEW Palazzo	28
Paris	20
Planet Hollywood	18
Signature/MGM Grand	27
Skylofts/MGM Grand	-
Treasure Island	-
NEW Trump Int'l	21
☑ Venetian	27
☑ Wynn	28

WEST OF STRIP
Orleans	18
Palms	20
Rio All-Suite	20

Let your voice be heard – visit ZAGAT.com/vote

Hotel Special Features

Listings cover the best in each category and include hotel names, locations and Room ratings.

ADDITIONS

Alexis | **E of Strip**	15
Hooters | **S of Strip**	14
Palazzo | **Strip**	28
Trump Int'l | **Strip**	21

BUTLERS

⚡ Ritz-Carlton | **Henderson**	27
Skylofts/MGM Grand | **Strip**	—

CASINOS

Bally's | **Strip**	16
⚡ Bellagio | **Strip**	26
⚡ Caesars | **Strip**	22
Flamingo | **Strip**	13
Golden Nugget | **Downtown**	22
Green Valley | **Henderson**	24
Hard Rock | **E of Strip**	20
Hooters | **S of Strip**	14
Imperial Palace | **Strip**	11
JW Marriott | **NW**	27
Las Vegas Hilton | **E of Strip**	—
Loews | **Henderson**	22
Luxor | **Strip**	17
⚡ Mandalay Bay | **Strip**	24
MGM Grand | **Strip**	19
Mirage | **Strip**	19
Monte Carlo | **Strip**	18
New York-NY | **Strip**	17
Orleans | **W of Strip**	18
NEW Palazzo | **Strip**	28
Palms | **W of Strip**	20
Paris | **Strip**	20
Planet Hollywood | **Strip**	18
Red Rock | **NW**	27
Rio All-Suite | **W of Strip**	20
Riviera | **E Side**	12
Skylofts/MGM Grand | **Strip**	—
South Point | **SW**	21
Treasure Island | **Strip**	—
⚡ Venetian | **Strip**	27
Westin Casuarina | **E of Strip**	19
⚡ Wynn | **Strip**	28

CITY VIEWS

⚡ Bellagio | **Strip**	26
⚡ Four Seasons | **Strip**	27
Golden Nugget | **Downtown**	22
Green Valley | **Henderson**	24
Hard Rock | **E of Strip**	20
JW Marriott | **NW**	27
Luxor | **Strip**	17
⚡ Mandalay Bay | **Strip**	24
MGM Grand | **Strip**	19
Mirage | **Strip**	19
Monte Carlo | **Strip**	18
New York-NY | **Strip**	17
NEW Palazzo | **Strip**	28
Palms | **W of Strip**	20
Renaissance | **E of Strip**	26
Rio All-Suite | **W of Strip**	20
Signature/MGM Grand | **Strip**	27
Skylofts/MGM Grand | **Strip**	—
Treasure Island | **Strip**	—
⚡ Venetian | **Strip**	27
Westin Casuarina | **E of Strip**	19
⚡ Wynn | **Strip**	28

DRAMATIC DESIGN

⚡ Bellagio | **Strip**	26
NEW Palazzo | **Strip**	28
Paris | **Strip**	20
Red Rock | **NW**	27
⚡ Ritz-Carlton | **Henderson**	27
Skylofts/MGM Grand | **Strip**	—
NEW Trump Int'l | **Strip**	21
⚡ Venetian | **Strip**	27
⚡ Wynn | **Strip**	28

FISHING

Loews | **Henderson**	22
⚡ Ritz-Carlton | **Henderson**	27

HIKING/WALKING TRAILS

Loews	**Henderson**	22
⭐ Ritz-Carlton	**Henderson**	27

MOUNTAIN SETTINGS/VIEWS

Golden Nugget	**Downtown**	22
Green Valley	**Henderson**	24
Hard Rock	**E of Strip**	20
JW Marriott	**NW**	27
Loews	**Henderson**	22
Luxor	**Strip**	17
Red Rock	**NW**	27
Treasure Island	**Strip**	–

OFFBEAT/FUNKY

Hard Rock	**E of Strip**	20
Planet Hollywood	**Strip**	18
Rio All-Suite	**W of Strip**	20

POWER SCENES

⭐ Bellagio	**Strip**	26
NEW Palazzo	**Strip**	28
Palms	**W of Strip**	20
Skylofts/MGM Grand	**Strip**	–
NEW Trump Int'l	**Strip**	21
⭐ Venetian	**Strip**	27
⭐ Wynn	**Strip**	28

ROMANTIC

Platinum	**E of Strip**	–
Red Rock	**NW**	27
Skylofts/MGM Grand	**Strip**	–

SAILING

Loews	**Henderson**	22

SPA FACILITIES

Bally's	**Strip**	16
⭐ Bellagio	**Strip**	26
⭐ Caesars	**Strip**	22
Flamingo	**Strip**	13
⭐ Four Seasons	**Strip**	27
Golden Nugget	**Downtown**	22
Green Valley	**Henderson**	24
Hard Rock	**E of Strip**	20
Hooters	**S of Strip**	14
Imperial Palace	**Strip**	11
JW Marriott	**NW**	27
Las Vegas Hilton	**E of Strip**	–
Loews	**Henderson**	22
Luxor	**Strip**	17
⭐ Mandalay Bay	**Strip**	24
MGM Grand	**Strip**	19
Mirage	**Strip**	19
Monte Carlo	**Strip**	18
New York-NY	**Strip**	17
Orleans	**W of Strip**	18
NEW Palazzo	**Strip**	28
Palms	**W of Strip**	20
Paris	**Strip**	20
Planet Hollywood	**Strip**	18
Platinum	**E of Strip**	–
Red Rock	**NW**	27
Rio All-Suite	**W of Strip**	20
⭐ Ritz-Carlton	**Henderson**	27
Riviera	**E Side**	12
Signature/MGM Grand	**Strip**	27
South Point	**SW**	21
Treasure Island	**Strip**	–
NEW Trump Int'l	**Strip**	21
⭐ Venetian	**Strip**	27
Westin Casuarina	**E of Strip**	19
⭐ Wynn	**Strip**	28

SPA FACILITIES: WEIGHT LOSS

JW Marriott	**NW**	27
NEW Palazzo	**Strip**	28
⭐ Venetian	**Strip**	27

SPA FACILITIES: YOGA

Green Valley	**Henderson**	24
JW Marriott	**NW**	27
Loews	**Henderson**	22
⭐ Mandalay Bay	**Strip**	24
NEW Palazzo	**Strip**	28
Palms	**W of Strip**	20
⭐ Ritz-Carlton	**Henderson**	27
⭐ Venetian	**Strip**	27

Let your voice be heard – visit ZAGAT.com/vote

TRENDY PLACES

Z Bellagio | **Strip**	26
Hard Rock | **E of Strip**	20
NEW Palazzo | **Strip**	28
Palms | **W of Strip**	20
Red Rock | **NW**	27
Skylofts/MGM Grand | **Strip**	–
NEW Trump Int'l | **Strip**	21
Z Wynn | **Strip**	28

WATER VIEWS

Loews | **Henderson**	22
Z Ritz-Carlton | **Henderson**	27

ALPHABETICAL PAGE INDEX

Adventuredome, The	132
Agave	19
Agent Provocateur	114
NEW Ago	19
Ah Sin	19
AJ's Steakhouse	19
Alan Albert's	20
al Dente	20
Z Alex	20
Alexis Park Resort	146
A Little White Wedding Chapel	132
Alizé	20
All-American Bar & Grille	20
Along Came a Spider	114
America	21
Z André's	21
Angel Park, Mountain	140
Angel Park, Palm	140
Anne Fontaine	114
NEW Annie Creamcheese	114
Antonio's	21
NEW Anya Hindmarch	115
Applebee's	21
AquaKnox	22
Archi's Thai Kitchen	22
Artem	22
Artisan Lounge	90
Z Art of Shaving, The	115
a. testoni	115
Atomic Testing Museum, The	132
Attic, The	115
Auld Dubliner Irish Pub	22
Z Aureole	22
Austins Steakhouse	23
Auto Collections/Imperial Pal.	132
A/X Armani Exchange	115
Baccarat	116
Bahama Breeze	90
Baja Fresh Mexican Grill	23
Bali Hai	140
Bally of Switzerland	116
Bally's Las Vegas	146
Bally's Steakhouse	23
Z B&B Ristorante	23
NEW Bank Nightclub, The	90
Bar at Times Square	90
Bare	91
NEW Barneys New York	116
Bartolotta Ristorante di Mare	24
Z Bass Pro Shops	116
Battista's Hole in the Wall	24
NEW Bauman Rare Books	116
Bay Side Buffet	24
Bear's Best Las Vegas	141
Beatles REVOLUTION Lounge	91
Beauty Bar	91
Z Bellagio Buffet	24
Z Bellagio Conserv./Gdns.	133
Z Bellagio Hotel	146
Benihana	24
Big Al's Oyster Bar	25
Big Dog's	25
Big Kitchen Buffet	25
Bill's Gamblin' Hall	91
Billy Bob's	25
Binion's Ranch Steakhouse	25
Black Mountain Grill	26
NEW BLT Burger	26
Blush	91
Boa Steakhouse	26
Bob Taylor's Ranch House	26
Body English	91
Bonanza Gifts	117
Bonefish Grill	26
Bootlegger Bistro	27
Border Grill	27
BOSS Hugo Boss	117
Bottega Veneta	117
Z Bouchon	27
Z Bradley Ogden	27
NEW Brand Steakhouse	27
Brass Lounge, The	92
Breeze Bar	92
Brendan's Irish Pub	92
Z Brioni	117
NEW Brio Tuscan Grille	28
Broiler	28
Brooks Brothers	117
Buffalo Exchange	117
Buffet, The (Wynn)	28
Buffet, The (Golden Nugget)	28
Buffet, The (Hilton)	28
Bulgari	118
Bunkhouse Saloon	92
NEW Burberry	118
Burger Bar	28
Buzio's	29
Z Caesars Palace	147
Cafe, The	29
Cafe Ba Ba Reeba!	29

ALPHA INDEX

Café Bellagio	29
Cafe Heidelberg	29
Cafe Lago	30
Cafe Martorano	30
Café Wasabi	30
California Pizza Kitchen	30
NEW Caminos de Morelia	30
Canaletto	30
NEW Canali	118
Canal Street	31
Canter's Deli	31
NEW Canyon Club	92
Canyon Ranch Café	31
NEW Canyon Ranch Grill	31
Capital Grille, The	31
Capriotti's Sandwich Shop	31
Caramel Bar & Lounge	92
Caribe Café	32
Carluccio's Tivoli Gardens	32
Carnaval Court	92
Carnegie Deli	32
NEW Carnevino	32
Carnival World Buffet	33
Carson Street Cafe	33
Z Cartier	118
Casa Nicola	33
Z Cascata	141
Cathay House	33
NEW Catherine Malandrino	118
NEW CatHouse	33, 93
Champagnes Cafe	93
Chanel	119
Chang's	34
Charlie Palmer Steak	34
CH Carolina Herrera	119
Cheesecake Factory	34
Cheetah's	93
Cherry	93
Chevys Fresh Mex	34
Chicago Brewing Company	34
Chicago Joe's	35
Chili's Grill & Bar	35
China Grill	35
Chin Chin	35
Chinois	35
Chipotle	36
NEW Chloé	119
Chocolate Swan	36
Chopard	119
NEW Christian Audigier	93
NEW Christian Louboutin	119
Chrome Showroom	93
Circo	36
Claim Jumper	36
Cleopatra's Barge	94
C Level	119
Club, The	94
Club Paradise	94
Coffee Pub	36
NEW Company American Bistro	37
Coyote Ugly	94
Craftsteak	37
Cravings	37
Crazy Armadillo	94
Crown & Anchor British Pub	37
NEW CUT	37
NEW Dal Toro	38
Z Daniel Boulud Brasserie	38
David Burke	38
De Beers	120
Z Del Frisco's	38
Z Delmonico Steakhouse	38
Diablo's Cantina	39
Diablo's Cantina	95
NEW Diane von Furstenberg	120
Dick's Last Resort	39
Diego	39
Dino's Lounge	95
Dior	120
Divebar	95
NEW DJT	39
Dolce & Gabbana	120
Donald J Pliner	120
Doña Maria	39
Don Miguel's	40
NEW Dos Caminos	40
Double Down Saloon	95
Downtown Cocktail Room	95
Dragon Noodle Co.	40
Drop Bar	95
Egg & I	40
Eiffel Tower	40
Eiffel Tower Experience	133
Elephant Bar	40
El Jefe's	41
Ellis Island Lounge	96
El Sombrero Café	41
Z Emeril's Fish House	41
Empress Court	41
Enoteca San Marco	41

Let your voice be heard - visit ZAGAT.com/vote

Envy Steakhouse 41	Girls of Glitter Gulch 97
Escada 121	Gold Coast Lounge 97
ESPN Zone 96	NEW Gold Diggers 97
Ethel's Chocolate Lounge 42	Golden Nugget Hotel 147
eyecandy sound lounge & bar . . . 96	Golden Steer Steak House 47
☑ Falls/Lake Las Vegas 141	Gondola Adventures 134
Famous Dave's 42	Gondola Rides at the Ventian . . . 134
FAO Schwarz 121	Gordon Biersch 98
Fatburger 42	Graceland Wedding Chapel . . . 134
Feast, The 43	Grand Lux Cafe 47
Feast Around The World Buffet . . 43	Grape Street Café 47
Fellini's 43	Green Valley Ranch 148
Fendi 121	Griffin, The 98
Ferrari Store 121	Guadalajara Bar & Grille 48
Ferraro's 43	☑ Guy Savoy 48
Festival Buffet 43	Hamada 48
Fiamma Trattoria 44	H&M 122
Field of Dreams 121	Hank's 48
Fin 44	Hard Rock Cafe 49
Firefly 44	Hard Rock Hotel & Casino 148
Firelight Buffet 44	Harley-Davidson Cafe 49
Fix 44	☑ Harry Winston 122
Flamingo Las Vegas 147	Hash House A Go Go 49
Flavors Buffet 45	NEW Hawaiian Tropic Zone . . . 49
Fleming's 45	☑ Hermès 122
Fleur de Lys 45	Hofbrauhaus Las Vegas 98
Flight 96	Hogs & Heifers 98
Flirt 96	Hooters Casino Hotel 148
Florida Café 45	☑ Hoover Dam 134
Floyd Lamb Park 133	☑ House of Blues 98
NEW 4949 Lounge 96	☑ Hugo's Cellar 49
☑ Fountains of Bellagio 133	Hush Puppy 50
☑ Four Seasons 147	Hyakumi 50
Freakin' Frog 97	NEW I-Bar 98
Fred Leighton 122	Il Fornaio 50
☑ Fremont Street Experience 133	Il Mulino New York 50
French Market Buffet 45	I Love Sushi 50
Fusia 45	Images Lounge 99
Gaetano's 46	Imax Theatre 135
NEW Galerias Gourmet 46	Imperial Palace 148
Gallagher's Steakhouse 46	India Palace 51
GameWorks 134	Indigo Lounge 99
Gandhi India's Cuisine 46	In-N-Out Burger 51
Garden Court Buffet 46	Intermix 123
Garduño's 46	Isla 51
Gaylord's 47	Ivan Kane's Forty Deuce 99
☑ ghostbar 97	NEW Jade Dim Sum Noodles . . . 51
Giorgio Armani 122	Japonais 51
Giorgio Ristorante & Caffè 47	Jasmine 52
Gipsy 97	J. C. Wooloughan's 99

Jean Philippe Patisserie	52
Jessica McClintock	123
JET Nightclub	99
Jillian's	99
Jimmy Buffett's Margaritaville	52
Jimmy Choo	123
ⓏJoël Robuchon	52
Joe's Sea/Steak/Crab	52
Johnston & Murphy	123
John Varvatos	123
Joint, The	100
Joyful House Chinese Cuisine	53
J-POP Sushi Bar and Lounge	100
Juicy Couture	124
JW Marriott Resort & Spa	148
NEW Kabuki	53
Kahunaville	100
Kate Spade	124
Kathy's Southern Cooking	53
Kenneth Cole	124
Kiehl's	124
King's Fish House	53
NEW Koi	53
Kona Grill	53
Krave	100
Lacoste	124
Lake Mead Cruises	54
NEW La Madonna	54
La Perla	125
La Salsa	54
La Scena Lounge	100
Las Vegas Golf & Tennis	125
Las Vegas Hilton	149
Las Vegas Mini Grand Prix	135
Las Vegas Nat. History Mus.	135
Las Vegas Paiute, Snow	141
Las Vegas Paiute, Sun	141
ⓏLas Vegas Paiute, Wolf	142
Las Vegas Premium Outlets	125
ⓏL'Atelier de Joël Robuchon	54
NEW Lavo	55
Lawry's The Prime Rib	55
LAX	100
ⓏLe Cirque	55
Legacy, The	142
NEW Le Golosita	55
Leiber	125
Le Provençal	55
Les Artistes Steakhouse	55
Le Village Buffet	56
Liberace Museum	135
Lied Children's Mus.	135
Lindo Michoacan	56
Lion Habitat	135
Little Buddha	56
Little Church of the West, The	136
Loews Lake Las Vegas Resort	149
Lombardi's	56
ⓏLotus of Siam	56
NEW Louis's Las Vegas	57
Lucille's Smokehouse Bar-B-Que	57
NEW Lucio Ristorante	57
Luna Rossa	57
Luxor Las Vegas	149
Madame Tussauds	136
Maggiano's Little Italy	57
Makino	57
ⓏMandalay Bay Resort	149
Manolo Blahnik	125
Marché Bacchus	58
Marc Jacobs	126
Market City Caffe	58
Marrakech	58
Marriott Las Vegas Suites	149
Martinis	58
McCormick & Schmick's	58
NEW McFadden's	101
Medici Café	59
Melting Pot	59
Memphis Barbecue	59
Mermaid	101
ⓏMesa Grill	59
Metro Pizza	59
MGM Grand	150
MGM Grand Buffet	60
NEW Michael Kors Collection	126
ⓏMichael Mina	60
ⓏMichael's	60
Mikimoto	126
Mirage Hotel	150
MiraLago	60
Mist	101
ⓏmiX	60
ⓏmiX Lounge	101
ⓏMon Ami Gabi	61
Montblanc	126
Monte Carlo Resort & Casino	150
Montesano's	61
Moon	101
NEW Morels	61

Let your voice be heard – visit ZAGAT.com/vote

Morton's The Steakhouse 61	Penazzi 67
Mr. Lucky's 24/7............ 61	NEW Penthouse Club........ 103
Mystic Falls Park 136	☑ Peppermill Fireside Lounge... 103
Nanette Lepore 126	Petrossian Bar............. 103
Napoleon's Champagne Bar ... 101	NEW Piaget................ 127
☑ Neiman Marcus 126	☑ Picasso 67
Neon Museum, The 136	Piero's Italian Cuisine......... 67
Neros 62	NEW Pie Town Pizza 68
Nevada State Museum 136	Ping Pang Pong 68
NEW New Orleans Connection ... 62	Pink Taco 68
New York-New York Hotel 150	Pinot Brasserie 68
Niketown 127	Planet Hollywood 68
Nine Fine Irishmen 62, 102	Planet Hollywood Resort 151
N9ne Steakhouse 62	Platinum Hotel & Spa......... 152
Nobhill Tavern............... 62	☑ Playboy Club 103
☑ Nobu 63	Poetry 103
Noir Bar 102	Polly Esthers 104
Noodles 63	Postrio 68
Noodle Shop 63	Potato Valley Café 69
Nora's Cuisine............... 63	Prada 127
Nora's Wine Bar & Osteria..... 63	☑ Prime Steakhouse 69
☑ Nordstrom................ 127	NEW Privé................. 104
Nove Italiano 63	Pullman Grille 69
☑ Okada 64	☑ PURE 104
☑ Olives 64	Pussycat Dolls Lounge 104
Olympic Garden 102	Raffles Café................ 69
Onda 64	Railhead, The 104
Origin India 64	Rain Nightclub 104
Orleans Hotel & Casino 151	Range Steakhouse 69
Osaka Japanese Bistro 64	Rao's 70
Osaka Japanese Cuisine....... 65	Red 8 Asian Bistro 70
☑ Oscar de la Renta 127	☑ Red Rock Canyon 137
Outback Steakhouse.......... 65	Red Rock Casino Resort & Spa ... 152
Ovation 102	☑ Red Square 105
P.F. Chang's China Bistro 67	Red, White and Blue......... 70
Pahrump Valley Winery 65	Redwood Bar & Grill......... 70
NEW Palazzo Resort......... 151	☑ Reflection/Lake Las Vegas ... 142
Palm, The................... 65	☑ Rehab 105
Palms Casino Resort 151	Renaissance 152
Palomino Club 102	NEW Restaurant Charlie 70
Pampas Churrascaria 65	Revere, Concord 142
Pamplemousse 66	Revere, Lexington........... 142
Panevino 66	Rick Moonen's RM Seafood.... 71
Paris Las Vegas 151	Rick's Cabaret.............. 105
Pasta Mia West.............. 66	Rincon Criollo 71
Pasta Shop & Ristorante 66	Rio All-Suite Hotel & Casino ... 152
NEW Payard Pâtisserie & Bistro... 66	☑ Rio Secco 143
Paymon's Mediterranean Café ... 66	Risqué 105
Pearl....................... 67	☑ Ritz-Carlton Lake Las Vegas .. 152
Pearl, The.................. 103	Riviera Hotel & Casino....... 153

ALPHA INDEX

Roadrunner	71
Roberto Cavalli	128
NEW Rok	105
Roller Coaster at NY-NY	137
Romance	105
Romano's Macaroni Grill	71
Z Rosemary's	71
Rosewood	72
NEW Rox	106
Roxy's Diner	72
Royal Links	143
Roy's	72
NEW RUB BBQ	72
Rubio's Fresh Mexican Grill	72
Z rumjungle	106
Ruth's Chris Steak House	73
Z Saks Fifth Avenue	128
Salt Lick Bar-BQ	73
Samba Brazilian Steakhouse	73
Sammy's Woodfired Pizza	73
Sam Woo BBQ	73
Sand Dollar Blues	106
Sapphire	106
Sapporo	74
NEW Scoop	128
Seablue	74
Seahorse Lounge	106
Seamless	106
Second Street Grill	74
Secret Garden Store	128
Sedona	107
Sen of Japan	74
Sensi	74
Z Sephora	128
Settebello	75
Shadow	107
Z Shadow Creek	143
Shanghai Lilly	75
Shark Reef	137
Shark Reef Aquarium Gift Shop	129
Shibuya	75
Show in the Sky	137
Sidebar	107
Siegfried/Roy's Gdn./Dolphin	137
Siena	143
Signature at MGM Grand	153
NEW Simon	75
Skylofts at MGM Grand	153
Smith & Wollensky	75
Social House	75
South Point	153
Spago	76
Spearmint Rhino	107
Spice Market Buffet	76
Spiedini	76
Springs Preserve	138
Stack	76
Stage Deli	76
Steak House	77
Steak House, The	77
Steakhouse46	77
Sterling Brunch	77
St. John	129
NEW Stoney's Rockin' Country	107
Stratosphere Tower & Rides	138
NEW Stratta	77
Strip House	77
StripSteak	78
Studio 54	107
NEW Sugarcane	108
Sushi Roku	78
NEW SushiSamba	78
SW Steakhouse	78
Z Tableau	78
NEW Table 10	78
Table 34	79
Tabú	108
Tamba Indian Cuisine	79
NEW T&T (Tacos & Tequila)	79
Tao	79
Z Tao	108
Z Tao Beach	108
Taqueria Cañonita	79
Taryn Rose	129
Z T-Bones Chophouse	80
Terra Verde	80
T.G.I. Friday's	80
Thai Spice	80
32 degrees	108
Z Tiffany & Co.	129
Tillerman, The	80
Tinoco's Bistro	80
Tintoretto Bakery & Café	81
Toby Keith's	109
Todai	81
Z Todd's Unique Dining	81
Togoshi Ramen	81
NEW Tommy Bahama's Café	81
NEW Tommy Bahama's Emp.	129
Tommy Rocker's	109

Let your voice be heard – visit ZAGAT.com/vote

Tony Roma's	81
Top of the World	82
NEW Torrid	109
NEW Tory Burch	130
Trader Vic's	82
Trattoria del Lupo	82
Treasure Island	153
Trevi	82
Triple George Grill	83
Triple 7 Restaurant & Brewery	83
Triq	109
Truefitt & Hill	130
NEW Trump Int'l Hotel	154
Z Tryst	109
Valentino	83
Z Valley of Fire State Park	138
V Bar	109
Vegas Indoor Skydiving	138
Z Venetian Hotel	154
Ventano	83
Verandah, The	83
Versace	130
Vic & Anthony's Steakhouse	83
Vintner Grill	84
Viva Mercado's	84
Z VooDoo Lounge	110
NEW V Thai Cuisine, The	84
NEW Wasted Space	110
Westin Casuarina Hotel	154
West of Santa Fe	130
NEW White Chocolate Grill	84
'wichcraft	84
Wildlife Habitat	138
Wing Lei	84
Wolfgang Puck Bar & Grill	85
NEW Woo	85
Z Wynn Casino Resort	154
Wynn Las Vegas	143
NEW Yellowtail	85
Yolie's Brazilian Steakhouse	85
NEW Yolos	85
Zeffirino	85
Z Gallerie	130
NEW Zine Noodles Dim Sum	86
Zuri	110

ON THE GO.
IN THE KNOW.

ZAGAT TO GO℠

Unlimited access to Zagat dining & travel content in hundreds of major cities.

Search by name, location, ratings, cuisine, special features & Top Lists.

BlackBerry,® Palm,® Windows Mobile® and mobile phones.

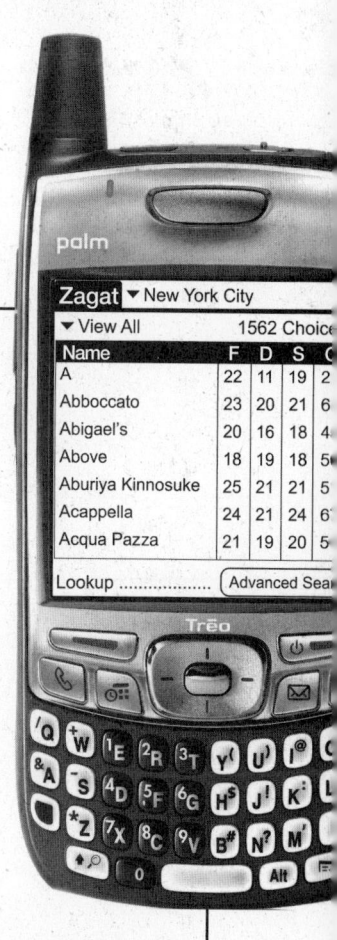

Get it now at **mobile.zagat.com** or text* **ZAGAT** to **78247**

*Standard text rates apply. Check with your carrier.